Campus

The Architectural History Foundation is a publicly supported, not-for-profit foundation.

Special thanks go to the National Endowment for the Arts, whose generous grant helped make possible the publication of this book.

Campus

An American Planning Tradition

Paul Venable Turner

The Architectural History Foundation
New York

The MIT Press
Cambridge, Massachusetts,
and London, England

Paul Turner is Professor of Architectural History at Stanford University.

Designed by Marc Treib

Unattributed photographs and plans are by the author.

Printed in the United States of America

Library of Congres Cataloging in Publication Data

Turner, Paul Venable.
Campus: an American planning tradition.
(The Architectural History Foundation/MIT Press series; 7)
Bibliography: p. 330

1. Campus planning—United States—History. 2. Universities and colleges—United States—Design and construction—History. 3. Universities and colleges—Social aspects—United States. I. Title. II. Series. III. Series: (Architectural History Foundation (New York: N.Y.))
LB3223.3.T87 1987 690'73'0973 86-28846

ISBN 0-262-20047-3
ISBN 0-262-70032-8 pbk

Contents

For my father and mother

Acknowledgments

In 1976, while preparing an exhibition and publication on the architecture of Stanford University, I discovered that no history of the American campus existed, and I decided to undertake a study of the subject. In the time since then, as I researched and wrote this work, a large number of people and institutions assisted me in the project. I have tried to mention as many of these as possible here; and I also thank all those whom it is impossible to name individually.

A National Endowment for the Humanities fellowship enabled me to spend the 1977–1978 academic year planning the project and conducting preliminary research. As one means of gathering information, I sent a questionnaire to about 500 colleges and universities (over 350 of which responded), asking about their physical character and planning. I thank all the people who responded to this questionnaire and in many cases sent me additional information about the history of their campuses. Later that year, I traveled around the United States, visiting schools and conducting research at a number of institutions. Among the people who helped me during this stage of the project were: Adolf K. Placzek, Librarian, and Herbert Mitchell, Curator of Drawings, Avery Architectural Library, Columbia University; Professor Harry Wells Langworthy III, Cleveland State University; Roy E. Graham, Colonial Williamsburg Foundation; Professor William Crelly, Emory University; Professors James S. Ackerman and John P. Coolidge, Harvard University; Wolfgang Freitag, Head Librarian, Fine Arts Library, Harvard; Karen Lewis, Harvard University Archives; Eleanor Garvey and David Becker, Houghton Library, Harvard; Christopher Hale, Graduate School of Design Library, Harvard; Dr. Laurence Homolka; Professor Frederick Kirchhoff, Indiana University-Purdue University; Professor Richard Longstreth, Kansas State University; C. Ford Peatross, Curator of the Architectural Collections, and Mary Ison, Prints and Photographs Division, Library of Congress; Charles Brownell, Maryland Historical Society; the staff of the Massachusetts Historical Society; David Kiehl and William P. Rieder, Metropolitan Museum of Art, New York; Robert B. Rettig, National Register of Historic Places; Professor Bainbridge Bunting, University of New Mexico; W. E. Bigglestone, Oberlin College Archives; Artemas Richardson, Olmsted Associates;

Robert Judson Clark, Princeton University; J. E. Robinson, Sasaki Associates; Professor Willard Spiegelman, Southern Methodist University; William Beiswanger, Thomas Jefferson Memorial Foundation; Professor Tony Smith, Tufts University; Ruth Ann Evans and Frances D. Miller, Shaffer Library, Union College; Professors Frederick D. Nichols and Dora Wiebenson, University of Virginia; Professor Buford L. Pickens, Washington University; and Judith Schiff, Manuscripts and Archives, Yale University Library.

After 1978, as I carried out further research and began writing sections of the work, I corresponded and spoke with many people who provided me with information and advice. These included: Professor William H. Jordy, Brown University; Frances D. Ferguson, Vice President for Academic Affairs, Bucknell University; Sally Woodbridge, University of California, Berkeley; Professor Chalmers G. Davidson, Archivist, Davidson College; Albert Bush-Brown, Chancellor, Long Island University; Professor Daniel D. Reiff, State University of New York, College at Fredonia; Professor Sarah Bradford Landau, New York University; Professor Geoffrey Blodgett, Oberlin College; Jean R. France, University of Rochester; Philip C. Williams, Director of Planning, Stanford University; Peter J. Knapp, Archivist, Trinity College; Ellen Fladger, Archivist, Union College; Professor Frederick D. Nichols, University of Virginia; Rolfe P. Kellor, Campus Planning Officer, University of Washington; Professor James O'Gorman, Wellesley College; Eric Johannesen, Western Reserve Historical Society; Karin M. E. Alexis; and Charles L. Dibble.

In the course of writing the work, I showed portions of it to other historians whose fields of expertise were relevant to the subjects involved. Among those who read parts of the manuscript and gave me valuable suggestions were: Professor Charles C. McLaughlin, The American University; Professor Spiro Kostof, University of California at Berkeley; Professor Robert Bruegmann, University of Illinois at Chicago Circle; Professor Richard Longstreth, Kansas State University; Professor Bainbridge Bunting, University of New Mexico; Professor Leland M. Roth, University of Oregon; Professor Robert Judson Clark, Princeton University; Professor David Tyack, School of Education, Stanford University; Professor Margaret Henderson Floyd, Tufts University; Professor Thomas J. McCormick, Wheaton College; Professor James D. Kornwolf, College of William and Mary; and Elizabeth Mills Brown.

I also thank the organizers of several conferences on college planning in which I participated, especially, Professor François-Auguste de Montêquin of Skidmore College, who organized a symposium on collegiate architecture at that school in 1978; and Susan E. Ryan of the University of Michigan, who chaired a session on campus planning at the 1982 annual meeting of the Society of Architectural Historians. I am also grateful to Professor Daniel Robbins and President John S. Morris of Union College, where I presented the Walter C. Baker lecture in 1981, on the topic of the designs of Union College and the University of Virginia.

Locating and acquiring illustrations was a laborious part of the project. Among the numerous people who assisted me in this activity were: Robert L. Norris, Vice Provost, and Ann Stevens, Office of University Relations, The American University; Nina Myatt, Curator, Antiochiana, and Irwin Inman, Director, Office of Information, Antioch College; Walter Frese, Architectural Book Publishing Co., Inc.; Mildred Schmertz, Executive Editor, *Architectural Record*; Angela Giral, Librarian, Avery Architectural Library, Columbia University; Todd H. Bullard, President, Bethany College; Barbara Chapman, Billboard Publications, Inc.; Professor Gerald S. Bernstein, Brandeis University; Frederick Koeper, Dean, School of Environmental Design, California State Polytechnic University; Professors Kenneth Cardwell and Stephen Tobriner, James R. K. Kantor, University Archivist, and Jeffrey Johnson, Documents Collection, College of Environmental Design, University of California, Berkeley; Elwin V. Svenson, Vice Chancellor, University of California, Los Angeles; Charles M. Sullivan, Executive Director, and Paul Bockelman, Assistant Director, Cambridge Historical Commission; Daniel Meyer, Joseph Regenstein Library, University of Chicago; Patricia G. Maccubbin, Colonial Williamsburg Foundation; Francesco Passanti, Columbia University; Professor Kermit C. Parsons and Marguerite J. Pack, Cornell University; Kenneth C. Cramer, Archivist, Dartmouth College Library; Dr. Chalmers G. Davidson, Archivist, Davidson College; M. Charles Seller, Executive Assistant to the President, and John E.

Ross, Director, Public Information Services, Dickinson College; William E. King, Archivist, Duke University; Lee Kline, Director of Public Relations, Elmira College; Linda M. Matthews, Head, Special Collections, Emory University; Joan Green, Public Information, Foothill College; Bruce Brooks Pfeiffer, Director of Archives, Frank Lloyd Wright Memorial Foundation; Shary Page Berg, Frederick Law Olmsted National Historic Site; R. Barry Wood, Director of Public Relations, University of Georgia; Rhoda M. Dorsey, President, Goucher College; Ralph Stenstrom, Librarian, Hamilton College; Robin McElheny, Harvard University Archives; Grace W. Choi, Harvard University News Office; Susan C. Metzger, Harvard University Press; Nicholas Mascari, Hobart and William Smith Colleges; Daniel H. Woodward, Librarian, and Harriet McLoone, Assistant Curator, The Huntington Library; Professor Kevin Harrington and William T. Covington III, Illinois Institute of Technology; Julia B. Morgan, Archivist, Johns Hopkins University; Thomas B. Greenslade, Archivist, Kenyon College; Paul G. Sifton, Manuscript Division, C. Ford Peatross, Curator of Architectural Collections, and Mary Ison, Prints and Photographs Division, Library of Congress; John D. Cushing, Massachusetts Historical Society; Warren Seamans, Director, and Michelle Bagdis, Massachusetts Institute of Technology Museum; David Kiehl, Print Room, Metropolitan Museum of Art, New York; Clinton N. Hewitt, Assistant Vice President, Physical Planning, University of Minnesota; Thomas D. Grischkowsky, Museum of Modern Art, New York; Terrie Nault, Office of Information, University of Nevada, Reno; Tobin A. Sparling, Print Room, New York Public Library; Jerry W. Cotten, Photographic Archivist, University of North Carolina; Dr. Wendy Clauson Schlereth, Archivist, and Richard M. Cochran, Assistant Archivist, University of Notre Dame; Dr. G. V. Bennett, Librarian, New College, and C. G. Cordeaux, Bodleian Library, Oxford University; Raymond J. Christina, Department of News and Publications, University of Pittsburgh; Earle E. Coleman, Archivist, and Charles E. Greene, Keeper of the Rare Books, Princeton University; Professor Emerita Dorothy O. Johansen, Archivist, Reed College; O. Jack Mitchell, Dean, School of Architecture, and Nancy Parker, Director, Woodson Research Center, Rice University; William Ramirez, Chief, San Francisco Public Library; Ellie Reichlin, Curator of Photographic Collections, Society for the Preservation of New England Antiquities; Roxanne Nilan, Archivist, Stanford University; Albert W. Fowler, Friends Historical Library, Swarthmore College; Albert B. Fink, Jr., Assistant to the President, Sweet Briar College; Barbara J. McSpadden, Information Services, Transylvania University; Peter J. Knapp, Archivist, Trinity College; Jean Mayer, President, Tufts University; Jean C. Pelletière, Director, Shaffer Library, and Peter Blankman, Publications Office, Union College; Richard J. Hellinger, Chief Archivist, and Joanne M. Nocton, United States Military Academy; Edmund Berkeley, Jr., Curator, and Gregory A. Johnson, Manuscripts Department, Alderman Library, University of Virginia; Professor Buford L. Pickens, Washington University; Jeffery G. Hanna, Director, University News Office, Washington and Lee University; Kathleen East and Karen D. Drickamer, Williamsiana, Williams College; Jack A. Siggins and Judith Schiff, Yale University Library.

Also, the following architects and architectural firms: The Architects Collaborative; Edward Larrabee Barnes Associates; Judy K. Miller, Gunnar Birkerts & Associates; Franklin D. Lawyer; Caudill Rowlett Scott; Art Sweeney, Evans, Mills, Gardner, Architects; Ulrich Franzen, Ulrich Franzen / Keith Kroeger & Associates; Robert Geddes, Geddes Brecher Qualls Cunningham, Architects; George Saire, Don H. Hisaka & Associates; Charles W. Moore; I. M. Pei & Partners; William L. Pereira Associates; Kevin Roche, Kevin Roche, John Dinkeloo & Associates; Paul Rudolph; Skidmore, Owings & Merrill; Sprankle, Lynd & Sprague; Edward Durell Stone Associates; William Turnbull.

The following professional photographers: Morley Baer, Orlando R. Cabanban, George Cserna, Balthazar Korab, Norman McGrath, Hosmer McKoon, Fred Stone, George E. Thomas, and Nick Wheeler. I also thank Joel Leivick, instructor in photography at Stanford University, who helped me with various aspects of the photographic work for the book.

At Stanford University, many of my colleagues and friends have assisted this project in numerous ways. Some of them are mentioned elsewhere in these acknowledgments. In addition, I want to thank Joan Coppock and Elizabeth Martin of the

Art Department; Alex Ross and Marguerite Grady of the Art Library; Barbara Van Deventer and the staff of the Cubberley Education Library; and David Rozkuszka of Government Documents, Green Library. I am grateful to the School of Humanities and Sciences for its support of my project in various ways, and to the generosity of Ruth Halperin toward the Art Department. I also wish to acknowledge Professor Tilmann Buddensieg, who taught at Stanford in 1970–71, and conducted research on the design of its campus, which aided me in my own subsequent studies.

I thank the many students I have had over the years, in lecture courses on American architecture and seminars on campus planning and related subjects, who have contributed significantly to my work by their intelligent questions, their research papers, and their fresh outlook that serves as an antidote to the maladies that can afflict a prolonged study.

I also thank the editors of the Architectural History Foundation, for their confidence in my work and their superb editorial advice and collaboration; and Marc Treib, the designer of the book, for his skill in correlating textual content and visual images.

Finally, I want to express special gratitude to several people who have given me help and moral support from the earliest stages of the project: Professor Albert Elsen and Lorenz Eitner, Chairman, the Department of Art, Stanford University; Professor Emeritus Buford L. Pickens, Washington University; Michael E. Moors; and the late Bainbridge Bunting, whose encouragement and good cheer I sorely miss.

Paul Venable Turner
June 1983

Campus

1

1 University of Virginia, Charlottesville. Designed by Thomas Jefferson, 1817. (Printing Services Records, University of Virginia Archives)

Preface

The American Campus as an "Academical Village"

While designing the University of Virginia, Thomas Jefferson described his goal as the creation of an "academical village" (Fig. 1).[1] This term expressed Jefferson's own views on education and planning, but it also summarizes a basic trait of American higher education from the colonial period to the twentieth century: the conception of colleges and universities as communities in themselves—in effect, as cities in microcosm. This reflects educational patterns and ideals which, although derived from Europe, have developed in distinctively American ways. As a result, the physical forms of American colleges and universities—their buildings, grounds, and spaces—are different from anything elsewhere, and thus they provide an excellent opportunity to examine the ways in which architectural design is shaped by the character of a particular type of institution.

Throughout its history, American higher education has largely adhered to the "collegiate" ideal rooted in the medieval English universities, where students and teachers lived and studied together in small, tightly regulated colleges. Beginning in the colonial period, American colleges followed this English model as closely as possible, and even when large universities developed in the United States in the late nineteenth century, they took on many collegiate characteristics, in contrast to the typical pattern of continental European universities, which more often concentrated on academic matters and paid little attention to their students' extracurricular lives. Therefore, American colleges and universities, like those in England, have required not only classrooms and other academic spaces, but dormitories, dining halls, and recreational facilities as well, making the architect's job not only the design of individual buildings, but the creation of a whole community. Even with the more recent appearance in America of commuter schools and other educational institutions that are fundamentally noncollegiate, the collegiate spirit has persisted, manifesting itself in such things as student unions, social clubs, and athletic programs, seldom found in the traditional European university.

In its faithfulness to the collegiate spirit, America followed English precedent, but in many ways American higher education developed its own character. Starting in the colonial period, Americans departed from tradition by creating individual colleges in separate locations rather than clustering them at a university, and thus they intensified the autonomous nature of each college as a community in itself. They strengthened it further by another innovation, the placing of colleges in the countryside or even in the wilderness, an unprecedented break with European tradition. The romantic notion of a college in nature, removed from the corrupting forces of the city, became an American ideal (Figs. 2,3). But in the process, the college had to become even more fully a kind of miniature city. And its design became an experiment in urbanism.

Another trait that typifies American college planning is its spaciousness and openness to the world. From its very beginning, at Harvard in the seventeenth century, the American college has largely rejected the European tradition of cloister-like structures in favor of separate buildings set in open green space. This ideal is so strong in America that even those schools located in cities, where land is scarce, have often gone to considerable expense or inconvenience to simulate a rural spaciousness.

European visitors have remarked on the distinctive physical character of the American college. Charles Dickens in the 1840s was struck by the appearance of Yale, with its buildings "erected in a kind of park . . . dimly visible among the shadowing trees" (Fig. 4).[2] The English architect Charles R. Ashbee wrote in 1912 that American university design expressed "the feeling that here is a community, working on certain fixed principles."[3] And Le Corbusier, after traveling in America in the 1930s, observed that "each college or university is an urban unit in itself, a small or large city. But a green city. . . . The American university is a world in itself."[4]

The word *campus*, more than any other term, sums up the unique physical character of the American college and university. When it was first used to describe the grounds of a college, probably at Princeton in the late eighteenth century, *campus* had simply its Latin meaning, a field, and described the green expansiveness already distinctive of American schools.[5] But gradually the word assumed wider significance, until at most colleges it came to mean the entire property, including buildings, so that one could speak even of an "urban campus" that might possess nothing remotely resembling a field (Fig. 5). In 1925, the German city planner Werner Hegemann, writing about America, defined *campus* for his countrymen as "a piece of land that is covered with the buildings of an American university."[6] But beyond these purely physical meanings, the word has taken on other connotations, suggesting the pervasive spirit of a school, or its *genius loci*, as embodied in its architecture and grounds. *Campus* sums up the distinctive physical qualities of the American college, but also its integrity as a self-contained community and its architectural expression of educational and social ideals. As early as the 1870s the term was so evocative that an observer of one American college could write, "There is no spell more powerful to recall the memories of college life than the word Campus."[7]

Despite its continuity over the centuries, the American campus has experienced major changes in its form which reflect not only evolving notions of architectural planning but changing educational and social principles as well. This study examines the relationship between ideas and physical environments in selected cases of college planning throughout American history. It focuses largely on plans and designs—more than on the problems of executing them—because it has often been the dreams of educators and their architects, whether fully realized or not, that have expressed most clearly the correlation of educational ideals to physical planning.

Historians have given little attention to American college planning. Except for studies of the architecture of individual schools and portions of books written by planners on how to design colleges, almost nothing has been published on the history of the campus.[8] A dissertation written in 1958 by Albert Bush-Brown, on American collegiate architecture in the nineteenth century, has been the only study so far of a broad spectrum of academic designs.[9] The general neglect of the subject may be due in part to a belief that there has been little real planning of American colleges. It is often assumed that until recently, and with a few exceptions like the University of Virginia, colleges have simply grown haphazardly, without conscious design. In reality, campus planning in America has a long and full history. "Planning," of course, can mean many different things, ranging from the design of a single building to the creation

2

3

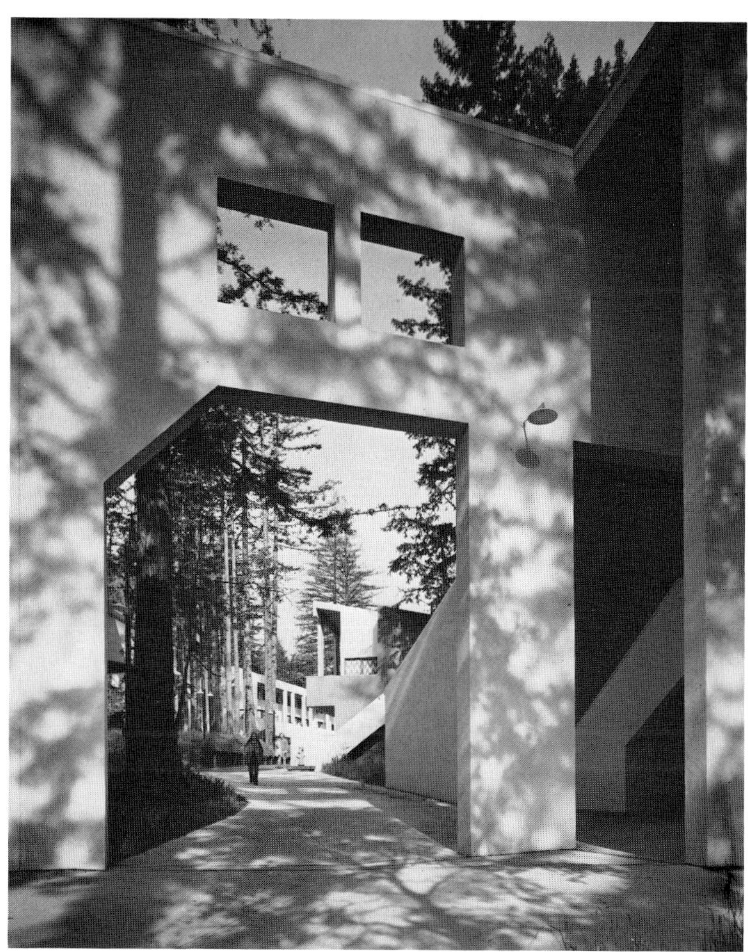

2 Dartmouth College, Hanover, New Hampshire, ca. 1850. *From left*: Wentworth Hall, 1828; Dartmouth Hall, 1784–1791; Thornton Hall, 1828; and Reed Hall, 1839. The architect of Dartmouth Hall is unknown; the other three buildings were designed by Ammi B. Young. (*Gleason's Pictorial Drawing-Room Companion*, October 29, 1853, p. 280)

3 Kresge College, University of California at Santa Cruz. Designed by Charles W. Moore and William Turnbull (of Moore Lyndon Turnbull Whitaker), 1965–1972. (Photograph: © Morley Baer)

of a master plan involving many structures, their surrounding environment, and the gradual execution of the plan over a period of time. But even by the most demanding definitions, college planning can be shown to have existed in America from the earliest period.

There also can be various definitions of a college or a university. The educational community today makes relatively clear distinctions between colleges, universities, academies, and other kinds of schools, but their definitions have varied widely in different times and places. In order to avoid repeating "college and university" with awkward frequency, the term *college* is sometimes used in this work in a broad sense, as including most schools of higher education in America—although merely framing a definition of "higher education" is difficult, given the changes, over time, in the ages of students, types of curricula, and academic degrees.[10]

Geographically, the scope of this study is the area presently comprising the United States. For the colonial period, this might seem somewhat artificial as it does not cover all the English colonies in America; in reality it is not a problem, since with only one or two exceptions (such as Codrington College in Barbados), there were no English colonial colleges before 1776 outside of what is now the United States.[11] Spanish and French schools in the New World, though often having ancient histories (there were at least three "universities" in Latin America before the English colonies even were settled), were so different from English schools and had so little intercourse with them, that it makes sense to examine the English collegiate tradition in America as a relatively isolated subject.

The relationship to Great Britain, of course, is important to the story—although decreasingly so after the early colonial period. In the mid-nineteenth century, the German university system began to influence American education in significant ways, but architecture and planning were not commensurately affected. To a remarkable degree, college planning in America has an independent history, evolving its own forms and producing its own innovations, less subject to European fashion than other fields of architecture and design. The educational institutions of Europe simply were not appropriate models for American schools, which developed their own original character, requiring new forms of physical planning. The American campus, from the beginning, has been shaped less by European precedents than by the social, economic, and cultural forces around it. As a result, it has been the laboratory for perhaps the most distinctively American experiments in architectural planning.

It would be impossible in a single work on the American campus to survey the subject fully, or even to begin to include all of the significant collegiate plans. Of necessity, this study is highly selective, with only a few schools or plans examined in any detail in each period.[12] These choices naturally reflect my own background and interests, as well as my interpretations of the historical forces that have shaped collegiate design. I hope that by suggesting the richness of the American campus tradition, this work will stimulate further studies, differing interpretations, and increased interest in this surprisingly neglected part of the American environment.

4 Yale College, New Haven, Connecticut, seen from New Haven Green, ca. 1850. Buildings, known as the Old Brick Row, were constructed from 1750 to the 1820s. (*Gleason's Pictorial Drawing-Room Companion*, December 6, 1851, p. 505)

5 Columbia University, New York City. Rendering of Low Library and central part of the master plan for the campus by Charles F. McKim (of McKim, Mead & White), ca. 1894, as viewed from West 116th Street. (*Architectural Record*, May 1895; courtesy of Francesco Passanti)

4

5

6

Introduction

The British College on the Eve of American Colonization

6 New College, Oxford. Fourteenth-century quadrangle, as seen in a drawing in the Chandler Manuscript, ca. 1465. In foreground are the fellows of New College and its warden, or head. (The Bodleian Library, and New College, Oxford University)

At the beginning of the seventeenth century, the universities of Oxford and Cambridge were at a high point in their development. The political and religious turmoil of the Reformation had disrupted their medieval traditions, but they had emerged revitalized. Their curricula were reformed and their enrollments were larger than ever before, reflecting a new popular enthusiasm for education. All of this was to be significant for the colleges in colonial America, which would be patterned on those of Oxford and Cambridge and also to some extent on the Scottish universities. Architecturally, too, the English colleges were undergoing changes that established models for America.[1]

The sixteenth century saw the full development of the English "collegiate" system of university education. At their origins in the twelfth and thirteenth centuries, Oxford and Cambridge had been modeled on the University of Paris, both in their curricula, based on the dialectical analysis of Christian doctrine, and in their methods of operation. Students attended the lectures of chosen teachers, but their living arrangements were their own concern and, except for students attached to monastic houses, there were few structured social institutions. At first students generally lodged with townspeople, but soon "halls" or "hostels" became more common; these were buildings rented by groups of students, sometimes under the direction of a master, where the students slept and took meals but in which there was little social or educational structure. In the mid-fifteenth century there were about seventy of these halls at Oxford. But by then colleges had made their appearance: permanent establishments endowed by benefactors, often expressly for poor scholars, with specific regulations of discipline and study. The first was probably Merton College at Oxford, founded in 1264 by the King's Chancellor, who drew up statutes regulating its government and discipline.

Merton and succeeding colleges for a century provided lodging only for masters (those studying for higher degrees), not for undergraduates. But in 1379, William of Wykeham founded New College at Oxford, with emphasis on the education and housing of undergraduates. A former Surveyor of the King's Works, Wykeham took a special interest in the physical planning of his college.[2] The buildings formed an enclosed quadrangle, containing all the major collegiate requirements:

a chapel, a hall (used for dining, lectures, and other assemblies), scholars' and masters' chambers, and quarters for the head of the college (Fig. 6). In the next two centuries about eighteen more colleges were founded at Oxford and Cambridge, for the most part following the patterns laid down at New College, both in their organization (with teachers and undergraduates living together), and in the quadrangular arrangement of their buildings.

There were several reasons for the use of the enclosed quadrangle or courtyard at English colleges.[3] One was the tradition of the cloistered monastery. Although English colleges were not as thoroughly patterned on monastic models as is sometimes supposed, the influence was strong and several of the colleges were actually founded in, or later took over, monastic structures. Simply from an architectural point of view, the monastic and collegiate "programs" were nearly identical: the housing of a community of unmarried men and boys, with spaces for sleeping, eating, instruction, and religious services. Furthermore, the enclosed quadrangle functioned as defense against potential enemies, who included the townspeople themselves as much as outside armies. The early histories of Oxford and Cambridge abound in incidents of town-gown antagonism leading to fighting, warfare, and murder on both sides. The ability to close off a college at a few gate-points also gave college authorities the advantage of greater control over the students, a concern that was a major factor in the growth of the collegiate system. At Oxford in 1410, the desire to control disorder and whoring produced an edict requiring all students to reside in either a hall or a college.[4] The fact that colleges provided more control than halls was one of the reasons for the gradual dominance of the college.

Moreover, the quadrangular form made sense simply in terms of planning and land use. In the crowded towns of Oxford and Cambridge, colleges made the best use of small lots by building around their perimeters, thus getting the maximum building space for the acreage. At first, this practice often resulted in misshapen quadrangles (such as the fourteenth-century Old Court of Corpus Christi College, Cambridge), revealing in the builders of the time little of the concern for architectural regularity that later ages would display (Fig. 7). As new colleges were founded and existing ones ex-

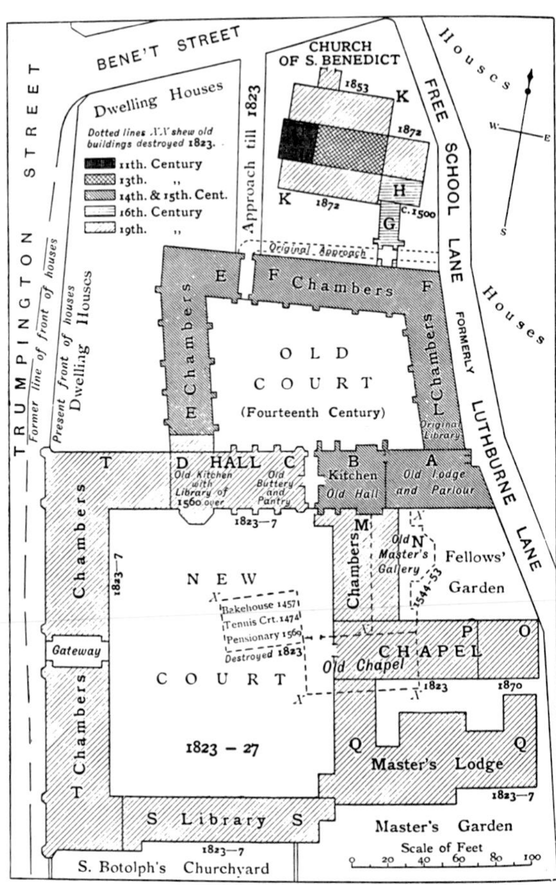

7 Plan of Corpus Christi College, Cambridge, as it evolved from the fourteenth to the nineteenth centuries. (Thomas D. Atkinson, *Cambridge Described and Illustrated*, London, 1897, p. 344)

8 Portion of David Loggan's map of Oxford, from *Oxonia Illustrata*, 1675. Collegiate quadrangles shown include those of University College (1), Merton College (3), Oriel College (5), Queen's College (6), New College (7), All Souls College (9), and Christ Church College (13).

8

panded, space became scarcer while the desire grew for larger quadrangles and more uniform architecture. Maps and aerial views, such as David Loggan's seventeenth-century engraving of Oxford, show the colleges vying with each other for space within the confining medieval walls of the city (Fig. 8).[5] At Cambridge, the land-use pattern of many of the early colleges was somewhat different, with narrow frontages on the main street and lengthy gardened "backs" extending down to the River Cam behind. But the buildings themselves were generally arranged around quadrangles as at Oxford.

In the mid-sixteenth century, an innovation in the quadrangular form appeared that would be important for later collegiate planning in America as well as in England. When Dr. John Caius, a graduate of Gonville Hall at Cambridge who had studied medicine in Italy and become court physician after returning to England, endowed and refounded his old school as Gonville and Caius College in 1557, he had a new court built adjacent to the old one (Fig. 9). Unlike earlier quadrangles, the new Caius Court was open on one side, bounded only by a wall and a monumental gate. The doctor's ostensible reason for leaving the courtyard open was health. He expressly forbade buildings on the open side "lest the air, from being confined within a narrow space, should become foul."[6] But, as Nikolaus Pevsner has pointed out, there was also probably a more formal motive for this design, as the three-sided courtyard was typical of the fashionable new chateaux in France, such as those of Bury and Anet.[7] Whatever practical advantages it may have had, Caius's open quadrangle created an architectural impression very different from that of the medieval enclosed court and represented a new, Renaissance notion of planning. It created the possibility of focal points and axial organization not inherent in the closed, equilateral cloister. And its openness suggested a more sympathetic and less defensive attitude toward the world outside the college.

In the late sixteenth century, two more colleges were founded at Cambridge (the last new foundations there until 1800): Emmanuel in 1584 and Sidney Sussex in 1596, both of which followed the open-courtyard pattern established by Dr. Caius (Fig. 10). Both also were centers of Puritanism, and Emmanuel had special links with New England and Harvard College in the following century. The three-sided courtyard was to play an important role in American college planning, and Emmanuel was probably the transmitter of this form to the New World.

Oxford, during this period, was more conservative than Cambridge, theologically, politically, and architecturally. It resisted the reforms of Protestantism and Puritanism more tenaciously than did its rival, and it was disrupted more seriously by the civil war in the 1640s. In its physical planning, Oxford perpetuated the enclosed quadrangle, using it in virtually all of its newly founded colleges: St. John's, 1555; Trinity, 1555; Jesus, 1571; Wadham, 1610; and Pembroke, 1624. In terms of architectural style, it is remarkable how long Oxford resisted the Renaissance and persisted in building in the Gothic manner—well into the seventeenth century—although much of this seems to be a consciously antiquarian "revival" rather than a true continuation of the Gothic tradition.[8] But despite the retention of Gothic details and enclosed quadrangles, Oxford revealed a new architectural mentality. Courtyards were now planned symmetrically, with axes emphasized by prominent entry gates placed at the midpoints of the ranges,

9 Gonville and Caius College, Cambridge. View from Loggan's *Cantabrigia Illustrata*, 1688. Open courtyard in foreground was constructed ca. 1560–1580. Behind it is older quadrangle of Gonville Hall. *Extreme right*: Perse and Legge buildings (dormitories, built 1617–1619), to which extensions later were made that created another quadrangle.

10 Emmanuel College, Cambridge. View from Loggan's *Cantabrigia Illustrata*, 1688. Most of these buildings were constructed soon after the founding of the college in 1584. Main entrance, through gate at the left in this view, led into three-sided courtyard opening to the left. Central courtyard also was originally open on one side, but was closed, about 1670, by the erection of the chapel, designed by Christopher Wren (seen at top in this view).

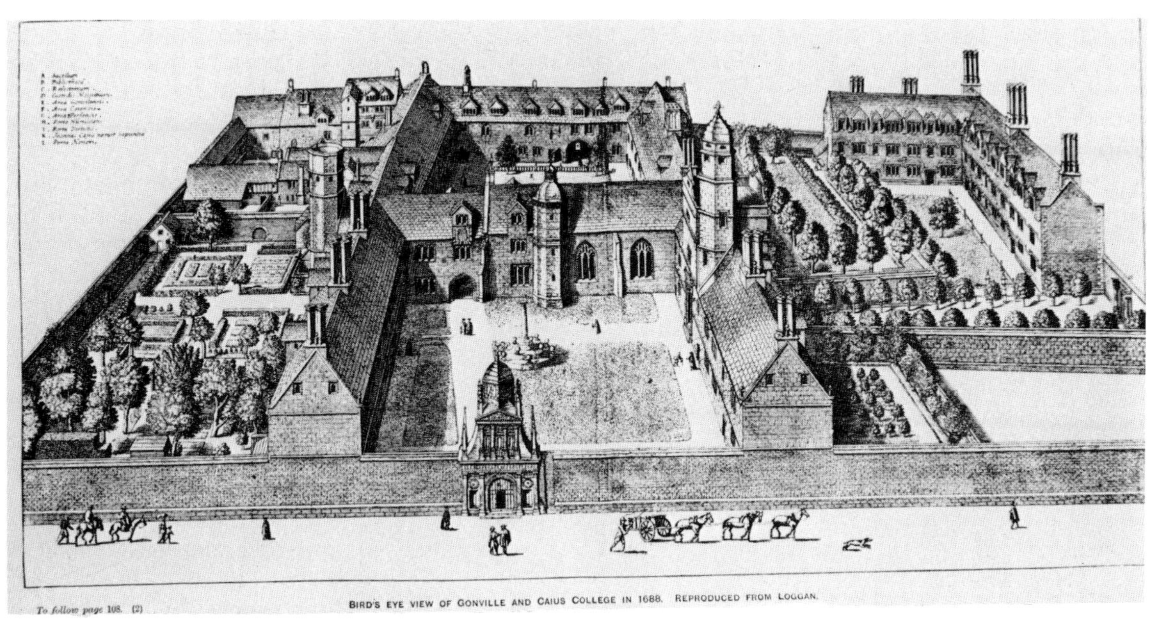
To follow page 108. (2)
BIRD'S EYE VIEW OF GONVILLE AND CAIUS COLLEGE IN 1688. REPRODUCED FROM LOGGAN.

9

10

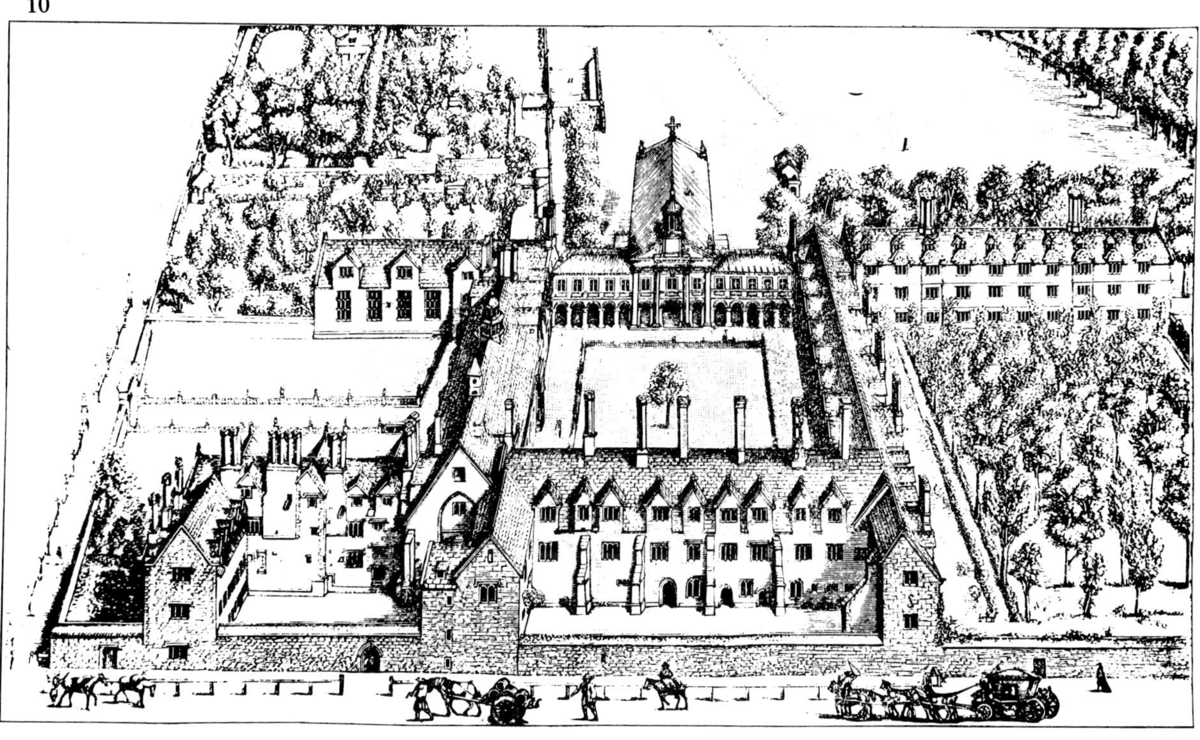

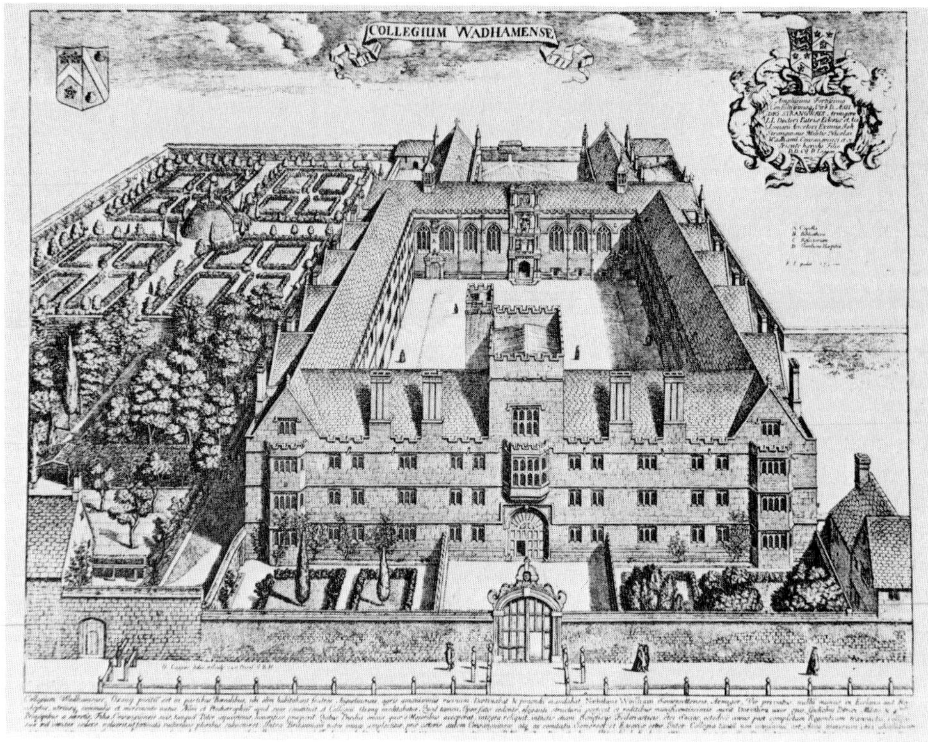

11

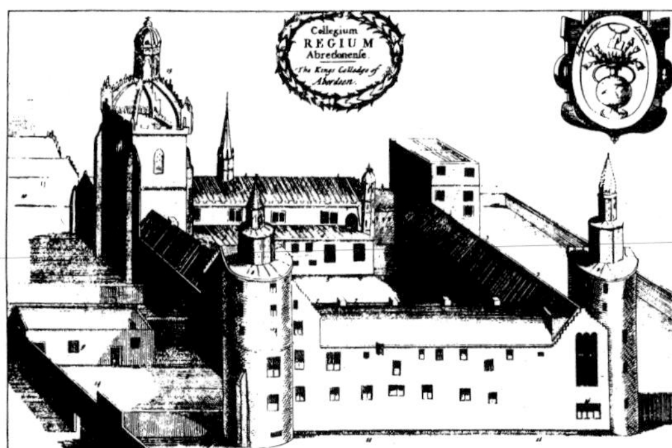

12

13

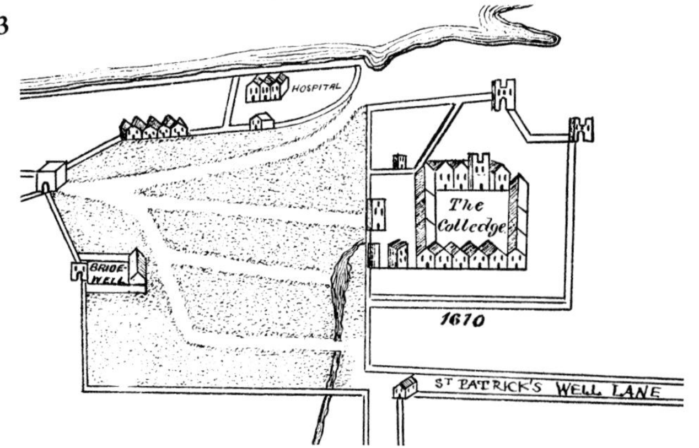

11 Wadham College, Oxford, constructed 1610–1613. View from Loggan's *Oxonia Illustrata*, 1675.

12 King's College, Aberdeen. View from a map of 1661 by James Gordon. (Peter J. Anderson, ed., *Studies in the History and Development of the University of Aberdeen*, Aberdeen, 1906, opp. p. 369)

13 Trinity College, Dublin. View from a map of 1610. (John W. Stubbs, *The History of the University of Dublin*, Dublin, 1889, frontispiece)

as in the quadrangle of Wadham College, constructed about 1610, and the Canterbury Quad of St. John's College of the 1630s (Fig. 11).[9] The new formal treatment of the enclosed quadrangle also is found at Cambridge, most strikingly in the series of axially aligned courtyards of St. John's College.

Despite the religious and political turmoil of the late sixteenth and early seventeenth centuries, Oxford and Cambridge came through the period educationally strengthened. Their curricula were reformed, with the introduction of some science and the suppression of medieval scholasticism.[10] The reformers also had social goals. They reminded the universities that many of the colleges had been founded originally for the education of poor children and that they had a responsibility to train greater numbers of them. Toward the other end of the social scale, the aristocrats, gentry, and affluent merchant class began sending more of their sons to the universities, reflecting a widespread enthusiasm for education that was unknown earlier. The early seventeenth century saw a greater proportion of the English population receiving higher education than ever before—greater, in fact, than at any later time until the twentieth century.[11] This popular enthusiasm for education was exported to the American colonies, and became an important force in the early establishment of colleges there.

Thus, both educationally and architecturally, the English college underwent major transformations just before and during the first wave of American colonization. In some ways the architectural developments can be seen as expressions of the educational ones. Particularly at Cambridge, the three-sided courtyard, open to the community and the world, reflected the new intellectual ideals and the rejection of the medieval monastic tradition.

Higher education in Scotland was different from that in England in a number of ways that may have influenced colonial America.[12] In contrast to the two centralized English institutions, Scotland had four relatively small universities (founded between 1411 and 1582): St. Andrews, Glasgow, Aberdeen, and Edinburgh. Typically, these had only two or three colleges each, and Aberdeen had only one until 1593. Consequently there was some confusion in Scotland between "college" and "university," which was to be true also in America. There was also a difference between the geographical settings of English and Scottish universities, the latter being generally located in or near the main town of a region.[13] That fact, combined with their smaller size, made Scottish universities more urban in character, or at least less dominant over their urban environments. Partly as a result of this (and also because of a greater reliance on European models of education), the Scottish schools were less collegiate than the English, in that the English ideal of a tightly regulated college community did not hold sway. Scottish students were freer to live in town rather than at their colleges, and in this way their lives were more like those of continental students. Architecturally, this meant that fewer collegiate buildings were required. But the form of Scottish colleges was not very different from the English form; normally it was an enclosed, or nearly enclosed, quandrangle of buildings (Fig. 12).[14]

Another school of higher education in the British sphere during the period before American colonization was Trinity College in Dublin, founded in 1591.[15] In a number of ways, it was similar to the American colleges that would follow. It was small; it was originally not a university, but just a single college; and its location was in effect colonial. Furthermore, at its foundation it had a strong Puritan bias and was run by Cambridge alumni, as Harvard was to be. Despite this, there is no evidence that the architecture or planning of Trinity College was influential in America. The original Trinity buildings, though humble in comparison with contemporary construction at English colleges, were arranged in the traditional enclosed quandrangle, a form that was to find little favor in colonial America (Fig. 13). From its start, the American college would devise new physical forms suitable to its own special needs.

14

14 "The Founding of Dartmouth College in 1769." Engraving by S. E. Brown, 1839, showing Eleazer Wheelock with his white and Indian students in the wilderness of New Hampshire. (Dartmouth College)

I. The Colonial College

The importance of education to the founders of the English colonies in America is shown by how quickly they created colleges. In 1640, a mere ten years after the settling of the Massachusetts Bay Colony, when its population was only about 12,000, a college was already established and fully operating. In Virginia, an attempt to start a college was made even earlier, although it did not succeed at first. Thus the enthusiasm for education in England at the time was exported to the colonies, especially to New England, where the Puritans put a special emphasis on learning, and where there was an unusually high proportion of university men in the population.[1]

This enthusiasm persisted throughout the colonial period. By the time of the Revolution there were nine degree-granting colleges in the colonies, a remarkable number in proportion to the total population.[2] These were Harvard College in Massachusetts, founded in 1636; the College of William and Mary in Virginia, 1693; Yale College in Connecticut, 1701; the College of New Jersey (later Princeton), 1746; King's College (later Columbia) in New York, 1754; the College of Philadelphia (later the University of Pennsylvania), 1755; the College of Rhode Island (later Brown), 1765; Queen's College (later Rutgers) in New Jersey, 1766; and Dartmouth College in New Hampshire, 1769.[3] Already, a pattern was established that would characterize American education from then on: many separate colleges, widely dispersed and responding to different local needs rather than centralized in one or two universities as in England.

Architecturally, the importance of education in the American colonies is suggested by the sheer size of the college buildings in relation to other structures. When erected in the late 1630s, the first Harvard building was the largest edifice in New England (Fig. 21).[4] Forty years later it was replaced by a new building, which in turn was the "most imposing structure in the English colonies" (Fig. 22).[5] The main building at William and Mary, constructed at the end of the seventeenth century, was "the largest building yet erected in Virginia and probably in any of the colonies" (Fig. 27).[6] And Nassau Hall at Princeton is said to have been the largest building in North America when it was built in 1753 (Fig. 43).[7] Thus, during most, if not all, of the colonial period, the biggest buildings in the colonies were educational, a fact that reveals a commitment to education—and to its physical needs—that was to be a particularly American trait.[8]

The importance of education in colonial America is also seen in the dispersal of colleges throughout the colonies. Except for the underrepresented South, the colonies had colleges more or less evenly distributed among them (one each in Massachusetts, Connecticut, Rhode Island, New Hampshire, New York, Pennsylvania, Virginia, and two in New Jersey). In this respect the American colonies were more like Scotland, with its four relatively small universities. But in America the tendency to decentralize was much stronger, and after the Revolution colleges proliferated throughout the country.

Related to this was an American tendency for colleges to be located on the frontier rather than in the cities. At first, this was motivated by the goal of training Indians for missionary work. The first college planned for the English colonies was conceived by the Virginia Company of London in 1618; its primary purpose was to convert and train "infidel children," and its site was to be in the wilderness at Henrico, eighty miles inland from Jamestown.[9] Funds were collected, land acquired, and bricks made for a building or buildings, but after the Indians massacred the colonists at Henrico in 1622 the Virginians began thinking less favorably of the native Americans.[10] In the following years, both in Virginia and in New England, further attempts were made to establish Indian colleges or schools (the intended level of instruction was always rather vague). However, the promoters were usually idealistic authorities in London; most of the colonists were unenthusiastic, the Indians were uninterested, and the projects proved unproductive. Nevertheless, the notion persisted that American higher education ought somehow to include the Indian. The most notable efforts in this area were those of the Reverend Eleazer Wheelock in the mid-eighteenth century, first in his academy at Lebanon, Connecticut, then in Dartmouth College, chartered by the province of New Hampshire in 1769 and purposely located in the wilderness in order to make contact with the Indians (Fig. 14).[11]

By the mid-eighteenth century, two other factors contributed to the rural placement of schools: a distrust of cities, which were viewed as centers of irreligion and discord, and an attraction to the supposed purity of nature. New Light Presbyterianism was the major manifestation of the evangelical spirit in America at this time, and the schools it established usually were well removed from cities; notable examples are William and Gilbert Tennents' seminary at Neshaminy, Pennsylvania, started in 1727, and the College of New Jersey, founded in 1746 and placed at Princeton several years later.[12] The Tennents' school was housed in a simple log cabin in the woods along the Neshaminy Creek, and this humble architecture was made a virtue by the New Light leaders, who proudly christened their institution "the Log College." Technically, perhaps, it was not a college, but the term happily expressed the ironic combination of primitive purity and higher learning. From then on, the virtuous "log college" and its variants held a fascination for Americans, becoming common images in collegiate mythology (Fig. 15).[13] The romantic ideal of the college in nature, removed from the distractions of civilization, has persisted up to the present time and has determined the locations of countless institutions.

In curriculum, the colonial colleges largely perpetuated the traditional classical format, based mainly on Latin and Greek studies and theology. But some innovations were instituted or proposed. As early as 1672, a Harvard president called for a broad increase of scientific studies.[14] The main innovations came in the mid-eighteenth century, notably with Benjamin Franklin and William Smith at the College of Philadelphia, where practical training and the study of English began to be admitted along with the classical courses. Smith, one of the most original educators of the period, published in 1753 a proposal for an ideal American college, which he called "the College of Mirania"; trades were to be taught along with the classics, a spirit of semidemocracy was to prevail, and "Imagination" would be encouraged among the students.[15] But in contrast to the innovative curriculum, the physical plan of Smith's proposed school, which he described in some detail, was thoroughly conventional—simply the English enclosed quadrangle.[16] Much more innovative were the plans of the actual colleges that existed in America at Smith's time.

The most remarkable thing about the architecture and planning of the nine colonial colleges is

15 Ædificium Primum. Æd. 1836.

16

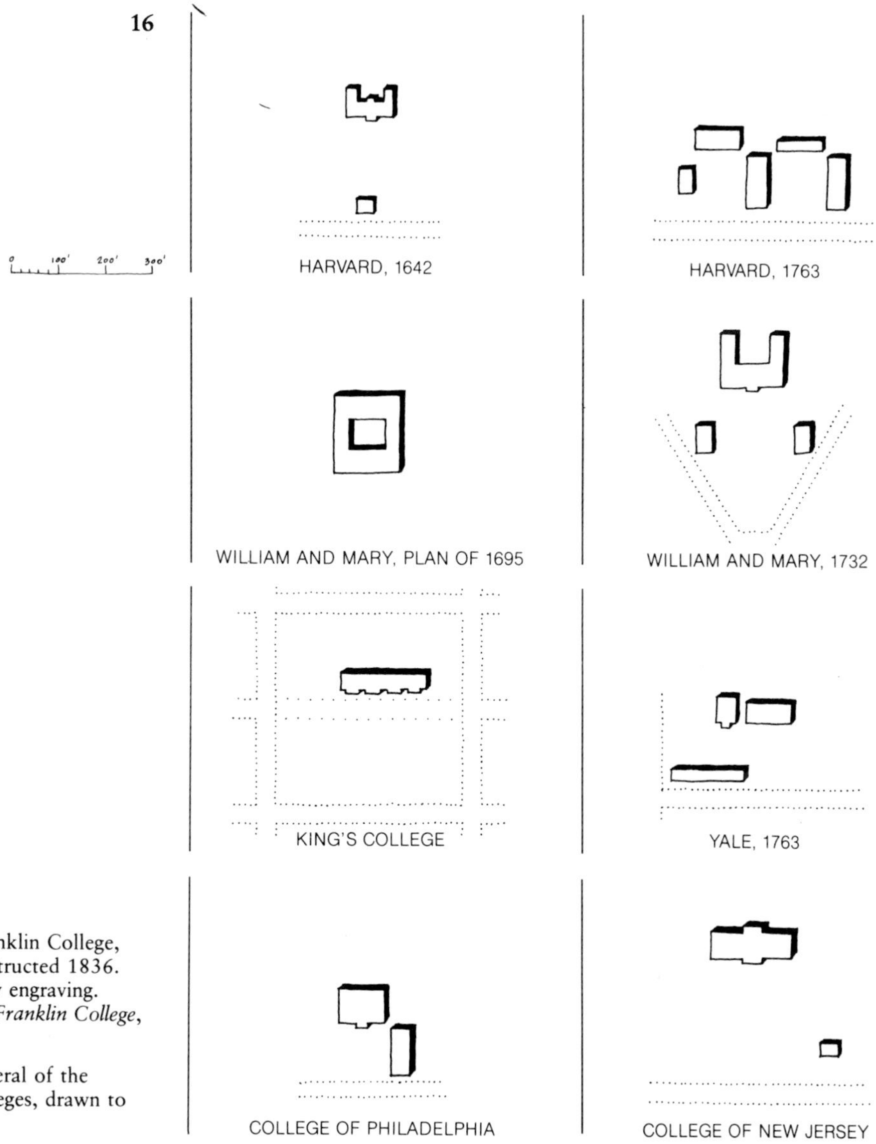

0 100' 200' 300'

HARVARD, 1642

HARVARD, 1763

WILLIAM AND MARY, PLAN OF 1695

WILLIAM AND MARY, 1732

KING'S COLLEGE

YALE, 1763

COLLEGE OF PHILADELPHIA

COLLEGE OF NEW JERSEY

15 "First building" of Franklin College, Franklin, Indiana, constructed 1836. Late-nineteenth-century engraving. (*First Half Century of Franklin College*, Cincinnati, 1884)

16 Schematic plans of several of the colonial American colleges, drawn to the same scale.

17

18

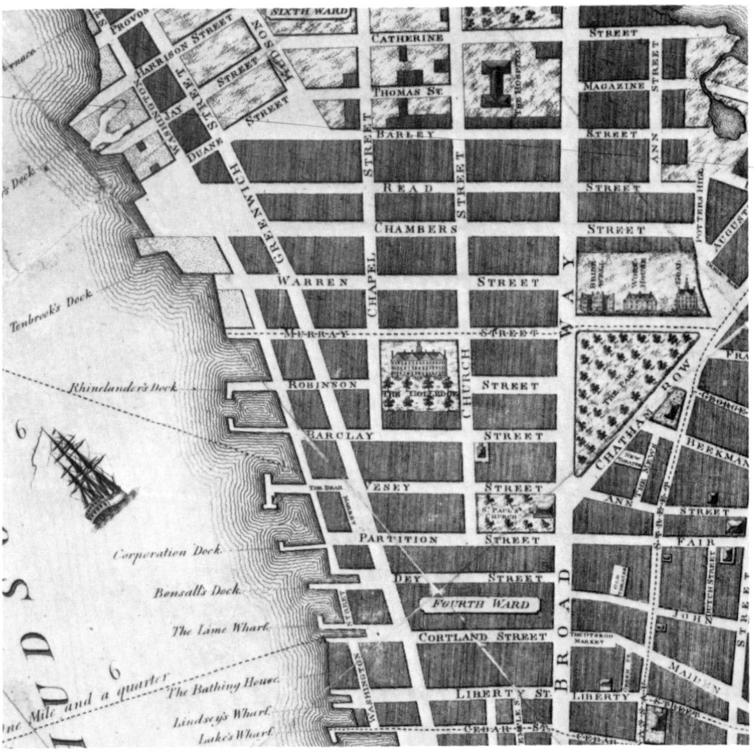

17 First buildings of the College of Philadelphia (later the University of Pennsylvania), as shown in a nineteenth-century view based on a drawing by Pierre-Eugène du Simitière. Academy (*left*), built in 1740 as a charity school, and dormitory (*right*), built in 1762, designed by Robert Smith. Both demolished in the 1840s. (George B. Wood, *Early History of the University of Pennsylvania*, Philadelphia, 1896, p. 11)

18 Detail of Taylor-Roberts map of New York City, 1797, showing (*center*) the first building of King's College (now Columbia University), constructed 1756–1760, demolished 1857. College was bounded by Murray, Church, Barclay, and Chapel streets, near present location of the World Trade Center in lower Manhattan. (I. N. Phelps Stokes Collection, New York Public Library, Astor, Lenox, and Tilden Foundations)

their diversity (Fig. 16). The three-sided courtyard was used at Harvard, first singly and then in a double form (Figs. 22, 25). The two colonial buildings of the College of Philadelphia may represent this plan in an unfinished state (Fig. 17).[17] The College of William and Mary produced two very different types of plans: the Oxford-like enclosed quadrangle of its original scheme, never completed; and its executed plan with a large building flanked symmetrically by small structures (Figs. 26, 29). The first buildings of Dartmouth College were simple structures which, together with barns, a blacksmith's shop, and other wilderness necessities, formed a village-like compound dominated by the college president's "Mansion House."[18]

Several of the colonial colleges had a single large building containing most of the collegiate functions, but among these there were significant differences. The long, narrow building constructed for King's College in lower Manhattan in 1756 was originally intended to form part of a three-sided quadrangle; since this plan was never fully executed, the building was left with an open space in front of it (called the "College Green"), but the school nonetheless quickly assumed an urban character as the city expanded around it and streets were laid out on all sides (Fig. 18).[19] In contrast, Nassau Hall at rural Princeton was purposely set far back from the road, creating a large greensward or field (the first college grounds to be called a "campus"), to which the building acted as a defining backdrop (Fig. 43). This pattern, which had no exact precedent in the British universities, was to be used at many subsequent American colleges—including Brown in Rhode Island (where the building now called University Hall was built in 1770) and, after the Revolution, at Dartmouth (Dartmouth Hall, 1784–91) and Rutgers (Old Queen's, 1809) (Figs. 45, 46).[20] Yale began with a single building directly on the New Haven Green, but then constructed two buildings behind it, the beginning of the "Old Brick Row" of aligned buildings, another pattern that had no European collegiate precedent and was to be repeated often in America (Fig. 35).

The originality seen in these diverse plans is probably greater than that of any other type of colonial American architecture, and reveals a highly inventive search for new forms to embody new educational requirements and ideals. In particular, the colonial plans of Harvard, William and Mary, Yale, and Princeton are significant, and will be examined here in some detail.

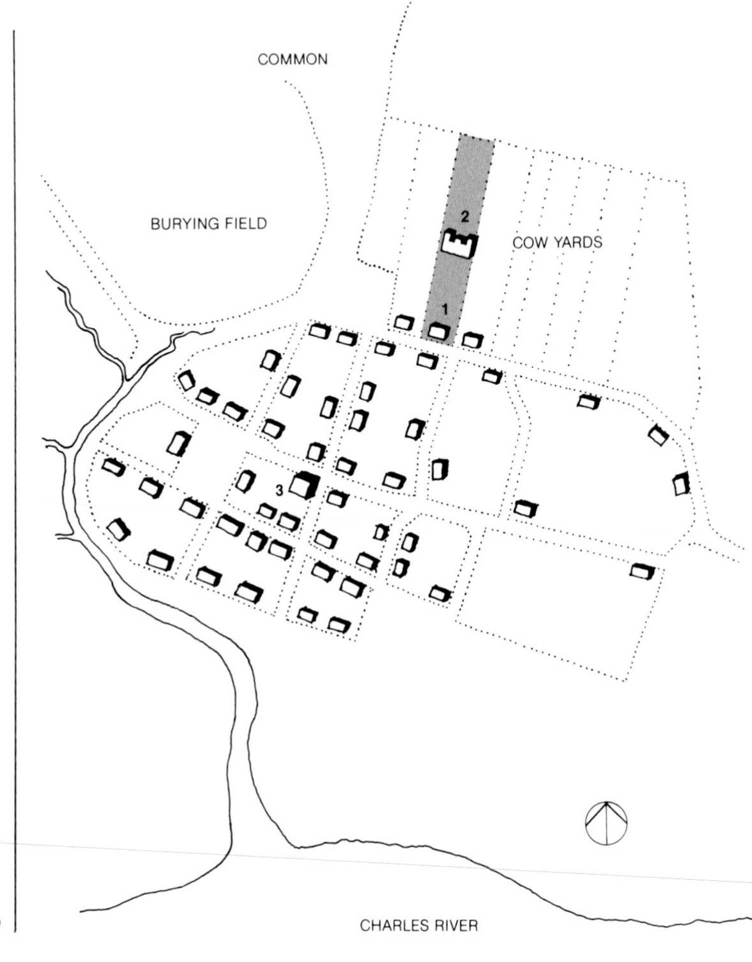

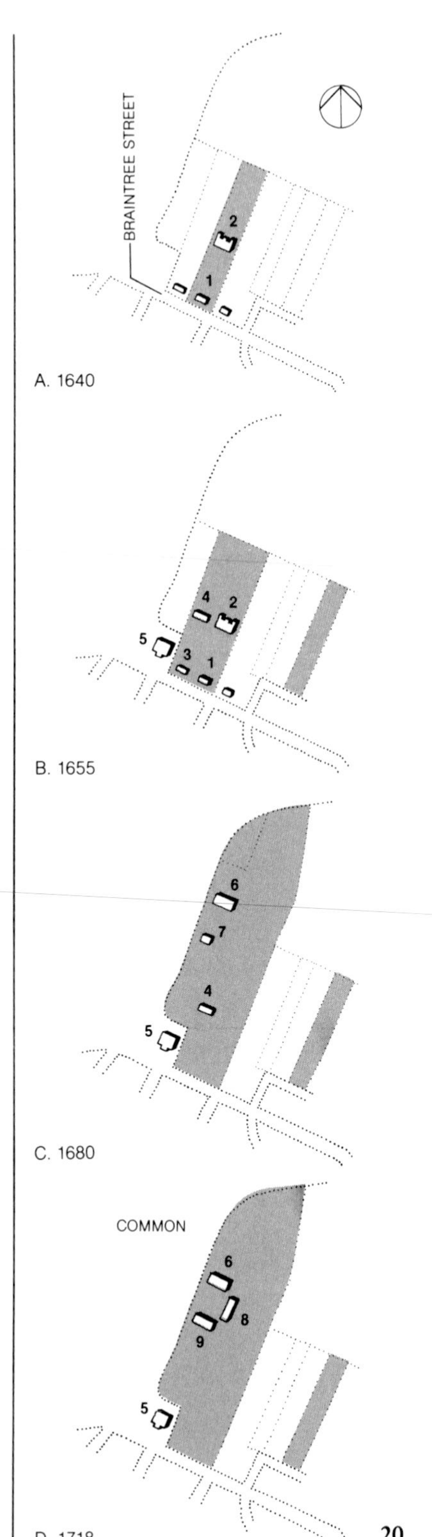

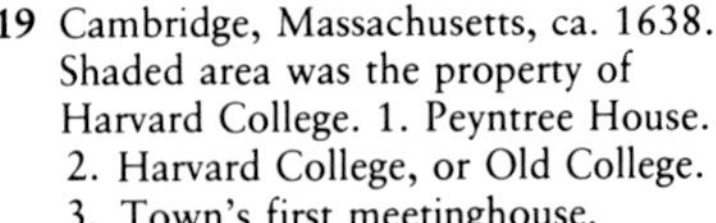

19 Cambridge, Massachusetts, ca. 1638. Shaded area was the property of Harvard College. 1. Peyntree House. 2. Harvard College, or Old College. 3. Town's first meetinghouse.

20 Plans showing growth of Harvard College from 1640 to 1720. 1. Peyntree House, acquired by college in 1637. 2. Old College, 1638–1642. 3. Goffe College, acquired 1651. 4. Indian College, 1655. 5. The town's new meetinghouse, 1651. 6. New College, or Harvard Hall, 1672. 7. President's House, 1680. 8. Stoughton College, 1697. 9. Massachusetts Hall, 1718.

Harvard

In October 1636, only six years after the settlement of the Massachusetts Bay Colony, its General Court voted to establish a college and a year later decided to place it at Newtowne, a village on the Charles River four miles inland from Boston. Several months after that, Newtowne was renamed Cambridge, reflecting the high proportion of Cambridge alumni among the leaders of the colony. One of these, John Harvard, died in 1638 and left half of his estate and his library to the new school, which in gratitude was promptly named in his memory. (Thus the English tradition of naming colleges or individual buildings for benefactors was brought to America, where it became a popular practice and a common device for attracting contributions. At the beginning of the eighteenth century, Cotton Mather told Elihu Yale that having a college named for him would be "much better than an Egyptian pyramid.")[21]

The determination to create this college in the wilderness was a strong expression of the Puritan beliefs of the Massachusetts Bay colonists, namely, their emphasis on community cohesion and religious conformity, and their conviction that higher learning was essential to these ideals.[22] A major motive for the college was the traditional one of training clergymen, but Harvard was more than just a religious seminary; it served important secular functions in the colony, with its graduates entering careers in government, teaching, and business as well as the ministry.

From the start, Harvard made a firm commitment to the English collegiate system. It would have been much easier and cheaper for the founders to adopt the continental or Scottish mode of having students room and board in the town, leaving the school with the sole responsibility of teaching. But the founders were resolute in the collegiate belief that higher education is fully effective only when students eat, sleep, study, worship, and play together in a tight community. The governing board of Harvard explicitly stated this in 1671:

> It is well known . . . what advantage to Learning accrues by the multitude of persons cohabiting for scholasticall communion, whereby to acuate the minds of one another, and other waies to promote the ends of a Colledge-Society.[23]

Cotton Mather, in the 1690s, specifically called this the "Collegiate way of Living."[24] Firmly established at Harvard, this principle set the pattern for later colleges and has remained an American educational ideal ever since, despite changing circumstances (such as the increase in student ages, now about three or four years older than in the seventeenth and eighteenth centuries).[25] At Harvard, the collegiate commitment was very demanding from the beginning, requiring that a large proportion of available funds be spent on construction. When the college opened in the late summer of 1638, it was quartered in the Peyntree House, a dwelling provided for the first professor (Figs. 19, 20-A). But already a large multipurpose building was planned by the college's Board of Overseers. Its construction was started without delay, and it was completed in 1642.[26]

The form of this building—called at first "Harvard College," then "Old College" after additional buildings were constructed—is not known from any contemporary plans or drawings, but its design has been reconstructed from seventeenth-century descriptions and other evidence (Fig. 21).[27] Old College was on a long, narrow, one-acre lot that was the college's only property at this time (Fig. 20-A). It was set back well behind the Peyntree House and Braintree Street (now Massachusetts Avenue), leading an English visitor in the 1650s to write: "The scituation of this Coledg is very pleasant, at the end of a spacious plain, more like a bowling green, than a wilderness."[28] The odd shape of the lot resulted from one of the land-division patterns in the colony, by which individual residents were allotted narrow strips of pasture land at the edge of the town for their cattle. The Peyntree House and its contiguous strip of the "Cow-Yard" were thus Harvard's first land, an accident that gave for all time the homely word *Yard* to its central property. This word was to be borrowed by several other American colleges (William and Mary and Yale, for example, used it well into the nineteenth century), until it was superseded by the more learned-sounding *campus*, which apparently was first used at Princeton in the 1770s.[29]

This first building at Harvard was a three-story wooden structure, containing virtually all of the college's functions except the president's quarters, which stayed in the Peyntree House (and a new building that replaced it in 1645). During its brief life of forty years, Old College was the most ambitious building in New England, described by an English captain as "thought by some to be too gorgeous for a Wilderness, and yet too mean in others apprehensions for a Colledg."[30] The first floor contained a "spacious Hall," the center of college life, serving as lecture hall, dining room, and general living space. No other large classrooms were needed, because lectures were only a small portion of the collegiate curriculum, which put more emphasis on "recitation" in which students recited memorized passages from textbooks. Also on the first floor were the kitchen, the "buttery" (for the storage of foods and beverages), other storerooms, and two or three student chambers. The second floor contained the library and most of the building's dormitory chambers, the remaining ones being in the attic.

These chambers were of varying sizes, and altogether must have accommodated about fifty persons (seldom did the enrollment at Harvard exceed that in the seventeenth century, and it was usually far less). The smaller rooms, with one or two occupants, were normally for the tutors or "fellows," assistant teachers who aided the president (there were no other professors), and for privileged students. The largest chamber, on the second floor, held about fifteen students (the freshman class may have been put there); each of the remaining chambers housed three or four students and had a separate partitioned "study," only a few feet square, for each occupant. Thus the students were thrown together for sleeping, usually two to a bed, but were given private spaces for studying. In these regards, Harvard followed the standard practice of English colleges.[31]

However, there was no separate college chapel at Harvard, as there normally was in England. Students attended religious services with the citizens of Cambridge in the town's meetinghouse, which was originally in the center of town but in 1650 was rebuilt at the western edge of Harvard's property, with a special student gallery paid for by the college (Fig. 20-B). Harvard considered itself an inseparable part of the larger religious community; it built its own chapel only after doctrinal uniformity ceased in Cambridge.

The overall plan of Old College formed a kind of E, with short wings and a central staircase turret extending from the main block. This form does not seem to derive from the colleges of Oxford or Cambridge; it has been compared to a type of Elizabethan manor house and also to a fifteenth-century building at Eton.[32] Already, the American college was experimenting architecturally.

But the next stage of Harvard's growth introduced a more important innovation, one that set a pattern for American colleges: the creation of separate buildings, rather than the linked structures of English colleges. In 1650, the college acquired the adjacent Goffe lot to the west, whose house, renamed Goffe College, was used for extra college space (Fig. 20-B). In 1655, another building was erected, probably on the new Goffe lot, expressly for the housing and instruction of Indian students (although almost no Indians attended, and the building was used mainly to house the college printing press). Except that it was made of brick, little is known about the form of this "Indian College."[33] But it is clear that it was completely separate from the Old College. A visitor in 1655 wrote that, "At Cambridg they have a wooden Colledg, and in the yard a brick pile . . . for the Indians."[34]

21 Reconstructed view of Cambridge in 1668, looking from the northeast toward the Charles River. In foreground are the four buildings of Harvard. The largest is Old College, which probably stood about where Grays Hall is now, in Harvard Yard. To right of it is the Indian College. On the street are Peyntree House and Goffe College. Square building where streets intersect is town meetinghouse. Many features of this reconstruction are conjectural, since no contemporary visual records of the buildings exist. Drawing by Harold R. Shurtleff.
(Harvard University Press)

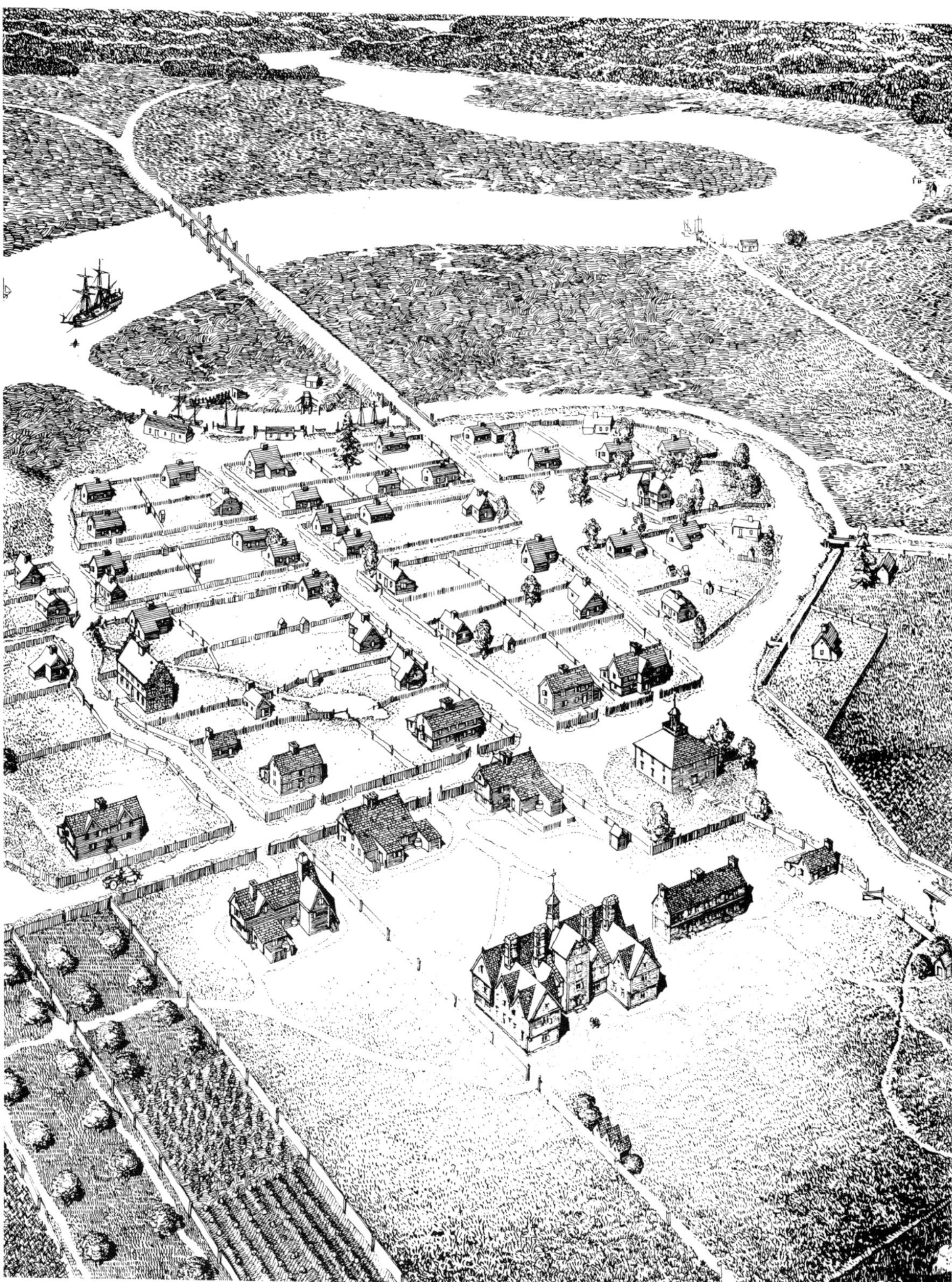

21

22

22 "A Prospect of the Colledges in Cambridge in New England." Engraved view, looking east, by William Burgis, 1726. *From left*: second Harvard College, 1672–1682, burned 1764; Stoughton College, 1697–1699, demolished 1781; and Massachusetts Hall, 1718–1720, which replaced the President's House built on this site in 1680.
(Massachusetts Historical Society)

By 1655 Harvard thus had four buildings—Old College, the Indian College, the President's House, and Goffe College—all of them separate structures (Fig. 21). This contrasts with the English colleges, where buildings normally were constructed in linked series, forming enclosed quadrangles. Beginning with Harvard, American schools favored a very different spatial pattern, with separate buildings set in an open landscape. As a result, the typical American college has been extroverted and expansive, in contrast to the inward-turning English school.

There were no doubt several reasons for this momentous departure at Harvard. One was perhaps a sense that the vastness of the American landscape required a commensurately large vision of planning. A more practical concern was the danger of fire. Unlike the masonry structures at the English colleges, most of Harvard's early buildings were made of wood, and therefore separating them lessened the risk of total disaster. The new pattern of planning also probably had religious significance. The Puritans may have associated linked buildings and enclosed quadrangles with monastic models, and rejected them because of the Catholic connotation. It was no accident that in England the three-sided courtyard was favored by the Puritan colleges. The Harvard planners probably wanted to divorce their school even further from the tradition of the monastic cloister by separating the buildings altogether. (In the late nineteenth century, an observer of American colleges suggested this factor, when he characterized the pattern of separate structures as "Congregational," in contrast to the "Anglican" pattern of linked buildings around a quadrangle—"like a group of Anglican communities under a bishop.")[35] Moreover, anything suggesting that the college was cloistered or isolated would have been repugnant to the Puritan sense of the integrity of the whole community. Harvard was meant to serve the community and be a part of it, a purpose for which inward-turning groups of buildings were inappropriate.[36]

Finally, another likely motive for the separation of buildings at Harvard is suggested by the odd use of the word "college" to designate individual structures at the school. This usage was apparently unknown in England (where *hall* was the normal word for a college building) and was invented at Harvard with the names Goffe College, Indian College, and Old College.[37] In the case of the Indian College, it is possible that the Harvard authorities actually thought of it as a separate college in the English sense, for it had its own teachers and the Indian students were supposed to live together in the building. It was therefore natural to build the Indian College separate from the main building. In this sense, Harvard was more like a university than simply one college. And, in fact, there is evidence that as early as the 1640s Harvard asserted some university degree-granting privileges that technically were beyond its jurisdiction.[38] In the realm of architectural planning, Harvard's self-image as a near-university could have been expressed by the separation of buildings and by their designation as "colleges." Educational changes soon made the issue of university powers less relevant and the original motive was no doubt forgotten, but the peculiar use of the word *college* persisted at Harvard, as shown in the engraving made by William Burgis in 1726, entitled "A Prospect of the Colledges in Cambridge in New England" (Fig. 22). Other American schools followed the example, especially in the early nineteenth century, and several old campuses still have buildings called "colleges"—although Harvard itself no longer does.[39]

It is clear that even in its early years, Harvard's physical layout was the result of conscious and long-range planning, rather than simply haphazard responses to needs as they arose. By 1672 a wholesale reorientation and rebuilding program was under way, which took several decades to complete and which reveals a controlling design or master plan (Fig. 20-C, D). The new construction was required by the poor condition of Old College, which already in the 1650s was described as being "in a very ruinous condition, . . . not fitt for Scholars long to abide in."[40] Rather than simply build a new structure near it on the same lot, the Board of Overseers chose a separate location, and planned a much grander group of buildings. In 1660 they acquired new parcels of the Cow-Yard, which provided frontage to the west, facing the town Common and the road connecting Cambridge with the main highway.

On this land a new brick building was begun in 1672, which was to succeed Old College as the largest structure in New England.[41] Called variously New College, Harvard College, or Harvard Hall, it took ten years to finish, but even before completion it began to receive students from the collapsing Old College. Like its predecessor, it had a multipurpose hall and a kitchen and buttery on the ground floor, a library and chambers on the second floor, and above that two more stories of chambers.

The location of this new building is significant. It did not face west toward the street and Burying Ground, but was oriented south, in a position that makes sense only as part of a preconceived three-sided courtyard, of which it was to be the northern building. In the next several decades, all construction at Harvard was in fact directed toward the completion of this master plan. In 1680 a new President's House was built to the south of Harvard Hall. In 1697 the old Indian College was torn down and its bricks used to construct the eastern component of the new group, Stoughton College. And in 1718 the President's House was replaced by a more substantial structure, Massachusetts Hall, which alone of these buildings still stands (Fig.23).[42]

By this time there were increased enrollments at Harvard. Stoughton College, built with a donation from the lieutenant-governor of the colony, was devoted exclusively to students' rooms, with four chambers per floor (each housing two or three students), served by two stairways, as in the typical plan of English college dormitories. Massachusetts Hall provided even more chambers, as well as tutors' quarters and an "Apparatus Chamber" for the study of science. In 1726 a new president's residence (now Wadsworth House) was built to replace the house torn down for Massachusetts Hall. (The fact that Harvard took such care to provide a president's house on college property is another example of English tradition perpetuated in America under changing circumstances. In England, the collegiate principle required all faculty members to live with the students. Of these faculty, only the head of the college was allowed to marry, and therefore a residence for his family had to be provided in the college quadrangle. Most early American colleges continued this tradition by providing a president's house on their land, and maintained the practice well after all faculty were allowed to marry, with the incongruous result that even today many colleges keep their presidents on campus while allowing all other professors to live anywhere they wish.)

Harvard, Stoughton, and Massachusetts halls were completely separate buildings, but their overall pattern continued the tradition of the three-sided quadrangles of Cambridge University. Indeed, the space enclosed by the Harvard buildings was almost identical in form and area (about 100 feet square) to that of Emmanuel College at Cambridge (Figs. 24, 10). Of all the English colleges, Emmanuel had the most alumni, including John Harvard, among the members of the Massachusetts Bay Colony. And Emmanuel alumni during most of the seventeenth century dominated Harvard's Board of Overseers, the group that had the real power in decisions affecting the school and which took charge of the planning of Harvard Hall in 1672.[43] At this time, at least five of the Overseers were from Emmanuel, including Governor Simon Bradstreet and Richard Saltonstall, both of whom served on the Board from the 1640s to the 1680s and had great influence on the affairs of the college.[44] They were probably the main authors of the master plan that resulted in the Emmanuel-like grouping of Harvard, Stoughton, and Massachusetts halls.

In the eighteenth century, a second open courtyard was created by the addition of two more buildings to the north: Holden Chapel, built in 1744, and Hollis Hall, another dormitory, built in 1763 to accommodate students who had been lodging in private houses in town. The two new buildings are seen in Paul Revere's engraved view of the college in 1767, which also shows a new Harvard Hall on the site of its predecessor, which was destroyed by fire in 1764 (Fig. 25). All three of these buildings exist today, although the orientation of Holden Chapel and Hollis Hall was altered in the nineteenth century when their entrances were moved from west to east as part of a redirection of the college inward toward the Yard (an area that in the eighteenth century was simply the muddy rear of the college, with pumps and privies).

The overall pattern of buildings completed by Holden and Hollis was like that of the double courtyards of Sidney Sussex College at Cambridge, but by now the similarity to the English prototype was much less pronounced. Diminutive Holden Chapel was relatively far from Hollis, decreasing

23

24

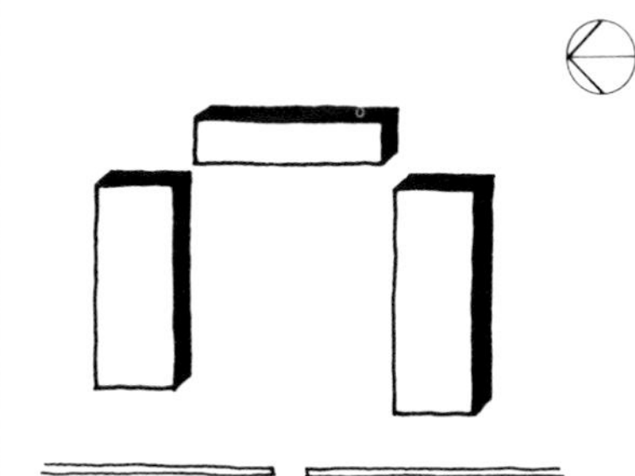

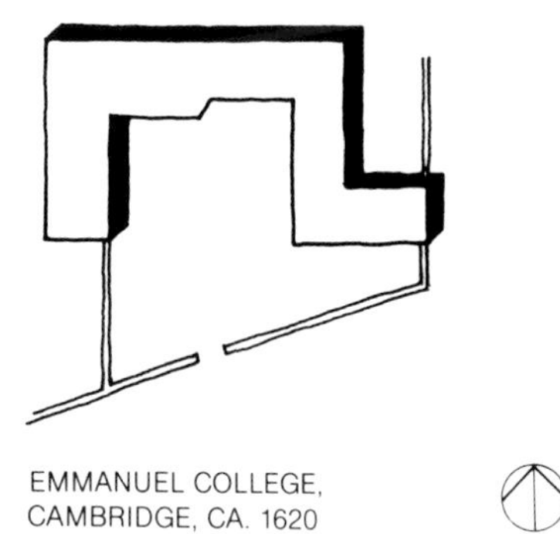

23 Massachusetts Hall, Harvard. Built 1718–1720, with £3500 appropriated by the provincial legislature. The plan for the building may have been drawn by President Leverett of the college. The building contained rooms to house sixty students and a couple of tutors, and a scientific "Apparatus Chamber"; rooms were arranged around two stairways. The building still stands, although its interior plan has been much altered over time. (Moses King, *Harvard and Its Surroundings*, Cambridge, 1882, opp. p. 19)

24 Comparison of plans of Harvard College, ca. 1720, and north court of Emmanuel College, Cambridge, ca. 1620, drawn to the same scale.

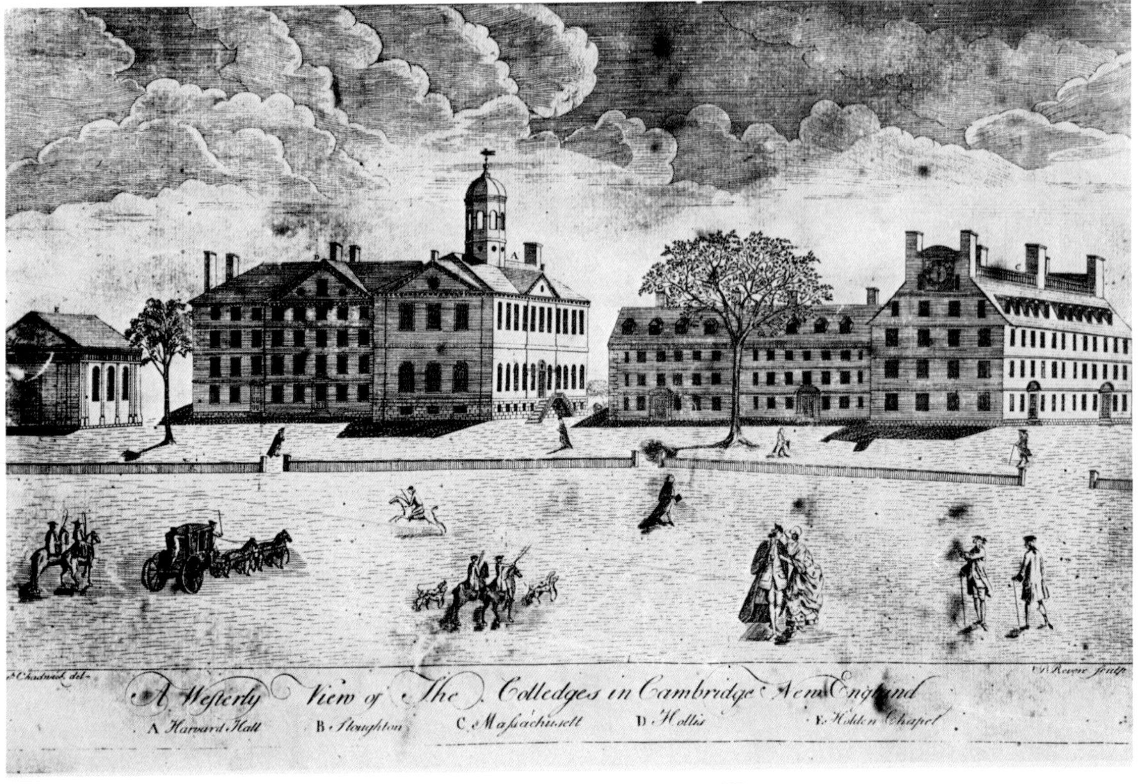

25

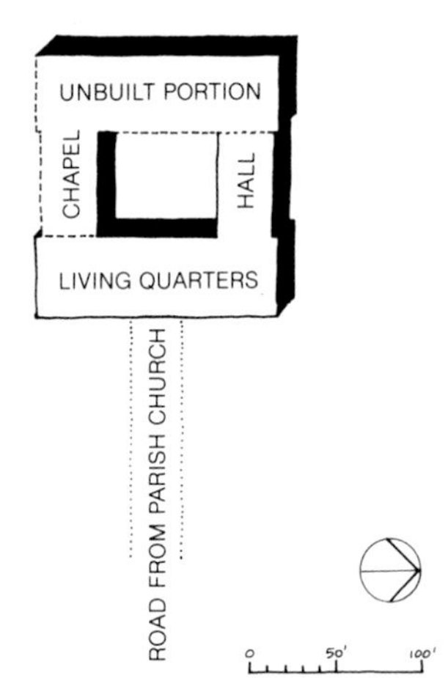

26

25 "A Westerly View of the Colledges in Cambridge New England." Engraving by Paul Revere, 1767, based on a drawing by Joshua Chadwick. *From left*: Holden Chapel, 1744; Hollis Hall, 1763; Harvard Hall, 1764; Stoughton College; and Massachusetts Hall. The new Harvard Hall, designed by the Royal Governor, Francis Bernard, contained classrooms, the college library, and a dining hall. Hollis Hall was devoted wholly to dormitory rooms. All of these buildings, except Stoughton, still stand. (Harvard University)

26 College of William and Mary, Williamsburg, Virginia. Conjectural reconstruction of plan of the first building, based on Bland Map of 1699 and proportions of the structure as it was rebuilt after the fire of 1705. Originally, only about half of this plan was constructed.

its effectiveness in defining a courtyard. And its entrance was not from the courtyard, but from the west, an orientation emphasized visually by the carved arms on its western, pedimented facade. Hollis echoed this with a pedimented central section, very different in character from the uniform facades of the earlier dormitories. Both buildings thus had an emphatic orientation to the west, with the effect that they were more like parts of a row than sides of a courtyard. The arrangement of college buildings in a row was to become very popular in America in the following decades, and especially in the early nineteenth century. This placement of Holden and Hollis oriented the college firmly toward the Cambridge Common and the public road, strengthening its outward-turning character.

The buildings of Harvard at the end of the colonial period thus embodied several concepts of planning. The underlying pattern was a continuation of the English collegiate quadrangle, as revised and opened up in the Puritan colleges at Cambridge. The memory of this tradition was still strong at Harvard in the late seventeenth century, when the courtyard bounded by Harvard, Stoughton, and Massachusetts halls was planned. When Holden Chapel and Hollis Hall were built in the next century, this tradition still determined their general placement, but the buildings were conceived more as elements in a row, all facing out to Cambridge and the world. Essential to this opening-out process was the separation of buildings, an innovation that had appeared even at the earliest stages of Harvard's growth.

This extroverted attitude toward planning clearly reflected Harvard's educational and social ideals. While committed to the collegiate ideal of students and teachers living together, the school also considered itself an integral part of the larger community. This was to become typical of American colleges. With few exceptions, the American college was to turn outward rather than inward, directing itself to the community or to nature. And its physical plan was to be the clearest evidence of this orientation.

William and Mary

Like Harvard, the College of William and Mary transformed patterns of planning taken from the English universities. But the results were very different from those at Harvard, due to the different natures of the two schools. William and Mary was Anglican rather than Puritan, its educational roots were in Oxford rather than Cambridge, and land and settlement patterns in Virginia were different from those in Massachusetts. For these and other reasons, William and Mary produced its own innovations in planning that were significant for later American colleges.[45]

The attempts to found a college in Virginia, made first at Henrico around 1620, bore fruit at the end of the century. James Blair, a Scottish-educated Anglican minister and deputy of the Bishop of London in Virginia, was the prime mover of the project and became the college's first president, overseeing most of its growth in the colonial period (his tenure lasting fifty years). By 1690, he and Francis Nicholson, lieutenant-governor of the colony, had organized support for a college among Virginians, and from 1691 to 1693 Blair was in London where he succeeded in raising funds and obtaining a royal charter from the co-reigning monarchs for whom the college was named. There is evidence that while in England Blair also engaged in some kind of architectural planning for the college, but its nature is unknown.[46] It had to be siteless planning in any case, for not until Blair returned to Virginia was the decision made to locate the college at Middle Plantation, later renamed Williamsburg. Situated about midway on the peninsula between the York and James rivers, Middle Plantation was considered a central location. The site was typical of the Virginia settlements at this time—which were mainly scattered plantations rather than real towns as in New England—and consisted merely of a parish church and widely separated farms linked by a road that ran along a ridge in the land. Probably for the first time anywhere, a college was founded in a truly rural environment. The school preceded the town, a sequence that was to become common in America.

The college acquired 330 acres west of the church, and in 1695 construction began. Several years of financial and political difficulty followed, with Blair returning to London to lobby for his interests, but by 1700 the college was ready for

27

28

27 Wren Building, College of William and Mary. Erected 1695–1700; burned and rebuilt in 1705 and twice in nineteenth century; restored 1928–1933. (Colonial Williamsburg photograph)

28 Williamson Building, Queen's College, Oxford, erected 1671. Designed possibly by Christopher Wren. Detail of David Loggan's view of Queen's College, in *Oxonia Illustrata*, 1675.

occupancy. The building, which burned in 1705, is known only through a drawing made by a Swiss traveler in 1702 and a map of 1699 that shows the ell-shaped structure as part of a larger plan for an enclosed quadrangle, the unbuilt portion indicated by dotted lines (Fig. 26).[47] There are also contemporary written references to the "square" or "quadrangle" of which only two sides were built.

Thus, in contrast to Harvard's use of the three-sided courtyard of Puritan Cambridge, the College of William and Mary originally intended to follow the conservative tradition of the fully enclosed quadrangle more typical of Oxford. William and Mary's educational roots were in fact mostly at Oxford, especially in Queen's College, whose alumni included several early supporters of the Virginia school.[48] One of these was Henry Compton, Blair's superior as Bishop of London and first chancellor of William and Mary, the person most likely to have advised Blair on the original planning of the college between 1691 and 1693.

This first William and Mary building contained the College Hall in the northern wing and living quarters in the three-story main block. After it burned in 1705, the building was rebuilt on the same foundations, but apparently the interior plan was changed, the exterior proportions were made more classical, and a projecting gabled pavilion was added to the center of the facade.[49] This second building, with the addition of a chapel wing in about 1730, remained until the mid-nineteenth century, when it was destroyed twice again by fires and was rebuilt in different styles. The Colonial Williamsburg restoration of 1928–33 returned the structure to its second stage, so that what exists today is based on the form of the building from 1705 to 1859 (Fig. 27).

This structure is called the Wren Building by the college. The controversial attribution of the design to Christopher Wren derives from a 1724 book on Virginia by a professor at the college who stated:

> The Building is beautiful and commodious, being first modelled by Sir Christopher Wren, adapted to the Nature of the Country by the Gentlemen there; and since it was burnt down, it has been rebuilt, and nicely contrived, altered, and adorned by the ingenious Direction of Governor Spotswood, and is not altogether unlike Chelsea Hospital.[50]

Wren held the position of Surveyor-General of the King's Works when Blair was in London in 1691–93, and it is possible that he, or his office, would have produced plans for a royally chartered college.[51] However, the enclosed-quadrangle design of the first structure at William and Mary is a type of plan that Wren is known to have disliked for colleges. (When asked his opinion on the matter, he wrote that if a college insisted on having a quadrangle, "let them have . . . a lame one, somewhat like a three-legged table," that is, open on one side.)[52] The building as it was reconstructed after the fire of 1705 is closer in spirit to Wren's work, but Wren is not likely to have produced a design at that time, for he was in his seventies and doing almost no work. In any case, it is possible that the reconstruction of 1705 was influenced by other works of Wren and his office, such as the Williamson Building at Queen's College, Oxford (the English college most closely tied to the college in Virginia), a building that was similar to the second William and Mary structure in general form and proportions (Fig. 28).[53]

More significant than the precise role that Wren may have played in the design of the building at William and Mary is the building's reflection of a new attitude toward collegiate architecture, which Wren exemplified. From the 1660s to 1690s, he designed at least seven buildings for the colleges at Oxford and Cambridge, and his influence transformed the look of the English universities.[54] Wren's disapproval of the medieval enclosed quadrangle resulted from his Baroque preference for openness, directional spaces, vistas with focal points, and hierarchical organization. Before Wren, the ranges of buildings in the English colleges, whether or not classical in detail, were nearly always uniform longitudinally, with little or no central emphasis or axiality. In contrast, most of Wren's designs for Oxford and Cambridge have strong central emphasis, based on pedimented forms—for example, at Oxford in the Sheldonian Theatre and the Williamson Building, and at Cambridge in the Pembroke College Chapel and the chapel range at Emmanuel College (Fig. 10). These designs introduced a new type of spatial organization to the English college, replacing medieval uniformity and closure with directionality and axial focus.

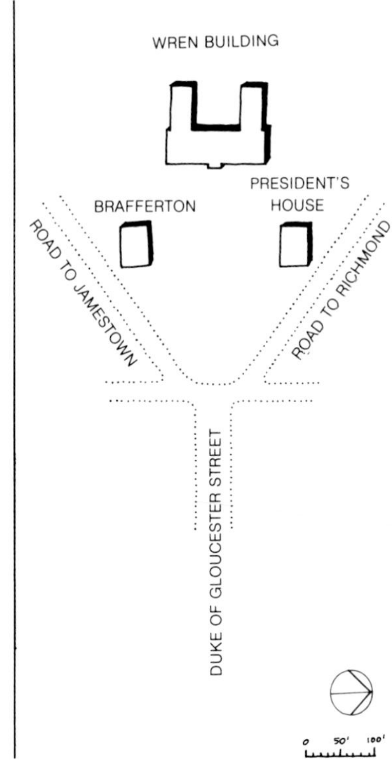

29

29 Plan of the College of William and Mary, after 1732. Wren Building was rebuilt in the decade after fire of 1705, and its chapel wing was added in 1728. Brafferton Hall, originally intended for Indian students, was built in 1723, and the President's House in 1732.

At William and Mary, there was a similar shift in thinking between the original design of 1693—the uniform enclosed quadrangle—and the second building with its new axial orientation eastward. This is confirmed by the fact that in the 1720s, when the college undertook a new building program, it altogether ignored the original plan, which would have located new construction to complete the quadrangle to the west of the built portion, and instead erected to the east two new buildings that strengthened the axiality and Baroque nature of the college (Figs. 29, 30).

This reorientation was a response to the newly laid-out plan of Williamsburg to the east. It is the most striking example up to this time, either in England or America, of collegiate planning as an integral component of a grand urban design. Francis Nicholson, who as lieutenant-governor had supported Blair in the founding of the college, was reassigned to Maryland in 1693. There he first indulged his fascination with city planning by laying out Annapolis in an eccentric pattern of circles and radial streets inspired by the plans for London, after the fire of 1666, by Wren and John Evelyn.[55] Nicholson returned to Virginia as governor in 1698, just as the statehouse at Jamestown burned down, providing an opportunity he and Blair immediately seized for moving the capital to Williamsburg. The resulting conjunction of government and education went against English tradition (the closest British parallel being in Blair's alma mater, Edinburgh), and established an American precedent that was to be followed occasionally, especially at state institutions, despite the ingrained Anglo-American suspicions about education in large urban centers.

As it happened, Williamsburg never developed into a major city. But Nicholson believed it would, and he conceived an appropriately ambitious plan for it, whose main feature was a broad street nearly a mile long (the Duke of Gloucester Street), connecting the college at the west and the Capitol at the east, with public squares and cross-axes at points along this main axis (Fig. 31). Such a monumental city plan demanded that the college assume a form appropriate to its focal position. This urbanistic consideration surely contributed to the suspension of plans for the enclosed quadrangle and to the Wren-like transformation of the building after the fire of 1705. Nicholson was relieved

30

31

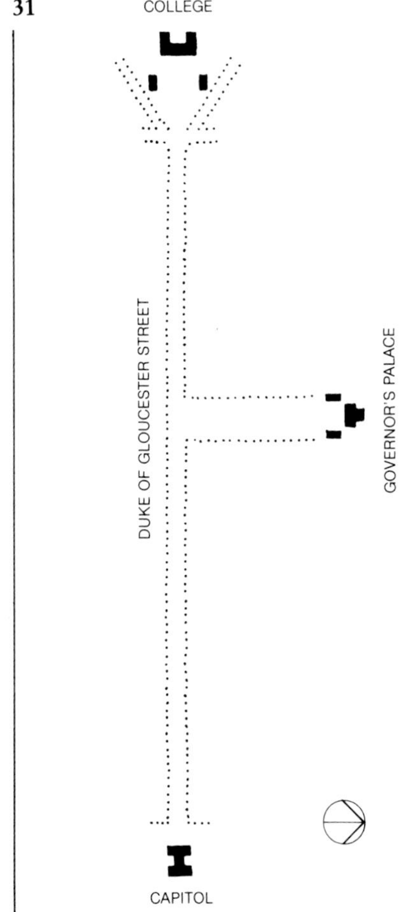

30 College of William and Mary, in the mid-eighteenth century. Portion of the "Bodleian Plate," engraved ca. 1740. *From left*: Brafferton Hall, Wren Building, and President's House. (Colonial Williamsburg photograph)

31 Schematic plan of colonial Williamsburg, with College of William and Mary, Capitol, and Governor's Palace. Buildings are shown somewhat larger than actual size.

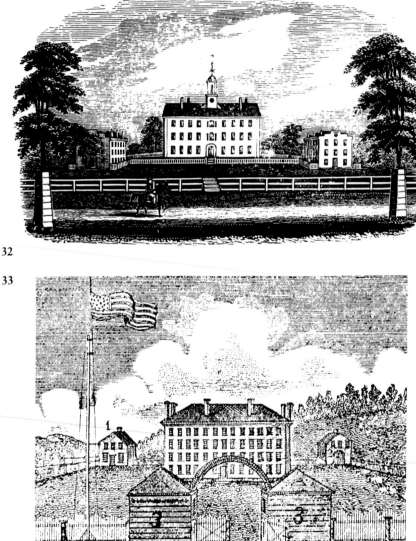

32

33

32 Ohio University, Athens, Ohio. Engraving by Henry Howe, 1846. In center is Cutler Hall (originally called simply the College Edifice), erected 1816, designed by Benjamin Corp. To left and right are Wilson and McGuffey halls (originally called East Wing and West Wing), 1837 and 1839. All three buildings still stand.
(Henry Howe, *Historical Collections of Ohio*, Cincinnati, 1847, p. 50)

33 American Literary, Scientific, and Military Academy (later Norwich University), Norwich, Vermont, in 1820. Buildings were erected 1819–1820, the central one containing classrooms, dormitory rooms, and an armory.
(G. M. Dodge and W. A. Ellis, *Norwich University, 1819–1911*, Montpelier, 1911, p. 8)

of his post right before the fire, and Alexander Spotswood, who assumed the governorship in 1710, has been credited with redesigning the college. But Nicholson may well have proposed changes in the college as part of his overall plan for the town, changes that were carried out only after his departure. Regardless of who was directly responsible, the resulting scheme, including the two flanking structures added to the main building in the 1720s and 1730s, can be understood only in terms of Nicholson's Baroque vision of the whole town.

With the addition of these flanking buildings—the President's House and Brafferton—William and Mary assumed a form unprecedented in collegiate planning. Brafferton, or the Indian School, was built in 1723 with income from a bequest intended expressly for the education of Indians, although as at Harvard, the enterprise proved unsuccessful and the building was eventually used for other purposes. In 1732 the nearly identical President's House was begun.[56] These two buildings were based on provincial domestic architecture of the period in England.[57] But more significant was their relationship with the main building. At first glance the three separated buildings appear to form a quadrangle of the Harvard type, based on the Puritan colleges at Cambridge, but they are very different in nature. The William and Mary group is not composed of equal members, having instead one major structure and two small appendages to it. This tripartite scheme is in the tradition of the English country house with flanking outbuildings, ultimately derived from Andrea Palladio's designs for villas in sixteenth-century Italy. The domestic character of the William and Mary scheme is underscored by its similarity to the Governor's Palace in Williamsburg—a main house flanked by kitchens and stables, built prior to Brafferton and the President's House at William and Mary and by the same master builder, Henry Cary.[58] (This pattern of buildings was later used, especially in the early ninteenth century, by several other American schools, such as Ohio University and Antioch College in Ohio, Norwich University in Vermont, and Marshall College in Pennsylvania [Figs. 32, 33].)[59]

That the College of William and Mary at this stage of its planning drew from domestic, rather than traditionally collegiate, models of architecture, was due perhaps to the college's provincial setting and its sheer physical distance from collegiate prototypes, or perhaps to the fact that neither Nicholson nor Spotswood was a university man. But it also may have reflected the educational character of the college, in particular the desire that the school be more oriented toward the community and less reclusive than the traditional college. It has been suggested that the liberal educational ideals of John Locke were to some degree embodied in the College of William and Mary, as Locke himself had ties with the school through Blair and Nicholson.[60] The provincial problems with which the college had to contend, especially in its difficult early years, inclined it to temper the rigidity of the traditional classical curriculum in order to appeal to its colonial constituency. The school espoused a somewhat more worldly and pragmatic program, better suited to the down-to-earth affairs of Virginia. This was one of the stated motives for bringing the capital from Jamestown to Williamsburg, as expressed in a student speech of 1699 (generally assumed to have been ghost-written by Blair or Nicholson), which noted:

> Another great benefite to the students at this place, would be the conveniency of good company and conversation; For in such a retired Corner of the world, far from business, and action, if we make scholars, they are in danger of proving meer scholars, which make a very ridiculous figure: made up of Pedantry, disputaciousness, positiveness, and a great many other ill qualities which render them not so fitt for action and conversation.[61]

One way of emphasizing this goal of intercourse between college and community, and of repudiating the pedantic excesses of traditional European education, was to replace the conventional architectural forms of the English college with more familiar and homely forms. In this sense, the early development of the William and Mary plan—from the original enclosed quadrangle to progressively more open and domestic forms—represented not only an architectural transformation, but a change in traditional educational ideals in response to the practical requirements of the colonial condition.

Yale

Despite their differences, the architectural plans of Harvard College and the College of William and Mary both rejected the inward-turning enclosed quadrangle of English colleges and turned to the world around them. The other colonial American schools devised their own ways of doing basically the same thing. Yale College in New Haven, Connecticut, developed a type of plan that had a great influence on later American college planning.[62]

Founded in 1701 by Congregational ministers wanting a college in Connecticut independent of Harvard, Yale was briefly located at Saybrook. But in 1717 several towns in the colony vied for the honor of being the permanent home for the college, and New Haven was chosen, largely because it had optimistically begun constructing an imposing edifice for the school on donated land in a prime location facing the large town green (Fig. 34).[63] New Haven, one of the first geometrically planned cities in the English colonies, had been laid out in 1638 as nine squares of land, the central one being the Green with the church at its center. It has been suggested that this form was inspired by biblical references to the plan of Jerusalem and the camp of the twelve tribes of Israel, and also by contemporary visions of utopian Christian communities.[64] One of these utopias, Johann Valentin Andreae's "Christianopolis"—which was apparently known to the Puritan founder of New Haven, John Davenport—had a "Collegium" directly on the sides of a central square that contained a church. As it happened, Yale College was laid out in a similar way, facing the New Haven Green, in a linear fashion that was unprecedented in earlier college planning.

The first Yale building in New Haven, constructed in 1717 by the town as an inducement to the college to settle there, contained an assembly hall, library, dining hall, kitchen, and twenty-two chambers each housing two students.[65] This building had a peculiarly long and narrow shape—162 feet by 23 feet—which may have resulted partly from the arrangement of rooms around multiple entries, but also probably reflected a desire to present an elongated face to the Green for a more imposing appearance (Fig. 35). This motive continued to dominate the physical planning of the college and ultimately produced the full Yale Row (or Old Brick Row, as it came to be called at the school), consisting of seven buildings in a line along the western side of the New Haven Green (Figs. 4, 39).

The remarkable notion of an alignment of collegiate buildings perhaps was conceived by Thomas Clap, president of Yale in the mid-eighteenth century. In 1750 he began construction of Connecticut Hall (partly with funds raised through a lottery authorized by the colonial assembly), similar in form to Harvard's Massachusetts Hall, to house sixty-four students; and about twelve years later he erected a chapel that also contained the college library (Fig. 36). These two buildings were constructed side by side, set back from the Green and partially hidden behind the original Yale building, a pattern that makes sense only if the original building was expected to be removed (as it was in 1782) so the new buildings could be seen from the Green as an aligned pair.[66] In fact, President Clap later wrote that when he built Connecticut Hall, he planned it so that "when the old College should come down, another college or chapel or both should be set [next to it]."[67]

In 1792 Yale College consisted of three buildings: Connecticut Hall, the chapel, and behind them a one-story dining hall, later used as a laboratory. Only about half the students could be housed in Connecticut Hall, the rest lodging in town in violation of the collegiate principle. To correct this, the Yale Corporation (the college's governing body) at first decided to construct a new building nearly as long and narrow as the original Yale building, apparently to be placed at right angles to Connecticut Hall.[68] But this plan aroused criticism, and James Hillhouse, a member of the Corporation and treasurer of the college, assumed the task of devising a new plan—and also raised the money for its execution. Hillhouse consulted the painter and amateur architect John Trumbull (son of the governor of Connecticut), who by December 1792 produced two sheets of plans that reinforced the concept of an alignment of buildings, and which also, incidentally, constitute probably the oldest surviving master plan for an American college (Figs. 37, 38).[69]

Trumbull had studied painting in London, but except for the landscaping he included and some of the architectural details, his drawings show little influence from England or Europe. In fact, Hillhouse, who was interested in town planning and

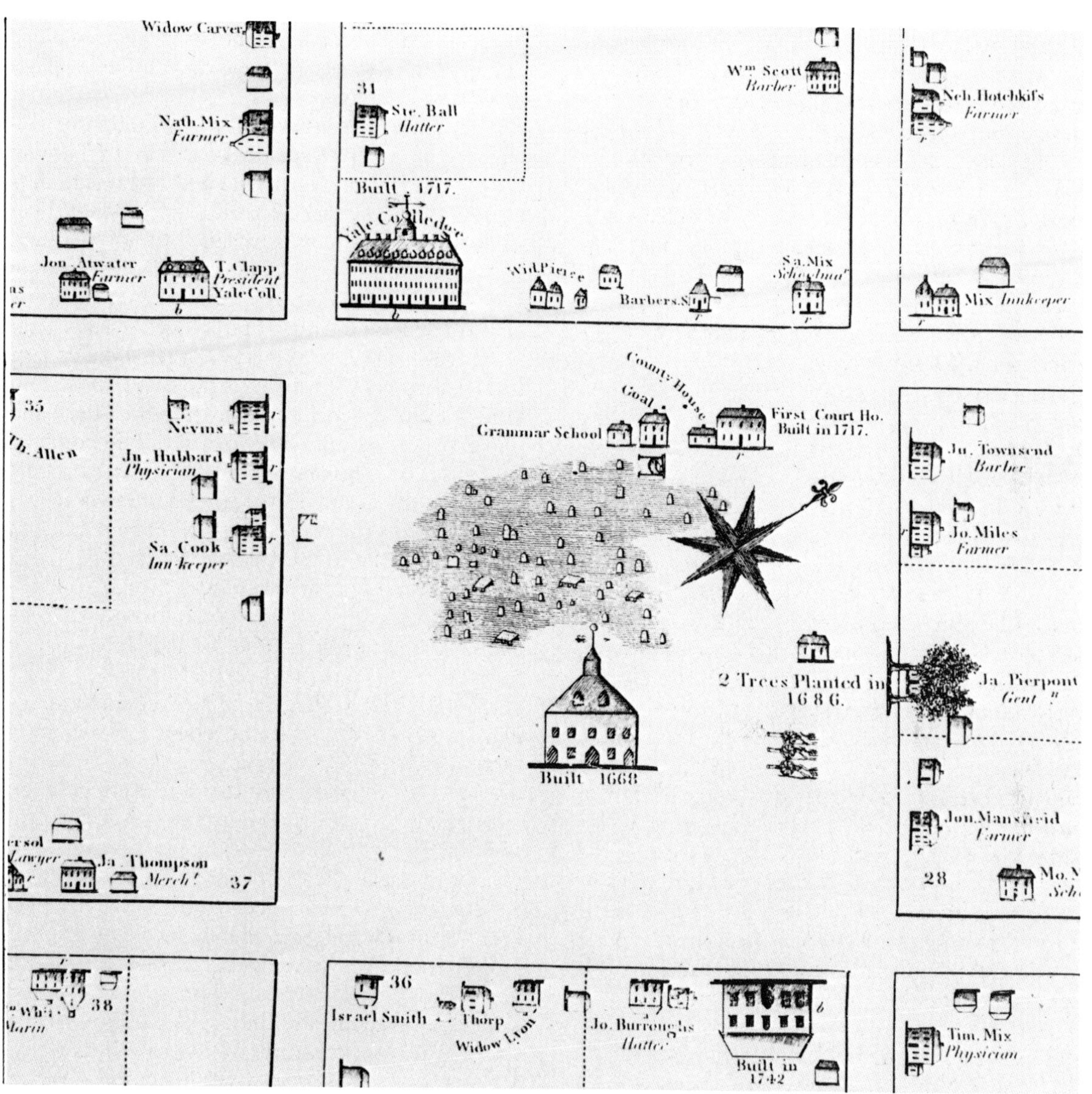

34

34 Central part of New Haven, Connecticut, in 1748. At upper left edge of the Green is first Yale College building, constructed 1717 by master builder Henry Caner. Large building in the Green is the town meetinghouse. Detail of an engraving by William Lyon, of 1806, based on a drawing by James Wadsworth, Yale class of 1748.

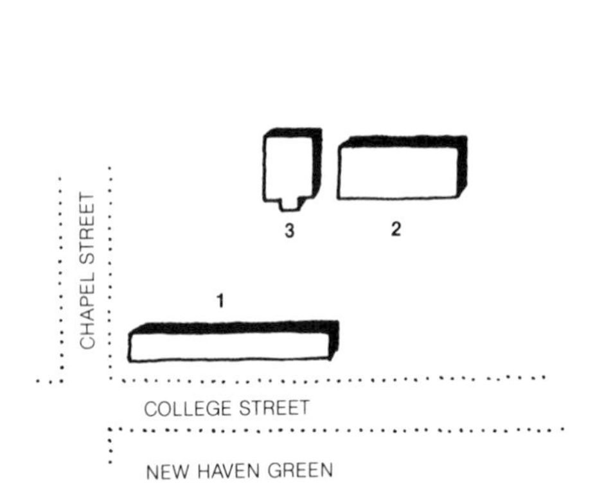

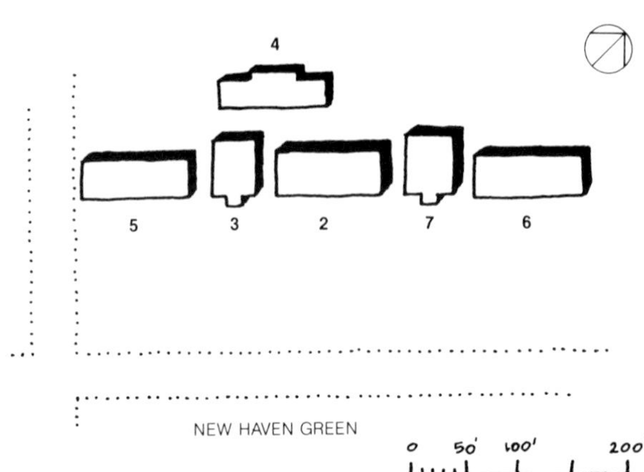

35

36

35 Plans showing the growth of Yale College from 1717 to 1803. 1. First Yale College building, 1717, demolished 1782. 2. Connecticut Hall, 1750. 3. First Chapel (later the Athenaeum), 1761, demolished 1893. 4. Dining hall (later a laboratory), 1782, demolished 1888. 5. South College, 1793, demolished 1893. 6. Berkeley Hall, 1801, demolished 1895. 7. Lyceum, 1803, demolished 1901.

36 Yale College in the 1780s. View based on a woodcut of 1786. At left is the Chapel, which was remodeled in 1824 as classrooms and dormitory rooms and renamed the Athenaeum. At right is Connecticut Hall (called South Middle College in the nineteenth century). Remodeled at various times, it was restored to its colonial appearance in 1905.
(*Harper's New Monthly Magazine*, May 1865, p. 699)

was promoting the redesign of the New Haven Green at this time, may have contributed as much to the basic idea as Trumbull.[70] Five aligned buildings were shown: the existing chapel and Connecticut Hall; the proposed new dormitory, labeled "Projected Building," to the south; and to the north, two "Buildings which may be erected hereafter," another dormitory, and a structure containing recitation rooms and a library. The three new buildings were made to conform as much as possible, within the architectural dictates of the time, to the existing structures. Trumbull gave the new recitation-library building the same shape as the chapel (minus its tower). The new dormitories were made similar to Connecticut Hall, a point Trumbull emphasized in a note written below the plan, although he criticized Connecticut Hall's gambrel roof as "inconvenient and expensive Gothicism," and recommended that "the uniformity of the . . . Buildings may be compleated by taking off the Roof from the present College and carrying up the Walls."

The proposed new dormitory had a significant innovation in its interior plan. In place of the traditional arrangement—used in Connecticut Hall and the Harvard dormitories—of rooms sleeping two or more students, with tiny adjacent studies, Trumbull proposed suites housing four students each, consisting of "a large common Parlor, & two Bedrooms, serving as studies also." Trumbull claimed that this plan (similar to what would later be common at many American colleges) is more easily heated and cooled, and thus more "pleasant and agreeable to the Scholars at all seasons."[71]

Trumbull's overall site plan reveals a strong interest in landscaping (Fig. 37). In the open space between the line of buildings and the New Haven Green, Trumbull showed rows of trees around the edges of rectangular lawns, and behind the buildings was a large area laid out with meandering paths and irregular beds of planting—an early example in America of the romantic "English garden," which Trumbull had seen during his travels abroad. He clearly was delighted with the idea of this garden, as shown by the notes he wrote on the plan, describing the "irregular and winding" walkways, specifying the types of plants to be used, and recommending that this planting be made to hide the college privies, which Trumbull discreetly named with a Latin euphemism:

> The Temples of Cloacina, (which it is too much the custom of New England to place conspicuously) I would wish to have concealed as much as possible, by planting a variety of shrubs, such as Laburnums, Lilacs, Roses, Snowballs, Laurel, &c. &c.—a gravel walk should lead thru the shrubbery to these buildings. The Eating Hall should likewise be hidden as much as the space will permit with similar shrubs.[72]

Trumbull's notes also defended the linear arrangement of the buildings. He stressed the undesirability of placing a new building at an angle to the existing ones, and he advocated the straight alignment on both aesthetic and practical grounds:

> if the [projected] Building be placed at an angle with the existing one, it will preclude the Possibility of reconciling the whole University to any degree of Elegance or Uniformity . . . and is certainly less agreeable to the Eye.—But an arrangement similar to that meditated above—would unite Utility with Ornament,—and would admit of being pursued gradually, and whether partially or compleatly executed, would be in all its stages handsome.[73]

This is probably the first recorded instance in American college planning of a concern that a master plan be devised in such a way that it would be visually satisfactory at each stage of its execution. This consideration, along with the unlimited extensibility of a row of buildings, must have been persuasive to the Yale Corporation, for Trumbull's plan was eventually executed, over a period of ten years, although the individual buildings were not constructed exactly as he designed them (Fig. 39). Until all of them—except for Connecticut Hall—were demolished at the end of the nineteenth century, these five aligned buildings (plus two others built in the 1820s), constituted the most memorable feature of Yale's campus, despite the addition of other buildings behind them and to the north.

Especially in the early nineteenth century, the form of this Yale Row was repeated at many other schools. These included Dartmouth in New Hampshire, Brown in Rhode Island, Amherst College in Massachusetts, Colby and Bowdoin colleges in Maine, Hamilton and Hobart colleges in New York, Washington (later Trinity) College and Wesleyan University in Connecticut, St. John's and

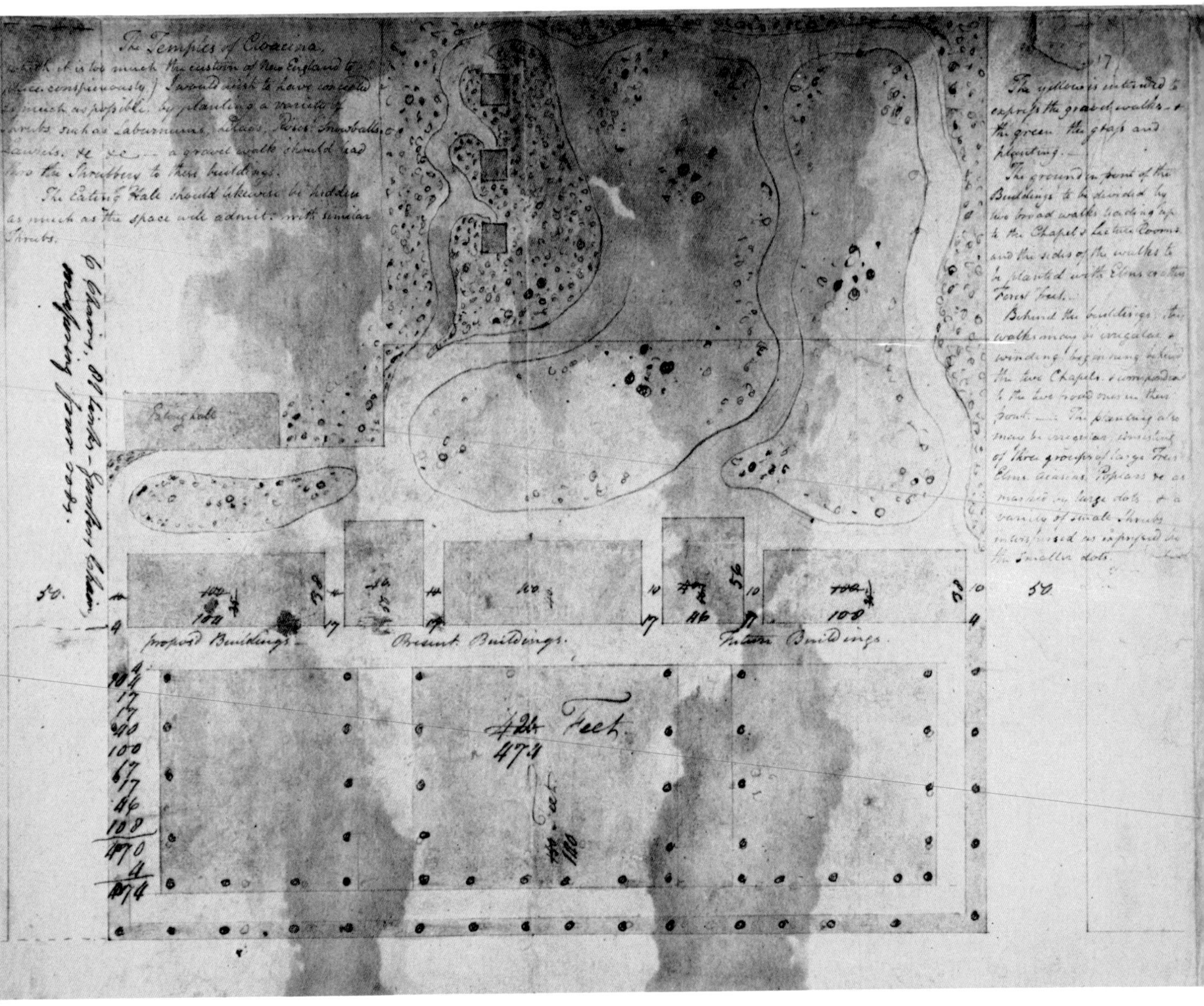

37 Master plan for Yale, drawn by John Trumbull, 1792. Site plan, in ink and watercolor. At bottom (east) is New Haven Green, called by Trumbull "Grand Square." In center are the "present buildings," flanked by three "proposed buildings." Behind proposed building at left is school's dining hall, and at the top of the sheet, three privies (or "Temples of Cloacina," as Trumbull ennobled them), to be concealed by plantings in a naturalistic garden. (Yale University Library)

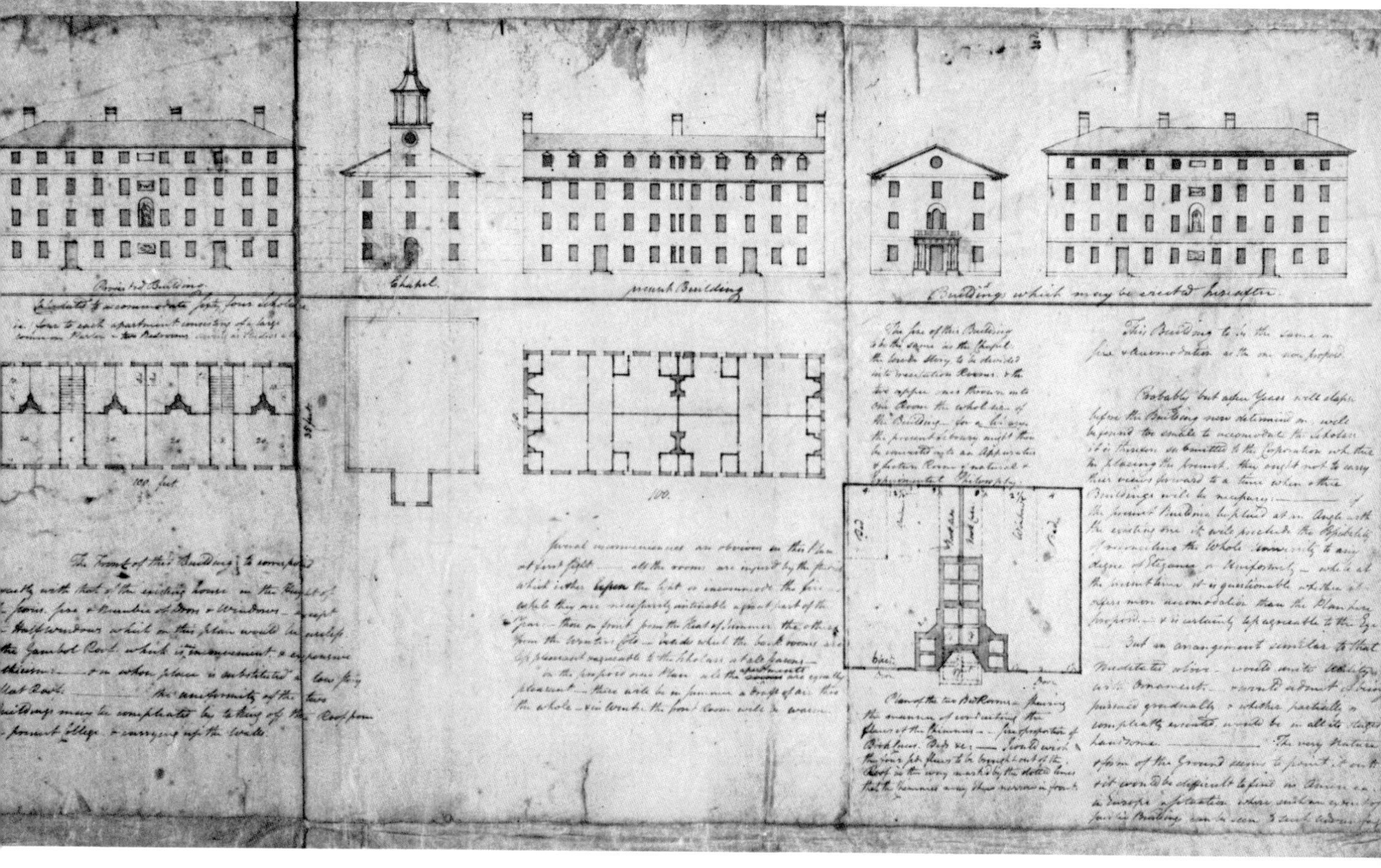

38

38 Trumbull's master plan for Yale. Plans and elevation drawings of buildings, with notes. At center is the existing Connecticut Hall; left of it, the existing Chapel. The other three buildings are the projected structures: two dormitories (each to house sixty-four students) and a building corresponding to the Chapel, to contain recitation rooms and the library. (Yale University Library)

39

40

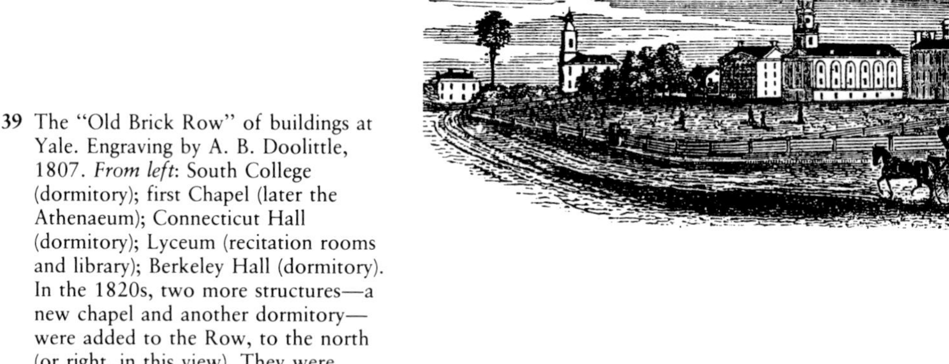

41

39 The "Old Brick Row" of buildings at Yale. Engraving by A. B. Doolittle, 1807. *From left*: South College (dormitory); first Chapel (later the Athenaeum); Connecticut Hall (dormitory); Lyceum (recitation rooms and library); Berkeley Hall (dormitory). In the 1820s, two more structures—a new chapel and another dormitory—were added to the Row, to the north (or right, in this view). They were demolished around 1900, as were the rest of the buildings, except for Connecticut Hall, which still stands. (Yale University Library)

40 Progeny of the Yale Row. Amherst College, Amherst, Massachusetts. Engraving after drawing by Alexander Jackson Davis, ca. 1828. The buildings in the row, are, from left: North Hall, ca. 1827; North College, 1821–1823; Chapel, 1826; and South College, 1820–1821.
(John Howard Hinton, *The History and Topography of the United States*, vol. 2, London, 1832, pl. 41)

41 Progeny of the Yale Row. Western Reserve College, Hudson, Ohio, ca. 1845. This group of buildings was called the "Monumental Row" or "Brick Row." *From left to right* (excluding the building at extreme left): Athenaeum, erected 1840–1843 as classrooms; President's House, 1830; North College, erected 1838 to house the students of divinity; Chapel (also containing the school's library), 1836; Middle College, 1826, demolished 1912; and South College, ca. 1830, demolished 1884. Buildings were designed and built by Lemuel and Simeon Porter, father and son masterbuilders from Connecticut. Originally there were plans to continue the row, to the left, with extra buildings. In the 1880s the college moved to Cleveland; surviving buildings are now used by Western Reserve Academy.
(Henry Howe, *Historical Collections of Ohio*, Cincinnati, 1847, p. 473)

42

Washington colleges in Maryland, Middlebury College in Vermont, the University of Vermont, and Ohio Wesleyan, Marietta, and Western Reserve colleges in Ohio (Figs. 2, 40–42, 162).[74] Many of these schools even copied Yale's a-b-a-b-a pattern of alternating the flat sides of buildings with the gabled ends of buildings, producing a rhythm of long and narrow facades.

Later in the nineteenth century, the Yale Row came to be considered monotonous and old-fashioned, as more complex (and inward-turning) patterns of campus planning became popular.[75] Some schools that had erected rows of buildings followed Yale's example and demolished them, or abandoned them and moved to new sites (as did Trinity College in Hartford and Western Reserve College in Hudson, Ohio). But when the Yale Row was conceived in the eighteenth century, it was a bold and impressive innovation in collegiate planning, and was also an integral part of its urban environment. Just as the buildings at William and Mary created a focal point at the end of the axial vista that was the main element in the plan of Williamsburg, so the Yale Row created a boundary along the New Haven Green, helping to define this open space which was the main urbanistic element in New Haven's plan, and giving the college a commanding position at the heart of the community.

42 Progeny of the Yale Row. Trinity College, Hartford, Connecticut, ca. 1850. *From left*: Jarvis Hall, 1824; Seabury Hall, 1824; Brownell Hall, 1845. In 1872, the college sold its campus (for $600,000) to the State of Connecticut, which constructed its present Capitol on this site, and the college moved to a new location outside Hartford.
(*Gleason's Pictorial Drawing-Room Companion*, November 1, 1851, p. 281)

Princeton

At Princeton, another pattern of placing a college in open space was devised. When the College of New Jersey, founded in 1746 by a group of Yale graduates who were converts to the evangelical New Light Presbyterianism, decided in 1753 to establish itself at Princeton, the place was not a town like New Haven or Cambridge, but simply a small village along the "high road" (Nassau Street), more analogous to Middle Plantation at the time of the founding of the College of William and Mary.[76] This, in fact, was one of the advantages of the location to the trustees, who were seeking a place "more sequestered from the various temptations attending a promiscuous converse with the world, that theatre of folly and dissipation."[77] The trustees immediately began planning a large building, Nassau Hall (190 by 50 feet in the original plans—later reduced somewhat in size, but still the largest building in the English colonies at the time), and erected it a good distance from Nassau Street, on the four-and-one-half-acre lot donated to the college by a local landowner (Figs. 43, 44).

The space thus created was different from the three-sided courtyards of Harvard or the English colleges. It was larger, and there is no evidence that buildings originally were planned for its sides (only in the nineteenth century were flanking buildings erected). The original college consisted simply of Nassau Hall and the President's House on the street. Perhaps the model was the New Haven Green, or New England commons in general; the Princeton trustees simply created a village green since none already existed. As at Yale, the college was ranged along one side of the green, although it was housed in one large structure rather than in a row of buildings.

The spaciousness of the area between Nassau Hall and the road and the generally rural character of the College of New Jersey were appropriately expressed by the term *campus*, which was coined, probably around 1770, to describe the school's grounds. The earliest record of this usage of the word is found in a letter written by a Princeton student in January 1774, recounting an event evidently inspired by the Boston Tea Party:

> Last week to show our patriotism, we gathered all the steward's winter store of tea, and having a fire in the Campus, we there burnt near a dozen pounds, tolled the bell and made many spirited resolves.[78]

Before this time, the college at Princeton had used Harvard's word *yard*, or simply *grounds*, to designate the area around Nassau Hall. After the Revolution, *campus* superseded these terms at Princeton, and by the 1820s, the new word (or rather, its new usage) had been borrowed by other schools, including the distant College of South Carolina.[79] In the mid-nineteenth century, *campus* became the most popular term for American college grounds. (At the end of the century, a survey of 359 colleges and universities in the country found that the word was employed at 320 of them—the only major category of schools not using it being Roman Catholic institutions.)[80] Invented at colonial Princeton as a Latinism, perhaps alluding to the Campus Martius of ancient Rome, *campus* expressed perfectly the open, semirural environment of the College of New Jersey and the physical qualities that would characterize so many American schools.

Nassau Hall itself, probably designed by the Philadelphia master builder Robert Smith, is of the tripartite, center-pediment type that was introduced into American collegiate architecture at the College of William and Mary, although at Princeton it was handled in a more sophisticated manner, adhering more faithfully to the proportions of English prototypes like James Gibbs's designs for King's College, Cambridge.[81] Inside, it originally contained virtually all the college's functions: classrooms, dining hall, chapel, and students' rooms on the upper floors. In its simple logic of housing everything under one roof, and with its impressive pedimented facade, Nassau Hall struck a chord with many Americans of the period as the perfect collegiate building, and in the late eighteenth and early nineteenth centuries it was imitated more often than any other college edifice. Among the structures that shared its general form were Hollis Hall at Harvard (1762), University Hall at Brown University (1770), Dartmouth Hall at Dartmouth College (1784–91), Old North Building at Georgetown University in the District of Columbia (1790s), Rutledge Hall at the University of South Carolina (1803), Old Queen's College at Rutgers University (1809), the original

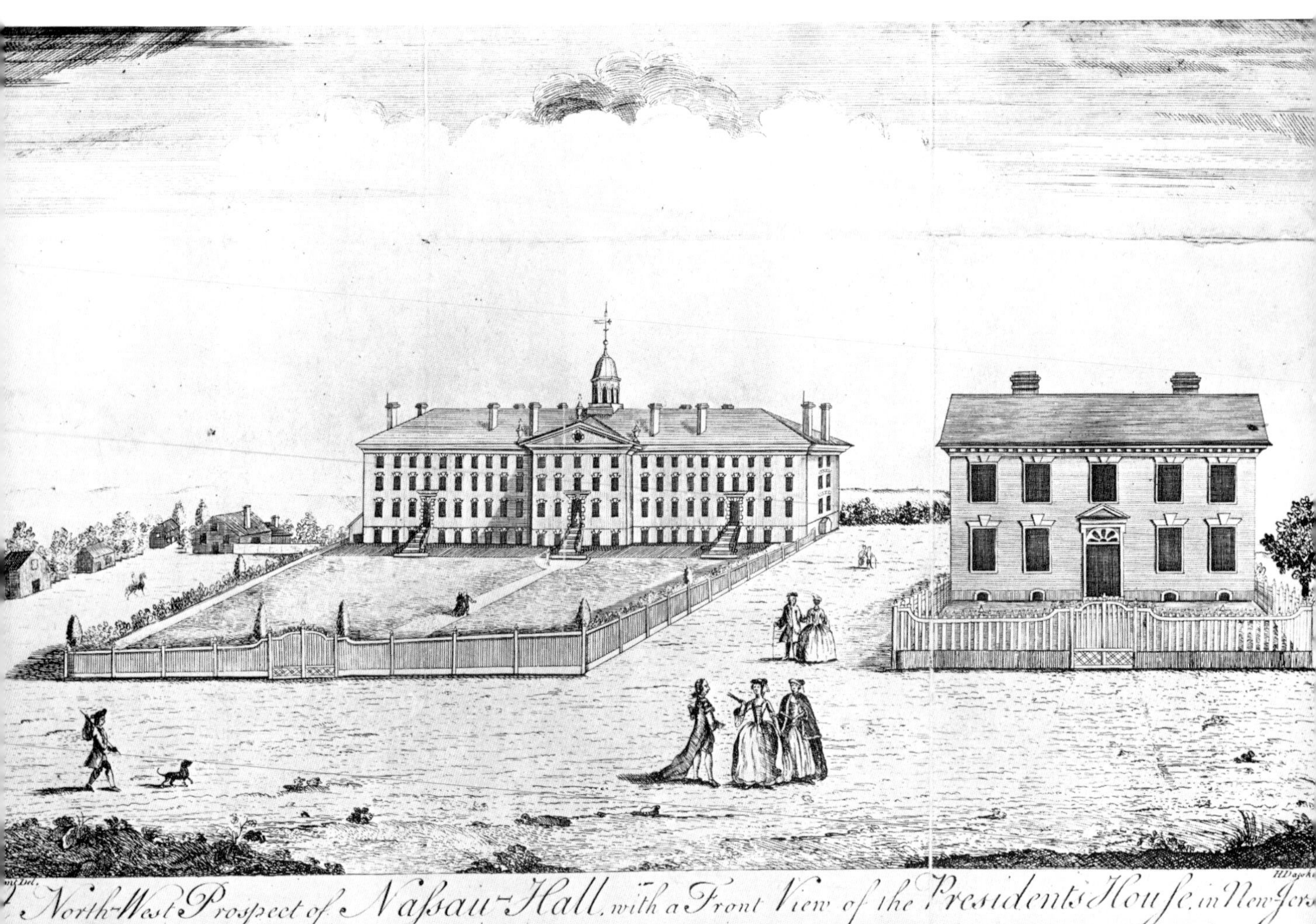
North-West Prospect of Naſsau-Hall, with a Front View of the Presidents Houſe, in New Jers

44

43 College of New Jersey, Princeton. Engraving of 1764, by Henry Dawkins. At left is Nassau Hall (named in honor of King William III, of the house of Nassau), designed and executed 1755–1757, principally by Robert Smith, carpenter-architect of Philadelphia. The basement contained kitchen, dining room, and steward's quarters. On upper floors were the chapel, library, and forty-two chambers, some used as recitation rooms but most as dormitory rooms. At right is the President's House (now Dean's House), also built by Robert Smith, 1756. The area in front of Nassau Hall came to be called "the Campus" in the 1770s—apparently the first use of this term to designate college grounds. The fence partially surrounding the Campus, in this view, was probably a creation of the artist's imagination.
(Samuel Blair, *An Account of the College of New Jersey*, Woodbridge, N.J., 1764, frontispiece. Princeton University Library)

44 Nassau Hall and the Campus, at Princeton. After a fire in 1855, additions were made to Nassau Hall by the architect John Notman, including the tall tower and enlarged main entrance seen in this photograph.
(Princeton University Archives)

Main Building of Transylvania College in Lexington, Kentucky (1816), the Academy Building at Wesleyan University in Connecticut (1824), and Griffin Hall at Williams College in Massachusetts (1828) (Figs. 25, 45–47, 104).[82]

Many American colleges also were shaped by the example of Nassau Hall's setting: its spacious village green, or "campus," symbolically setting the college apart from the traffic of the world, yet—in contrast to the cloistered European quadrangle—able to survey its domain and the country beyond. Like Harvard, William and Mary, and Yale, the College of New Jersey at Princeton invented a distinctive physical environment, expressive of its own character and of a new, expansive, American temperament.

45 College of Rhode Island (later Brown University), in Providence. Engraving of ca. 1790. At right is University Hall, built in 1770 following designs by a building committee that included Joseph Brown, benefactor of the school. At left is the President's House, built at about the same time as University Hall, later moved to another site.
(Brown University)

46 Dartmouth Hall, Dartmouth College, Hanover, New Hampshire. Built 1784–1791, burned 1904, rebuilt 1904–1906. Designer of the building is unknown. Photograph before the fire of 1904.
(Dartmouth College)

45

46

47

47 Williams College, Williamstown, Massachusetts. View of ca. 1830. Building with a tower is Griffin Hall, erected 1828 (for $6,000) to house the chapel, library, and classrooms. At right is West Hall, built 1790 as an academy, which became the principal building of the college when it was founded in 1793.
(Williams College)

II. Schools For A New Nation

In the first several decades after the Revolution, numerous colleges were founded in the United States, including the first state universities, and plans for a National University were widely discussed.[1] The enthusiasm for creating an educational system worthy of the new republic was reflected in the physical planning of these institutions. Moreover, the process of college planning itself was transformed, mainly as a result of the advent of the professional architect. In the colonial period, the president or trustees of a school usually determined the placement and overall form of new buildings and left the details of their design to a master builder. After the Revolution, the design of college campuses and buildings increasingly was given over to architects—either true professionals, such as Benjamin Henry Latrobe and Joseph-Jacques Ramée, or talented amateurs such as Thomas Jefferson. The designs produced by these men naturally had a more sophisticated and unified character than the colonial plans, as well as an architectural grandeur that was an appropriate expression of the ambitious educational goals of the new American nation.

The number of colleges in the United States grew steadily, from the nine colonial institutions to about twenty in 1790, and at least forty-five by the mid-1820s (counting only the schools that still survive).[2] These were located not only in the states that had colonial colleges, but also in Maine, Vermont, Kentucky, Tennessee, North and South Carolina, Georgia, Alabama, Louisiana, Ohio, and the District of Columbia. The geographical dispersion of the colonial colleges was thus continued into the new regions being settled; indeed, the early nineteenth-century American college has been called "typically a frontier institution, . . . shaped and adapted to the peculiar needs of an advancing people."[3]

Except for the state institutions, nearly all of the new colleges were founded by religious denominations, and this was a factor in the proliferation of schools, since each sect wanted its own college in every part of the expanding country. The sectarian rivalry was criticized by some educators, such as Philip Lindsley, president of the University of Nashville, who in 1829 blamed it for "the excessive multiplication and dwarfish dimensions of western colleges," and also charged the sects with putting their schools in "small villages or retired parts of the country" in order to control their students' minds more effectively.[4] Lindsley argued that colleges should be in cities, a view that was shared by some other progressive and secularly oriented educators. The state colleges and universities often were founded in cities, but the majority of new schools were in essentially rural locations (Figs. 47, 48).

48

The issue of urban versus rural locations was part of a larger controversy over the validity of the traditional collegiate system of education. It was criticized for its religious orientation, its elitism, its strict discipline, and the narrowness of its curriculum—still largely based on recitation, and with virtually no student choice of studies. Some educators, such as George Tichnor of Harvard, advocated more specialized professional training and research, as in Göttingen and other German universities; but there was only slow progress in this direction until later in the nineteenth century.[5] The traditional collegiate system remained dominant in America. Its endurance was symbolized by a widely hailed report issued by the faculty of Yale College in 1828, which fully endorsed the classical curriculum, the recitation method, and the college's need to substitute for "parental superintendence."[6]

The controversy about the collegiate system had many implications for the physical planning of schools, especially in the matter of dormitories. The desirability of dormitories was questioned widely in the decades after the Revolution. A few of the detractors were moral extremists, such as the Ohio minister Manasseh Cutler, who in 1800 attacked college dormitories as "the secret nurseries of every vice and the cages of unclean birds."[7] But since the alternative was to let students find their own lodgings off campus, thus escaping collegiate supervision, most of the traditionalists strongly favored dormitories. Their major critics were the progressives and reformers, such as Benjamin Rush, founder of Dickinson College in Pennsylvania, who called dormitories a product of "monkish ignorance," or Francis Wayland, president of Brown University, who considered them "unnatural" and a waste of money.[8] But the strength of the collegiate ideal of students residing together, under paternalistic supervision, forced most schools to construct dormitories. As the Yale Report of 1828 stated, "The parental character

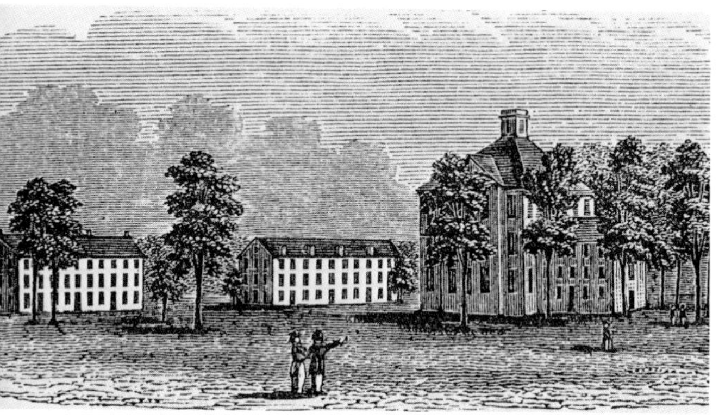

49

of college government requires that the students should be so collected together as to constitute one family. . . . This renders it necessary that suitable buildings be provided for the residence of the students."[9]

On the other hand, the collegiate system and classical curriculum did not demand much in the way of academic facilities. Since course offerings were minimal, only a few classrooms were needed. And as the classes relied on a small number of standard texts, large libraries were unnecessary. In fact, the typical college library in the early nineteenth century could be accommodated easily in a single room, which was open to the students for only a few hours a week, or even just part of one day a week.[10]

The colleges founded in the first several decades after the Revolution showed great diversity in their physical plans and architecture. Some perpetuated the colonial models, such as the Yale Row, the Nassau Hall type from Princeton, or the Palladian pattern from William and Mary (Figs. 32, 33, 40–42, 47, 104, 162).[11] Even the old building type of Massachusetts and Connecticut halls from Harvard and Yale were used, as at George Washington University in the District of Columbia (in its original building, constructed in 1820), at Illinois College (Beecher Hall, 1829), and at Miami University in Ohio (Elliott and Stoddard halls, 1827–35 [Fig. 49]).[12] But this conservatism, understandable especially at frontier institutions, was in sharp contrast to the originality of campus planning at many other schools.

Particularly innovative were the plans for some of the early state universities, and for the proposed National University. The first state institution to plan a campus and erect buildings was the University of North Carolina, which in 1792 acquired a tract of land on a ridge called Chapel Hill, in the central part of the state.[13] The site was rural (North Carolina having decided to separate its university from the state capital and other urban centers), and from the beginning the plans included laying out a village adjacent to the university. Construction of the first college building began in 1793, and a map drawn two years later showed a plan for three large buildings on the hill, forming a wide three-sided space facing north toward the village (Fig. 50). Another early map showed dotted lines extending the sides of this space toward the

48 Bentley Hall, Allegheny College, Meadsville, Pennsylvania. School was founded in 1815, in the semiwilderness of western Pennsylvania. Five years later, work began on Bentley Hall, designed by the college's first president, Rev. Timothy Allen.

49 Miami University, Oxford, Ohio. View of ca. 1845. *From left*: Elliott Hall, 1827–1829; Stoddard Hall, 1835; Harrison Hall (now demolished). Elliott and Stoddard, both dormitories, have almost exactly the same dimensions as Connecticut Hall at Yale, on which they were probably based.
(Henry Howe, *Historical Collections of Ohio*, Cincinnati, 1847, p. 79)

village (identifying this area as "Grand Avenue"); and in 1795 a chapel was constructed along one of these lines (Fig. 51).[14] Implicit in these plans was the notion of a mall: two rows of buildings facing each other across an open space, and capable of being extended. This type of plan, later to become tremendously popular at American schools, seems to have appeared first at Chapel Hill, although the North Carolina campus did not ultimately develop in exactly this manner (Fig. 52).

It is not known who conceived this pattern at the University of North Carolina, but it was probably the Board of Trustees, who made most of the early planning decisions.[15] Princeton alumni figured prominently among the founders of the university, and the mall-like plan may have resulted from a merger of the notion of a large village green—like the area in front of Nassau Hall—with the axiality of the arrangement at William and Mary, the college that North Carolinians would have known best. (One also wonders if Charles-Pierre L'Enfant's nearly contemporaneous plan for Washington, D.C., with its great mall extending from the Capitol, might have provided an inspiration for the new type of campus plan.) In any case, the mall form soon was adopted by other American schools, the first of which was probably South Carolina College.

South Carolina College (now the University of South Carolina) was founded in 1801 by the state legislature, which decided to locate the school in the newly laid-out capital of Columbia. The following year, the college trustees announced a competition for "the best original plan of a College," perhaps the first architectural competition sponsored by an American school.[16] The prize was awarded to Robert Mills, a native of South Carolina, who later had a distinguished architectural career but at this time was merely twenty years old, studying in Washington and working on architectural projects for Thomas Jefferson.[17] Mills's design, following the competition instructions, was for a single large building accommodating all of the college functions; it consisted of a central pavilion with a cupola, and two long wings with an open arcade on the ground floor, giving access to the classrooms.[18] But by the time the awards were announced, the trustees had apparently changed their minds about the type of design they wanted, for they put the winning plans aside and proceeded

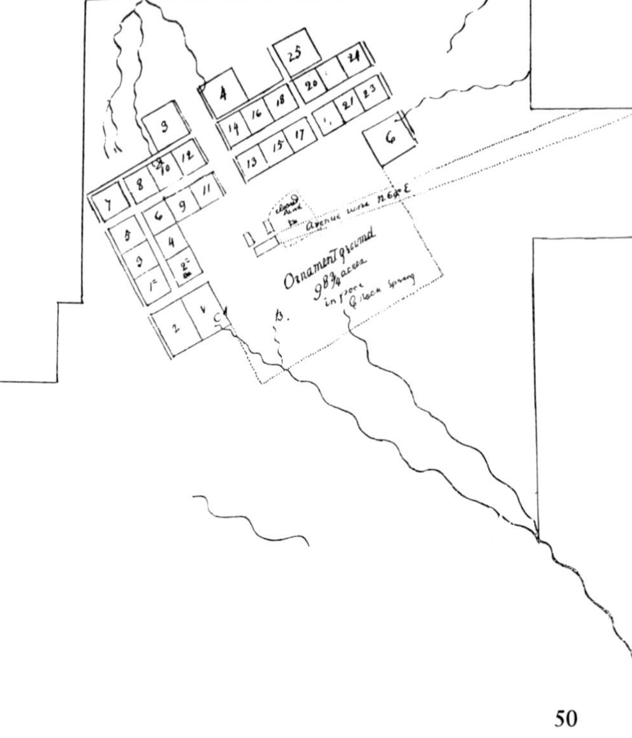

50

50 University of North Carolina, Chapel Hill. Master plan, entitled "A plan of the situation of ye University—ye ornamental ground, ye adjacent village . . . ," and dated 1795. Drawn probably by Charles W. Harris, at the direction of the university's trustees. In middle of the "Ornamental ground," three university buildings are shown, forming an open quadrangle. Numbered squares north and west of campus are house lots in the proposed adjacent town.
(North Carolina Collection, University of North Carolina Library, Chapel Hill)

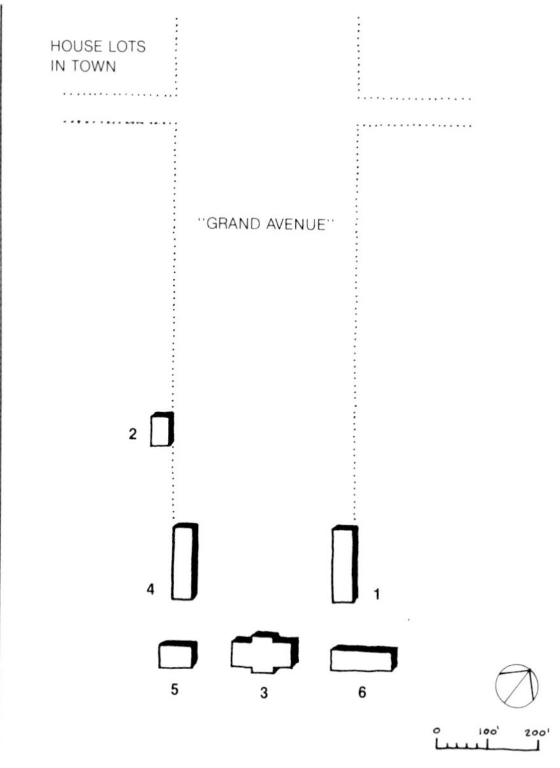

51

52

51 Plan showing early growth of the University of North Carolina. 1. Old East, 1793. 2. The Chapel, 1795. 3. South Building, 1798. 4. Old West, 1822. 5. Gerrard Hall, 1822. 6. Smith Hall, 1851. The "Grand Avenue" was indicated on a plan of the campus of about 1800.

52 Lithographic view of the University of North Carolina campus, looking south along the "Grand Avenue," ca. 1860. *From left*: Old East, South Building, and Old West. The northern ends of Old East and Old West were additions made in 1844 to house the school's two literary societies.
(North Carolina Collection, University of North Carolina Library, Chapel Hill)

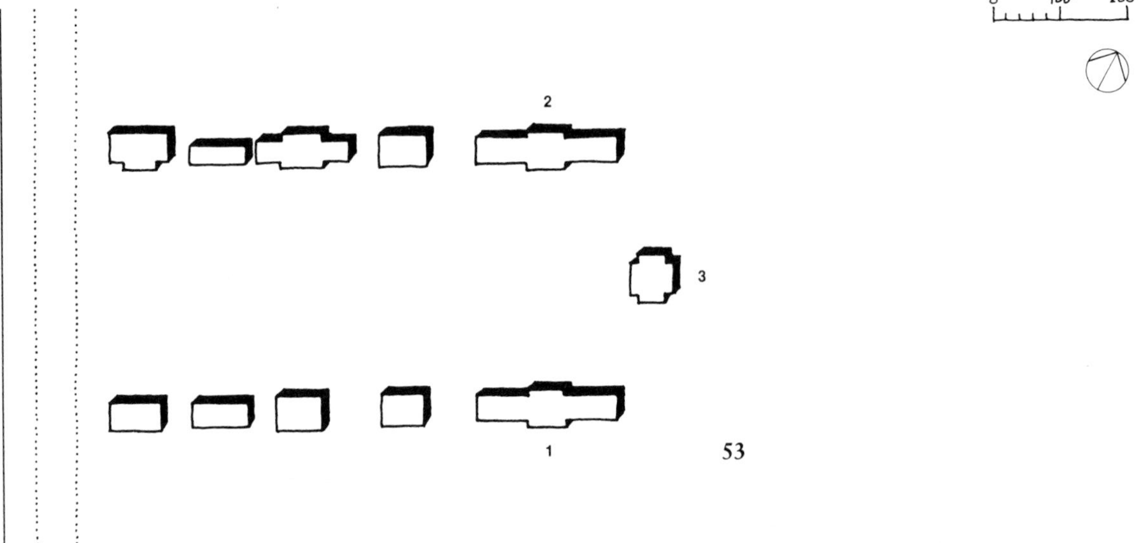

53

54

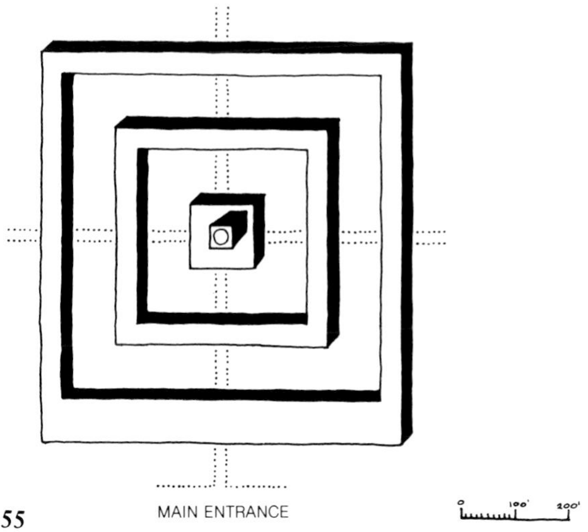

55

53 South Carolina College (now the University of South Carolina), Columbia. Plan showing early growth of the campus. 1. Rutledge College, erected beginning in 1803.
2. DeSaussure College, 1804.
3. President's House, 1807. The other buildings around the mall, or "Horseshoe," were constructed from about 1806 to the 1840s.

54 South Carolina College, as shown in a lithographic view of Columbia, 1872. At end of the mall is the President's House (now replaced by a library). On the two sides of the mall, closest to the President's House, are DeSaussure College and Rutledge College, the first two buildings constructed at the school.

55 Plan of Samuel Knox's proposed national university, reconstructed from his description of 1799. Outer square of buildings was meant to include professors' houses and their classrooms, the library, museum, public halls, and president's and vice-president's houses. The middle square was to contain students' lodgings and dining rooms. Inner square was to have facilities for the arts and printing, a book shop, and an astronomical observatory in a domed tower.

to construct several structures arranged in a pattern that came to be called "the horseshoe," but which was in effect a mall—two rows of buildings facing one another across a greensward, with the president's house at the center of one end, and the entrance from the town at the other end (Fig. 53). Beginning in 1805, buildings were gradually added along the sides of this space, producing a campus pattern similar to the one that was conceived but never fully executed at Chapel Hill (Fig. 54). The mall plan, which a decade later was used so brilliantly by Jefferson at the University of Virginia and which ultimately became one of the most popular forms for the American campus, was thus apparently first executed at South Carolina College.

In the early years of the Republic, much attention was given to proposals for a National University, an idea that was supported by the first several presidents of the United States, although it was never realized.[19] An essay published in 1799 by Samuel Knox, a minister and educator, included a written description of the ideal National University (to be located "a few miles" from the capital, in order to be close to the government and yet removed from the "profligacy" and "vicious corruption" of the city), and specified enough architectural details that its plan can be sketched (Fig. 55).[20] Knox's vision was of a series of enclosed quadrangles set within one another, with access from all four sides by passages through each quadrangle. There seems to be no precedent for this odd pattern—except possibly a grandiose plan for a university formed of concentric circles by Giovanni Battista Piranesi in the mid-eighteenth century.[21] In Knox's scheme, the outer quadrangle was to contain assembly halls, the president's and vice-president's houses, a library and museums, and along the sides, classrooms for all the professors, "contiguous to or adjoining their private apartments"—just as Jefferson was to do at the University of Virginia.[22] One hundred feet inside, there was to be another quadrangle, containing the students' lodgings and dining rooms, and at the center of the whole scheme, facilities for teaching "the ornamental arts," as well as a printing office, bookstore, and an astronomical observatory situated in a dome on the top of a "magnificent steeple . . . with a proper bell."[23]

Knox's proposal, while architecturally naive, represented an imaginative approach toward campus planning that is found also in the work of the professional architects who worked in America during this period. In 1812, Harvard engaged the Boston architect Charles Bulfinch to design a building containing new dining facilities, classrooms, a chapel, and the president's office. The instruction that Bulfinch was to determine both "the form and site" of the new structure reveals that the architect addressed the full scope of the design, including aspects of site planning that earlier would normally have been handled by the college authorities.[24] Moreover, the Harvard trustees specified that the design should "have reference to other buildings that may in future be erected"—that is, that a master plan be made. Bulfinch produced at least three such plans, which still exist.[25] In all of them, he took advantage of recently acquired tracts of land by orienting the college inward around the Yard (hitherto simply the land behind the westward-opening courtyards). The plan that appears to be Bulfinch's first is awkward in some respects, but it contains an extraordinary feature: a monumental dormitory, in the shape of a semicircle 280 feet in diameter, framed by two colonnaded buildings (probably to house the dining halls and other facilities the college required) (Fig. 56).

The source of this design was no doubt the Royal Crescent at Bath, built forty years earlier, which Bulfinch knew from his travels in England.[26] But the form was unprecedented for a collegiate structure, as was its tremendous scale. The building would have made an impression of luxurious grandeur unheard of at American colleges, especially for a dormitory. The Harvard authorities must have considered it excessive, for Bulfinch abandoned the crescent and produced new master plans, concentrating on the western part of the Yard, where he created a large symmetrical quadrangle of buildings by mirroring the existing structures (Fig. 57). He placed the required dining-classroom-chapel building in the center of this arrangement, on the axis created by the space between Massachusetts and Harvard halls and surrounded by an ellipse of trees, a faint echo of the lost crescent. This building, University Hall, was constructed in 1813, with light granite walls and Ionic pilasters, in striking contrast to the plain brick structures of colonial Harvard (Fig. 58). Today, University Hall is still the focal point of the Yard into which Bulfinch redirected Harvard's activity.

56 Master plan for new buildings at Harvard, probably by Charles Bulfinch, 1812. At left (west) are four structures that already existed in 1812 (Harvard and Hollis halls and two other dormitories). The rest of the buildings shown on the plan were projected. The large semicircular building (never constructed) was to be a dormitory, with nine separate entrances and stairways. Drawing in ink. (Harvard University Archives)

57 Master plan for new buildings at Harvard, by Charles Bulfinch, 1812. Identified structures already existed; the rest were proposed. Building in center of the ellipse of trees was subsequently erected, as University Hall. Drawing in ink. (Harvard University Archives)

The New College
Hollis
Harvard

56

57

HOLWORTHY
STOUGHTON
HOLLIS
HARVARD
MASSACHUSETS
HARVARD COLLEGE LIBRARY

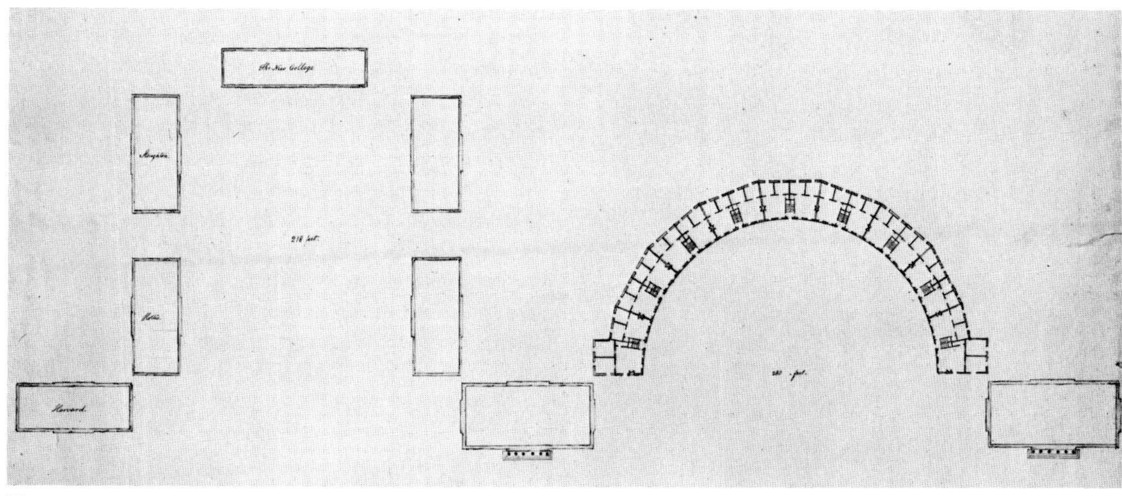

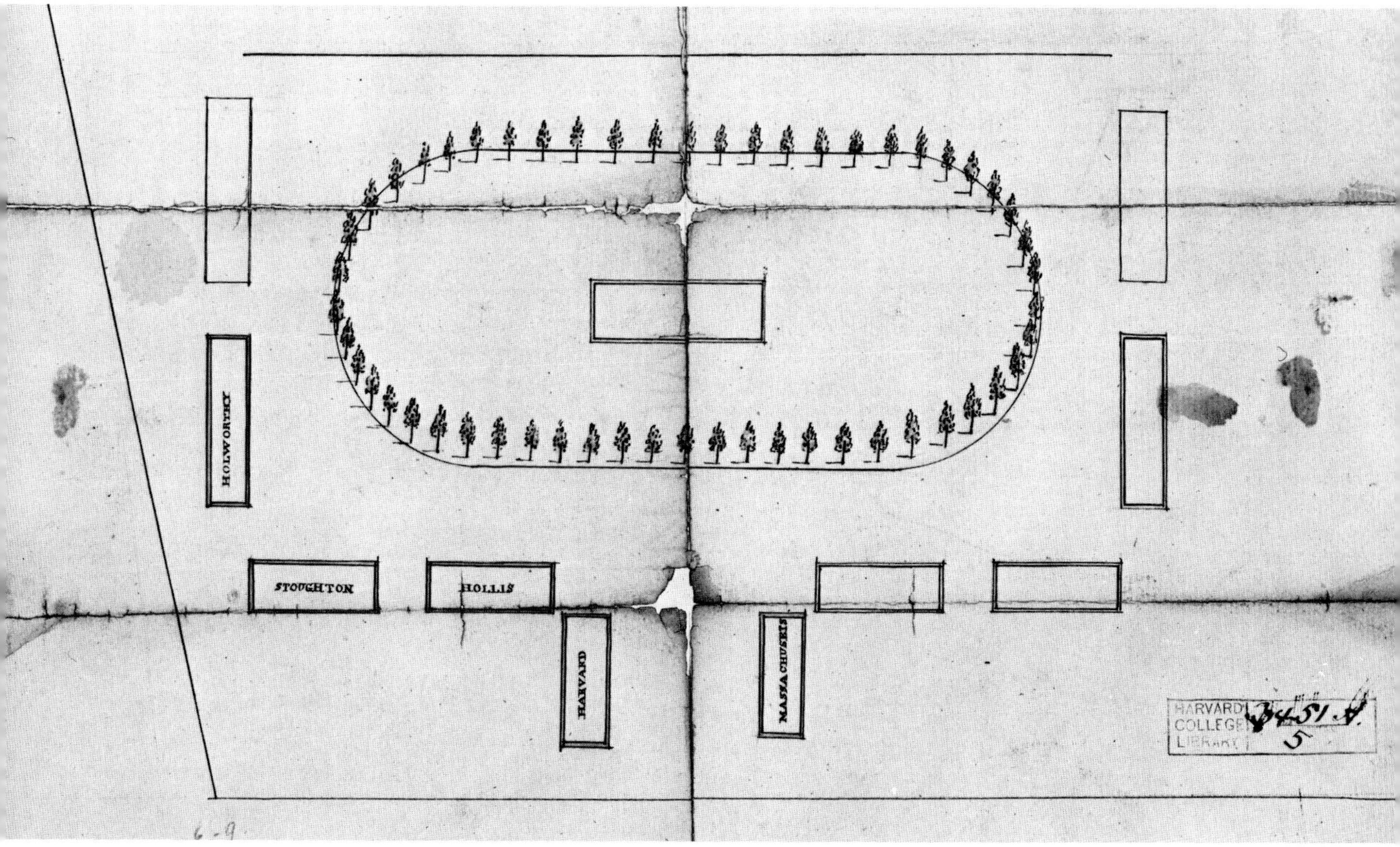

58

58 University Hall, Harvard. Designed by Charles Bulfinch, constructed 1813–1814. Building originally contained the college chapel, dining hall, and classrooms. (Harvard University News Office)

59 Design for a military academy, by Benjamin Henry Latrobe, 1800. Plan of the ground floor. In center of main block are a dining hall and a semicircular lecture hall. The rest of the rooms are principally classrooms. Upper floor was to be devoted mainly to dormitory rooms. (Library of Congress)

60 Latrobe's design for a military academy, 1800. Elevation drawing of north side of building, looking into courtyard. (Library of Congress)

Latrobe's Collegiate Designs

Benjamin Henry Latrobe exemplified the new breed of professional architects in America.[27] He had been raised in Germany, learned the practice of architecture in England, and emigrated to America in 1795. During his relatively brief but prolific career, Latrobe was involved in the design of at least eight colleges; the jobs ranged from remodeling existing buildings to planning an entire campus. In 1800 he designed a military academy and undertook work for the University of Pennsylvania, remodeling for its use the Executive Mansion that remained from Philadelphia's period as capital of the United States, and later adding to it a domed medical school (Figs. 59–61).[28] In 1802, Nassau Hall at Princeton was damaged by fire, and Latrobe rebuilt it, changing some of its details for bolder effect.[29] At Princeton he also designed Stanhope and Philosophical halls, the two small buildings symmetrically flanking Nassau Hall, which were erected in 1803–4 to house the college library, dining hall, and other functions (only Stanhope now survives).[30] In 1802 he submitted a design in the South Carolina College competition, and the following year he designed a building for Dickinson College in central Pennsylvania, which still stands (Fig. 62).[31] In 1812 he produced a design, now lost, for a building at Transylvania College in Kentucky.[32] In 1816 he drew an elaborate plan for a National University to be located in the city of Washington, in the middle of the Mall (Fig. 63).[33] And the following year, he made recommendations to Thomas Jefferson for the design of the University of Virginia (Fig. 78).[34] In view of the quantity and variety of his collegiate works, Latrobe might be considered America's first professional campus planner.

The collegiate designs by Latrobe that survive reveal certain patterns. Nearly all took the form of a building with a central section and two perpendicular wings creating a three-sided courtyard, although in the case of the modest Dickinson building, the wings were very short. The central block usually featured a dome—merely a domed cupola at Dickinson, but large and prominent domes in Latrobe's designs for a military college and the National University and in his recommendations to Jefferson. The three-sided courtyard may recall Harvard's colonial plan, but Latrobe's courtyards were always formed by connected parts,

59

North
No I
Gates
Lodge
Lodge
Ditch
Ditch
Square
Laboratory
Chemical Lecture Room
Piazza
Piazza
West
East
Dining Hall
Lecture Room
South
Principal Story of a Military School
BHLatrobe architect

60

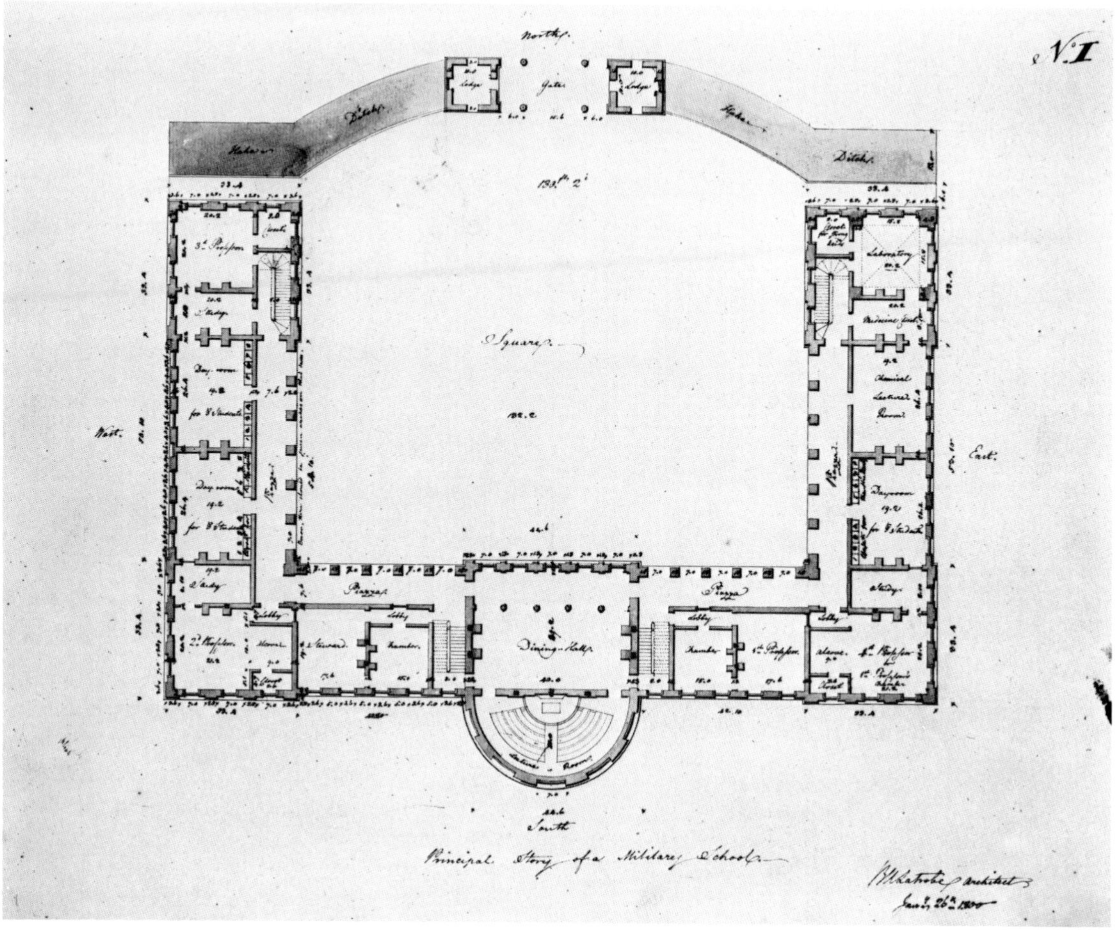

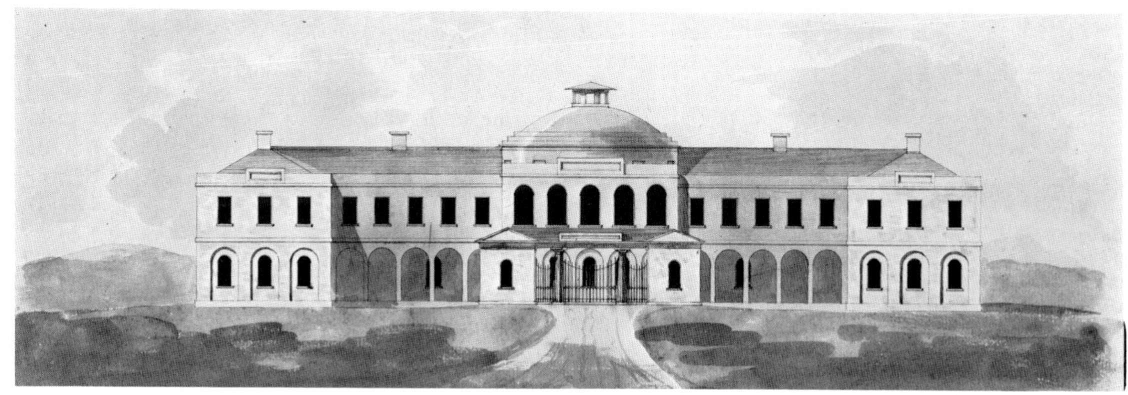

THE UNIVERSITY OF PENNSYLVANIA, 1802-1829.
(ERECTED FOR THE PRESIDENTIAL MANSION.)

61

61 Buildings used by the University of Pennsylvania in Philadelphia in early nineteenth century. Larger structure, erected as the United States President's House when Philadelphia was the national capital, was purchased by the University in 1800 and used as its main building until 1829. Domed structure is addition Latrobe designed in 1805 to house the university's medical school. Engraving, based on a drawing by William Strickland.
(George B. Wood, *Early History of the University of Pennsylvania*, Philadelphia, 1896, opp. p. 133)

62 

62 Dickinson College, Carlisle, Pennsylvania. Old West, designed by Latrobe in 1803 to replace the school's original building, which had been destroyed by fire. Two short wings on the rear of Old West create a shallow courtyard. Structure was designed to accommodate the college chapel, dining hall, recitation rooms, student dormitory rooms, and even faculty residence quarters. Today it contains administrative offices and some classrooms. Among those who donated money to erect the building were Thomas Jefferson, James Madison, and John Marshall.
(Dickinson College)

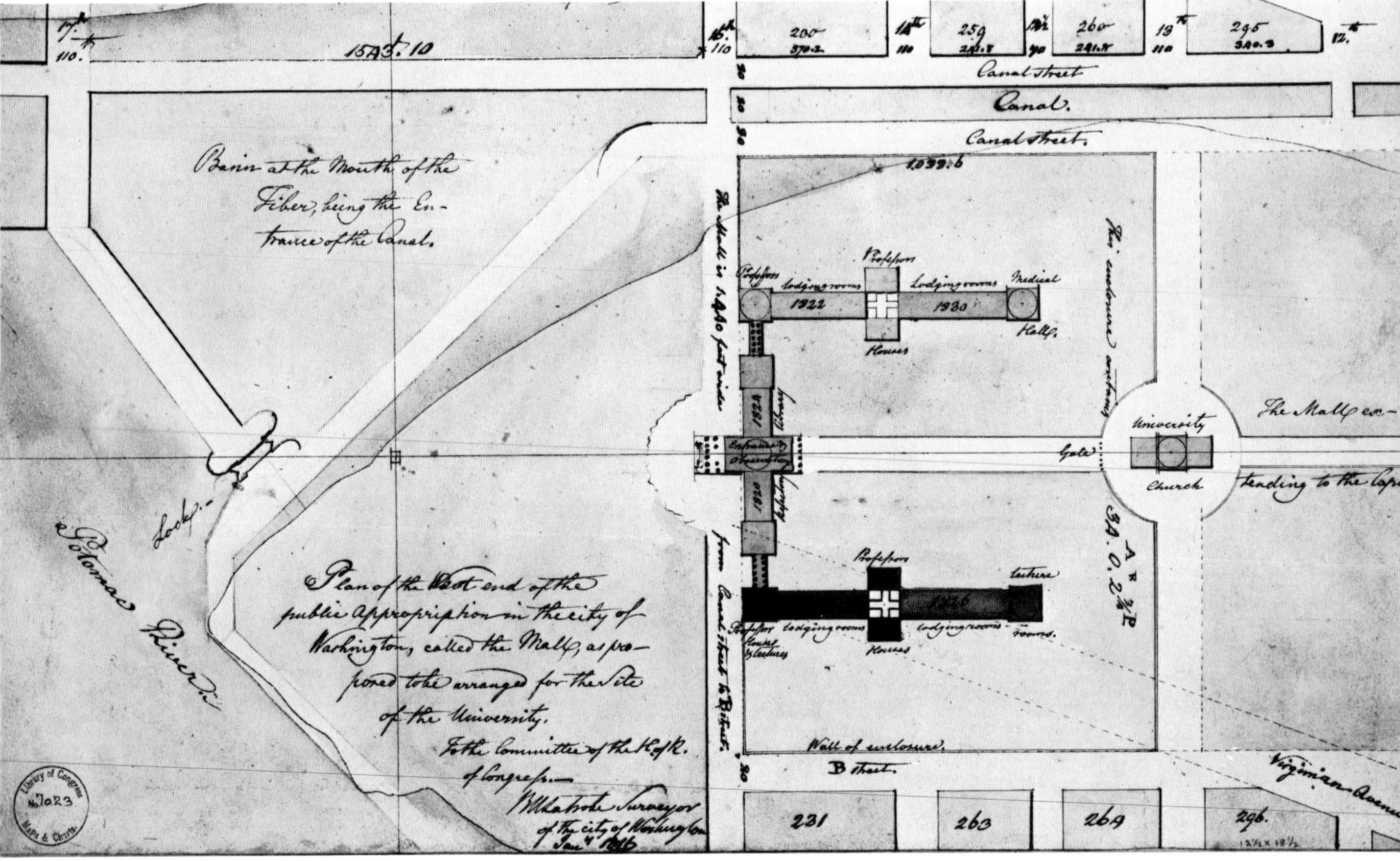

63

63 Plan for a national university in Washington, D.C., by Latrobe, 1816. Intended location was on the Mall, roughly in the area now between the Washington Monument and Smithsonian Institution. Main structure was to contain the library, classrooms, dining hall, and an observatory, with wings devoted mainly to students' rooms and professors' lodgings. Separated from main group of buildings is "University Church."
(Library of Congress, Geography and Map Division)

in contrast to the typical American pattern of separated buildings.

Among the innovations that Latrobe attempted to introduce into American college planning were new ideas about dormitory accommodations. The typical English system of dormitories—which was adopted at colonial Harvard and Yale and later at other American colleges—had students' rooms arranged around stairways with direct access from outside (this is often called the "separate entry" system). Nassau Hall at Princeton, and dormitories at many other colleges after the Revolution, used another, more economical system, with long corridors lined on both sides by rooms (the "double-loaded corridor" system). Latrobe liked neither of these systems. In a letter to one of the trustees of Dickinson College, he wrote that the Nassau Hall model "has many disadvantages, the chief of which are the noise, & the necessary darkness, of the passage, and the bad aspect of one half of the rooms" (by "bad aspect" he meant the north side, which he considered too cold and drafty in American winters).[35] Latrobe preferred dormitory rooms ranged along one side of a corridor—the south side, if possible. He also expressed a preference for what he called the "German" system, large rooms that could accommodate many students under better supervision, in contrast to the "French" system of more private rooms—although he recognized American adherence to the latter.[36]

The largely European nature of Latrobe's college designs is underscored by the fact that all of their distinctive traits were established already in his plans of 1800 for a military college, done before Latrobe had any professional contact with American schools (Figs. 59, 60).[37] This design, which was never built but probably was meant for the national military academy later established at West Point, summed up Latrobe's notion of a college. Entered through the courtyard, the main floor contained classrooms and a dining hall; the second floor had dormitory rooms on one side of the corridor and a library; both floors had lecture halls in the semicircular projection under the dome. The ground floor corridor opened onto the courtyard through an arcade, a feature not found in Latrobe's other known college designs, but similar to Jefferson's later colonnade at the University of Virginia.

Despite the general influence of Latrobe's work on American architecture, his collegiate designs probably did not have a great effect on college planning in the United States. His concept of a college as a single structure, with wings forming a courtyard, was essentially European and was at variance with the American tradition of separate buildings in a landscape.[38] However, Latrobe did play an important role in Jefferson's design for the University of Virginia; and his plans were a kind of premonition of patterns of collegiate design that were to appear in America about a century later.

Union College

In 1813, the most ambitious American college plan up to that time was produced for Union College in Schenectady, New York. Drawn by Joseph-Jacques Ramée, a French architect working in America, the plan was partially executed and still forms the core of the school's campus.[39] Historians have assumed that the design was totally the work of Ramée, but there is evidence that the president of the college played an important role in its evolution and that it reflected his progressive educational ideals. Along with Thomas Jefferson's plans for the University of Virginia of four years later, the design for Union College epitomizes the visionary collegiate dreams of the early American Republic.

Union College was founded in 1795 and represented many of the liberal ideas in American education of the period.[40] It was nonsectarian; it made efforts to modernize the classical curriculum, for example, by offering French as an elective alternative to Greek; and it considered itself more democratic than its rival Columbia College, with whom it contended in the New York state legislature for grants and the right to hold lotteries to raise money for the construction of buildings. (Lotteries were a common fund-raising device for colleges at this time.) In 1804, after three short-term presidents had come and gone, the college hired Eliphalet Nott, an eloquent young preacher, who was destined to remain as president for sixty-two years, the longest tenure in American college history. Nott brought to the job unbounded optimism, energy, and a combination of religious fervor and patriotism that had transmuted his childhood Calvinism into a millennial faith that America was to be the "new Zion."[41]

Nott continued Union College's policy of curricular innovation and liberalized the rules governing student behavior. But at the same time he strengthened the school's collegiate character by instituting a plan intended to create a family-like community. Announced by Nott when he took office, this plan specified that students were to be "separated from the great world," that each class was to constitute "the family of the officer who instructs them," that the students, president, faculty, and their families were to "lodge in college and board in commons," and that emphasis would be on "the decorum, ceremony, and politeness of refined domestic life."[42] Over the years, Nott became famous for putting this familial policy into practice himself, by being a friendly and tolerant father figure to his students, in contrast to the traditionally stern college authority. Thus Nott fashioned a highly personal merger of liberal and conservative educational principles, combining a freedom in matters of curriculum and discipline with a reaffirmation of the communal spirit of the collegiate tradition. There was something consummately American in the formula, and its success at Union was to influence numerous other colleges in the nineteenth century.

When Nott assumed the presidency in 1804, Union College had just occupied a new building in the town of Schenectady, a stone structure patterned on Princeton's Nassau Hall and nearly as large.[43] Nott's popularity soon swelled the student ranks, and additional quarters were needed. Nott decided that the college should have a new, spacious location outside of town—no doubt to facilitate its "separation from the great world"—and in 1806 he began acquiring a large tract of land on a hill overlooking the Mohawk Valley. In 1812, foundations were laid for new buildings on this hill.[44] But the intended structures never were completed, for at this point Joseph-Jacques Ramée appeared on the scene.

Ramée, an architect and landscape designer trained in Paris, had worked in Germany and Denmark after the French Revolution. He came to America in 1812, and was introduced to Eliphalet Nott the following January. Nott must have recognized in Ramée the right man to give physical form to his grand collegiate vision, for he hired him (for the princely fee of $1,500) to draw plans. Ramée worked on the project for about a year, experimenting with several designs, parts of which survive in drawings that were discovered at the college in 1932.[45] These range from thumbnail sketches to site plans and detailed working drawings of individual buildings, but it is unclear how the varying schemes relate to one another, and there have been different interpretations of the evolution of Ramée's design.

The surviving site plans all show a group of buildings arranged to form a courtyard open on one side, with a circular structure in the center. The nature of the scheme is seen best in Ramée's final design, shown in a plan he later published, and in an engraving apparently based on one of

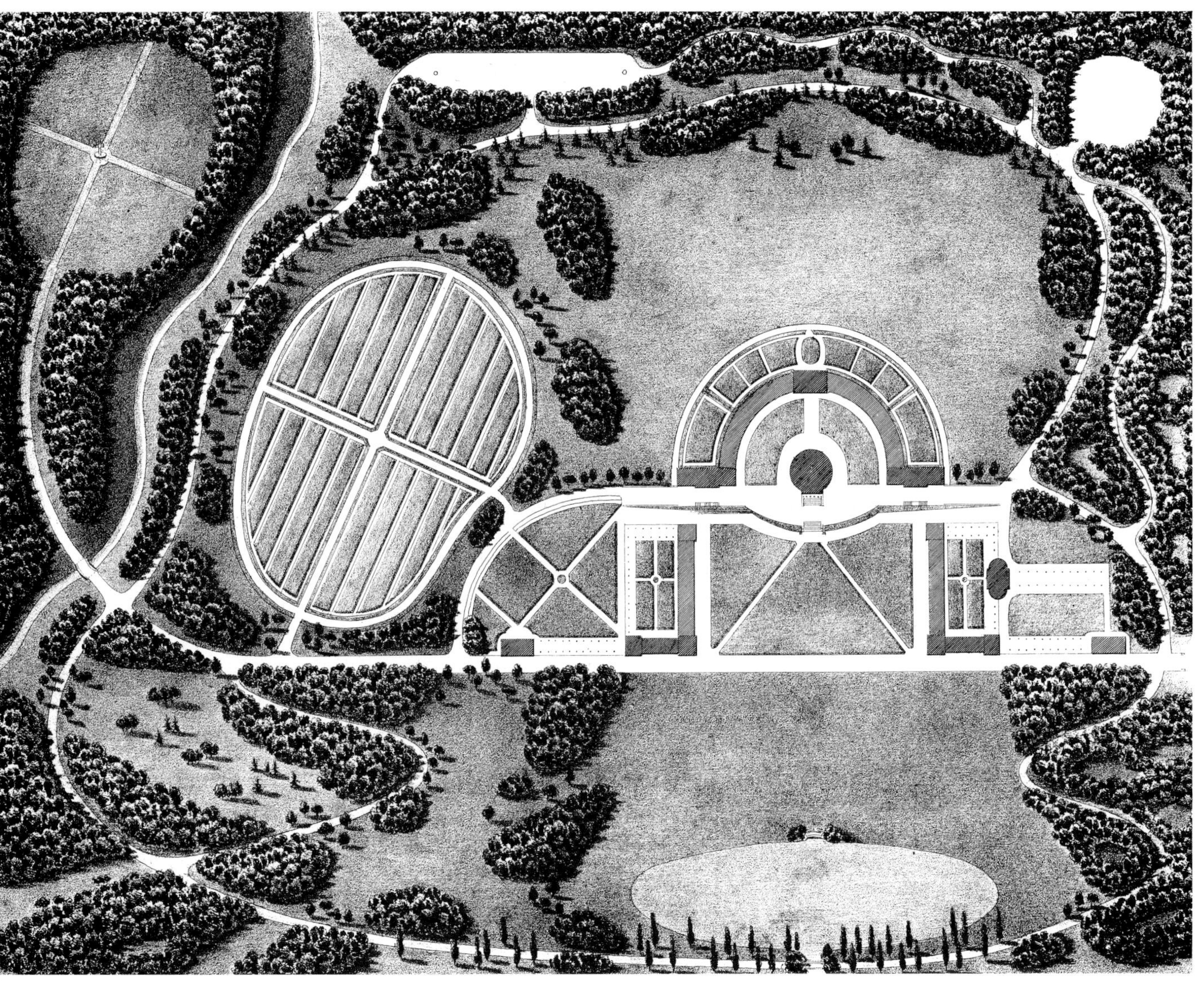

64

64 Site plan for Union College, Schenectady, New York, by Joseph-Jacques Ramée, 1813. Buildings, on a terraced hill, form a courtyard open to the west, looking over the Mohawk Valley. Engraving, published in Ramée's *Parcs et Jardins, Composés et Exécutés dans Différentes Contrées de l'Europe et des Etats Unis d'Amérique*, after Ramée returned to France.
(Shaffer Library, Union College)

65

65 Union College. Engraving by J. Klein and V. Balch, ca. 1820, representing Ramée's design. To left and right are North and South colleges (dormitories and faculty residences), erected beginning in 1812. The two small structures connected to them by arcades (used mainly as classrooms) also were executed. Circular building in center (probably intended as a chapel) was constructed in the late nineteenth century, but in a modified form. The two large buildings and connecting arcade in the background never were erected. This view was probably based on a drawing by Ramée, now lost. (Shaffer Library, Union College)

his lost drawings (Figs. 64, 65).[46] The immense courtyard—600 feet in width and open toward the west—occupies a terrace created by leveling the hilltop. Linking the buildings are arcades, one of which forms a semicircle at the back of the court, with the President's House at its easternmost point. In the center of the court is a domed Pantheon-like structure, which probably was meant to be the chapel.[47] At the western end of the courtyard are the only two buildings that were constructed immediately: North College and South College, each of which contained dormitory rooms in the center and faculty residences at the ends, in accordance with Nott's desire that the professors and students should live and dine together (Fig. 66). (Somewhat later, shortened versions of the arcaded structures along the sides of the court also were constructed, and in the mid-nineteenth century the central rotunda was built, but in a modified, Ruskinian Gothic form [Fig. 67].)[48]

Many elements of Ramée's scheme are clearly derived from European designs of the period: the crisp, simplified classicism of the architecture itself; the three-sided courtyard that recalls a French *cour d'honneur*; and surrounding it all, an extensive "English garden." But the plan also reflects American traditions and ideas. In particular, there is evidence that North and South colleges were erected on the foundations that President Nott had laid in 1812, before Ramée arrived.[49] Nott probably insisted, for economy's sake, that Ramée incorporate these buildings into his plan, and this is confirmed by the fact that in all the varying site plans, North and South colleges remain in the same places, the only constants in the plans (Fig. 68). In fact, the position and form of these two buildings are not very typical of French traditions of planning. What they do suggest is a Yale-like row of college buildings, of which they were to be the two ends. It seems likely that Nott originally planned an alignment of buildings similar to the Yale Row (the most popular campus model in America at that time), but that Ramée convinced him to transform it into a much grander scheme. This also helps to explain a number of mysterious aspects of Ramée's design, including a group of detailed drawings for a large building that does not appear in any of the surviving site plans (Fig. 69).[50] This building was to contain all of the college facilities except the dormitories, and was apparently to be connected with North and South colleges by arcaded passageways, in a pattern that makes sense as a transition between Nott's original plan and the final design (Fig. 70).

Thus, the design for Union College resulted from a process of compromise between Ramée's French principles of planning and Nott's American concepts. And a good deal of Nott survived in the final design. The predetermined placement of North and South colleges strongly affected the nature of the whole scheme. As vestiges of a Yale-like row of buildings, they looked out on the world in the extroverted manner typical of the American college. Moreover, their distance from each other established a scale so vast (compared with the limited amount of construction the college could undertake), that no matter how many arcades Ramée invented in an attempt to knit everything together in good French fashion, the final impression inevitably was one of separate buildings in open space—the distinctively American collegiate pattern. And it is significant that North and South colleges were the only major elements of Ramée's plan that Nott actually constructed. For they embodied the most crucial part of his educational philosophy, the family-like collegiality of faculty and students living together. The design for the Union College campus, traditionally ascribed to Ramée, in fact owed as much to Eliphalet Nott and his ideals. His vision of a community of scholars, "separated from the great world" and yet contemplating the grandeur of the "new Zion," was fittingly embodied in this spacious architectural ensemble on a hilltop facing the American West.

66

67

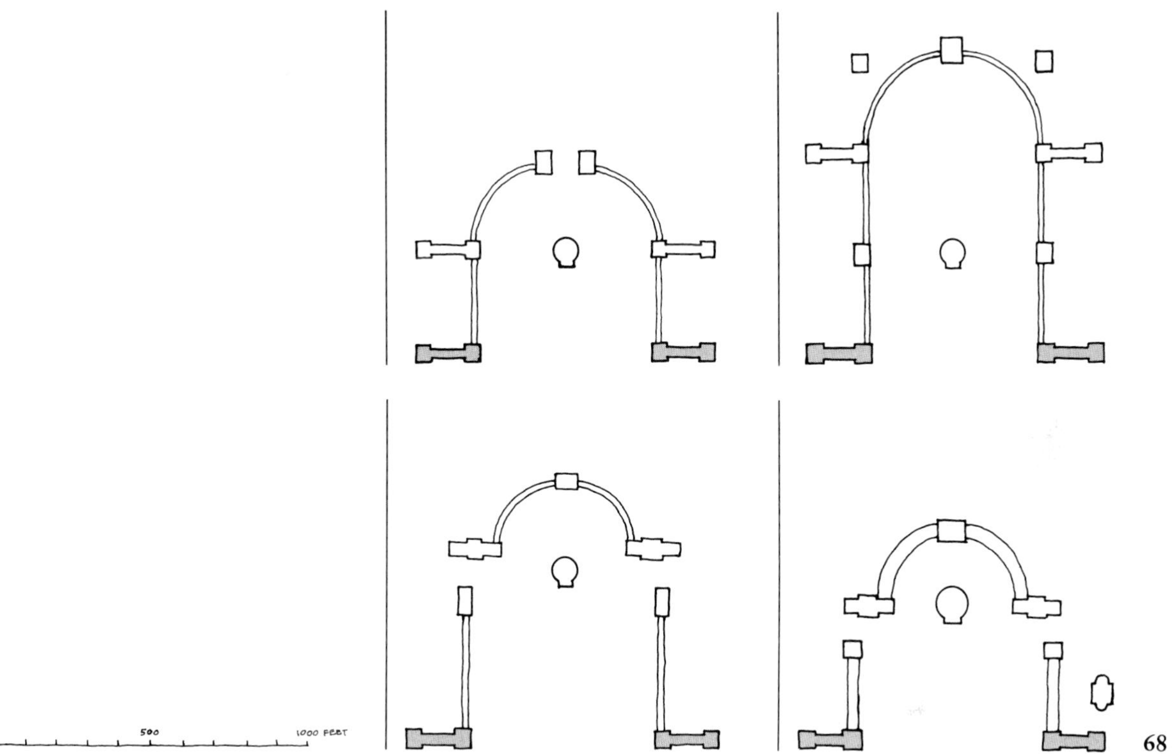

66 Union College. South College, erected 1812–1814, to house students in the central portion and professors in the two houses at the ends. This structure and the similar North College still serve the same functions. (Union College Publications Office)

67 Aerial view of Union College, ca. 1950. To left and right are North and South colleges, with academic wings extending behind them. In center is Nott Memorial, erected 1858–1870s (designed by Edward Tuckerman Potter), in place of Ramée's circular chapel. Behind it is Powers-Washburn Hall (erected 1880, demolished 1960), whose curving arms faintly echoed the semicircular arcade in Ramée's plan. (Union College Publications Office)

68 Schematic versions of four of Ramée's site plans for Union College, drawn to same scale. Shaded buildings are North and South colleges.

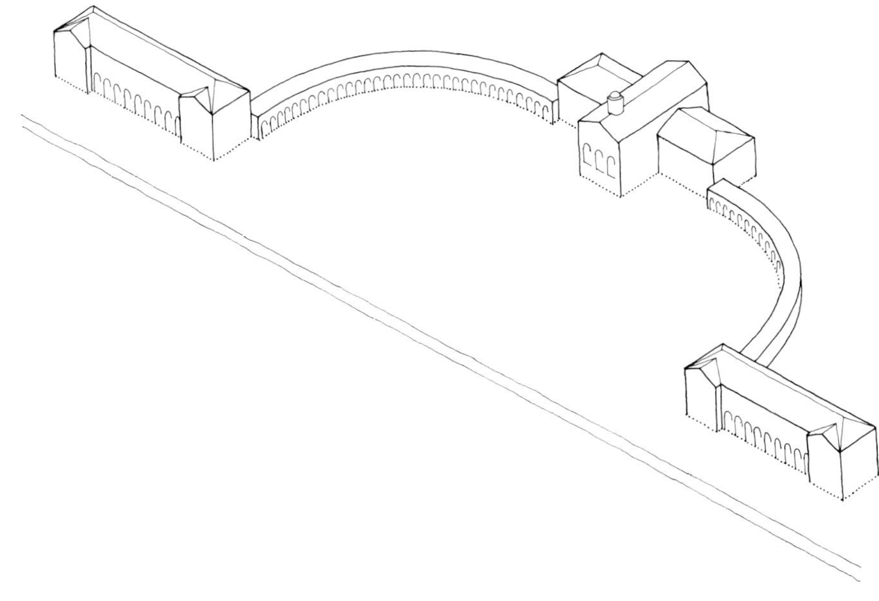

70

69 Elevation drawing, by Ramée, for a Union College building to contain the chapel, dining hall, classrooms, offices, library, and other functions. This structure was probably the centerpiece of his first design for the college. Visible at the edges of the drawing are portions of arcades, perhaps meant to connect this building to North and South colleges. (Shaffer Library, Union College)

70 Conjectural reconstruction of Ramée's first plan for Union College, 1813. At the ends are North and South colleges. At center is the building for which detailed drawings by Ramée survive, but which does not appear in Ramée's surviving site plans.

Jefferson and the University of Virginia

In 1817, construction began for the buildings of Central College, soon renamed the University of Virginia, and eight years later the school was ready to open. Located on a small hill outside the town of Charlottesville, only four miles from the home of its founder and architect, Thomas Jefferson, the institution consisted of a series of professors' houses (the "Pavilions"), alternating with groups of students' rooms, along the colonnaded sides of a mall (the "Lawn"), terminating at the north in a domed library (the "Rotunda"), and flanked to the east and west by gardens and outer rows of buildings (Figs. 1, 71, 72).[51]

The similarities between this design and the Union College plan are striking, and the possibility of a connection between them has been mentioned. (One historian, Talbot Hamlin, even suggested that Jefferson may have borrowed Ramée's drawings of the central rotunda at Union and neglected to return them, thereby explaining their absence from the Union College archives.)[52] But there is no evidence that Jefferson knew of Ramée's plans; and in fact, the evolution of Jefferson's design reveals that nearly all of the features it shares with Ramée's can be explained independently. The University of Virginia campus, like Union's, was an expression of architectural and educational principles of the period. Also like the Union College plan, Jefferson's design has traditionally been seen as having its sources principally in Europe, whereas in many respects it has a distinctively American character.

Jefferson was involved in college planning long before he designed the University of Virginia. His first major architectural undertaking (aside from his own house, Monticello) occurred in 1771, when he was twenty-eight years old and was asked by the royal governor of Virginia to draw plans for an addition to the Wren Building at William and Mary, his alma mater. Jefferson produced a design, of which the ground floor plan survives, and recent excavations have shown that construction actually was begun, although in 1776 the work was discontinued, "on Account of the Present Troubles" (as noted in the college records of that year), and it was never resumed (Fig. 73).[53]

Jefferson had attended William and Mary from 1760 to 1762, and later wrote of the strong influence on his education exerted by William Small, a Scottish liberal and enthusiast of science, who recognized the young Jefferson's talents and gave him special attention. Small introduced his student into the circle of cultivated gentlemen of Williamsburg, and it was here that Jefferson first became acquainted with architectural books and ideas. Later, in his *Notes on Virginia*, he criticized the buildings at William and Mary for lack of architectural refinement ("rude, mis-shapen piles, which, but that they have roofs, would be taken for brick-kilns").[54] But in his plans of 1771 for extending the Wren Building, he adhered to the original plan of 1693 for an enclosed courtyard, except that he increased its size by doubling the length of the side wings to accommodate extra classrooms and dormitory space. Jefferson also recommended extending the arcaded passageway, which was on one facade of the existing building, around all four sides of the courtyard. Throughout his life, he was to be especially fond of arcades and colonnades in his architectural designs; and their inclusion in his plan for William and Mary foreshadowed the importance of colonnades at the University of Virginia.

In 1779, as governor of Virginia, Jefferson presented to the state legislature a proposal for reforming public education by creating an extensive state system of free schools that would culminate in a university.[55] He originally intended William and Mary to be this university, but his proposed reforms of it were not enacted, and henceforth he devoted himself to the creation of a totally new state institution.

Jefferson's service as Minister to France from 1785 to 1789 gave him the opportunity to visit Roman buildings he had known only from books, such as the Maison Carrée in Nîmes, on which he modeled his design for the Virginia State Capitol at Richmond. But his exposure to contemporary French architecture was equally important, as revealed by his later use of a design by Claude-Nicolas Ledoux as a model for one of the professors' houses at the University of Virginia.[56] It is also likely that Jefferson was interested in the architectural debates in Paris over the plans for the new hospital of the Hôtel-Dieu, which called for a "pavilion" system of linked structures—rather like his own later plan for the university.[57]

After returning to America, Jefferson again took up educational issues, including the proposal to establish a national university. George Washington

71 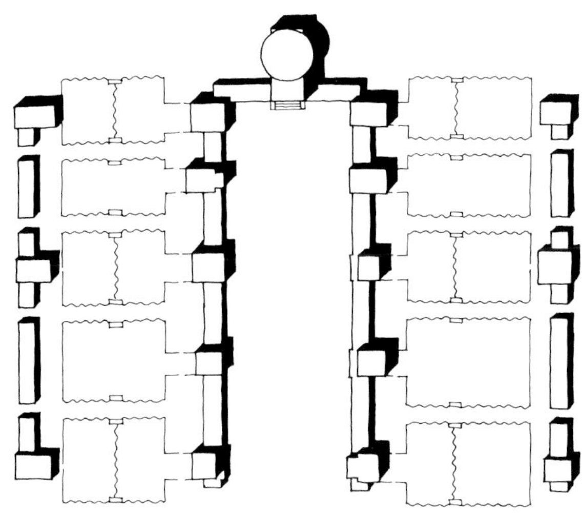

71 University of Virginia, Charlottesville, designed by Thomas Jefferson, 1817. Schematic plan, based on the Maverick engraving of 1822. Central space, called the Lawn, is flanked by ten Pavilions (each serving as a professor's house and classroom), linked by colonnades onto which students' rooms open. At north end of Lawn is domed Rotunda, serving principally as the library. Behind Pavilions are gardens, enclosed by serpentine brick walls. Beyond these are extra students' rooms and dining halls.

72 University of Virginia, as shown in an engraving by B. Tanner of 1827. Several of the Pavilions are seen here with their original roof parapets and the colonnades with flat roofs, which later were altered.
(University of Virginia Library)

72 

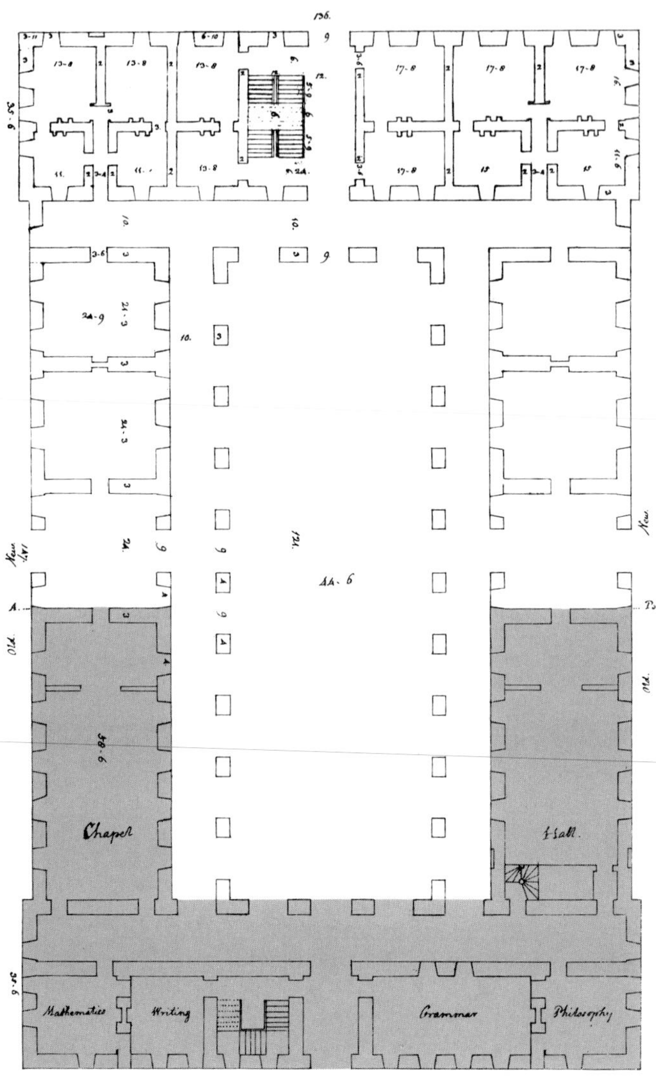

73

73 Plan for extension of the Wren Building at the College of William and Mary, by Thomas Jefferson, ca. 1771. (Shading has been added to indicate existing building.) Construction of proposed addition was begun but was discontinued in 1776, "on Account of the Present Troubles," as college records of that year stated. (The Huntington Library)

supported the idea strongly, and about 1795 Jefferson corresponded with him on the subject, taking the position that a national institution must be a true university in the European sense, with high standards of scholarship, professional studies, and scientific investigation, a type of institution still unknown in America. In 1797, as Vice-President of the United States, Jefferson oversaw the competition held by the American Philosophical Society for essays on a national university, in which Samuel Knox took a prize for his proposal (described earlier), which included a description of concentric quadrangles, the outer one containing professors' houses contiguous to their classrooms (Fig. 55), as Jefferson was to do in the University of Virginia. Jefferson may have gotten this idea from Knox, but since they were acquaintances, it is also possible that Jefferson first suggested it to Knox.

During his presidency, from 1801 to 1809, Jefferson continued to develop his ideas about a university for Virginia, and about college architecture in general. In 1802, his young friend Robert Mills, who was studying architecture and helping Jefferson with plans for Monticello, submitted his design in the South Carolina College competition, a design that featured arcaded passageways connecting the classrooms, and for which Jefferson may have made suggestions.[58] Jefferson was no doubt aware of the campus plan that South Carolina College soon began executing, the "horseshoe" arrangement of buildings around three sides of an extendable mall, as Jefferson himself was to do at the University of Virginia (Fig. 53). In 1805, when an acquaintance wrote to Jefferson about a plan for establishing a lower school in central Virginia, Jefferson urged more ambitious plans, and included his most specific ideas so far about the physical design of a college:

> The greatest danger will be [the college authorities'] over-building themselves, by attempting a large house in the beginning, sufficient to contain the whole institution. Large houses are always ugly, inconvenient, exposed to the accident of fire, and bad in cases of infection. A plain small house for the school and lodging of each professor is best. These connected by covered ways out of which the rooms of the students should open would be best. These may be built only as they shall be wanting. In fact a university should not be a house but a village. This will much lessen their first expenses.[59]

Years later, Jefferson recalled this correspondence as the genesis of "the general idea of an Academical Village" for the University of Virginia.[60] A sketch by Jefferson exists, which may date from about this time, showing a one-story "Pavilion" and adjacent rows of "dormitories," although without the covered walk mentioned in the letter.[61] Jefferson's emphasis that his plan could be built easily in stages recalls John Trumbull's similar remarks about his 1792 design for Yale—with which Jefferson was surely familiar, since he and Trumbull were friends and had spent time together in France visiting architectural monuments.[62]

In 1810, Jefferson described his evolving plans more fully, in recommendations to the trustees of the newly founded East Tennessee College:

> I consider the common plan, followed in this country but not in others, of making one large and expensive building, as unfortunately erroneous. It is infinitely better to erect a small and separate lodge for each separate professorship, with only a hall below for his class, and two chambers above for himself; joining these lodges by barracks for a certain portion of the students, opening into a covered way to give a dry communication between all the schools. The whole of these arranged around an open square of grass and trees, would make it, what it should be in fact, an academical village. . . . Every professor would be the police officer of the students adjacent to his own lodge, which should include those of his own class of preference, and might be at the head of their table, if, as I suppose, it can be reconciled with the necessary economy to dine them in smaller and separate parties rather than in a large and common mess. These separate buildings, too, might be erected successively and occasionally, as the number of professorships and students should be increased, or the funds become competent. . . . Much observation and reflection on these institutions have long convinced me that the large and crowded buildings in which youths are pent up, are equally unfriendly to health, to study, to manners, morals and order.[63]

This describes the most essential features of the plan that Jefferson ultimately created for the University of Virginia. The concept of a large open space, surrounded by professors' houses serving also as classrooms and alternating with students' rooms, was unprecedented in educational planning. Historians have proposed numerous possible architectural sources of this concept, ranging from the lyceum and palestra of antiquity, to Louis XIV's chateau at Marly (with its main structure framed by rows of courtiers' pavilions), which Jefferson is known to have visited in 1786.[64]

But the evolution of Jefferson's design suggests that its sources are to be found closer to home. Whereas the final form of the University of Virginia does bear some resemblance to European monuments such as Marly or the pavilion plans of French hospitals, as mentioned earlier, Jefferson's original concept was very different in character (Fig. 74). It called for a large, tree-filled space—practically four times as wide as it was finally executed—surrounded on three sides by professors' houses considerably smaller than those that were built, and with no dominant Rotunda.[65] If the university had been built this way, it would have looked very much like a typical American village green, an expansive space surrounded by modest private houses. Thus, when Jefferson wrote about his vision of an "academical village," he was thinking quite literally of an American village or town. Among the many town greens that Jefferson knew well was the Palace Green in Williamsburg, whose overall dimensions and character are similar to Jefferson's original concept for his university (Fig. 75).[66] In fact, when Jefferson was a student at William and Mary, at least one of his professors, George Wythe, lived on the side of Palace Green and often invited Jefferson into his home. The memory of Palace Green in Williamsburg was surely one of the images that inspired Jefferson's vision of an "academical village."

Despite Jefferson's professed desire to create a true university on the European model, his concept of an "academical village" was in many ways more suited to the traditional American collegiate system—in its scale, rural location, small classroom assigned each professor in his pavilion, and especially in the familial relationship between the professor and his students. Jefferson's statement, that "every professor would be the police officer of the students adjacent to his own lodge, . . . and might be at the head of their table," is thoroughly collegiate in spirit, and recalls Eliphalet Nott's program for Union College stipulating that each class was to be part of "the family of the officer who instructs them," and that they all would "lodge in college and board in commons."

Despite Jefferson's criticism, in 1810, of American colleges for concentrating everything in "one large and expensive building," there were a number of American campuses that could have contributed to his ideas for the University of Virginia. The mall plan of South Carolina College has already been mentioned. And Jefferson was familiar with the appearance of both Harvard and Yale, neither of which was concentrated in one building (Figs. 25, 39).[67] Harvard's pattern of buildings around three sides of a courtyard was a kind of miniature prototype of Jefferson's plan. And the Yale Row, designed by Jefferson's friend John Trumbull, was similar to the University of Virginia plan not only in its ease of staged construction, but also in its linear alternation of classroom buildings and dormitory facilities (Fig. 76). Jefferson's fragmenting of the educational units was much more radical than anything that had been done earlier, but it was a continuation of a tendency that already existed in American college planning.

In 1814, Jefferson began to implement his educational ideas. He became a trustee of Albemarle Academy, which two years later was reconstituted as Central College, and finally became the University of Virginia. Much of the physical planning of the institution was accomplished in 1817. In May of that year, Jefferson submitted his site plan to the university trustees, who accepted the concept it embodied (Fig. 74).[68] The drawing shows nine pavilions, linked by dormitory rooms and colonnades, around three sides of a rectangular space 257 yards in width. As drawn, the colonnaded dormitories fade away at the ends, showing that the scheme was meant to be extended as new facilities were required. On the back of this sheet, Jefferson drew the plan and elevation of one of the pavilions and its adjacent dormitories (Fig. 77).[69] The pavilion is modest in size and design (still the "plain small house" Jefferson had described in his 1805 letter), with a classroom on the ground floor and two dwelling rooms on the floor above.

74 Site plan for Central College (later the University of Virginia), by Thomas Jefferson, presented to trustees of the institution in May 1817. Professors' houses alternate with series of students' rooms along three sides of a space measuring 257 yards across—nearly four times as wide as in final plan. (Thomas Jefferson Papers, University of Virginia Library)

75 Palace Green, Williamsburg, Virginia. At end of Green is the Governor's Palace, erected beginning in 1706. Building in foreground at left was home of George Wythe, one of Jefferson's teachers when he was a student at the College of William and Mary.

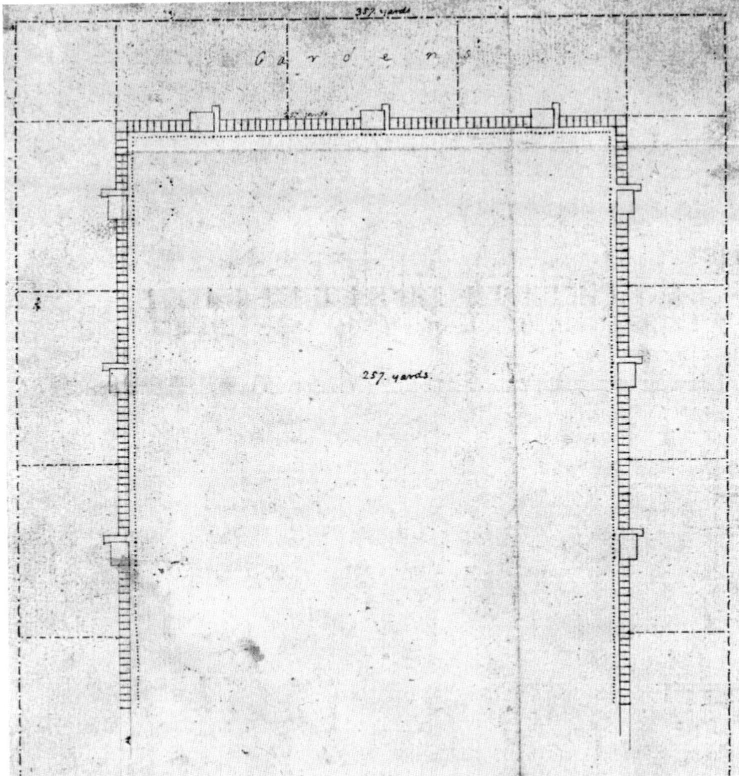

74

75

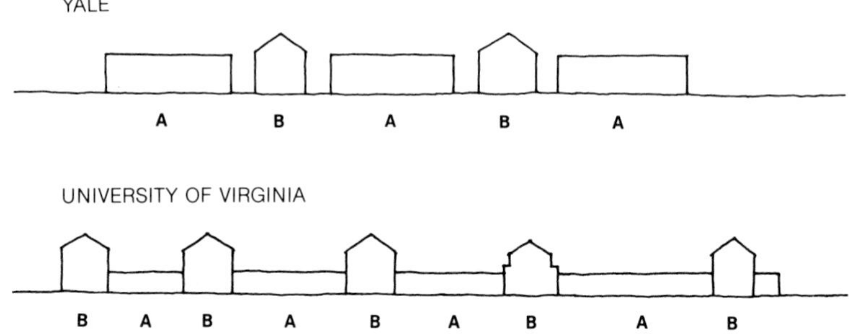

76

0 50' 100'

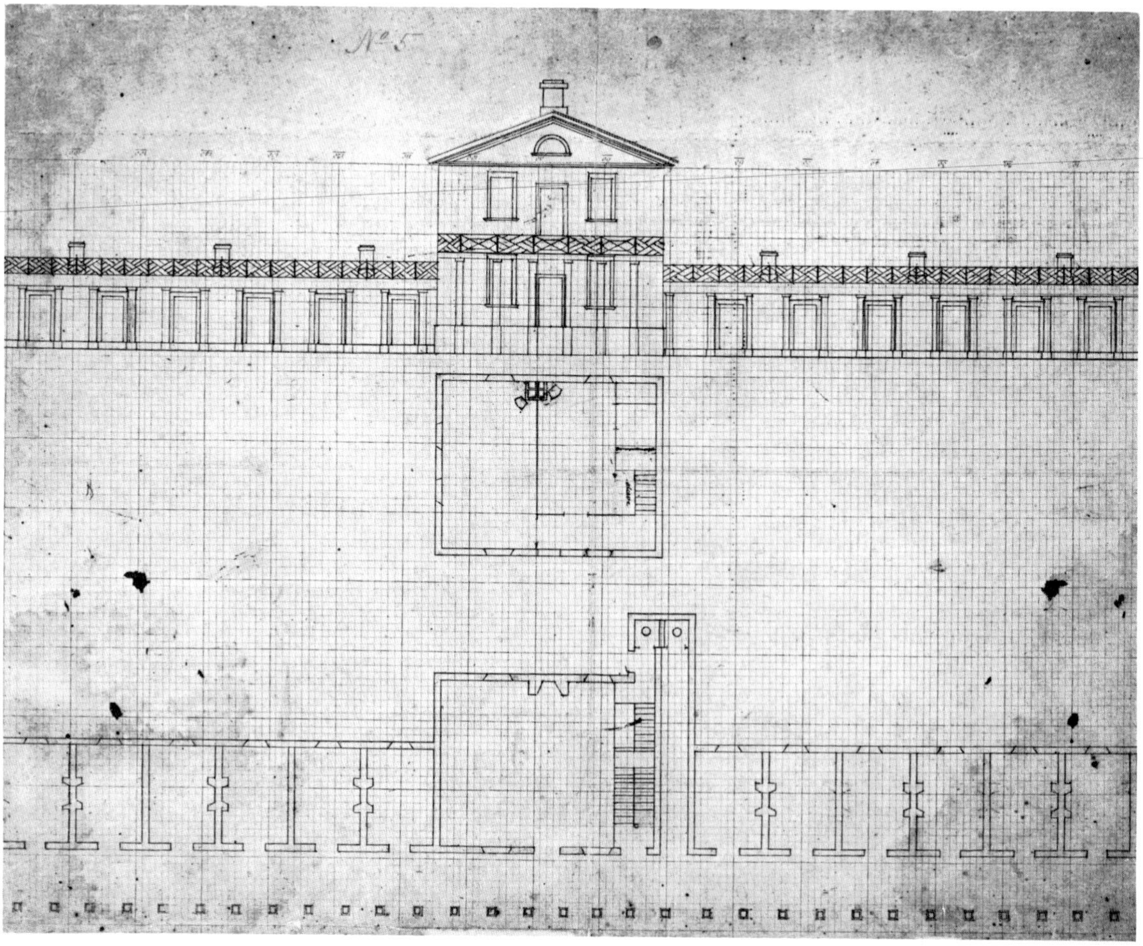

76 Schematic comparison of Yale Row and one side of Lawn at the University of Virginia. Buildings labeled *A* are student dormitories. Those labeled *B* contain classrooms and other functions.

77 Plan and elevation drawing of a professor's house and students' rooms, by Jefferson, probably 1817. Professor's house, with classroom on the ground floor, is considerably smaller than those finally executed. Attached to rear of house are two privies.
(Thomas Jefferson Papers, University of Virginia Library)

77

In May and June of 1817, Jefferson wrote to the architects William Thornton and Benjamin Latrobe, describing his plans, and asking for their suggestions.[70] In his letter to Thornton, he noted that he planned to give the pavilions "a variety of appearance, no two alike, so to serve as specimens for the Architecture lecturer." This was the first indication of Jefferson's intention to vary the designs of the pavilions, and it was an extraordinary notion, which violated the classical principles of uniformity and symmetry. Contrary to the advice of colleagues, Jefferson executed the pavilions this way, and several early visitors to the campus criticized this eccentricity.[71] It is an illustration of Jefferson's willingness to be nonconformist in matters of planning, in contrast to his concern for correctness in architectural details. But it also underscores the nature of Jefferson's design as literally an academic "village"—an informal group of buildings, each having its own independence and individual character, as in any American town.

Thornton and Latrobe made a number of suggestions that Jefferson approved, all of which increased the monumentality of the design and mitigated its modest village-like character. The pavilions were made larger and grander, and Latrobe proposed that the central building be an impressive domed structure—reminiscent of his own college designs, such as his national university plan of the year before (Figs. 78, 63).[72] Jefferson liked this idea and introduced the Rotunda into his design, although instead of making it a lecture hall as Latrobe proposed, he devoted it principally to the library. This was clearly an expression of Jefferson's aspiration to create a true university, where research played a role it never had in the traditional American college. For the first time on an American campus, the central focus was the library. Equally significant was Jefferson's omission of a chapel from his plans. He intended his institution to be fully secular and progressive, although based firmly on the residential collegiate tradition.

In the summer of 1817, land finally was acquired for the school outside Charlottesville, and construction of one of the pavilions was begun. But Jefferson discovered that the ridge on which the buildings were to be erected could not be graded to create the broad square he had envisioned. The distance between the colonnades had to be reduced to about 200 feet, and this required that all the pavilions be on the sides. Furthermore, the longer sides that resulted had to be placed on terraces that stepped down the hill, from north to south. Jefferson's original concept of a large village green was thus further obscured, although the unified architectural effect was heightened by the changes. The plan took its final form with the design of the ranges of buildings beyond the pavilions, to accommodate extra dormitories and dining halls. In 1819 Jefferson wrote, "It forms in fact a regular town, capable of being enlarged to any extent which future circumstances may call for."[73] By this time, several of the pavilions were under construction. The outer ranges were soon begun, and work on the Rotunda was started in 1821. The buildings were largely completed by the time the university opened in 1825, a year before Jefferson's death at the age of eighty-two (Figs. 79, 80).

The essential character of Jefferson's design for the University of Virginia was determined by his vision of the ideal education. In his own college years, Jefferson's most rewarding experiences had been in his personal relationships with his teachers. Later, in a similarly intimate way, he had acted as a teacher to young men such as Robert Mills, whom he often invited into his home. He evidently considered education to be best when familial in character and based on close personal relationships. The notion of separate pavilions serving as both the teacher's home and classroom, with students' rooms linked directly like guest wings, was the most logical physical expression of this ideal. That this model had little relevance to the modern European type of university Jefferson talked of emulating was a problem he never fully resolved.[74] His educational ideal was in fact largely American in spirit, and echoed the principles of other educators of the period, like Eliphalet Nott, in its collegiate commitment, its familial overtones, and its desire to withdraw from the life of cities and be a "village" unto itself.

The uncompromising way in which Jefferson translated these ideas into physical form proved to be both the strength and weakness of his design. The insistence on having professors live at the center of the campus, above their classrooms and next to their students, was too demanding and inflexible for most American institutions, and was almost never adopted elsewhere. In fact, soon after

Latrobe B. Henry. Rec'd July 24. 17.
ans'd Aug. 3.

86

A B E B A

C C

D D

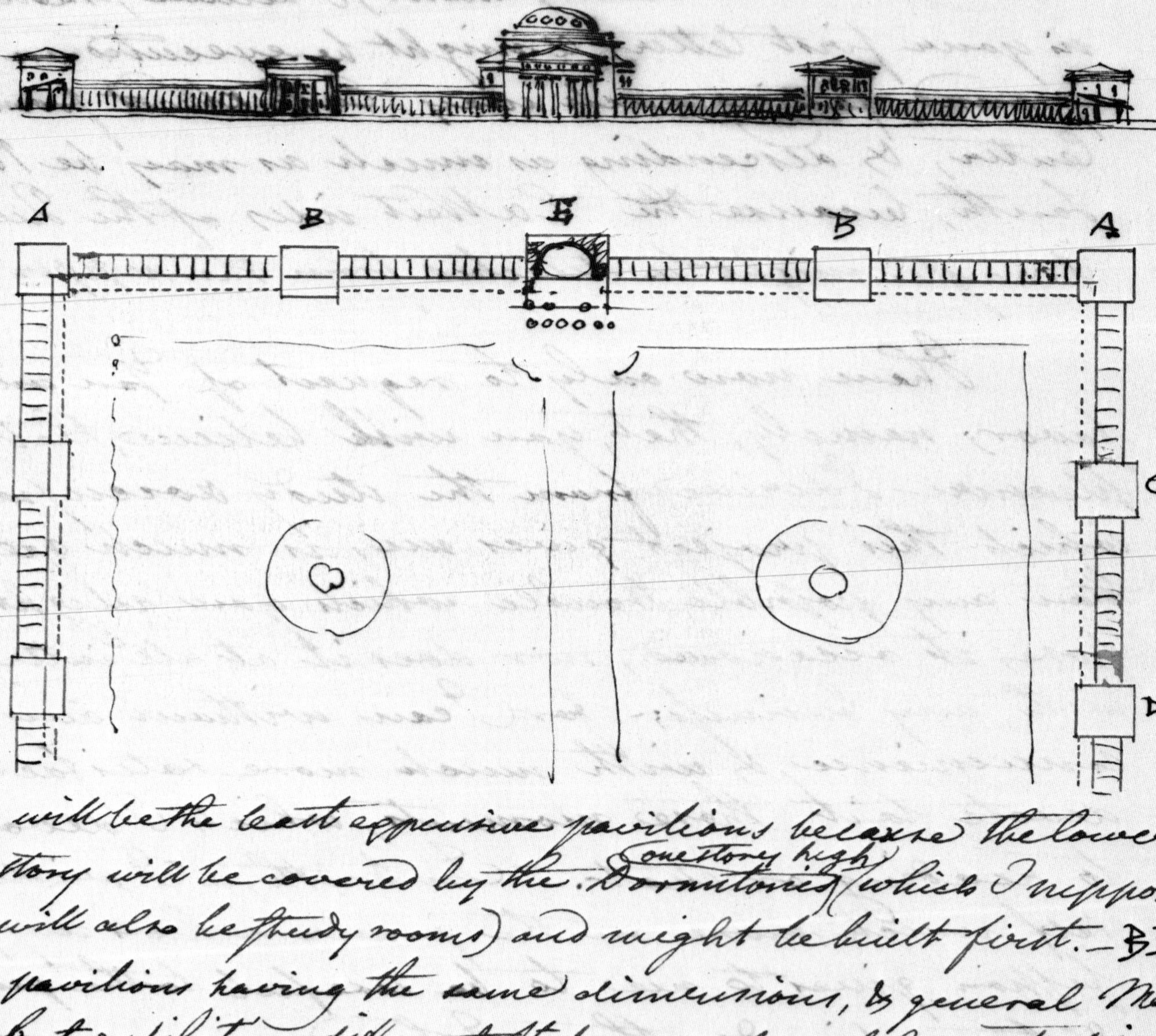

AA, will be the least expensive pavilions because the lower story will be covered by the Dormitories (one story high) (which I suppose will also be study rooms) and might be built first. — BB pavilions having the same dimensions, & general Plan but exhibiting different styles or orders of Architecture. CC do. do. ~~E~~ DD do. do. Center building which ought to exhibit in Plan & details as perfect a specimen of good Architectural taste as can be devised. I should propose below, a couple or 4 rooms for Janitors or Tutors,

79

78 Portion of letter from Benjamin Henry Latrobe to Jefferson, July 24, 1817, with proposals for design of the University of Virginia. Latrobe's principal suggestion was that a large domed structure be added (containing lecture rooms) at center of end of open square.
(Library of Congress)

79 View of the University of Virginia from the west. Lithograph by F. Sachse and Co., 1856. Behind Rotunda is the Annex, erected 1851–1853, containing classrooms and a public hall; was destroyed by fire in 1895. In background is the town of Charlottesville and, in the distance on a hill, Jefferson's home, Monticello. The scale of this view is somewhat inaccurate, showing the Rotunda larger in relation to other buildings than it actually is.
(University of Virginia Library)

80

81

the University of Virginia opened, most of the professors moved their classrooms from their pavilions to the Rotunda or other locations (reportedly at the insistence of their wives, who could not abide the continual presence of students in their homes).[75] But the notion of a collegiate town, composed of independent buildings around a village green, with the possibility of growth by extension, suited the American college perfectly.

The specific form of Jefferson's design—a mall lined with buildings, with a central structure as a focal point—was destined to have a curiously delayed influence on American college planning. Until the 1890s, it had little discernible effect on the planning of other colleges, with a few exceptions, such as William Nichols's plan for the University of Alabama in 1828 (Fig. 81).[76] Several campuses in the mid- and late-nineteenth century, such as the University of Wisconsin at Madison, the University of Notre Dame in Indiana, and Wilberforce University in Ohio, developed around malls of various kinds, but probably with little direct influence from the University of Virginia (Figs. 87, 99).[77] Around 1900, however, Jefferson's design was rediscovered and began to exert a great influence on college planning. Since that time, the appeal of the University of Virginia campus has grown steadily. Especially in an age of gigantic universities and the threat of impersonal education, Jefferson's "academical village" seems to embody perfectly the ideal of an intimate and enlightened dialogue between students and teachers.

80 University of Virginia. Rotunda and Pavilions on east side of Lawn. (Printing Services Records, University of Virginia Archives)

81 University of Alabama, Tuscaloosa. Engraved view, ca. 1837. Campus was designed by William Nichols in 1828, and most of the buildings were constructed in the following decade. In center is rotunda, containing library and assembly hall. At sides are dormitories, each accommodating about fifty students. In background are professors' houses and columned Lyceum, containing classrooms. Most of the structures were destroyed by fire in 1865. (Library of Congress, Prints and Photographs Division)

III. Expansion and Mythmaking

In the period from about 1820 to the Civil War, American higher education experienced tremendous growth but also found itself in crisis. The expanding American frontier, the rivalry of religious sects, and the ideal of democratic education all contributed to a proliferation of colleges in the country—perhaps as many as eight hundred being founded before the Civil War, although many of these were short-lived.[1] There was boundless enthusiasm in education, as in all aspects of American life, as Ralph Waldo Emerson commented in 1833: "It is a country of beginnings, of projects, of designs, and expectations."[2] Yet most schools perpetuated the traditional system of education, with its strict religious emphasis and narrowly classical curriculum, which many critics considered irrelevant to a society preoccupied with business, industry, expansion, and progress.

New types of schools did begin to appear: scientific and technical schools, agricultural schools presaging the later land-grant colleges, "manual training" schools, and women's seminaries. But the majority of colleges avoided experimentation and persisted in the old methods, as spelled out defiantly in the Yale Report of 1828.[3] The typical daily life of an American college student still consisted of compulsory chapel services, strict dormitory rules, and recitation classes in Latin, Greek, philosophy, and a smattering of other subjects. Intellectual interests falling outside the prescribed curriculum often were actually discouraged. Students vented their frustration in many ways, including vandalism and violence, which became serious problems in the American college for the first time. Riots and other disorders were not uncommon, sometimes resulting in the death of students, even of professors and of at least one college president.[4]

Concern for student order often affected architectural planning, as when authorities at South Carolina College decided to make all stairways fireproof and to design dormitories with separate entries in order to eliminate the corridors where rowdy students congregated.[5] Excessive collegiate regulations and discipline certainly provoked student unease, but the consequent disorders only encouraged greater restrictions. Perhaps not surprisingly, there is evidence that the architect Alexander Jackson Davis, who did much collegiate work during this period, thought of college buildings as belonging to an architectural category that also included prisons and asylums.[6]

More constructively, students began their own reshaping of the American college, creating alongside the official curriculum a renegade "extracurriculum." First established were the literary and debating societies, popular especially in the 1820s and 1830s; then the Greek-letter social fraternities; and later, organized athletics. College authorities often fought these intrusions, but they were unable to offset their appeal in satisfying real needs—intellectual, social, and physical. The literary society, for example, promoted debates and other intellectual activities often more relevant to modern life than the standard curriculum, sometimes built up a better collection of books than the college library itself, and usually had its own separate building, thus constituting almost an alternative, student-run college within the college.

Added to the curricular problems were conflicts between religious orthodoxy and academic freedom, the financial straits of many schools, and the widespread doubts in America about the value of higher education. In this embattled position, the American college reacted by creating a kind of mythology to sustain itself. Its main theme was the nobility and necessity of the traditional college with its classical curriculum. Supporting this was a reaffirmation of the collegiate principle that students should live together in a close-knit community, the college authorities acting *in loco parentis*. There was also the conviction that this community should be located in the countryside in order to escape the corrupting life of cities and to partake of the inherent purity of nature. There was an emphasis on the venerability of the American college, which as part of an ancient tradition of learning should display the supposed hallmarks and trappings of that tradition. There was a faith that despite its apparent elitism the institution was essentially democratic—as when the president of Amherst College wrote in 1856 that American colleges "are the people's colleges. . . . All classes have contributed . . . and all classes have reaped the benefits."[7] And there was a faith in the unlimited growth and grandeur of the American college. All of these ideas found expression in the architecture and physical planning of the mid-nineteenth-century American college.

The Classical Ideal

In the early decades of the nineteenth century the Greek Revival dominated American architecture and the American imagination. It was as much a state of mind as an architectural style, charged with connotations of Athenian democracy, purity, wisdom, and independence. At the height of its popularity, nearly all building types, from domestic to governmental, were forced into the temple form or other shapes thought to be "Greek."[8] In adopting this style of architecture, the college was therefore only following the fashion of the times (Fig. 82). But more than any other institution, the college had good reasons for embracing the Greek style—or generally, any architecture suggesting classical antiquity—since it fortified the ideal of the classical curriculum and its nobility. The college claimed preeminently to embody the wisdom of the Greco-Roman tradition, and in the early nineteenth century it reminded the public of this in every way possible, even to the point of giving the name Athens to the town in which it was located (as did Ohio University, the University of Georgia, and Athens College in Alabama), or by calling itself "The Athens of America" (Princeton), or "The Athens of the South" (the College of Charleston).[9]

The literary and debating societies—most early nineteenth-century colleges had two, into which the student body divided itself—usually were given Greek or Greek-sounding names, such as Demosthenian, Philanthropic, Dignothian, Atheneum, Alexandrian, or Philolexian.[10] When these societies erected their own buildings, they naturally chose the temple form in most cases, as did the Whig and Cliosophic societies at Princeton, Philanthropic and Eumenean at Davidson College in North Carolina, and Phi Gamma and Few halls at Emory College in Georgia (Figs. 83, 84).[11] These buildings were nearly always sited symmetrically, either side by side as at Princeton, or more often with their porticos facing one another, as at Davidson and Emory, neatly symbolizing the civilized dialogue between their memberships.

Other buildings at colleges of this period often were planned in a similar way, not only in their temple-like forms, but in their siting and relationship to each other. Symmetry and order governed the overall planning of schools more than ever before, as seen in a plan of the Princeton campus, drawn in 1836 by the pioneering scientist

82 Old Morrison at Transylvania College, Lexington, Kentucky. Designed by Gideon Shryock, erected 1830–1834. Originally called Morrison College, the building contained classrooms and a chapel, and later became the school's administration building.
(Transylvania College)

83 Whig and Cliosophic halls, Princeton, 1837–1838. These two society halls were positioned symmetrically behind Nassau Hall, so that each was visible from Nassau Street. In the 1890s, they were rebuilt and placed somewhat closer together.
(Princeton University Archives)

82

83

84

85

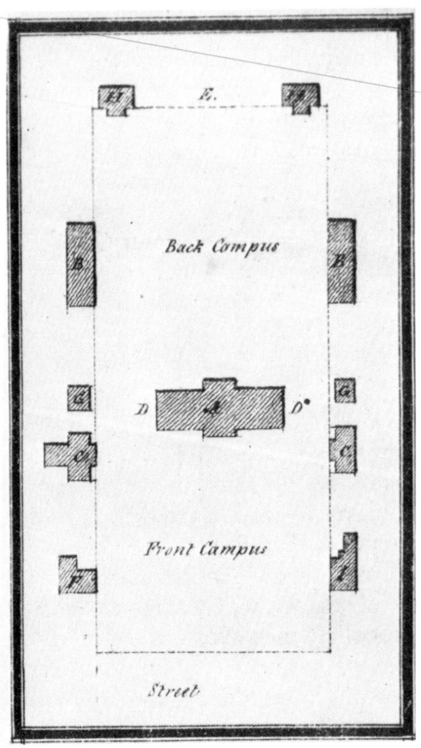

84 Eumenean and Philanthropic halls, Davidson College, Davidson, North Carolina, 1849–1850.

85 Plan of the Princeton campus, by Joseph Henry, 1836. Asked by student members of the Whig and Cliosophic societies to make recommendations for siting the proposed new society halls, Henry drew a plan, of which this is an engraved version used in a fund-raising letter to alumni. Besides indicating positions of the society halls (labeled H and H), Henry recommended moving two existing structures (a professor's house and the steward's house, labeled G and G), to increase symmetry of the campus and allow unimpeded sight lines for new society halls.
(Princeton University Archives)

Joseph Henry (who taught some architecture, as well as science, at the college), in which he sited the proposed Whig and Cliosophic halls and relocated a couple of the existing buildings in a manner that strengthened the classical order of the campus (Fig. 85).[12] Occasionally, colleges erected buildings principally to correct the asymmetry of an existing arrangement. (Nearly a century later, at Yale, a structure put up to mirror Connecticut Hall was ridiculed by the students with the slogan "For God, for Country, and for Symmetry").[13] In 1829, the University of Pennsylvania constructed two new buildings in Philadelphia, designed by William Strickland, whose identical appearance masked their very different functions—one housing the general collegiate program, the other the university's medical school (Fig. 86).[14] And in 1851, the University of Wisconsin at Madison had an architect prepare an ambitious master plan in which four aligned dormitories (of which only two were built) flanked a broad avenue leading to the main university building from the state capitol at the other end of the city, thus modifying the Yale Row pattern to achieve greater symmetry and axiality (Fig. 87).[15]

Another change was that buildings now tended to be placed at greater distances from one another, producing an impression that each was an independent object. The relatively tightly grouped buildings of colonial Harvard and Yale, or even of Jefferson's University of Virginia, were replaced by more isolated structures in open space, appropriate to the notion that each was a temple unto itself. This greater spaciousness can be seen at many schools, such as the University of Georgia, built up largely in the 1820s and 1830s (Fig. 88). Another southern school, the College of Charleston, achieved a different kind of evocation of antiquity by erecting in 1852 a triumphal arch through which one entered the campus, and by adding a monumental portico to the existing main building (Fig. 89).[16]

The tradition of housing many collegiate functions within one large structure was also encouraged by the classical ideal, since one dominating building could create a particularly noble and isolated impression. The more genuinely "Greek" of these buildings forced everything into a simple temple form—as at Girard College in Philadelphia (begun 1832), the University of Delaware (1834), and Westminster College in Missouri (ca. 1850) (Figs. 95, 90, 91). Other schools used more traditional or flexible plans, making them Greek by the inclusion of a robust colonnade or pedimented portico—as in the main buildings at Transylvania College in Kentucky (1830–34), Oglethorpe College in Georgia (1838), the University of Missouri (1840–43), and the University of Louisiana (1840s) (Figs. 82, 92, 93, 163).[17] Beginning in the 1820s, Washington College in Virginia (now Washington and Lee University) erected a monumental alignment of colonnaded structures that was like a Greek version of the Yale Row (Fig. 94), or perhaps of one side of Jefferson's Lawn at the University of Virginia.

Probably the most lavish Greek Revival academic architecture was created for Girard College in Philadelphia. It illustrates strikingly the use of classical forms to ennoble (or perhaps compensate for) an essentially modest educational program.[18] In 1831 the wealthy banker Stephen Girard died, having stipulated in his will that a college (or what would now probably be called an academy) be established for "poor white male orphans." Girard was known for his dislike of ostentatious architecture—as well as of organized religion, which he banned from the school—and he specified that the buildings be plain, utilitarian, and swiftly built. Despite this, the school's trustees held an architectural competition that elicited several grand designs; they gave the prize to Thomas U. Walter's scheme for a massive temple flanked symmetrically by additional buildings.[19] The president of the Board of Trustees, the amateur Hellenist Nicholas Biddle, persuaded Walter to embellish his design even further by transforming the central building into a full-fledged Greek temple, surrounded on all sides by a Corinthian colonnade, making it the most lavishly authentic "Greek" structure in America at that time. The final revised design for the campus replaced Walter's flanking structures with additional temple-like buildings, resulting in an unprecedented alignment of five temples (Fig. 95).

This design took fifteen years to execute, cost nearly the full $2 million that Girard had allocated for the entire college bequest, and stirred great controversy in the community. One local critic bitterly pointed out the contrast between Girard's original desire for a "humble but charitable college

UNIVERSITY OF PENNSYLVANIA. 86

87

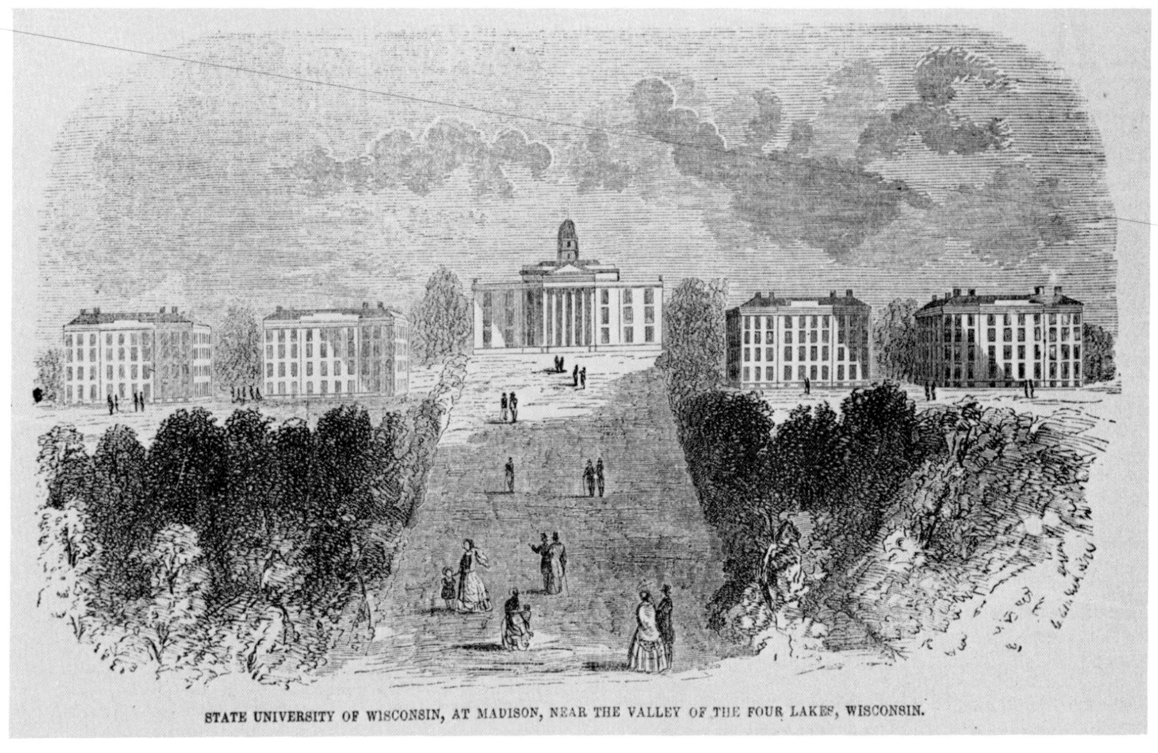
STATE UNIVERSITY OF WISCONSIN, AT MADISON, NEAR THE VALLEY OF THE FOUR LAKES, WISCONSIN.

88

86 College Hall and Medical Hall, the University of Pennsylvania. Designed by William Strickland and constructed 1829–1830, these buildings were located on Ninth Street between Chestnut and Market in Philadelphia, and were used by the university until it moved to West Philadelphia in 1872. (*Catalogue of the Trustees, Officers, and Students of the University of Pennsylvania, Session 1852–53*, back cover)

87 University of Wisconsin, Madison. Rendering of master plan by John F. Rague, 1851. At either side of main university building (later Bascom Hall) are four dormitories, only the two inner of which were constructed. The central axis leads to the State Capitol. (*Gleason's Pictorial Drawing-Room Companion*, October 25, 1851, p. 265)

88 University of Georgia, Athens, ca. 1840. *From left*: Phi Kappa Hall, built 1833 for one of the school's literary societies; Philosophical Hall (now Waddell Hall), built 1821 for science instruction; Old College (originally called Franklin College), built 1801–1806 to house all the collegiate functions; New College, built 1823, destroyed by fire and rebuilt 1832; Chapel, 1832; Demosthenian Hall, built 1824 for the other literary society; Ivy Building. (*Gleason's Pictorial Drawing-Room Companion*, May 13, 1854. Reproduction courtesy of the University of Georgia, Office of Public Relations)

89

90

89 College of Charleston, South Carolina. In foreground is Porter's Lodge (entry gate to the college), designed by E. B. White, erected 1852. In background (*left*) is the Main Building, designed by William Strickland, built 1829, portico added 1850.

90 Old College, University of Delaware, Newark, Delaware. Central section of this structure, erected in 1834 (with funds raised by a lottery), was school's principal building for half a century. Side wings were added in 1902.

91 Westminster College, Fulton, Missouri. Main building, erected ca. 1852. (M. M. Fisher, *History of Westminster College, 1851–1903*, Columbia, Missouri, 1903, p. xv)

92 Oglethorpe College, Milledgeville, Georgia, built 1838. (Robert Sears, *Pictorial Description of the United States*, New York, 1855, p. 393)

91

92

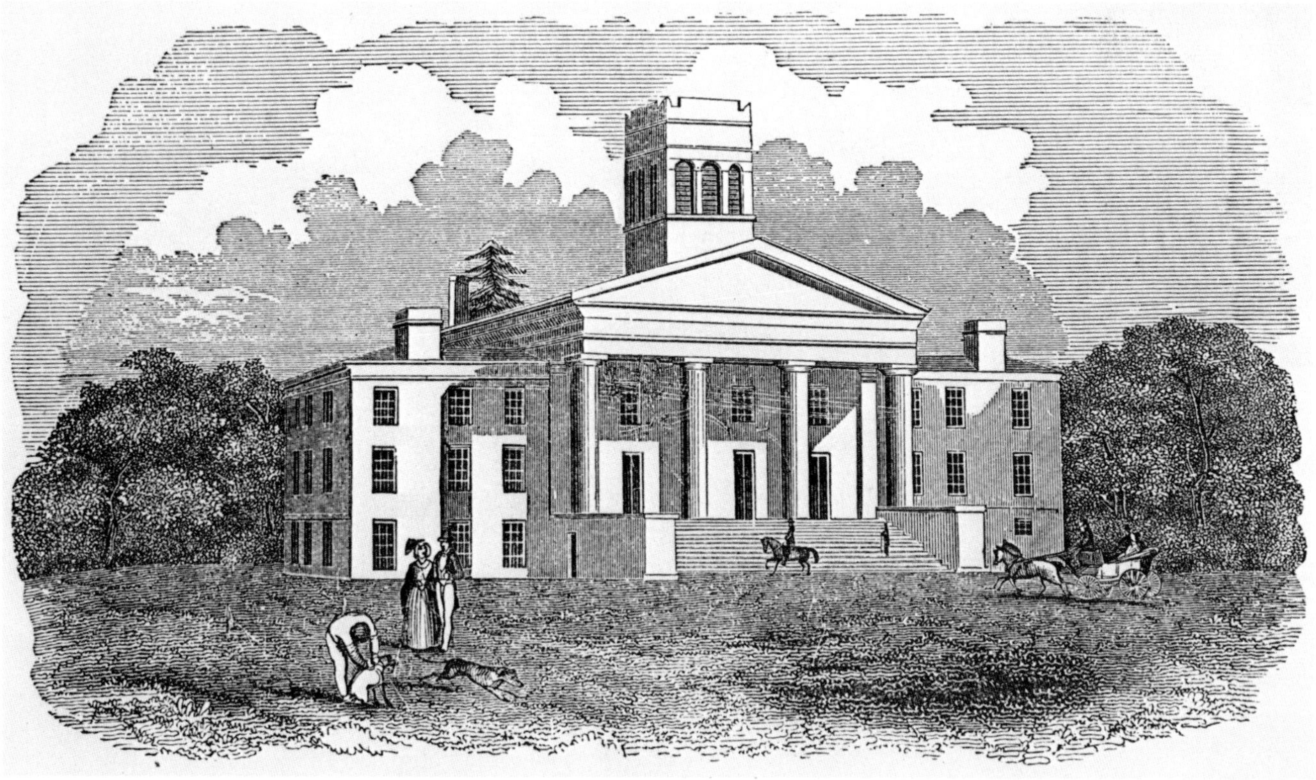

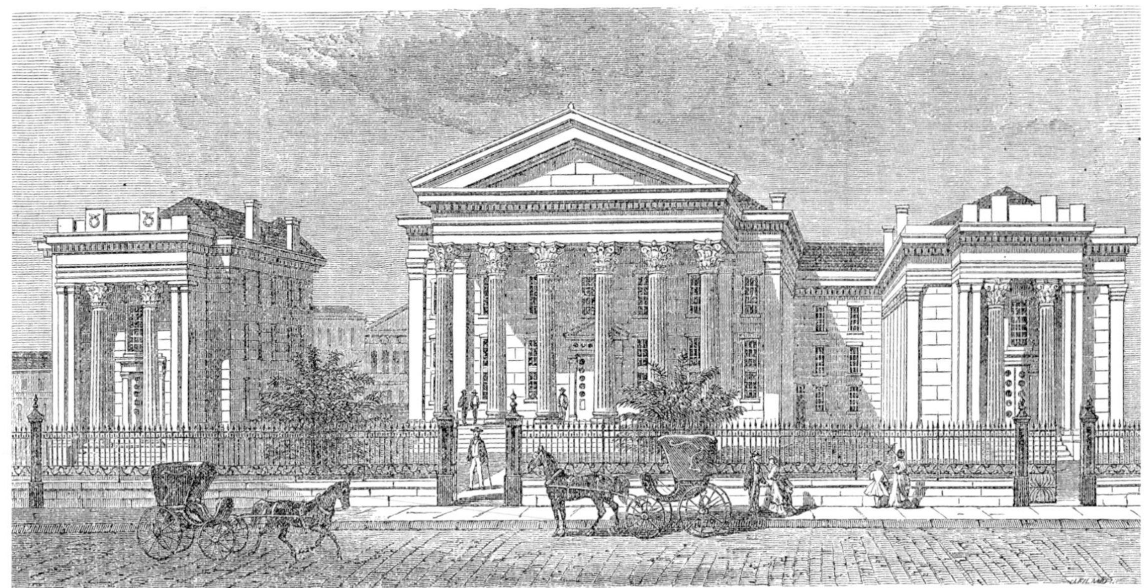
93

94

93 University of Louisiana (now Tulane University), New Orleans. Buildings designed by James Dakin in the 1840s. *From left*: Law Department, Medical Department, Academical Department. (*Annual Circular of the Medical Department of the University of Louisiana for the Session 1879–1880*, New Orleans, 1879, following p. 14)

94 Washington College (now Washington and Lee University), Lexington, Virginia. Engraving of ca. 1845. Pedimented building in center was erected in 1824, and contained principally classrooms. Structures linked with it to east and west, serving as dormitories and other functions, were added in the 1830s and 1840s.
(Henry Howe, *Historical Collections of Virginia*, Charleston, S.C., 1845, opp. p. 448)

95 Girard College, Philadelphia, Pennsylvania. Buildings designed by Thomas U. Walter and constructed 1833 to 1848, following architect's revised plan after the competition of 1832. Central building contained classrooms and administrative offices. Four smaller structures housed the student dormitories, dining facilities, and (in one of the buildings) four professors' residences.
(*The Girard College and Its Founder*, Philadelphia, 1869, frontispiece)

for fatherless and motherless children," and the trustees' preoccupation with architectural splendor, as revealed in their prediction that "this beautiful work of art will form . . . an object of the highest interest . . . inasmuch as no country on earth can boast a purer specimen of architecture, or a more substantial and elegantly wrought memorial, to convey to distant ages the 'spirit of the time.' "[20] Surely one aspect of the "spirit of the time," which this Girard College episode reveals, was the exploitation of classical architecture to transform modest educational operations into symbols of cultural aspiration.

Existing colleges also found the new spirit of classicism compelling. In the 1840s, the University of North Carolina hired the architect Alexander Jackson Davis to update its campus by making additions to the existing dormitories to house the two literary societies, and by rectifying an asymmetry in the campus with a new temple-form building, Smith Hall, to accommodate the two unlikely functions of library and ballroom.[21] The romantic ideal of antiquity was expressed in the design for an invitation to the school's commencement ball of 1844—in which the university was symbolized by a classical temple, alone in the wilderness and revealing through its open door the goddess of wisdom, Athena (Fig. 96).[22]

96

96 Engraved view on invitation to commencement ball at University of North Carolina, ca. 1844. Probably a fanciful representation of a projected building (to serve as library and ballroom) that was erected at the university several years later.
(North Carolina Collection, University of North Carolina Library, Chapel Hill)

ND

Sublime Nature

In the nineteenth century, the attraction of nature became one of the strongest motives in the location and planning of American colleges. When earlier schools had established themselves in the countryside, it was usually to avoid the evil influences of city life. This puritanical concern persisted in the nineteenth century at many colleges. But another, more aesthetic, motive was added to it, reflecting transcendental notions of nature as inherently more beautiful and uplifting than cities. Speaking in the 1830s of isolated Williams College in western Massachusetts, Henry David Thoreau said that "it would be no small advantage if every college were thus located at the base of a mountain (Fig. 47)."[23] And later in the century, James Garfield recalled his own student days at Williams, under its renowned President Hopkins, with the memorable statement, "The ideal college is Mark Hopkins at one end of a log and a student on the other."[24] The perfect education in nature theoretically did not even need architecture.

Often the aesthetic and moral advantages of nature were cited together, as when a popular nineteenth-century book on American colleges claimed, "If Yale were located at Williamstown, Harvard at Hanover, and Columbia at Ithaca, the moral character of their students would be elevated in as great a degree as the natural scenery . . . would be increased in beauty."[25] But even Yale, one of the more "urban" American colleges, appeared rather rural or park-like to Europeans (Fig. 4). Charles Dickens, in his *American Notes* of 1842, described his impression of Yale:

> The various departments . . . are erected in a kind of park or common in the middle of the town, where they are dimly visible among the shadowing trees. The effect is very like that of an old cathedral yard in England; and when their branches are in full leaf, must be extremely picturesque. Even in the winter time, these groups of well-grown trees . . . have a very quaint appearance, seeming to bring about a kind of compromise between town and country. . . .[26]

Some educators defended forthrightly urban colleges. Francis Wayland, the progressive president of Brown University, complained in 1842 that the typical American college was "isolated to a great extent from connexion with the community around it," and thus from the "salutary restraint of public observation."[27] But most nineteenth-century educators strongly favored rural colleges. Typical was the president of Central College in Iowa, the Baptist minister L. A. Dunn, who published a tract in 1876 purporting to demonstrate that rural colleges were successful, while schools in cities were educational and moral failures.[28]

The only religious denomination that tended to favor urban locations for its colleges was Roman Catholicism, whose educational traditions were generally more European than Anglo-American. The physical planning of urban Catholic colleges normally reflected this, with buildings closely grouped on city blocks—as at St. Louis University in Missouri, St. Xavier's College in Cincinnati, or St. Ignatius College (now the University of San Francisco) in California (Figs. 97, 98).[29] Some Catholic institutions were established in rural locations. The prime example is the University of Notre Dame, founded in 1842 by French missionaries in the wilderness of northern Indiana, next to two small lakes which the founders dedicated to the Virgin and St. Joseph. But as this school prospered and grew, it erected buildings that had an increasingly urban character and were densely grouped around the main structure and along the sides of a broad tree-lined avenue (Fig. 99).[30] The lofty main building erected in 1879 was itself a complex grouping of many wings and towers, with a cosmopolitan character typical of a category of Catholic collegiate structures of the period, which included the massive Healy Building at Georgetown College, begun in 1877, and the multiwinged structure that was planned in 1864 at Fordham University in New York, though never fully executed.[31]

The mystique of nature in the mid-nineteenth century can be seen in the visual representations of colleges. In the colonial period, views of colleges nearly always showed them in "civilized" settings (as in the Burgis and Revere views of Harvard, or the 1764 view of Princeton), regardless of their actual locations (Figs. 22, 43). But in the nineteenth century a pictorial manner became common that emphasized the natural environment. Examples are views of the United States Military Academy at West Point, Gettysburg College in Pennsylvania, Illinois College, and Mount St. Mary's College in Maryland (Figs. 100–102).[32] Even schools that

97

98

97 St. Louis University, St. Louis, Missouri. Engraved view of ca. 1860. (*Catalogue of the Officers and Students of the St. Louis University, 1860–61*, St. Louis, 1861, frontispiece)

98 St. Xavier's College, Cincinnati, Ohio, in the 1840s. (Henry Howe, *Historical Collections of Ohio*, Cincinnati, 1847, p. 219)

99 University of Notre Dame, South Bend, Indiana, in the 1890s. Largest building, at end of mall, is the Administration Building, designed by Willoughby Edbrooke and built in 1879 on the site of two earlier main buildings. To left is Sacred Heart Church, begun 1870. (Engraving by E. A. Wright, accompanying *Catalogue of the University of Notre Dame, 1897–98*)

100 United States Military Academy, West Point, New York. Engraving by Fenner, Sears & Co., 1831. The academy was established in 1802 at this site on the west bank of the Hudson River, also site of a fort during the Revolutionary War.
(John Howard Hinton, *The History and Topography of the United States*, vol. 3, London, 1832, pl. 11)

101 Gettysburg College, Gettysburg, Pennsylvania. View of ca. 1840. Designed by John C. Trautwine, 1835.
(Sherman Day, *Historical Collections of the State of Pennsylvania*, 1843, p. 59)

102 Mount St. Mary's College, Emmitsburg, Maryland. View of the 1850s.
(*Catalogue of the Officers and Students of Mount St. Mary's College, 1855–56*, Baltimore, 1856, frontispiece)

101

102

were actually in cities were often pictured falsely as being in nature, as was the case with the New York Free Academy (later the College of the City of New York), whose building at 23rd Street and Lexington Avenue was inaccurately shown in the midst of idyllic wilderness in a view of about 1850 (Fig. 103).[33]

Some colleges chose sites that possessed unusual natural beauty or the possibility of seeing nature from an especially good vantage point. Geneva College in New York (now Hobart and William Smith Colleges) established itself in the 1820s on a bluff overlooking Seneca Lake, with its buildings aligned so all could take advantage of the splendid view down the lake.[34] And it was in this period that the image of the "college on the hill" became a common ideal—examples being Georgetown College in the District of Columbia, Tufts College in Massachusetts, and East Tennessee College (now the University of Tennessee), which moved in 1826 from Knoxville to a hill outside the city (Figs. 104–106).[35]

In the 1830s a new type of building appeared at the American college that allowed an even grander and more sublime view of nature: the astronomical observatory. Beginning with the Williams College observatory in 1837 (reputedly the first permanent observatory in the United States), the fashion spread swiftly throughout the country; buildings to house telescopes were erected in 1838 at Western Reserve College in Ohio, the following year at Haverford College in Pennsylvania, and soon at dozens of other schools (Figs. 41, 107).[36] Religious reasons often were given to justify the expense and innovation, as when the speaker at the dedication for the observatory at Williams claimed that it would counteract materialism by elevating students' thoughts "toward that fathomless fountain and author of being."[37] More plausible motives were the attraction of nature itself and a burgeoning student interest in the neglected area of science. Sometimes the observatory was built close to the other college buildings, as at Western Reserve; but often, as at Georgetown College, it was set well apart, not only to escape distracting lights, but to allow the professor and his students to observe the universe in an inspiring scene of unspoiled nature (Fig. 108).[38]

The desire to escape from civilization, as well as from restrictive collegiate authority, found its most satisfying outlet, among students, in the Greek-letter social fraternities, which began to be popular in the middle decades of the nineteenth century.[39] College faculties at first usually banned these organizations or severely limited their activities, but this only heightened their appeal, and in the early days of fraternities many chapters met covertly, or even had their own secret lodges, as did the Delta Kappa Epsilon chapter at Kenyon College in Ohio, which in 1853 appropriated an abandoned cabin in the forest near the school for its meetings and rituals—thus indulging fully the American romance of collegiate life in the purity of nature (Fig. 109).[40]

103

104

105

103 New York Free Academy (later College of the City of New York). Romanticized view of ca. 1850. In reality, the building (designed by James Renwick, Jr., in 1849) was not in the countryside, as shown here, but at the busy intersection of 23rd Street and Lexington Avenue, in Manhattan.
(Henry Barnard, *School Architecture, or Contributions to the Improvement of School-Houses in the United States*, New York, 1854, p. 242)

104 Georgetown College (now Georgetown University), Washington, D.C., in the mid-nineteenth century. *At left*: Old South Building, 1788, and other structures; *right*: Old North Building, 1791–1808. Healy Building, constructed later, connected these buildings.
(Library of Congress, Prints and Photographs Division)

105 Tufts College, Medford, Massachusetts, ca. 1860. Main building (later Ballou Hall) was erected in 1853 to contain the chapel, library, recitation rooms, literary society rooms, and dormitory rooms.
(Alaric B. Start, ed., *History of Tufts College*, Medford, 1896, frontispiece)

106

107

108

109

106 University of Tennessee, on "University Hill," West Knoxville. Detail of lithographic view of Knoxville, of 1886. Institution moved to this site, next to the Tennessee River, in 1826.

107 Amherst College, Amherst, Massachusetts, ca. 1850. In center is octagonal scientific "Cabinet" with observatory, 1848. To right are North Hall, 1827; North College, 1821; Chapel, 1826; and South College, 1821. (Robert Sears, *A Pictorial Description of the United States*, New York, 1855, p. 105)

108 Astronomical Observatory, Georgetown College, 1841. View of ca. 1880. (*Catalogue of the Officers and Students of Georgetown College, 1879–80*, opp. p. 16)

109 Delta Kappa Epsilon's secret lodge, in forest near Kenyon College, Ohio, in 1853.
(William Bodine, *The Kenyon Book*, Columbus, Ohio, 1890, opp. p. 288)

Piety and Venerability

110 Just as the Greek Revival had special connotations that were exploited by the American college, so did the subsequent Gothic Revival. Gothic architecture became associated first with schools of specific religious denominations, and then with a desire that colleges project an image of age and respectability.

The first wave of the Gothic Revival in America occurred in the 1830s, but there were a few Gothic academic buildings even earlier. The first of these was probably the chapel of the Catholic St. Mary's Seminary in Baltimore, designed by the French architect Maximilian Godefroy in 1807, in which quasi-Gothic details simply were applied to a basically classical building form.[41] Besides Catholic schools, it was colleges with an Anglican or Episcopalian orientation that first employed the new style, no doubt reflecting the common belief at the time that Gothic architecture had been invented in England. In 1813 a young engineer named James Renwick (the father of the architect of the same name) produced a Gothic design for new buildings to house Columbia College in New York (Figs. 110, 111).[42] The plans called for a library reminiscent of King's College Chapel at Cambridge, flanked by two buildings containing classrooms, dormitories, and kitchens. Significantly, the three buildings were to be connected by a high wall to create an enclosed space (except for one open side), rather like an English college quadrangle. Renwick's design was a premature example of the association, which would later become common at American colleges, of Gothic architecture with the enclosed quadrangle.[43]

This design for Columbia never was executed, but in the following years, the Episcopalian bishop Philander Chase succeeded in building two Gothic Revival colleges. A man dedicated to the mission of establishing his denomination on the American frontier, Chase founded Episcopal colleges in Ohio and Illinois, in both cases using Gothic architecture to emphasize their ties with England. In 1824 he created Kenyon College in Ohio (named for one of his English financial backers), and engaged a fellow clergyman, Norman Nash, to draw a design for the main building, which was distinguished by simplified Gothic pointed windows and roof pinnacles (Fig. 112).[44] But the ground plan of the building was neither particularly Gothic nor English collegiate. It took the form of an H, not a

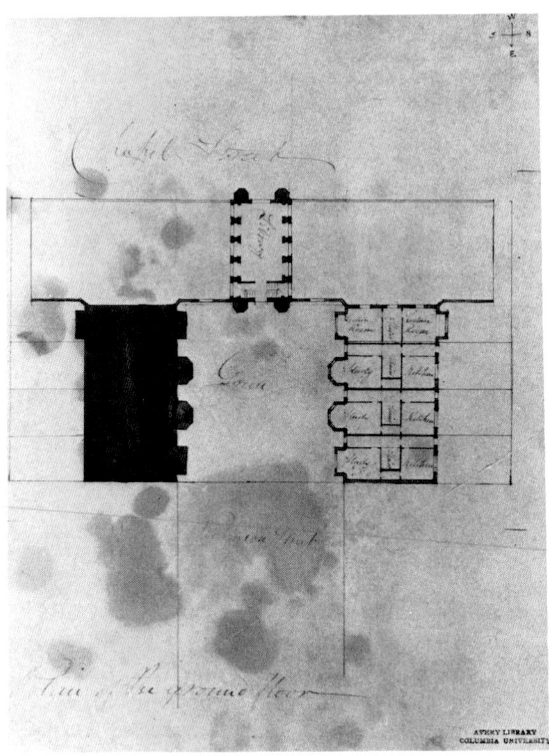

110

110 Columbia College, New York City. Plan for new buildings (not executed) at college's original site in lower Manhattan, by James Renwick, Sr., 1813. Shaded building at left was probably to be a residence hall for students. Building in center was to have college library on ground floor and hall above. Building at the right shows "studies," "lecture rooms," and "kitchens" on ground floor. The three structures were to be connected by a wall, enclosing one end of the courtyard.
(Avery Architectural and Fine Arts Library, Columbia University)

111 James Renwick's design for Columbia College, 1813. Elevation drawings of proposed building to house library and hall, showing walls that were to connect it to structures at the sides.
(Avery Architectural and Fine Arts Library, Columbia University)

Hall Window
Library Window
Hall & Library 54 ft
28 ft
32 ft
28 ft
Front of the Hall &c

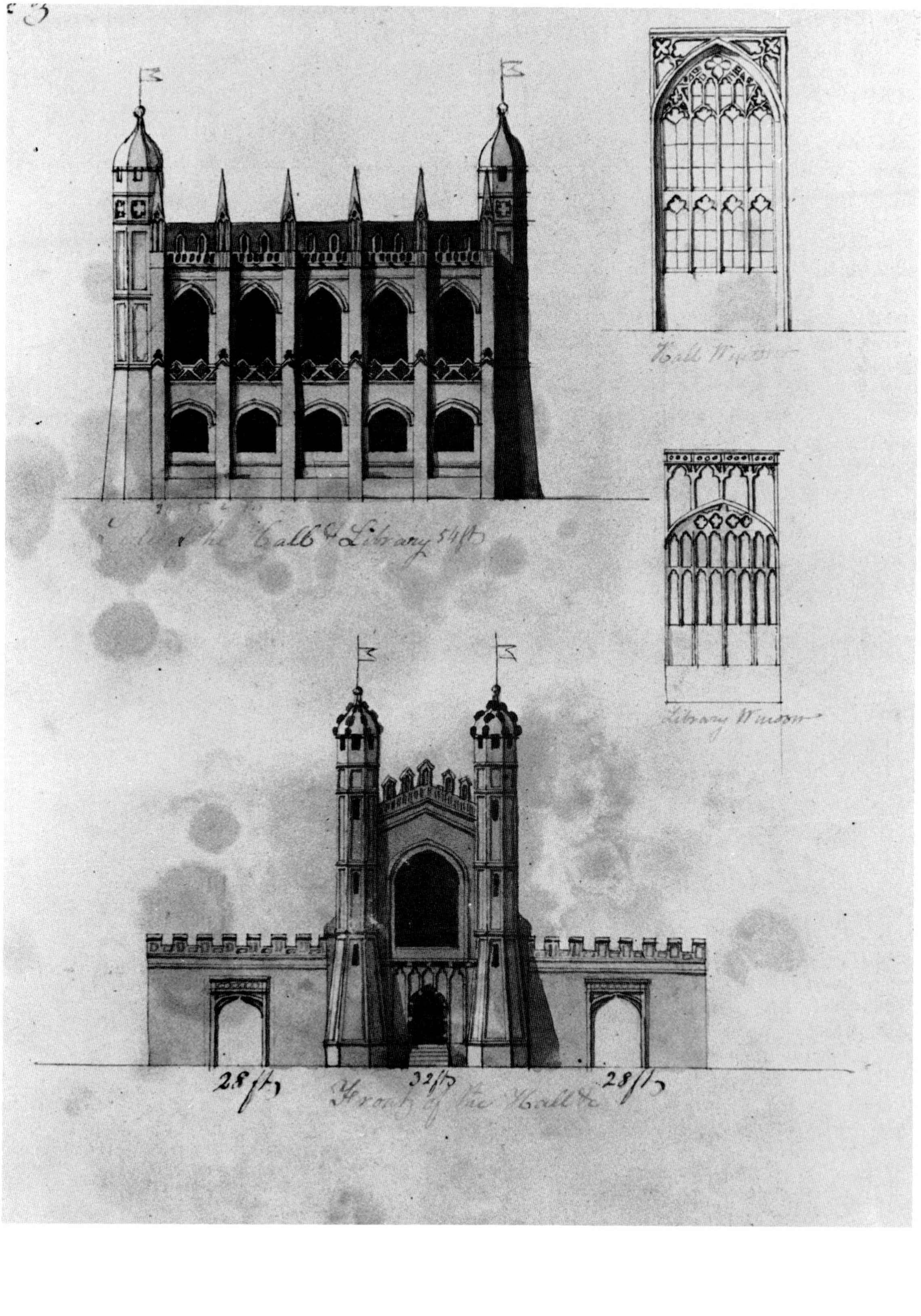

111

112

113

112 Kenyon College, Gambier, Ohio. Rendering of design by Norman Nash, of 1826, for the school's first building, now called Old Kenyon. Central block was meant to contain chapel, hall, dining facilities, and recitation rooms. Wings (much shortened when the building was constructed) were to contain dormitories. Engraving by Fenner, Sears & Co., 1831, based on a drawing by Nash. (Kenyon College Archives)

113 Old Kenyon, Kenyon College, 1827–1834. Photograph taken before building was destroyed by fire and rebuilt in 1949. (Kenyon College Archives)

114 Knox College, Galesburg, Illinois. Main building, 1856–1857. On the opposite side of the town square, a building housing the Knox Female Seminary also was erected in 1857. Both structures still stand. (*Catalogue of the Officers and Students of Knox College, 1867–68*, Galesburg, 1868, frontispiece)

115 Gore Hall, Harvard. Designed by Richard Bond, erected 1838, this was one of the first structures planned exclusively as a library at an American college. It was demolished in 1913. Engraving based on the design of Bond. (Josiah Quincy, *The History of Harvard University*, vol. 2, Boston, 1860, frontispiece)

116 Bowdoin College, Brunswick, Maine, in 1862. From left, the six buildings are: Adams Hall, 1861; Massachusetts Hall, 1798; Winthrop Hall, 1822; Maine Hall, 1808, rebuilt 1836; the Chapel, 1845 (designed by Richard Upjohn); and Appleton Hall, 1843. All still stand but are now part of a quadrangle started in the 1890s, when structures were erected in front of these. (*Memorial of the One Hundredth Anniversary of the Incorporation of Bowdoin College*, Brunswick, Maine, 1894, opp. p. lxxxiv)

114

115

116

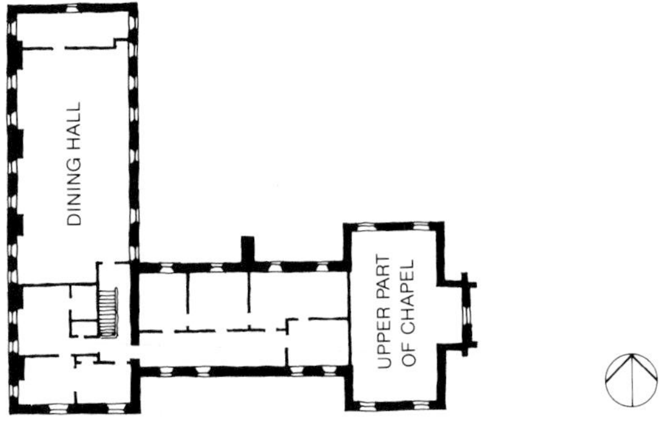

117

117 Jubilee College, Peoria County, Illinois. Plan of the upper floor of the main structure, probably designed by the school's first president, Bishop Philander Chase, in 1839. Smaller rooms are students' rooms. Lower story contains a hall, library, classrooms, kitchen, and chapel—part of which is two stories high. Drawing based on a plan made by the Historic American Buildings survey.

118 Jubilee College. View of main building, erected beginning in 1839, with chapel at right. Western wing (*left*), which housed the rest of the collegiate functions, burned in 1857 and was rebuilt. College later closed and buildings were abandoned, but they are now preserved as part of a state park. (Kenyon College Archives)

119 Yale College Library (now Dwight Chapel), designed by Henry Austin, 1842. Based roughly on King's College Chapel, Cambridge, this library was remodeled for use as a chapel in 1931 when Yale constructed a new library. (*Harper's New Monthly Magazine*, June 1858, p. 12)

quadrangle; and as executed, starting in 1828, the building's wings were cut short, making it even more like a traditional American college structure (Fig. 113). Moreover, the placement of the Kenyon College chapel—constructed beginning in 1829—at some distance from the main building, signaled that the college was not to develop as an enclosed quadrangle, and in succeeding years, new buildings were erected at intervals around a large rectangular green, on axis with the original building (rather as the main street of Williamsburg had been aligned with the buildings of William and Mary).

Thus, although the architectural details at Kenyon were "Gothic" and intended to evoke the image of English schools, the overall planning of the college was essentially open and American. This was to be true of nearly all Gothic Revival collegiate architecture in mid-nineteenth-century America. Other examples are the main building of Knox College in Illinois, built in 1857 (Fig. 114), a four-square structure facing a village green in the Princetonian tradition; and the three Gothic Revival buildings of Franklin and Marshall College in Pennsylvania, of the 1850s, lined up in a row like the buildings at Yale.[45] In the late 1830s, Harvard recognized the new Gothic fashion by building a library, Gore Hall, which was patterned roughly on the chapel of King's College at Cambridge University; but there was nothing particularly English or medieval about its relationship to the older buildings in Harvard Yard, which remained individual structures inhabiting a large, essentially open space in the American manner (Fig. 115).[46] Similarly, at Bowdoin College in Maine, the elegant chapel designed in 1845 by the preeminent Gothicist Richard Upjohn joined a row of existing structures, although it soared above them to become the dominant architectural focus of the school (Fig. 116).[47]

In 1831 Bishop Chase left Kenyon College and followed the moving frontier to Illinois, where in 1839 he founded Jubilee College on a wooded bluff overlooking the Kickapoo Creek. This time he acted as his own architect, and erected a Gothic-style chapel, classrooms, dining hall, and dormitory, all linked together to form an ell—which Chase apparently intended to be half of an enclosed English quadrangle (Figs. 117, 118).[48] But the quadrangle was never completed, despite the fact that Chase was a successful fund-raiser and

118

119

120

spent the rest of his years at Jubilee training ministers to proselytize the West. Perhaps the bishop came to realize that his school never could be—and never should be—exactly like an English college. The enclosed English quadrangle implied a turning inward, appropriate often for a college within a city, but not for Chase, the expansive missionary with his eyes on the frontier. Moreover, Chase fully shared his age's romanticism of nature. He described the Jubilee site as having "a fine grove of trees," being "in full view of the Robin's Nest" (his farm), and being blessed on the cornerstone-laying day with a "sky serene, and just enough wind to remind us of the breath of God."[49] Despite his loyalty to English collegiate traditions, Bishop Chase in his heart preferred the wilderness to the cloister.

By about 1850, Gothic Revival architecture was becoming common at colleges, and a new connotation became attached to it besides that of piety. American colleges increasingly sought the appearance of age and permanence; and whereas theoretically this could be achieved in any number of stylistic modes, the Gothic seemed especially appropriate. In 1847, an article in the *American Literary Magazine*, describing the new Gothic library at Yale (now Dwight Chapel), argued that "a college must have buildings . . . because there must be something to give the public a pledge of the permanency of the institution—and something that will be a centre of attachment for its members" (Fig. 119).[50] The notion that college architecture ought to serve affectional purposes became common in the following years, especially as the writings of John Ruskin were read in America.

In 1853, an article in the *Yale Literary Magazine* applied Ruskinian analysis to the two new Gothic buildings at the college, the library, and Alumni Hall.[51] The library was compared to Harvard's Gothic library, with the observations that the Harvard building satisfied Ruskin's "Lamp of Truth" better (since it was completely made of stone, with no falsity of materials), but that otherwise the Yale building was superior, being more complex in form, and having a surface texture that appeared "more venerable, while theirs, for sixty years to come, will show that newish exterior which cut granite retains so long." The other new building at Yale, Alumni Hall (designed by A. J. Davis), was similarly analyzed in terms of the appearance

120 Lehigh University, Bethlehem, Pennsylvania. Packer Hall, designed in 1865 by Edward T. Potter, constructed 1865–1868.
(*Harper's Weekly*, November 9, 1867, p. 709)

of age. Interior plastered walls were criticized for not giving "that substantial, venerable air" appropriate to "an old and honored university"; and the fear was expressed that the furnishings would be new and vulgar, without "one old, substantial thing, to embody the spirit of the old Collegiate Gothic," and without any "pleasing and strengthening associations." The anonymous author of this critique suggested that the whole expenditure for furnishings be devoted instead to carved wooden walls and ceilings, "substantial enough to last as long as the building will be used," and that "in a few years, other things . . . would be added piece by piece," in the manner of

> the glorious old cathedrals and town-halls of continental Europe, where one generation did one grand, substantial thing, and the next another, until there grew up the noble edifices we now see. So would we have each College generation make some single contribution and take pride in it.[52]

This desire that college architecture be "venerable" and "substantial," be laden with "associations," and testify to an "old and honored" institution, became common in the mid- and late-nineteenth century. The Gothic usually was considered best for creating this impression—along with other medieval styles, such as Romanesque, which was first used prominently in the many-turreted structure erected in 1852 at Antioch College in Ohio (Fig. 135).[53] Ironically, the earlier buildings at American colleges, despite their genuine age, often were considered incapable of evoking venerability because of their plainness. In the 1880s, President Abbott Lawrence Lowell of Harvard complained, "We have none, or next to none, of those coigns of vantage for the tendrils of memory or affection. Not any of our older buildings is venerable, or will ever become so. Time refuses to console them. They look as if they meant business and nothing more."[54] The plain utilitarianism of Harvard's early buildings had been lamented fifty years earlier, when history professor Henry Cleveland described them as "vast brick barns, destitute alike of symmetry, ornament, and taste; and with all their plain and uncouth proportions, there is a sort of horrible regularity and squareness about them, which heightens their deformity."[55]

Cleveland in 1836 was one of the first people to call publicly for the use of Gothic architecture at American colleges. In the following years, as the connotations of taste, piety, and venerability coalesced around the Gothic, it came to be used mainly by the more conservative and tradition-oriented schools. There were exceptions, such as the progressive New York Free Academy (later the City College of New York), which in 1848 executed a Gothic design by the architect James Renwick, Jr. (whose father had drawn the Gothic design for Columbia in 1813) (Fig. 103). And as the Gothic style became increasingly popular in America, it was used even by some of the new scientific and technical institutions, such as Lehigh University in Bethlehem, Pennsylvania, and the Free Institute of Industrial Science (now Worcester Polytechnic Institute) in Massachusetts, both of which built impressive Gothic structures in the 1860s (Fig. 120).[56]

But normally the Gothic was used to support the collegiate ideal of a community of scholars, living as a family, perpetuating the traditional curriculum, and united by a religious creed. William K. Pendleton, president of Bethany College in West Virginia, which in the 1850s was one of the earliest schools to plan a whole Gothic Revival campus, described his college as "a literary, moral and religious school, or the union of four institutions in one—the combination of the family, the primary school, the college, and the church in one great system of education."[57] After a fire destroyed Bethany's original buildings in 1857, Pendleton and the architectural firm of Walter & Wilson designed a long, picturesque, Gothic structure, giving the impression of a series of buildings constructed over time (thus providing an instant heritage to replace the lost college buildings) (Fig. 121). An arcade of pointed arches along one side of the structure suggested a medieval cloister—as well, perhaps, as being a kind of Gothic version of the colonnades of the University of Virginia, Pendleton's alma mater. But significantly, the building did not form an enclosed medieval quadrangle, and thus it was still faithful to the American tradition of expansive collegiate architecture.

The iconography of Gothic architecture at the American college was sometimes convoluted. In the 1870s, Harvard built Memorial Hall, a massive Ruskinian-Gothic structure designed by the firm

121

121 Main Building, Bethany College, Bethany, West Virginia. View of 1875. Designed by the architectural firm of Walter & Wilson, 1858. Row of connected structures, 420 feet long, originally housed the college's chapel, library, classrooms, society halls, offices, assembly hall, and some of the dormitory rooms. (Bethany College)

122 Memorial Hall, Harvard. Designed by Ware & Van Brunt, 1866–1868; constructed 1870–1878; tower destroyed by fire, 1956. (Moses King, *Harvard and Its Surroundings*, Cambridge, 1882, frontispiece)

123 Memorial Hall, Harvard. Dining hall. (King, *Harvard and Its Surroundings*, following p. 42)

122

123

of Ware & Van Brunt, and it soon was hailed as the most impressive American collegiate building (Fig. 122).[58] Its form was that of a medieval cathedral, with nave, transept, and semicircular choir. Even its east-west orientation was liturgically correct. Yet the function of the building had nothing to do with religion; its "nave" served as the college dining hall, its "choir" as a theater, and its "transept" as a hall memorializing Harvard's Civil War heroes (Fig. 123). The ecclesiastical shape of the building resulted from a combination of factors, including the popularity of Ruskin's writings and the congruity between the functions and the form. But most of all, it was due to the venerable connotations of the medieval cathedral, perfectly suited to the nineteenth-century college's longing for "the tendrils of memory and affection."

The Grand Plan and the Professional College Planner

The "excessive multiplication" of American colleges, as President Philip Lindsley of the University of Nashville called it in 1829, naturally produced a division of resources and students, resulting in the "dwarfish dimensions" of most institutions.[59] Yet in a strangely compensating manner, even the smallest of these dwafts tended to imagine itself a giant, and experienced delusions of grandeur. The historian Frederick Rudolph has said:

> College-founding in the nineteenth century was undertaken in the same spirit as canal-building, cotton-ginning, farming, and gold mining. In none of these activities did completely rational procedures prevail. All were touched by the American faith in tomorrow. . . . Reason could not combat the romantic belief in endless progress.[60]

Countless colleges viewed the future with boundless confidence and planned accordingly, often paying more attention to grand physical plans than to financial or even academic matters. As early as 1816, the American scholar George Ticknor complained, "We . . . build new colleges in abundance, but we buy no books," and "we think too much of convenience and comfort and luxury and show; and too little of real, laborious study."[61] Soon colleges began the practice of hiring architects to produce ambitious master plans, which no doubt impressed potential supporters, but often had little chance of being executed fully. This was in contrast to most of the earlier master planning of American colleges—such as Harvard's colonial plans, Trumbull's plan for Yale, or Jefferson's for Virginia, which were generally realistic in scale and were executed relatively quickly. Bulfinch's schemes for Harvard and Ramée's for Union, of 1812–13, were among the first examples of the new trend (Figs. 56, 57, 64). By the middle of the nineteenth century the grandiose collegiate plan was common.

Typical was a design for new buildings at Jubilee College, which Bishop Chase commissioned from the New York Gothicist Richard Upjohn in 1844 (Fig. 124). In contrast to the modest structure Chase and his students had just built with their own hands, Upjohn's lavish and monumental scheme was probably inappropriate for the pioneering school in the Illinois wilderness, and de-

124

124 Design for Jubilee College, Peoria County, Illinois, by Richard Upjohn, 1844. Lithograph by C. Hayard. Structure was meant to contain the college chapel, library, classrooms, dining hall, dormitories, and perhaps even professors' quarters. No part of the design was executed. (Kenyon College Archives)

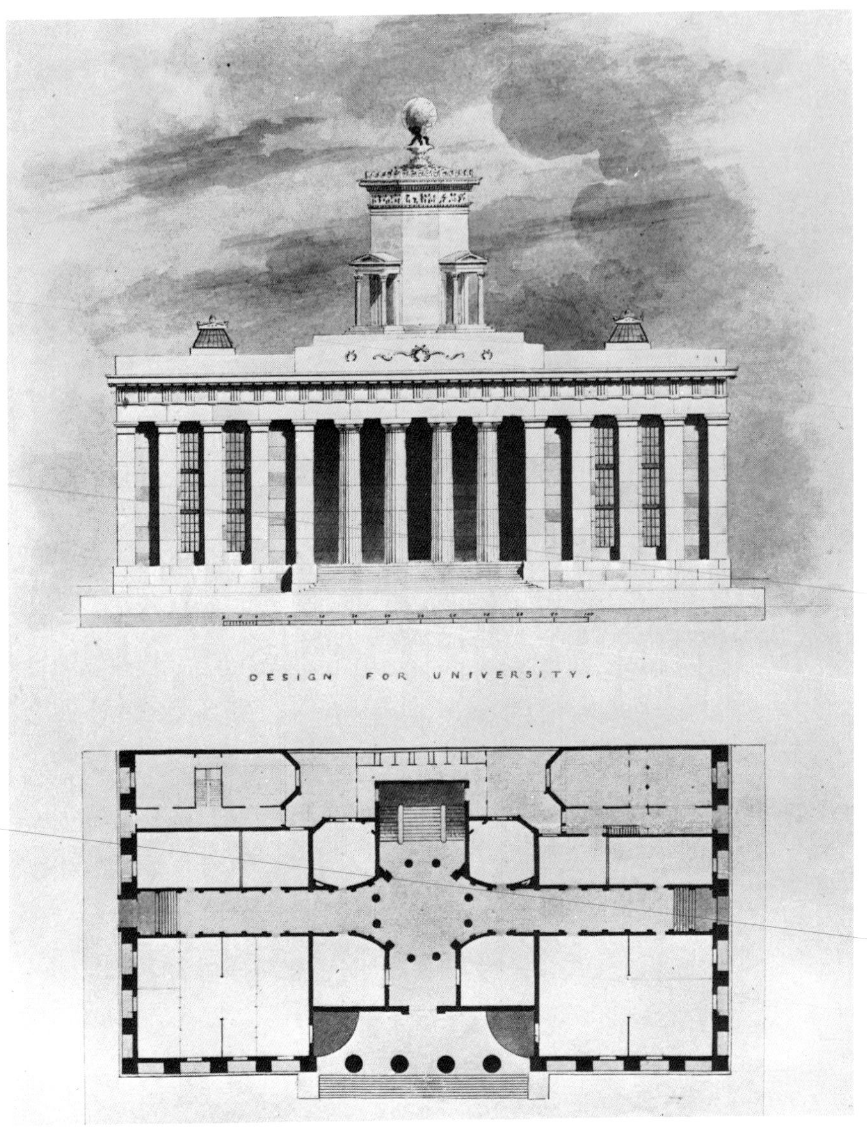

125

126

125 Design by Alexander Jackson Davis and his architectural firm, probably for New York University, 1831.
(The Metropolitan Museum of Art, Harris Brisbane Dick Fund, 1924)

126 New York University, on Washington Square in New York City. Designed by A. J. Davis and his associates, Ithiel Town and James Dakin, 1833; constructed 1833–1837; demolished ca. 1900. Lithographic view drawn by Davis.
(The Metropolitan Museum of Art, Bequest of Edward W. C. Arnold, 1954)

spite the Bishop's fund-raising abilities, the project never got off the ground.[62]

Thomas U. Walter's lavish design for Girard College, which has already been mentioned, was executed but only at the expense of a large part of the endowment that the founder had intended for the welfare of the indigent students (Fig. 95). The Girard competition launched Walter on a successful career of designing imposing structures for colleges and other institutions (his most famous work being the dome of the United States Capitol in Washington). In 1848, Walter designed a massive building for the University at Lewisburg (now Bucknell University) in Pennsylvania, consisting of a central pavilion with classrooms and a chapel-auditorium, and wings with dormitory rooms—one of the largest structures in the United States when it was built in the 1850s.[63] Walter also traveled in Europe, on a mission for the Girard College trustees in 1838, to examine school architecture there in search of ideas for the completion and furnishing of the Girard building.[64] Walter was one of a new breed of American architects who was considered as specializing in the design of colleges.

In the midwestern states, William Tinsley was perhaps the most popular collegiate architect in the middle of the century. He designed buildings in a variety of styles at Kenyon College in Ohio, Quincy College in Illinois, Indiana University and Wabash College in Indiana, Oskaloosa College in Iowa, and the University of Wisconsin.[65] Another midwestern architect, G. P. Randall, in 1868 published a book devoted in part to his designs for collegiate buildings.[66]

But it was Alexander Jackson Davis, one of the unsuccessful entrants in the Girard College competition, who emerged as the leading college architect of this period. From about 1830 to the 1850s, Davis and his New York office were involved in designs for at least a dozen colleges.[67] Some of these designs were for buildings at existing schools, such as his work, mentioned already, at Yale and the University of North Carolina. But others were master plans for newly founded colleges, or for schools embarking on major rebuilding programs. These included the University of Michigan, New York University, Bristol College in Pennsylvania, Davidson College in North Carolina, the Virginia Military Institute, and a proposed "Agricultural College" for New York State.[68]

Typical of the period, Davis showed an unabashed eclecticism; he was willing to design his colleges in a large number of variations of either the classical or Gothic styles, depending on circumstances and his clients' wishes. In some cases he even presented alternate schemes from which the school authorities could choose, as he did at the University of Michigan and New York University (Figs. 125, 126).[69] For Davis, architectural style was a kind of external clothing that could be changed more or less at will, although he personally preferred the Gothic, and in particular a mode of it he called "Collegiate Gothic." Davis was perhaps the first American architect to use this term, by which he seems to have meant the late medieval styles found at the English universities. But he used the term loosely to include various styles and building types, as indicated by a reference in his office diary to a building in a "Collegiate Gothic Villa Style."[70]

In his designs for colleges, Davis was less concerned with the niceties of historical styles than with creating standard types of plans appropriate to the functions of specific kinds of institutions. Urban schools naturally were more restricted by their sites, usually requiring compact rectangular plans to fit city blocks. This was true of the designs for New York University on Washington Square, done by Davis and his partners Ithiel Town and James Dakin in 1831–33, with circulation spaces and a large chapel in the center, flanked tightly by classrooms, library, and other functions.[71] The Gothic design was built by the school, and remained in use until it was demolished at the beginning of the twentieth century.

For sites in the open country, Davis developed more expansive and varied types of plans. In the mid-1830s he and his office made designs for at least three separate buildings at Bristol College in Pennsylvania, two in classical style and one "Collegiate Gothic," but all having basically the same plan: a large central structure for classrooms, with wings of dormitory rooms, using the separate-entry system.[72] It seems likely that in this case Davis was obliged by the college to produce individual buildings, for in virtually all of his other college plans he attempted to combine the collegiate functions into one grand building. In 1838 he was hired to design the new University of Michigan. He traveled to Ann Arbor to inspect the site and produced two designs, Greek and Gothic, his own preference being the Gothic (Fig. 127).[73] This design was similar to each of the Bristol buildings in having a central structure flanked by dormitory wings, but these wings turned at the corners and continued at right angles, creating an overall plan that suggested half of an enclosed quadrangle. In the following years, Davis took this idea to its logical conclusion, producing two fully quadrangular plans for colleges, at the Virginia Military Institute of 1848 and Davidson College in North Carolina of 1856 (Fig. 128).[74]

The design for Davidson College was the grandest of all of Davis's plans for colleges.[75] It consisted of a large temple-form structure containing classrooms and chapel, from which dormitory wings extended out and around to create a quadrangle roughly 600 feet square (in one of the versions), with extra classrooms at the corners and a circular dining hall opposite the main structure. Davis's perspective rendering of the design showed this complex in the midst of an idyllic landscape dotted with "villas" probably meant for the professors.[76] The design for the Virginia Military Institute was similar, although the quadrangle was smaller in scale, the style Gothic, and the circulation system open to the inner courtyard.[77]

These were probably the first designs for large-scale enclosed quadrangles in American college planning. At the end of the nineteenth century, the quadrangle would become popular in America as part of a conscious revival of the medieval colleges of Oxford and Cambridge. But Davis's quadrangles are quite different in character, in particular, his expansive and axially symmetrical composition at Davidson, with its temple-form structure at the center of the main facade. Davis may have been inspired, in fact, by more recent collegiate planning in Britain (where he traveled in 1829), especially William Wilkins's plans for Downing College at Cambridge of 1805, East India College in Hertfordshire of 1806, and University College in London of 1826, which recast the traditional English quadrangle in neoclassical form and enlarged its scale.[78] The enclosed quadrangle, however, was still too foreign and unfamiliar to Americans, who continued to favor the indigenous patterns of open-campus planning. This is surely one of the reasons that Davis's most ambitious master plans were not completed.

In any case, Davis apparently did not consider colleges as constituting an isolated building type, for he approached their design in essentially the same way he did other institutions housing large numbers of people, such as hospitals or prisons. Several of his plans for such buildings are similar in form to his college plans. In portfolios Davis compiled of his work, he emphasized this by grouping similar institutional building types together, illustrating on the same page his designs for Davidson College and the Hospital for the Insane in Raleigh.[79]

Typical of the overly optimistic college planning of the period, few of Davis's designs—quadrangular or otherwise—were fully realized. The University of Michigan, for lack of funds, was unable to build either his Gothic or his classical design. His plans for a New York Agricultural College also went unbuilt. Davidson College erected only the front part of his proposed quadrangle, although even that was tremendously impressive, leading Talbot Hamlin, the chronicler of the Greek Revival, to describe it as forming "a composition of power and scale that is almost unrivaled in the country," its "two long buildings flanking the central chapel, [with] a truly colossal Tuscan portico" (Fig. 129).[80]

Perhaps nothing epitomizes the ambitious mid-nineteenth-century spirit of American college building better than this design by Davis for Davidson College. The stark neoclassical forms fortified the myth of the classical curriculum with its roots in antiquity. The focal position of the chapel emphasized the fundamental religious purpose of the institution. The orderly arrangement of classrooms, dormitories, and dining hall, although unfamiliar in its quadrangularity, symbolized the collegiate system of a close-knit community. And the idyllic, rugged landscape in which Davis set the college expressed the American dream of living an heroic life in nature.

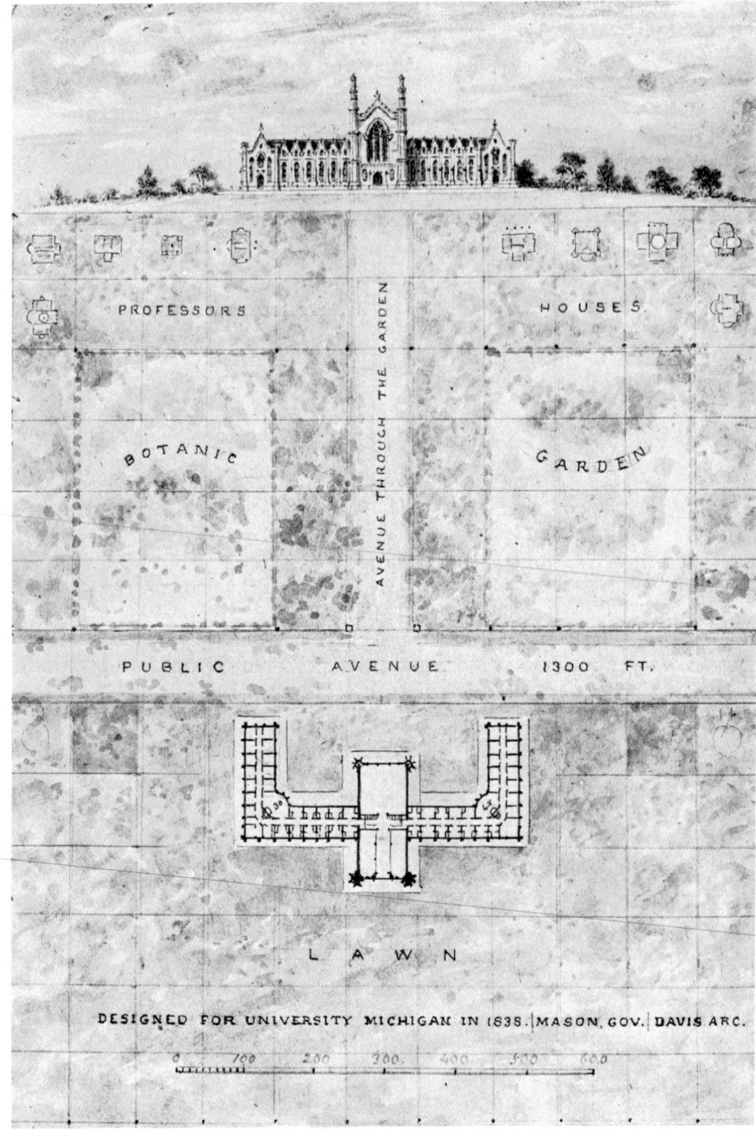

127

127 University of Michigan, Ann Arbor. Design by A. J. Davis, 1838, for the university building and surrounding grounds (including a "Botanic Garden") and professors' houses. This design was not executed, but the school did erect a large structure with wings, perhaps modeled in part on Davis's plan. (The Metropolitan Museum of Art, Harris Brisbane Dick Fund, 1924)

128 Design for Davidson College, Davidson, North Carolina, by A. J. Davis, ca. 1856. Only a portion of the front wing of the quadrangular structure was erected. (Avery Architectural and Fine Arts Library, Columbia University)

127

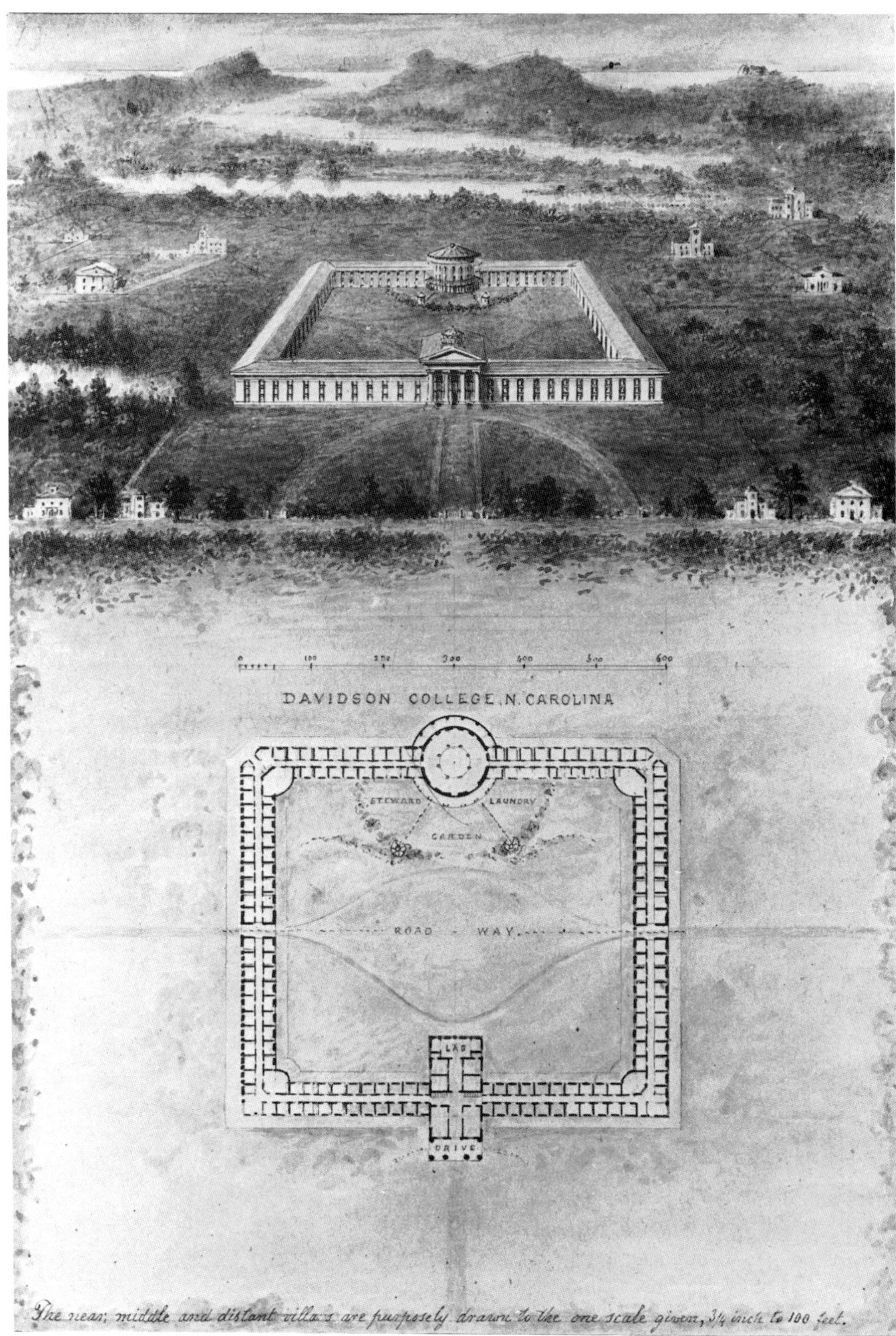
0 100 200 300 400 500 600
DAVIDSON COLLEGE, N. CAROLINA
STEWARD
LAUNDRY
GARDEN
ROAD WAY
LAB
DRIVE
The near, middle and distant villas are purposely drawn to the one scale given, 3/4 inch to 100 feet.

129

129 Chambers Hall, Davidson College. The only executed part of Davis's design, this structure was built in 1859 but burned in 1921.
(Davidson College Archives)

IV. The Democratic College

The Land Grant College Act, or Morrill Act, was passed by the Congress and signed by President Lincoln in 1862. It climaxed a long period of attempted reform of American colleges, and after the Civil War it became the major force in a shift toward more democratic education in the country. The traditional college, elitist by the nature of its curriculum and its function of producing primarily theologians, teachers, and lawyers, now was challenged by new educational systems that, though varying widely in form, all tended to broaden the scope of education and its constituency. These included agricultural schools, scientific and engineering programs, the elective system which freed undergraduates from the fixed classical curriculum, the opening of higher education to women, and colleges for blacks.[1] This educational revolution also produced important changes in the physical planning of colleges. More than any other person, the landscape architect Frederick Law Olmsted created a type of campus that reflected the new democratic impulses in education.

The Working Man's School

The revolution had been brewing for years. By the mid-nineteenth century it was common for educators, politicians, and writers to attack the traditional college as irrelevant to contemporary needs. The speaker at a Massachusetts state fair in 1855 said, "Colleges are made for professional men, not for the people, and their mission never was and never will be to educate the millions."[2] A California educator asked in 1858, "For what useful occupation are the gradutes of most of our old colleges fit?"[3] At the same time, Henry David Thoreau in *Walden* ridiculed his own Harvard education, suggesting that youths might avoid formal schooling altogether and simply "try the experiment of living."[4] But most critics supported new types of institutions, as Horace Greeley did in 1857, in championing the projected People's College in central New York State:

> Our present financial collapse results directly from the public want of such training as this College is destined to supply. . . . We need an education which will win the attention and aspirations of our enterprising youth [to] fertilizing and beautifying the green hills and rural valleys that surround their childhoods' homes; we want, in short, a People's College.[5]

130

131

130 Farmers' College, Hamilton County, Ohio. Building constructed 1846. At its founding, the school was described as "especially suited to the wants of the agricultural and business community." Financial problems in the 1850s led to its closing, but it was later revived and merged with the Ohio Military Institute. (Alexander B. Huston, *Historical Sketch of Farmers' College*, frontispiece)

131 Lawrence Scientific School, Cambridge, Massachusetts. Designed by Richard Bond and constructed in 1847 north of Harvard Yard. Wing served as the scientific professor's residence. Building later was used by Harvard for other purposes, and was demolished in 1970 after being damaged by fire. (Moses King, *Harvard and Its Surroundings*, Cambridge, 1882, following p. 40)

Pioneering agricultural colleges, such as this one in New York and the Farmers' College in Ohio, were founded in the 1840s and 1850s, but they had trouble attracting students and deciding what an agricultural school should be (Fig. 130). "Manual Labor Colleges," such as Wabash in Indiana and Knox in Illinois, both founded in the 1830s, also had trouble finding their identity, and usually reverted to more traditional formats of education. Significantly, when Wabash Manual Labor College and Knox Manual Labor College dropped the "Manual Labor" from their names, in 1851 and 1857 respectively, they erected large and impressive buildings in the fashionable styles of the day—Gothic Revival at Knox, Italianate at Wabash—as if to assert their new respectability and signal their return to traditional education (Fig. 114).[6]

In the meantime, scientific and technical schools made better progress. At the beginning of the nineteenth century, the United States Military Academy at West Point was the only place in the country that taught engineering and science; not until 1824, with the creation of the Rensselaer Polytechnic Institute in Troy, was there a successful model of specialized technical education.[7] Soon, both Harvard and Yale created their own scientific departments, although they were kept distinctly separate from the regular curriculum.

Even at these early stages of agricultural and scientific education, a notion arose of the appropriate type of architecture for it: one of plainness and utilitarian simplicity. This was simply a matter of necessity at many of the agricultural and manual training schools. But at the scientific schools, such as Harvard's Lawrence and Yale's Sheffield, it often reflected a conscious rejection of ostentatious architecture by scientists and engineers.[8] Typical was Joseph Henry, the pioneer of scientific education at Princeton, who had definite utilitarian ideas about architecture (despite his 1836 plan for the Princeton campus that emphasized formal symmetry). He stated in 1854 that "architecture should be looked upon more as a useful than a fine art. . . . In building, we should plan the inside first, and then plan the outside to cover it."[9] The structure built in 1847 to house the Lawrence Scientific School at Harvard reflected this attitude, with its straightforward containment of the varied functions required—which included the science instructor's residence attached to the main part of the building (Fig. 131).[10]

Professional architects who designed colleges, like Alexander Jackson Davis, would not have shared Henry's utilitarianism as a general principle, but many of them agreed that simplicity was appropriate to agricultural and technical schools. In 1849–50, Davis in collaboration with the landscape architect Andrew Jackson Downing produced designs (never executed) for the newly established New York Agricultural College (Fig. 132).[11] There were to be two buildings, one for classrooms and the other a dormitory, or "College Home." For them, Davis proposed a simplified and rustic Tuscan style, with a rugged character that he and the college trustees must have considered appropriate for an agricultural college.

Another aspect of the democratic reform of education at this time was the massive expansion of public grade schools, which stimulated innovation in educational planning. Books such as Henry Barnard's *School Architecture*, published in several editions starting in the 1840s, illustrated and described a large number of designs for schools, by various architects.[12] Much attention was given to practical problems like heating, ventilation, and sanitation; and the designs were described as corresponding closely to contemporary educational needs and theories. Many of the plans showed a concern for flexibility of planning, with large and small classroom spaces provided, and spaces that could be divided by curtains. Barnard also described a plan for classrooms that allowed them to be divided "by a frame partition, made to slide upon rollers in an iron groove."[13] Similar devices were described in an English book on school design, in its chapter on American schools.[14] Then as now, "flexible planning" may have caused teachers more trouble than it was worth, but it revealed the spirit of innovation and experimentation in American public education of the period.

132

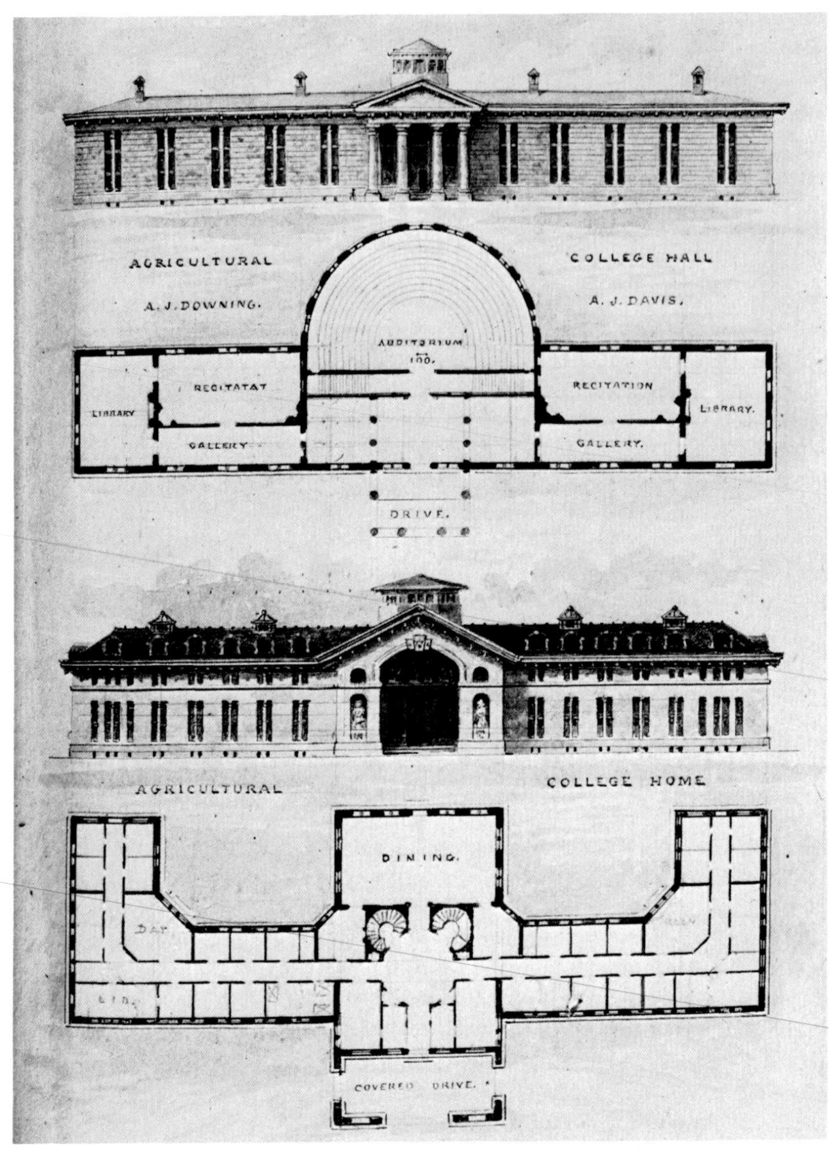

132 Designs of two buildings for a New York Agricultural College, by A. J. Davis and Andrew Jackson Downing, ca. 1849. "College Hall," or academic facility (*top*) and "College Home," or residence hall (*below*) apparently were never executed.
(The Metropolitan Museum of Art, Harris Brisbane Dick Fund, 1924)

Coeducation and Women's Colleges

Higher education for women was another innovation that made its appearance principally in the 1850s. "Female seminaries" had already existed for several decades, many of them located in town houses with a domestic character, as was Emma Willard's school in Troy, New York (Fig. 133). But the education these schools provided was usually very different from that of men's colleges.[15] In 1837, Oberlin College in Ohio took the unprecedented step of admitting women together with men, and included a "Ladies' Hall" among its first buildings, arranged around the village green of the town of Oberlin (Fig. 134).[16] Following this example, Antioch College in Yellow Springs, Ohio (which hired the progressive educator Horace Mann as president), erected in 1853 two identical dormitories, one for males, the other for females, flanking the school's lofty main structure—thus making new use of the Palladian pattern of buildings that went back to the College of William and Mary (Fig. 135).[17]

But coeducation was not widely popular. More successful at first were efforts to create separate women's colleges, about a dozen of which were founded in the 1850s. In 1861, the lavish endowment of Vassar College at Poughkeepsie, New York, and its quickly established reputation, created a model for female colleges that was emulated in succeeding years by others throughout the country.

The physical planning of these schools tended to follow certain patterns, reflecting attitudes toward women and their education. At the new women's schools, the generally antiurban prejudices of nineteenth-century educators were reinforced by a protective desire. A typical attitude toward female education was expressed in 1852 by the Valley Union Seminary in Virginia, in an advertisement describing the school and its location:

> [Its] remoteness from the peculiar temptations incident to towns and large cities, its romantic mountain scenery, its almost unbroken quietude, no less than its invigorating atmosphere and health-giving waters, adapt it . . . to the objects for which it has been selected. Here the pupil, secluded almost entirely from the engrossing scenes of active life, comfortable and agreeably provided for in every respect, may pursue her studies . . . without interruption or annoyance from the busy world around her.[18]

Thus, most of the early women's colleges and seminaries were placed in rural areas, although not too rural, lest they be considered remote or uncivilized. Architecturally, the most striking thing about them was that all their facilities—classrooms, dormitories, dining halls, administrative offices, and even professors' lodgings—usually were designed to be under one roof, either as one large building or as several buildings linked closely together, as at Stephens College in Missouri (Fig. 136). Elmira College in western New York State constructed in 1854 a remarkable structure formed of an eight-sided hub (reflecting the octagon-house fad of the 1850s), from which four wings were to extend like spokes, only three of which were built (Fig. 137).[19] Vassar's building, designed by James Renwick and built in the early 1860s, was grander still, a French mansarded structure containing virtually all the college's functions, and reputedly the largest building in the United States for a brief period until the Capitol in Washington was completed (Figs. 138, 139).[20]

The insistence on single all-inclusive buildings at women's colleges was motivated by a concern for the protection and safety of the students, as well as a desire to emphasize the family-like nature of the institution. Both motives were suggested by Matthew Vassar when he endowed his college in 1861, in his statement that the architecture of the school should "afford to the inmates the safety, privacy, and purity of the family."[21] Wellesley College in Massachusetts followed the example in 1875 with a rambling, palatial structure (which burned in 1914) sited picturesquely on a large estate, and containing under its one roof all the lecture and recitation rooms, dormitory suites, dining halls and kitchens, chapel, library, art gallery, music rooms, faculty quarters, gymnasium, and even a hospital provided with "adjoining rooms for visiting mothers of the sick" (Figs. 140, 141).[22]

Another type of education for women was provided by the "normal" colleges, whose main function was the training of public school teachers. The physical facilities of these colleges were usually more modest than those of the private women's schools, but they too often erected an imposing

133

133 Troy Female Seminary, Troy, New York, ca. 1850. Established 1821 by Emma Willard, the institution later closed, but the site and several of the buildings are now occupied by Russell Sage College.
(Library of Congress, Prints and Photographs Division)

134 Oberlin College, Oberlin, Ohio. View of 1846. *From left*: Oberlin Hall, 1833 (originally containing all the collegiate functions); Ladies' Hall, 1834 (women's dormitory); Colonial Hall, 1835 (chapel, classrooms, men's dormitory); Tappan Hall, 1836 (recitation rooms, men's dormitory); the Presbyterian Church of Oberlin.
(Henry Howe, *Historical Collections of Ohio*, Cincinnati, 1847, p. 315)

135 Antioch College, Yellow Springs, Ohio. Engraving of ca. 1855. Central structure, Antioch Hall, and two dormitories (for male and for female students) were designed in 1852 by Alpheus M. Merrifield, a building contractor from Massachusetts who was one of the school's founders. Arcades shown in this view, connecting the three buildings, never were constructed.
(Antiochiana, Antioch College)

134

135

136

137

136 Stephens Female College (now Stephens College), Columbia, Missouri. Lithographic view of ca. 1875. A portion of the structure was originally a private residence, built in 1841 and acquired by the college in 1857; additions were made in succeeding years. Part of the building still stands, surrounded by later structures. (Lithograph from *Boone County, Missouri, Atlas*, 1875. Library of Congress, Prints and Photographs Division)

137 Elmira Female College (now Elmira College), Elmira, New York. Early photograph of main building (now Cowles Hall), erected 1853–1855. Four wings originally were intended to extend from the octagonal core; two had been constructed when this photograph was taken, and a third was added later. Design of the building is attributed to Ward B. Farrar. (Elmira College)

138

139

138 Vassar College, Poughkeepsie, New York. Lithographic view of ca. 1865. Main building, designed by James Renwick, Jr., and constructed 1861–1865, was modeled in part on the Tuileries Palace in Paris. Upon completion, it was said to be one of the largest structures in America. (Library of Congress, Prints and Photographs Division)

139 Main entrance to Vassar College building. Engraving of ca. 1875. (*Harper's New Monthly Magazine*, February 1876, p. 348)

140

141

142

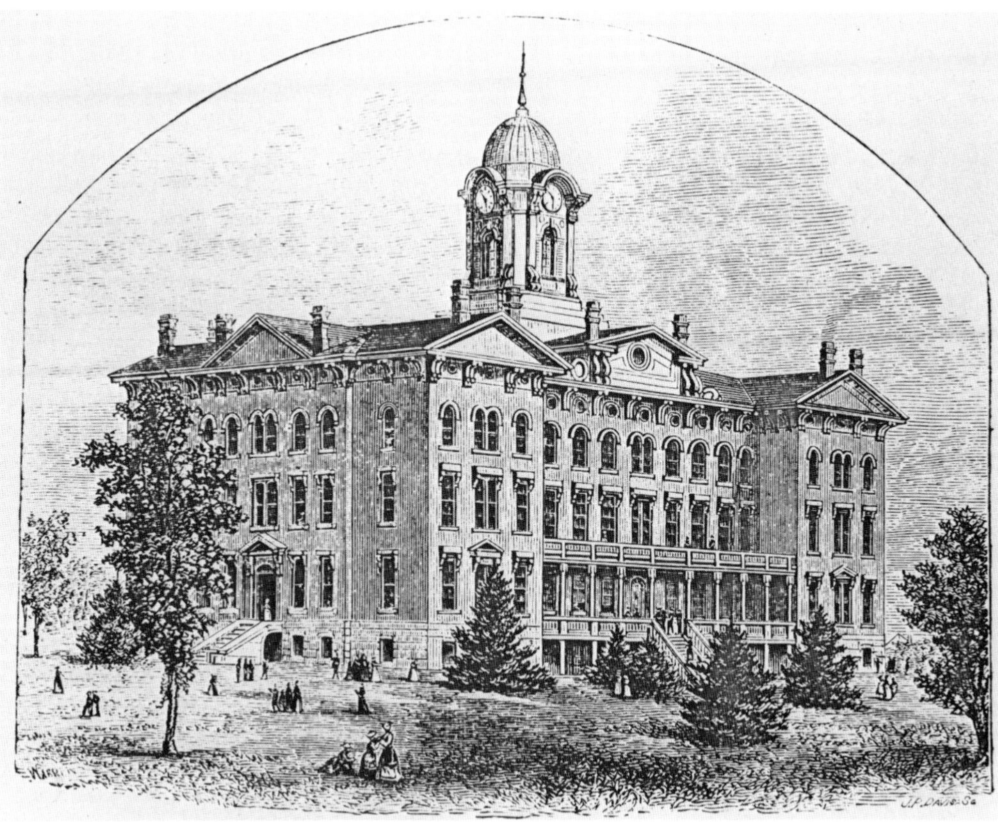

143

140 Wellesley College, Wellesley, Massachusetts. Engraving of ca. 1875, showing main building, College Hall, in the distance.
(*Harper's New Monthly Magazine*, August 1876, p. 321)

141 College Hall, Wellesley College. Designed by Hammatt and Joseph E. Billings, and erected in 1875, structure was destroyed by fire in 1914.
(*Views of Wellesley College, 1889*, Gardner, Massachusetts)

142 Illinois State Normal University (now Illinois State University), Bloomington, Illinois. Building erected 1857. Engraving of ca. 1879.
(Library of Congress, Prints and Photographs Division)

143 "Student's Parlor," Wellesley College, ca. 1875.
(*Harper's New Monthly Magazine*, August 1876, p. 329)

building that housed under one roof all the collegiate functions—as at the Illinois State Normal University in Bloomington (now Illinois State University) (Fig. 142).[23]

Large, all-purpose buildings were found also at many men's colleges of the period. But women's schools carried the concept to its extreme, and combined it with an emphasis on the home-like character of the institution. The buildings at Vassar and Wellesley, while featuring grand and impressive public spaces, also included many small "parlors" and "drawing rooms," to create an intimate and domestic atmosphere (Fig. 143). Thus the Anglo-American tradition of collegiate education, with students and teachers living and studying together in a close community, was perfectly suited to the needs of the early women's schools, especially as many people still questioned the advisability and propriety of women leaving home and going to college at all. The contradiction between the need for a large structure and the desire for a home-like atmosphere did not concern people much at first, although by the 1870s it was being mentioned. An observer of Vassar wrote in 1876 that "the plan of making one large family of four hundred students may be unwise," and she suggested that "the large body of students could have been divided into twenty different buildings."[24] Besides its specific relevance to women's colleges, this suggestion reflected new ideas about college planning in general. Promoted principally by Frederick Law Olmsted, these ideas were applied especially to a new type of institution in America, the land-grant college.

The Land-Grant Colleges and F. L. Olmsted

Many of the reforms of American higher education in the mid-nineteenth century coalesced in the Land Grant College Act, presented in Congress by Senator Justin Morrill in 1857 and enacted into law in 1862. The act allotted each state a share of government lands, which it was to sell, using the funds to establish colleges for agricultural and mechanical education. The states had different ideas of how to use these funds, some giving them to existing state universities, or even to private institutions, while others created new agricultural and mechanical colleges.[25] Despite the differences from state to state, the early land-grant schools shared certain basic goals, including the promotion of practical education, the right of education for all social classes, and the freedom of students to choose their courses of study. Ezra Cornell, benefactor of the school that became New York's principal land-grant enterprise, summed up the spirit in his motto, "I would found an institution where any person can find instruction in any study."[26] And the president of the University of Minnesota was said to be "interested in everything from Plato to hog cholera."[27] However, there was no consensus among the educators about the appropriate physical setting for this new type of institution. It took an idealistic landscape architect to create a campus for the "people's college."

Frederick Law Olmsted's work as a park planner has been studied closely in recent years. But the significance of his ideas on campus planning has not been recognized as fully. He was involved in the design of at least twenty schools of various types over the course of his career from the 1860s to 1890s, and he devoted particular attention to the design of land-grant colleges.[28] At root, Olmsted's interest in public parks and his concern for education had the same motives: a democratic idealism and a commitment to the welfare of the working classes, but also a belief that American society had to be "civilized" if democracy was to succeed. Moreover, beginning in his youth, Olmsted had questioned many aspects of the traditional collegiate system and had sought reforms of it or alternatives to it. Born in Hartford in 1822, he had avoided a normal academic program, although he attended classes for a while at Yale while his brother was a student there. Olmsted's disappointment with the restrictions and narrowness of the classical education system is reflected in a letter he wrote to his brother several years later, in which he proclaimed, "I do think colleges are a most gregious nuisance, and I'd almost make one of a mob to rase 'em all down about the besotted faculty's ears, if I could not make reason reach 'em any other way."[29]

While traveling in England in 1850, Olmsted was struck not only by the public urban parks in several cities, but by experiments in higher education for the laboring classes, such as People's College in Sheffield, which he visited.[30] After returning home, he must have followed closely the proposals for similar institutions in the United States. Among Olmsted's personal friends was the landscape planner Andrew Jackson Downing, who had just collaborated with A. J. Davis on the design of the New York Agricultural College.[31] Downing published Olmsted's observations about England in his magazine *The Horticulturalist*, in which he himself had already published an article on agricultural colleges.[32] In it, Downing spoke of the nobility of rural life and called for an agricultural education combining practical and theoretical training ("head and hands must work together"), as Olmsted was to do.

Two years after Congress enacted the Land Grant bill in 1862, Olmsted, who was working in California at that time, was hired by the College of California to survey its new site—soon named Berkeley—on the eastern shore of San Francisco Bay, and to make recommendations for its new campus.[33] Although this was a traditional private college (only later was it transformed into the public University of California), Olmsted developed ideas for it that he applied also to land-grant schools. In the summer of 1865, Olmsted visited the Berkeley site, a large area of farmland that sloped down toward San Francisco Bay and the Golden Gate. The following June, after returning to New York, he published his report to the trustees, along with his proposed plan (Fig. 144).[34]

The most remarkable thing about Olmsted's plan for Berkeley was its conception of the college not as a separate entity, but as an integral part of a larger community whose special physical character would promote a beneficial environment for the students. Olmsted began his report with the argument that colleges should be located neither in the country (divorced from "domestic life" and "civilization," and producing "the barrenness of monastic study"), nor in the midst of a city, with its distractions. The proper location was a planned suburb, of the sort that Berkeley, close to Oakland and San Francisco, could become. The main challenge was to plan a community that would attract the right kind of people, and to promote a refined and moral style of living. For Olmsted, the key to this was the proper integration of domestic life and nature, according to principles whose explanation took up the bulk of his report. In the resulting plan, the whole community, including the college, assumed the form of a naturalistic park—a concept Olmsted must have had in mind from the beginning, for he stated, in letters of early 1865, that he intended to lay out the College of California "on the Llewellyn plan," a reference to A. J. Davis's park-like design for a suburban town in New Jersey in the 1850s.[35]

The Berkeley trustees already had laid out a town adjacent to the college site, but its rectangular street grid was incompatible with Olmsted's concept, and he therefore decided to include residential areas in the college ground itself. These areas were to be separated by meandering roads and parkland, much of it meant for use by both the residents and the students, including "a suitable field for athletic games." The amount of land reserved specifically for the college was relatively small. It consisted of a rectangular open space, on axis with the view of the Golden Gate—with two main college buildings placed asymmetrically at its eastern end—and two other areas "reserved for college purposes."

One of Olmsted's innovative proposals at Berkeley concerned student lodgings. He rejected both the traditional dormitories ("large barracks"), and the turning loose of students to room in private houses. He suggested instead the erection of a number of buildings "having the general appearance of large domestic houses, and containing a respectably furnished drawing-room and dining-room for the common use of the students, together with a sufficient number of private rooms to accommodate from twenty to forty lodgers."[36] This notion, which Olmsted later called "the cottage system," was a natural outcome of his ideal of a college integrated into a humanly scaled domestic community. In justifying his concept of an informal campus to the Berkeley trustees, he wrote:

I would propose to adopt a picturesque, rather than a formal and perfectly symmetrical arrangement, for the two reasons that such an arrangement would better harmonize artistically with the general character desired for the neighborhood, and that it would allow any enlargement or modification of the general plan of building. . . . I may observe that in the large Eastern colleges the original design of arranging all the buildings . . . in a symmetrical way has in every case proved impracticable and been given up, while so far as it has been carried out it is a cause of great inconvenience.[37]

Thus Olmsted defended his new concept of a campus on both practical and aesthetic grounds. But it also had a moral basis, in his belief that a college planned as a domestically scaled suburban community, in a park-like setting, would instill in its students civilized and enlightened values.

While preparing his report on Berkeley in 1866, Olmsted was asked to make his first proposal for a land-grant school, the Massachusetts Agricultural College (now the University of Massachusetts) at Amherst. And other such commissions soon followed. This gave Olmsted the opportunity to combine his notions of college planning in general, as expressed in the Berkeley plan, with his developing ideas about the new land-grant institutions.[38] In May of 1866, Olmsted visited Amherst, conferred with the college authorities, and prepared a plan and a report that was published with the title "A Few Things to be Thought of Before Proceeding to Plan Buildings for the National Agricultural Colleges."[39] The authorities of the new Massachusetts Agricultural College had acquired land outside Amherst, with farm buildings on it, and were planning to erect one large college structure in the midst of a field. In his report, Olmsted strongly advised against this, arguing that a large building would be too expensive, was inappropriate to a rural location (unless it were "a jail or reformatory"), and would not be flexible enough to accommodate the unforeseen needs of the institution. Instead, he called for "a less formal and rigid plan."

Here, as at Berkeley, Olmsted's motives were as much ideological as practical. At Amherst, these motives specifically concerned his vision of agricultural education. He described two opposing social theories, one an elitist view that the working classes were totally separate from educated citizens, the other a democratic ideal in which "such artificial distinctions as exist between different members of society are considered undesirable." This egalitarian attitude, Olmsted observed, had already helped civilize the American laboring classes. To further this tendency, agricultural education should concern itself not only with "the farmer as a farmer," but also with "the things which belong to him as a man":

you must embrace in your ground-plan arrangements for something more than oral instruction and practical demonstration in the science of agriculture. . . . You must include arrangements designed to favorably affect the habits and inclinations of your students, and to qualify them for a wise and beneficent exercise of the rights and duties of citizens and of householders.[40]

As at Berkeley, Olmsted proposed creating a whole community rather than simply a school. But if Berkeley was to be a middle-class suburb, Amherst was to be a "model rural neighborhood." Olmsted's plan made the college an informal grouping of buildings along the main road, and around a village common that would serve also as a drill ground, in compliance with the Morrill Act stipulation that land-grant colleges provide military training (Fig. 145). The academic functions would be divided among four relatively small buildings. As for dormitories, Olmsted again rejected "the old college barracks," and proposed houses with "a domestic character," accommodating no more than thirty students each, which could be built "one after another, as required" along the road and on the common.

On receiving Olmsted's report, the Massachusetts college trustees were annoyed that he had not given them what they wanted—simply a plan for landscaping and roads around their projected large building. The president of the school found Olmsted's arguments compelling, but, partly because he supported Olmsted in opposition to the trustees, he was forced to resign.[41] In October 1866, *The Nation* published an article, probably written by Olmsted, entitled "How Not to Establish an Agricultural College."[42] It described the folly of the Massachusetts trustees in preferring "a large, unmanageable, and inappropriate struc-

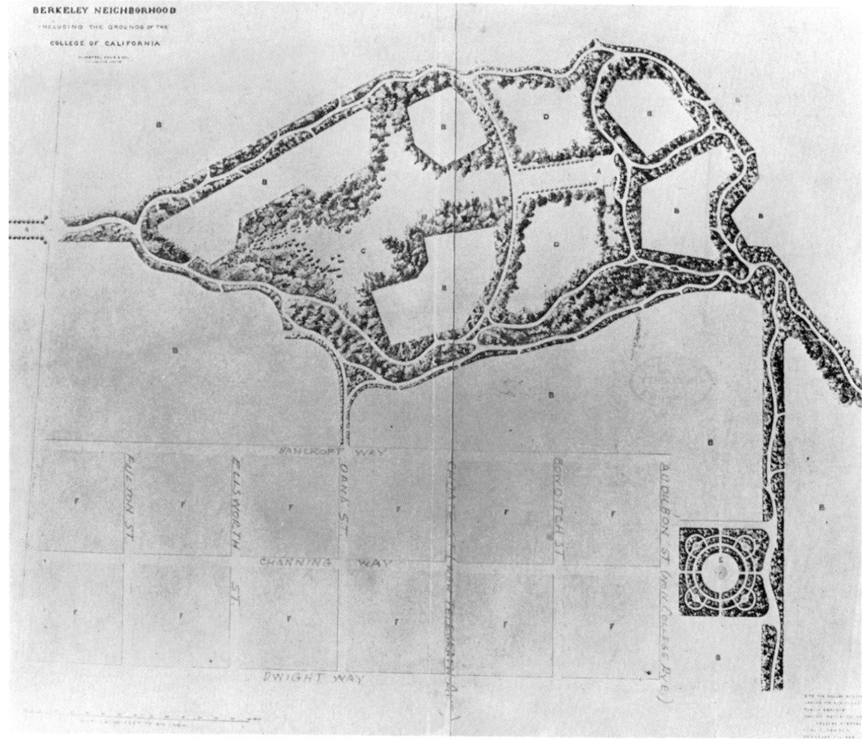

144

145

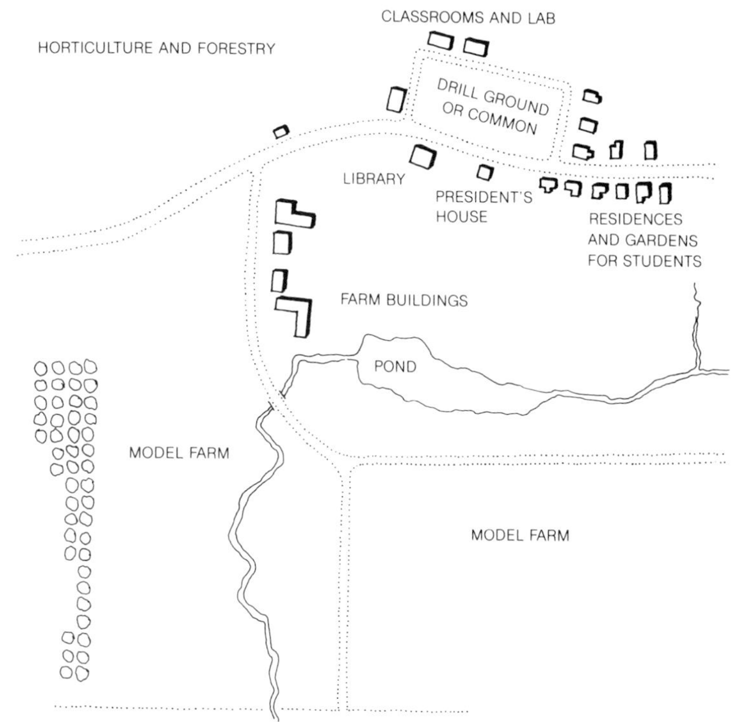

144 Plan for the College of California (later the University of California), Berkeley, by Frederick Law Olmsted, 1866. Area marked "A" and adjacent areas "D" were for the college itself. The rest of the park-like preserve was intended for residences and public ground. Rectangular lots to the south had been laid out before Olmsted was hired. (Olmsted, Vaux & Co., *Report upon a Projected Improvement of the Estate of the College of California at Berkeley, near Oakland*, San Francisco and New York, 1866. University of California, Berkeley, Archives)

145 Reconstruction of plan for Massachusetts Agricultural College (now University of Massachusetts), Amherst, by Olmsted, 1866. Drawn from plan by Frank A. Waugh, of 1911 (in the Olmsted Archives), based on Olmsted's written report to the college.

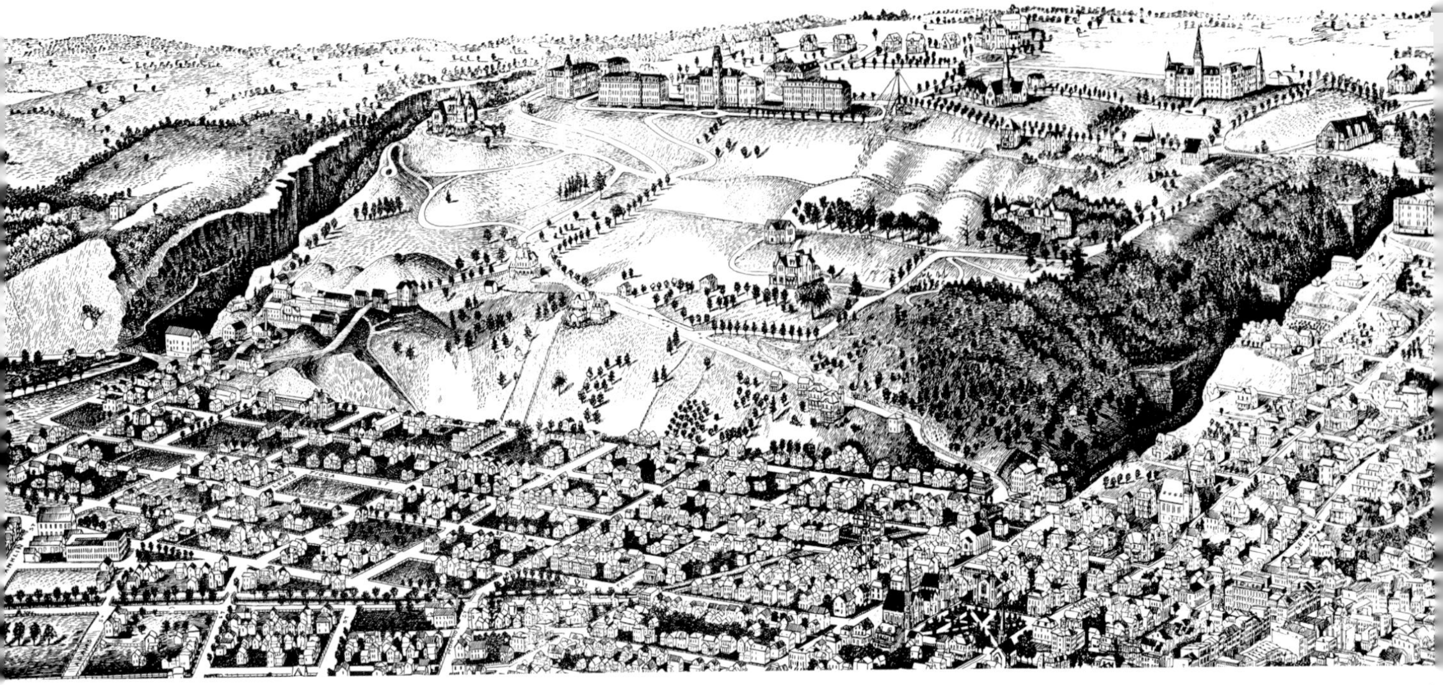

146

147

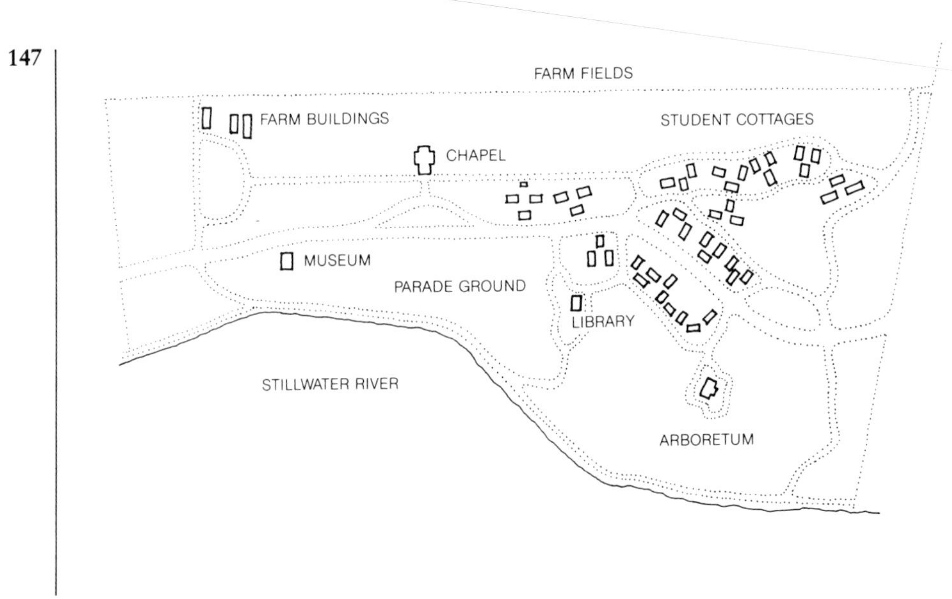

FARM FIELDS
FARM BUILDINGS
STUDENT COTTAGES
CHAPEL
MUSEUM
PARADE GROUND
LIBRARY
STILLWATER RIVER
ARBORETUM

146 Cornell University, Ithaca, New York, in the 1880s. The three buildings in a row (*center*), erected ca. 1866–1870, were to form one side of a planned quadrangle. Buildings to right (south) are Sage Chapel and Sage College (the women's residence), erected in 1872; they introduced a less formal pattern of planning at Cornell, reflecting the ideas of Olmsted and the school's president, Andrew D. White. Portion of a lithographic view of Ithaca by L. R. Burleigh, 1882.

147 Maine State College of Agriculture and Mechanic Arts (now University of Maine), Orono. Redrawn version of Olmsted's plan for the campus, of 1867, in Olmsted Archives, Brookline, Massachusetts.

148 Olmsted's plan for Maine State College. Redrawn detail of student residential clusters. Olmsted's plan identifies the buildings as follows: 1. "Cottages with sleeping rooms and parlors." 2. "Dining halls, with kitchens and study rooms." 3. "Wood sheds and water closets." Areas around the buildings are identified as "gardens."

148

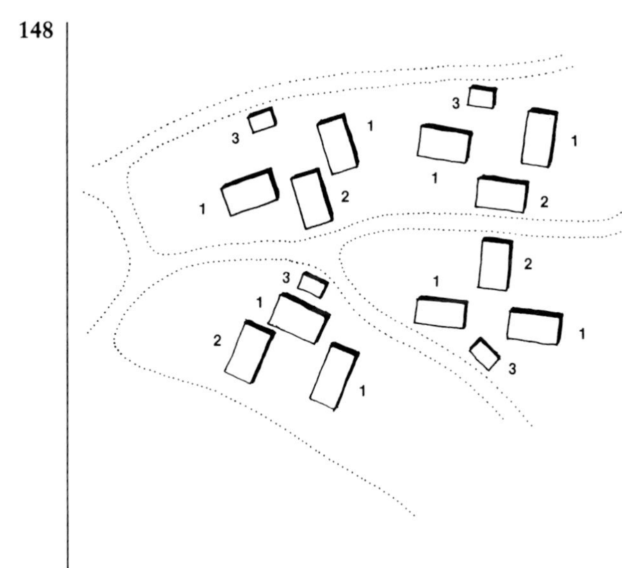

ture of stone" to the erection of "small, modest buildings, one after another, as needs became clearly known."

This article in *The Nation*, and Olmsted's published report on the Massachusetts Agricultural College (which also was reviewed favorably in *The Nation*), apparently attracted attention at the land-grant colleges and other schools around the country.[43] By the end of 1867, Olmsted had been asked to advise on planning at the Maine Agricultural College (later the University of Maine), the National Deaf-Mute Institute in Washington (later Gallaudet College), the Pennsylvania Agricultural College, the Hampton Institute in Virginia, and Cornell University.[44] He was even offered the presidency of a land-grant college, the Iowa State College of Agriculture and Mechanic Arts (later Iowa State University).[45]

At the newly founded Cornell University, in Ithaca, New York, Olmsted was called in by President Andrew D. White in 1867 to give advice on landscaping the school's projected quadrangle of buildings—an immense area 1,000 feet on each side (Fig. 146).[46] Typically, Olmsted advised that they rethink their plans completely. He argued against the quadrangle, or any rigid plan, calling instead for a "free, liberal, picturesque" arrangement that would be more suited to the rugged topography of Cornell's site, and also more flexible for future development. "Don't begin by tying yourself to formality and straight-lacing," he said.[47] White was sympathetic, but the quadrangular plan had been accepted by the school's founder, Ezra Cornell, and its execution had in fact begun, so Olmsted had to console himself with suggestions for refining the design of the quadrangle. In succeeding years, however, Olmsted's recommendations bore fruit in the addition of several buildings to the south, whose designs President White was able to control more carefully—notably the Ruskinian-Gothic Sage College (the women's dormitory) and Sage Chapel, whose arrangement White called the "informal grouping at Cornell."[48]

For the land-grant institution in the state of Maine—the College of Agriculture and the Mechanic Arts at Orono (now the University of Maine)—Olmsted presented a report in January 1867 and a plan four months later (Fig. 147).[49] The report was similar to the Massachusetts report, except for elaborating a kind of military system by which the students would be organized and self-disciplined. The design was the most extensive development, so far, of Olmsted's concepts of collegiate planning. He proposed that an existing road, parallel to the Stillwater River, become "the street of a village," flanked by the college buildings and student "cottages," with farm buildings and experimental fields to the east, and an "arboretum" and "parade ground" between the road and the river. The only formal part of the plan was an area between the parade ground and the largest building, which served as an armory, chapel, and assembly hall. Aside from this focal point, the plan had the studied irregularity of a naturalistic park, with the student cottages set seemingly at random along meandering paths. However, these buildings were organized according to a system of residential clusters, each cluster consisting of two sleeping cottages served by a small dining hall, and surrounded by gardens (Fig. 148).[50] Olmsted's plan was not adopted by the Maine college authorities, but his ideas began to influence college planning elsewhere.

In the 1860s and 1870s, practically every state founded at least one land-grant institution, or "Agricultural and Mechanical" college. Olmsted was the principal advocate of a method for planning these schools, and it is clear, from the large number of land-grant institutions that approached him for advice, that his ideas were widely known among the educators of the period. A survey of the campus plans of the early land-grant colleges reveals that his influence was significant.

To a remarkable extent, the early land-grant colleges were built as informal groups of buildings in park-like settings, very different from earlier American campuses, but fully in the spirit of Olmsted's proposals. Examples include the agricultural colleges of Michigan, Iowa, and Kansas (Figs. 150–156). Even the Massachusetts Agricultural College, which rejected Olmsted's proposals in 1866, actually produced a campus that had much of the village spirit suggested in his report (Fig. 149).[51]

In Michigan, the campus of the State Agricultural College (now Michigan State University) was developed, starting in the 1860s, on farmland outside the state capital, Lansing, with buildings placed irregularly along meandering roads, next to the Red Cedar River (Figs. 150, 151). A description in the school's catalogue of 1875 suggested the Olmstedian character of the place:

> The grounds have been laid out by a professional landscape gardener. . . . There are walks, drives, rustic bridges, lawns, flower borders, and groves in pleasing variety. The buildings, mostly of brick, stand upon a slight eminence among the forest trees, which have been purposely retained.[52]

The Iowa State College of Agriculture and Mechanic Arts, at Ames (now Iowa State University), was founded in 1858, although it did not open until eleven years later. The school typified the antielitism of the land-grant movement. When the Morrill Act placed funds at the state's disposal, the well-established University of Iowa attempted to share the wealth with the new agricultural school, but the latter garnered all the money after a campaign that "graphically pictured the contrast in organization, aims, and program between an urban centered, sophisticated university and a simple rural farmers' college."[53] In 1864, a large structure was begun, to house many of the college facilities (Fig. 152). By 1867, the college authorities must have become familiar with Olmsted's views on land-grant schools, since they reportedly offered him the presidency of the institution in that year.[54] And despite the *fait accompli* of the main structure, the campus in succeeding years evidently was shaped by Olmsted's principles, with modest buildings placed informally along meandering roads around a central park (Fig. 153).[55]

Even closer to Olmsted's ideas was the development at the Kansas State Agricultural College (now Kansas State University). Established at the town of Manhattan after the passage of the Morrill Act, the school's early growth occurred mainly in the 1870s, under the presidency of John Anderson, who represented a faction of the land-grant movement that might be called populist.[56] In the school's *Hand-Book* of 1874, he stated a policy of rejecting all vestiges of elitism and serving only the manual laboring classes:

> The difference between our line and that of other Agricultural Colleges seems to be this: They take as an objective point the graduation of agricultural experts. . . . We take as an objective point the graduation of a capable farmer. . . . Along the mechanical branch, they

149

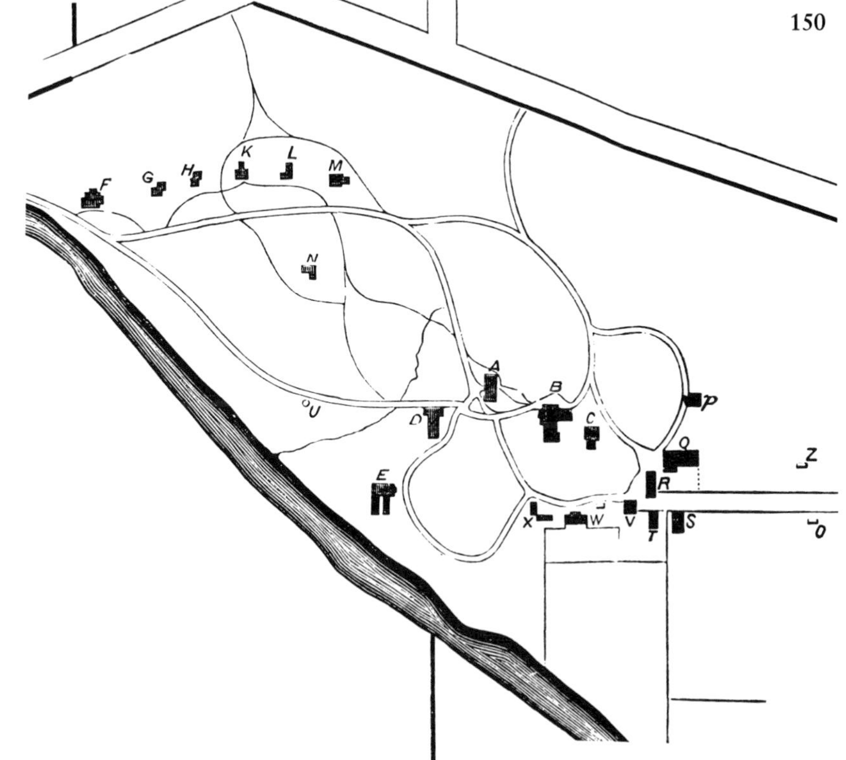

150

149 Massachusetts Agricultural College. Engraving of ca. 1870. In foreground is Durfee Plant-House; behind it, Botanic Museum. In background (*left*) are the classroom buildings (South College, North College, and College Hall) and (*extreme right*) one of the student "boarding-houses."
(*Seventh Annual Report of the Trustees of the Massachusetts Agricultural College*, Boston, 1870, frontispiece)

150 Michigan State Agricultural College (now Michigan State University), East Lansing. Plan of campus, on Red Cedar River, ca. 1875. A. College Hall, containing classrooms, offices, chapel, library, laboratories, museum, and garden shop. B. Boarding Hall, containing dining room, parlors, and rooms for about eighty students. C. Dormitory, with rooms for sixty students. D. Laboratory. E. Greenhouse. F-M. Professors' and president's houses. Q-Z. Farm buildings.
(*Annual Catalogue of the Officers and Students of the State Agricultural College of Michigan*, Lansing, 1875, following p. 42)

148

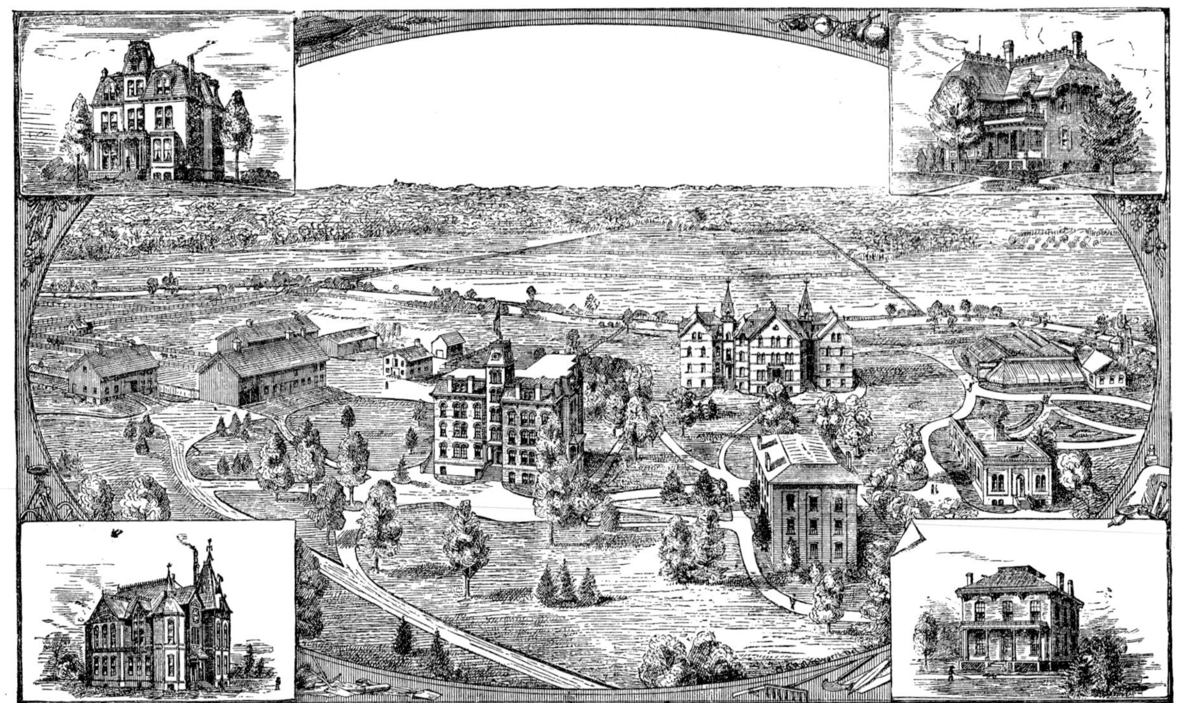

151

152

153

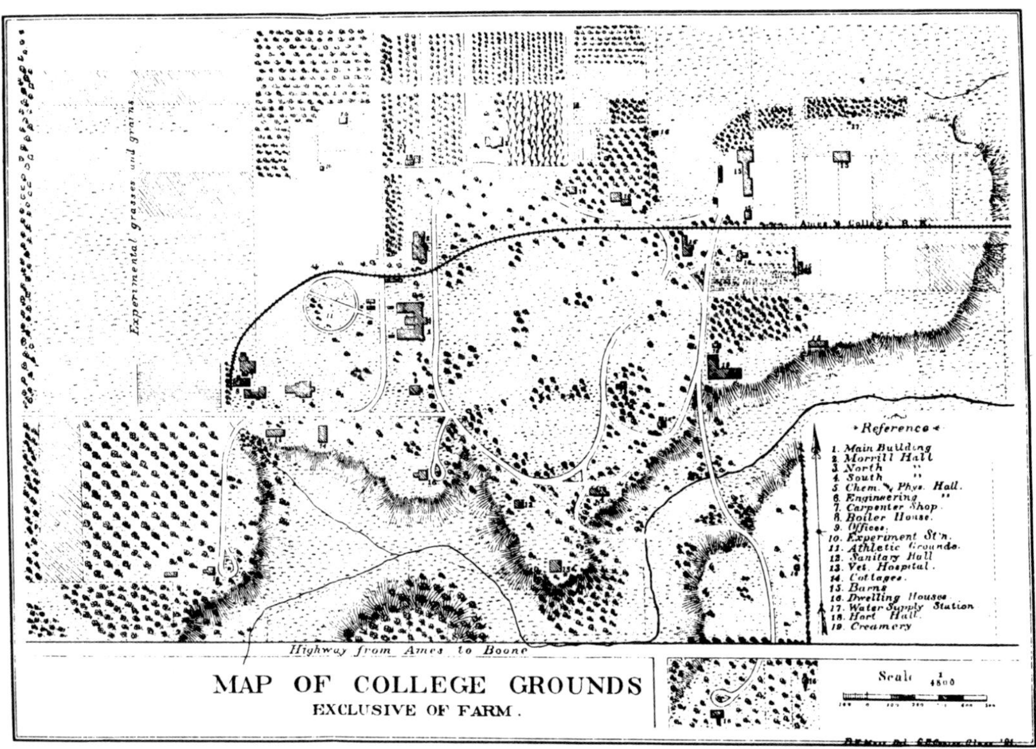

151 View of Michigan State Agricultural College in the 1870s. This area now forms the heart of the Michigan State University campus, and largely retains its original character, with buildings sited irregularly along winding roads in a wooded park.
(*Twenty-Third Annual Catalogue of the Officers and Students of the State Agricultural College of Michigan*, Lansing, 1879, frontispiece)

152 Main building of Iowa Agricultural College (now Iowa State University), Ames. Constructed ca. 1865.
(*Iowa State College of Agriculture and Mechanic Arts. Catalogue for the Year 1887*, Ames 1888, frontispiece)

153 Iowa Agricultural College, "Map of College Grounds, Exclusive of Farm," 1891.
(*Iowa State College of Agriculture and Mechanic Arts, Catalogue*, Ames, 1891, following p. 32)

> seek to graduate master builders or superintendents. . . ; we seek to graduate intelligent and skillful carpenters, masons or blacksmiths.[57]

Anderson proceeded to describe his vision of the physical form of his ideal land-grant school—in terms clearly recalling Olmsted's ideas:

> Some day and somewhere, there will be an Agricultural College looking so much like the grounds and buildings of a prosperous farmer . . . that we . . . would mistake it for a little hamlet of thriving artisans built in the heart of rich and well tilled fields. Nothing in its appearance would suggest our notion of the typical college. [It would have] cheap, stone buildings, one or two stories, scattered among the trees . . . no two alike. One would be used for teaching practical agriculture, but would as little prompt our idea of a recitation room, as the whole cluster would that of an imposing college edifice. . . . And there would be masons', carpenters' and smiths' shops . . . not requiring costly foundations and tall, heavy walls. . . . And they would not have been foreordained by men of a previous generation, who . . . could not possibly have foretold just what buildings such a college would need. As, in the process of its growth, a want had been felt, its shop was supplied. . . . No! it would not look like our great colleges.[58]

The buildings that Anderson erected for his school in the mid-1870s reflected this vision: small, modest structures, placed informally around a kind of village green.[59] Several years later, this scheme was modified somewhat, by the erection of a large central building (now called Anderson Hall), which still remains the focal point of the campus (Fig. 154).[60] But even with this dominant structure, the school retained an informal, rural character that was fully in keeping with Olmsted's concepts (Figs. 155, 156).

Thus, many of the early land-grant colleges apparently adopted from Olmsted—directly or indirectly—a new ideal of the campus as an irregular and picturesque arrangement of buildings in a setting suggesting a rural village or naturalistic park.[61] Of Olmsted's major principles of campus planning, only his injunction against large buildings, and his "cottage system" of housing, were not generally followed by the early land-grant colleges. Many of these schools erected large structures containing classrooms, offices, and sometimes dormitories on the upper floors—a continuation of the American tradition of single, all-inclusive collegiate buildings, although now they were often even larger and more complex structures, reflecting the architectural taste of the period. These are the "Old Mains" that stand as landmarks at so many institutions founded, or expanded, in the late nineteenth century (Figs. 157–160).[62]

As for Olmsted's "cottage system," very few schools adopted it in a consistent or wholehearted way. (Among those that did were a few women's colleges, notably Smith College in Massachusetts, whose founders in 1875 inaugurated a "cottage plan" of numerous home-like residences, which has been adhered to throughout the school's history.)[63] By coincidence, however, something very similar appeared unofficially at many institutions in the late nineteenth century, as the increasingly popular Greek-letter fraternities erected or purchased houses for their members on or near campus, each creating a domestically scaled residence where a small number of students could live and dine together in familial camaraderie, almost exactly as Olmsted had proposed (Fig. 161).[64]

There were no doubt several reasons why Olmsted's park-like model of campus planning appealed to the early land-grant colleges. Among them were the practical advantages that Olmsted had stressed in his reports, such as the ability of an informal plan to accommodate the unforeseeable future needs of an institution whose character was not yet fully defined. But more basic was the feeling among many educators, such as Anderson of Kansas, that an informal design was inherently appropriate to a land-grant institution as an expression of modest rural values, in contrast to the elitism and formality of the traditional colleges. Olmsted's park-like campus provided a tangible symbol for the new liberal and democratic ideals of education.

At about the same time, informal planning of a somewhat different type also appeared at traditional colleges, as part of the general popularity of naturalistic landscape and park design. After the Civil War, many colleges actually redesigned their grounds to reflect this new fashion. An example is Hamilton College in New York State,

154

155

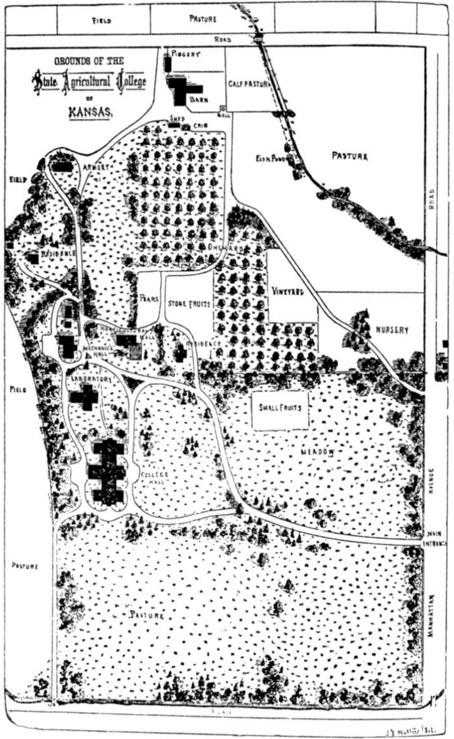

154 Kansas State Agricultural College (now Kansas State University), Manhattan. College Hall (now Anderson Hall), erected beginning in 1877 at a reported cost of $79,000. Building originally contained classrooms, administrative offices, library, chapel, and other functions.
(*Kansas State University*)

155 Plan of Kansas State Agricultural College, ca. 1889. The large building is College Hall.
(*State Agricultural College, Manhattan, Kansas, Seventh Biennial Report of the Regents and Faculty*, 1889–1890, p. 64)

156

157

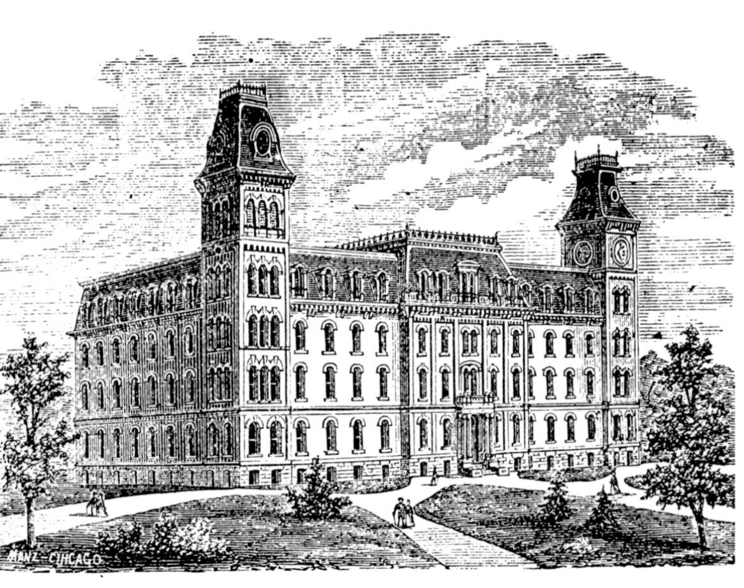

158

156 Kansas State Agricultural College. View looking north from College Hall, ca. 1885. In foreground is Chemical Laboratory. Behind it are Mechanics Hall and Horticultural Hall (*right*). (Kansas State University)

157 University Hall, Illinois Industrial University (now the University of Illinois), Urbana-Champaign. Designed by John M. Van Osdel, a member of school's board of trustees, the building was constructed in 1874, and originally contained classrooms, offices, chapel, museum, and other facilities. It was demolished in 1938. Reportedly, its plans also were used, in the late nineteenth century, for the main building at Arkansas Industrial University (now the University of Arkansas) at Fayetteville. (*Fifth Annual Report of the Board of Trustees of the Illinois Industrial University*, Springfield, 1873, p. 16)

158 Old Main Building, University of Texas, Austin. Designed by Frederick E. Ruffini (chosen in a competition), and constructed 1882–1898, the building originally stood alone on university property at the outskirts of Austin, facing the State Capitol in the center of town. It contained classrooms, laboratories, assembly hall, law school, library, and offices (the university originally had no dormitories). It was demolished in 1934, and replaced by present main building of the university. (*Catalogue of the University of Texas . . . for 1890–91*, Austin, 1891, frontispiece)

159 Morrill Hall, University of Nevada, Reno, 1885. (*University of Nevada*)

160 University of Nebraska, Lincoln, ca. 1880. Detail of lithographic view of the city of Lincoln. Main building, University Hall, was erected 1870–1871. School also possessed a 320-acre farm, outside the city.

159

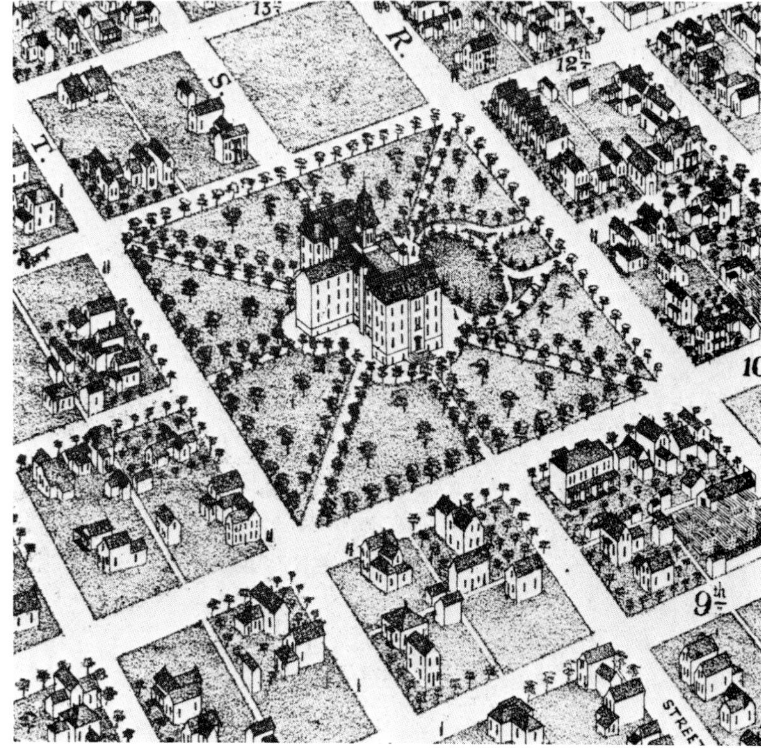

160

161

161 Fraternity houses at Stanford University, Palo Alto, California, in early twentieth century.
(*Stanford University Archives*)

162 Hamilton College, Clinton, New York. *Top*: plan of campus in 1853. Five main buildings, aligned in the manner of the Yale Row, were erected 1793–1827. *Bottom*: plan of campus in 1868; grounds had been redesigned, original academy building demolished, and several new structures erected. (*Documentary History of Hamilton College*, Clinton, 1922, following p. 254)

155
Well 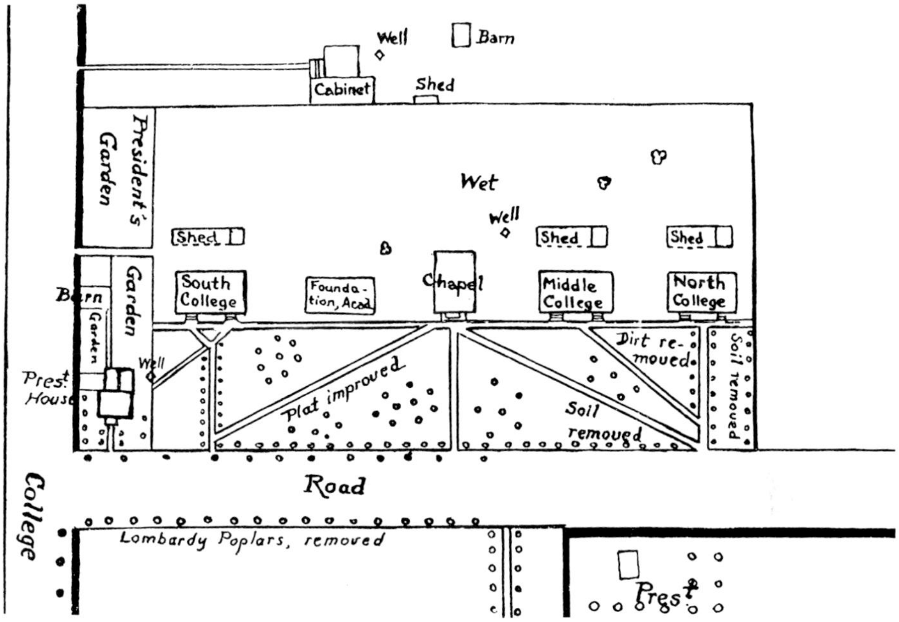
Barn
Cabinet
Shed
President's Garden
Wet
Well
Shed
Shed
Shed
South College
Founda-tion, Acad.
Chapel
Middle College
North College
Barn
Garden
Garden
Well
Prest. House
Plat improved
Dirt re-moved
Soil removed
Soil removed
College
Road
Lombardy Poplars, removed
Prest.
Woods 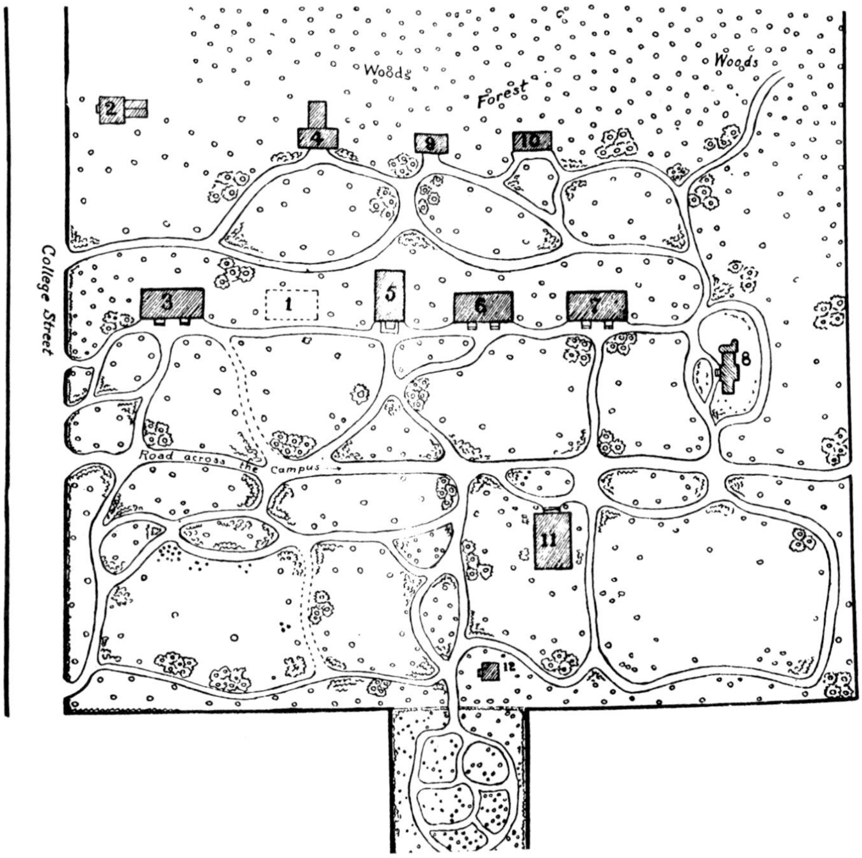
Forest
Woods
College Street
Road across the campus

156

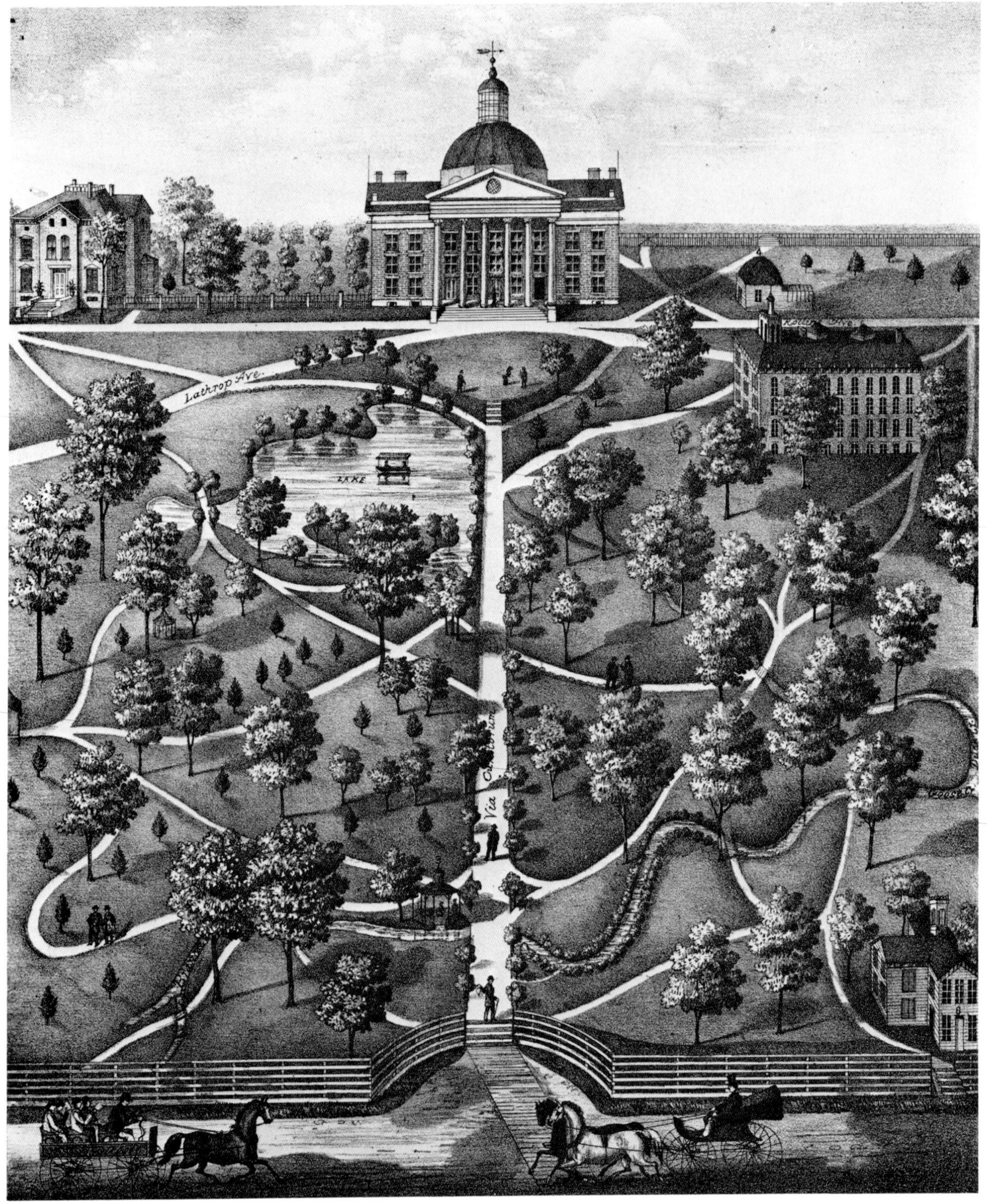

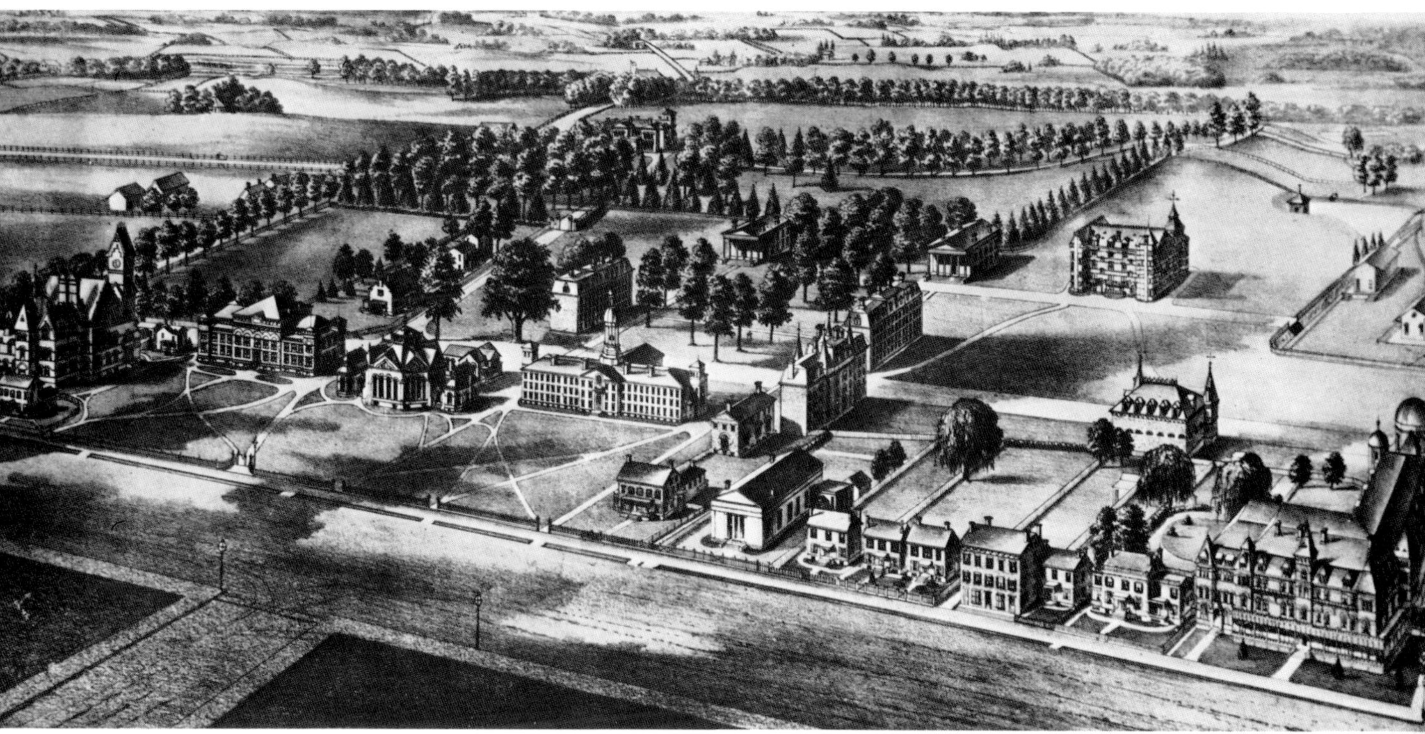

164

163 University of Missouri, Columbia. Lithographic view of ca. 1875. Main building, designed by Stephen Hills, was constructed 1840–1843. It burned in 1892, but its six Ionic columns have been kept standing ever since as a symbolic focal point of the campus. Other buildings shown in this view are President's House (upper left), the Observatory and Scientific Building (upper right), and Normal Building (lower right).
(*Boone County, Missouri, Atlas*, 1875, p. 24. Library of Congress, Prints and Photographs Division)

164 College of New Jersey, Princeton. Lithograph of 1875, by C. O. Hudnut. This view omits much greenery so that buildings can be seen more clearly. In center is Nassau Hall. To left of it is Chancellor Green Library, built in 1873, in place of demolished Philosophical Hall (thus destroying the symmetry of Latrobe's Philosophical and Stanhope halls). Further to left is Dickinson Hall, erected 1870 as a classroom building. Large structure in open field at upper right is Witherspoon Hall, a dormitory, anticipated in this view, since it was not built until 1877.
(Princeton University Archives)

which transformed its landscaping and road patterns, giving the campus a new, park-like character, despite the fact that the buildings remained in their Yale Row alignment (Fig. 162).[65] A similar naturalistic environment was created in the 1870s at the University of Missouri at Columbia, against the backdrop of the school's imposing Greek Revival main structure (Fig. 163).[66]

A dramatic transformation of this sort occurred at Princeton, under the presidency of James McCosh. In the 1870s, McCosh undertook a program that purposely destroyed the formal symmetry of the existing campus by demolishing one of the buildings framing Nassau Hall and adding new structures of picturesque form that adhered to no regular pattern of siting (Fig. 164).[67] Ironically, however, McCosh's reasons for remaking Princeton in this way had nothing in common with the populist or democratic motives of the land-grant educators. For McCosh, the informal campus evoked picturesque images whose nature was revealed by his remark, "I have laid [the campus out] on the model of the demesnes of English noblemen."[68] Thus, similar styles of campus planning could be employed to express antithetical ideas.

The Athletic Campus

At the same time that the land-grant schools appeared, athletic activities were being accepted and incorporated into the American college. Although the land-grant movement did not specifically promote collegiate athletics, both were in a sense manifestations of democratic trends in nineteenth-century American education, and the athletics phenomenon was exploited by the new institutions. It also had important effects on the form of the American campus.

The colonial and early nineteenth-century college normally made no provision for physical sports, and in fact usually discouraged them as unsuitable for educated gentlemen. The Princeton faculty in the 1780s denounced games as unworthy of its students, and in the 1820s Rensselaer Polytechnic Institute declared that physical exercise "detracts from that dignity of deportment which becomes a man of science."[69] Thomas Jefferson did suggest that the arcaded passageways on the ground floor of the Rotunda at the University of Virginia could be used by the students for exercise in bad weather, but he apparently was thinking principally of military drill.[70] The German gymnastics movement made a brief appearance at several New England colleges in the 1820s, and the progressive President Wayland of Brown even joined his students on the parallel bars, but the experiment was nipped in the bud by puritanical objections.[71]

Around 1850, gymnastics became popular again on the American campus, and this time the effects were lasting. The activities at first were held outdoors, as can be seen in a lithograph of the University of Virginia in 1856, in which students are shown exercising on bars and other equipment erected at the south end of Jefferson's Lawn (Fig. 165).[72] But in the 1860s, schools began to construct gymnasia, in which the various exercises were conducted in an orderly and decorous manner, sometimes to the accompaniment of music, as shown in an 1885 engraving of the spacious new gymnasium at Amherst College (Fig. 166).[73]

By this time, however, competitive sports had become more popular with students than gymnastics, and were being encouraged by the rivalry between colleges. The first intercollegiate baseball game occurred in 1859, and ten years later a football match between Princeton and Rutgers introduced the sport that was to transform campus

165 University of Virginia, Charlottesville. Detail of Sachse lithograph of 1856, showing gymnastic exercises at southern end of the Lawn.

166 Amherst College, Amherst, Massachusetts. Engraved view of Pratt Gymnasium, constructed in 1884. (*Harper's Weekly*, February 21, 1885, p. 125)

165

166

life.[74] Probably the greatest beneficiaries of the sports movement were the land-grant schools, which could compete in this area as equals with the traditional colleges. In 1870, a defeat of Harvard by the Massachusetts Agricultural College was celebrated as a victory for democracy, and the state legislature immediately increased its funding of the school.[75] In the following decades, land-grant schools throughout the country used sports to attract support and bolster their prestige. Within the traditional colleges, too, athletics played a democratic role by countering class distinctions with a new type of status. (In 1903, an athletic defeat of Bowdoin College by the University of Maine provoked a Bowdoin alumnus to call for relaxed admission standards, in order to "get some stock.")[76] The women's colleges also were caught up in the enthusiasm for sports, although they justified them at first more by motives of health than competition.

By the end of the nineteenth century, college athletics had become well organized, with full-time coaches, big budgets, and large numbers of spectators for intercollegiate events. All of this required extensive physical facilities: gymnasia, running tracks, playing fields, swimming pools, and other specialized accommodations. Boathouses were needed at the eastern schools where crew was a major sport; Princeton, which was near no body of water, even felt obligated to create an artificial lake in order to participate.[77] Alumni were normally delighted to pay for these things. More troublesome than cost was the large amount of land needed for these facilities—usually much larger than the area required for the rest of a school's buildings. Colleges with small campuses and no possibility of expansion were at a serious disadvantage. Urban sites were especially unfortunate, and thus another reason was added to the American preference for rural colleges.

Gymnasia were at first simple barn-like structures, clearly distinguishable from the rest of a college's buildings. But as athletics became fully accepted into the college, so were its buildings. By the end of the nineteenth century, gymnasia often were given picturesque and irregular shapes in an attempt to disguise their bulk and make them compatible with the rest of the campus (Fig. 167). The culminating architectural expression of collegiate athletics was the football stadium, whose scale was too great to be disguised. The first stadia were constructed around 1900, and in the next three decades about one hundred of them were built at major universities to accommodate the huge crowds of collegiate football fans (Fig. 168).[78] Their design usually was based on classical prototypes such as the Roman Coliseum and created impressions of strength and monumentality that perfectly suited the spirit of collegiate pride engendered by organized athletics. The state land-grant institutions had by now outgrown the modest aims of their early years, and Olmsted's rural village was superseded by the monumental stadium as the symbol of their ambitions.

After the architect Le Corbusier came to the United States in the 1930s and visited several colleges and universities, he wrote an effusive book about America with a chapter on colleges entitled "Everyone an Athlete."[79] He saw the American college as distinguished most by its "athletic" quality, by which he meant not only the interest in organized sports, but also the healthy and active lives of the students, and the park-like nature of the campus. To Le Corbusier, these were all part of the same essential character of the American college:

> Everything in the interest of comfort, everything for the sake of calm and serenity, everything to make solid bodies. Each college or university is an urban unit in itself, a small or large city. But a green city. Lawns, parks, stadiums, cloisters, dining halls, a whole complex of comfortable quarters. . . .
>
> The American university is a world in itself, a temporary paradise, a gracious stage of life. . . .[80]

Le Corbusier's romantic impressions reflected his own visions of the future as much as the real state of American higher education. But he saw clearly a special quality of the American college: its essentially democratic and utopian ideal of a perfect physical environment.

167

168

167 Hemenway Gymnasium, Harvard. Designed by Peabody & Stearns; built 1878; demolished 1933. (Moses King, *Harvard and Its Surroundings*, Cambridge, 1882, following p. 38)

168 Harvard Stadium, across Charles River from Harvard College. Designed by Charles F. McKim of the firm of McKim, Mead & White, and constructed 1899–1903, this was one of the largest structures in reinforced concrete at time of its completion. (*The American Architect*, August 18, 1920, p. 223)

V. The University As City Beautiful

The late nineteenth century saw the creation of the modern American university. Some earlier American schools had called themselves universities, but the term seldom had the English meaning of a degree-granting body for a group of colleges, or the German meaning of a collection of departmental faculties devoted to scholarship as well as teaching. Only in the late nineteenth century were there widespread and successful efforts in America to create universities that were significantly different from colleges.[1] The models at first were European, but they soon were transformed so radically that a new type of university was created, thoroughly American in its form and functions. Architecture, as usual, was enlisted to clarify and express the nature of this new institution, and by about 1900 new types of campus plans were being devised for the American university.

After the Civil War, the German university began to be emulated widely in America, as educators became increasingly concerned about the weakness of American scholarship and science. Johns Hopkins University, founded in 1867 in Baltimore, and other institutions that followed it, adopted the German system faithfully, concentrating on specialized graduate study and rejecting most aspects of the collegiate tradition. These schools were generally in cities. They purposely provided no dormitories and took no official interest in their students' extracurricular lives. And their physical planning made little attempt to create an integrated pattern to distinguish the school from the rest of the city. The early buildings of Johns Hopkins in Baltimore were simply separate structures on the city streets, with nothing in their overall plan to give the university a special physical character (Fig. 169).[2] In 1875 the English biologist Thomas Huxley visited Baltimore while on a lecture tour, and surprised his audience by praising the utilitarian buildings of Johns Hopkins and recommending that the school not waste its money on architects but merely hire "an honest bricklayer" as additional structures were needed.[3] Daniel Coit Gilman, president of Johns Hopkins, had been impressed with the practical laboratories of German universities, and frequently argued that American schools had no need for "splendid architecture," as he said in a speech in 1882 at Western Reserve University in Cleveland.[4]

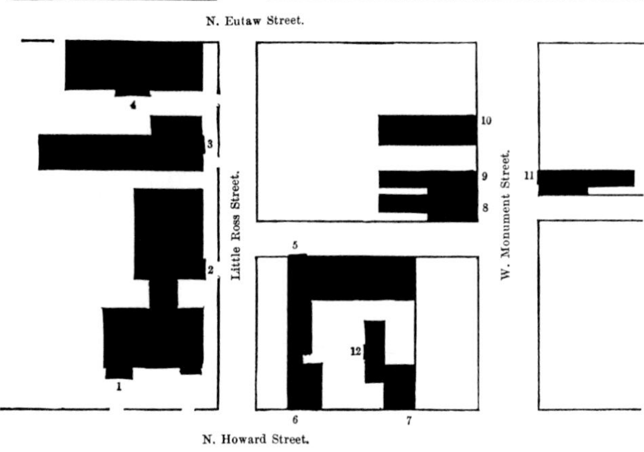

169

169 Johns Hopkins University, Baltimore, Maryland. Plan of buildings used by the university in 1884. Facilities included classrooms, laboratories, offices, library, mechanics' shop, and gymnasium—but no dormitories or dining hall. The institution was forthrightly a university, not a college.
(*The Johns Hopkins University Register, 1884–1885*, Baltimore, 1885, p. 37)

Other German-inspired schools, such as Clark University in Worcester, Massachusetts, erected one large structure to house most of their facilities, but these buildings usually had a plain and utilitarian character that reflected a scientific, down-to-earth reaction against the collegiate tradition (Fig. 170). Professional architects generally were avoided. The building at Clark was designed in 1887, apparently by the institution's founder, and during its construction the school's first president, the scientist G. Stanley Hall, concerned himself with practical problems like creating flexibility with the use of temporary partitions.[5]

The spirit of science and rationalism was naturally espoused also by the new technical schools, such as the Massachusetts Institute of Technology, which in its early days occupied disparate urban structures in Boston, several of which were designed by its engineering faculty.[6] In 1866, M.I.T. erected an elegant classical structure in Boston's newly laid-out Back Bay neighborhood (Fig. 171). But the Institute's catalogues for the next several years juxtaposed engravings of this building with views of the forthrightly inelegant metallurgy and mining laboratories in its basement (the only interior spaces pictured), thus suggesting an ambivalence about whether grandeur or stark utilitarianism was the proper image for a technical school (Fig. 172).[7]

Even the traditional colleges were caught up in some of the new trends. At Harvard, President Charles William Eliot in the 1870s dismantled much of the school's collegiate discipline, giving students unprecedented academic freedom with the elective system, and allowing them to live off campus. A professor at Columbia in 1884 predicted that the traditional college soon would be dead.[8] And the scientific fashion captivated a Princeton classics professor to the extent that he called his classroom a "laboratory" and his books "apparatus."[9]

Such zealous anticollegianism was short-lived, however. The German university model had great influence in America, but the collegiate tradition was too strong to be replaced by it, and ultimately the two systems merged and compromised with each other. The resulting institution, as it coalesced at the end of the nineteenth century, has been called a "marriage between collegiate and university ideals."[10] But it also had distinctive char-

170

170 Clark University, Worcester, Massachusetts. Main building, erected beginning in 1887. Reportedly designed by founder of the institution, Jonas Clark, with modifications during construction suggested by the school's first president, scientist G. Stanley Hall. (*Clark University . . . Register and Third Official Announcement*, April 1891, opp. p. 71)

171

172

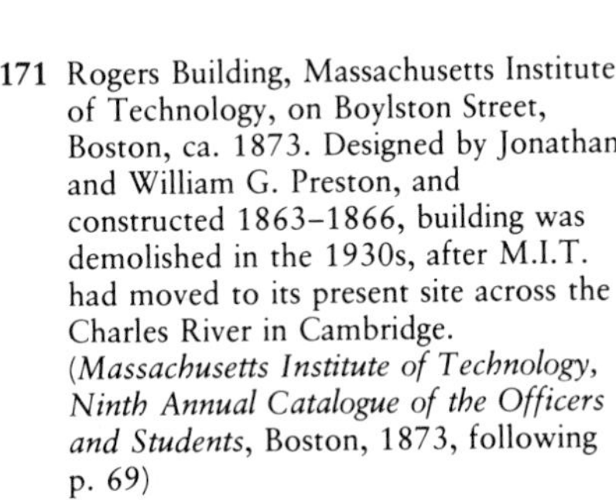

171 Rogers Building, Massachusetts Institute of Technology, on Boylston Street, Boston, ca. 1873. Designed by Jonathan and William G. Preston, and constructed 1863–1866, building was demolished in the 1930s, after M.I.T. had moved to its present site across the Charles River in Cambridge. (*Massachusetts Institute of Technology, Ninth Annual Catalogue of the Officers and Students*, Boston, 1873, following p. 69)

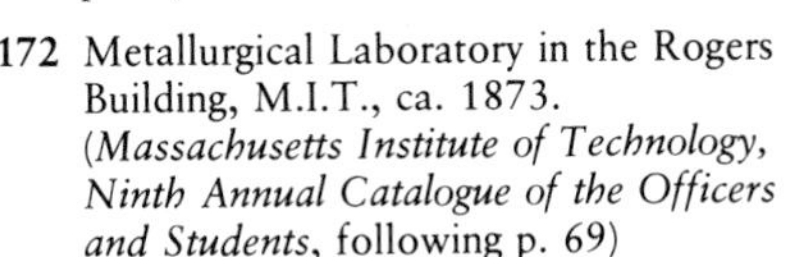

172 Metallurgical Laboratory in the Rogers Building, M.I.T., ca. 1873. (*Massachusetts Institute of Technology, Ninth Annual Catalogue of the Officers and Students*, following p. 69)

acteristics of its own. It promoted the goal of education for all in ways that even the land-grant schools had not done, and as a result it began accommodating vastly larger numbers of students than any earlier institutions. Because of this, and of the differing levels and aims of these students—graduate and undergraduate, technical and liberal arts, men and women—the university had to create a multiplicity of academic departments, programs, administrative offices, and housing facilities. In 1914, a trustee of Columbia University, in an article entitled "The Building of a University," suggested some of the factors that complicated the planning of this new type of institution:

> The ideal site should be large enough to contain all the departments of a university, not only the college, but the technical schools and law and medicine, thus concentrating all its faculties and students and bringing them within the university atmosphere, and yet should be so situated as to afford its technical students easy access to machine shops and factories, and its medical students the advantages of a nearby hospital.[11]

This new American institution quickly abandoned the disinterest in architectural matters that had typified the early German-inspired schools. In contrast to President Gilman of Johns Hopkins, the author of the article quoted above called for "a fine architectural effect which will represent to its students the ideals and purposes of a university and command the attention and admiration of the public." But it was clear that the forms of architectural planning now needed were very different from those of the earlier American college. To symbolize these differences, a new image or metaphor appeared for this large and complex institution. If the traditional college had been a "village," the new university would be a "city." Slogans like "City of Learning" and "Collegiate City" became common and began to influence the architectural form of the university.[12]

The Beaux-Arts Campus

By 1900, the Beaux-Arts system of architectural planning had come to the service of this new type of university. A major force in American design after the success of the Columbian Exposition in Chicago of 1893, the Beaux-Arts movement was well suited to express the character of the new educational institution. Its principles of monumental organization facilitated orderly planning on a grand scale and were capable of including many disparate buildings or parts within a unified overall pattern. Over the years, the Beaux-Arts system (developed at the Ecole des Beaux-Arts, the official French art school in Paris) had created and refined many such patterns—or *partis*—which constituted a repertoire of solutions to complex problems of planning (Fig. 173). The Beaux-Arts tradition also put great emphasis on city planning, and its principles of urbanism became the foundation of the "City Beautiful" movement in America in the years following the Chicago Fair. It was therefore natural that many of the new American universities, large both in size and ambition and thinking of themselves as cities of learning, should turn to the newly fashionable Beaux-Arts system to create their physical form and self-image.

Another factor helped shape the form of the American university at the same time: the philanthropic benefactor. Wealthy donors had endowed colleges since the colonial period, but in the late nineteenth century a new breed of philanthropist appeared, able to endow schools on an unprecedented scale, and enthusiastic about executing ambitious architectural plans. Before the Civil War, the twelve largest gifts to American schools had ranged from $20,000 to $175,000. Postwar benefactions soared; they included Ezra Cornell's of $500,000, Cornelius Vanderbilt's of $1 million, Johns Hopkins's of $3.5 million, Leland Stanford's of about $20 million, and John D. Rockefeller's (at the University of Chicago) of about $30 million.[13] Rather than simply give to existing schools, these men usually founded their own institutions, or else transformed existing colleges so radically that they became virtually new—as happened in the 1920s to little Trinity College in North Carolina, transformed by the Duke family into Duke University. These philanthropists often had a proprietary feeling about their creations, considering them almost as memorials to them-

173

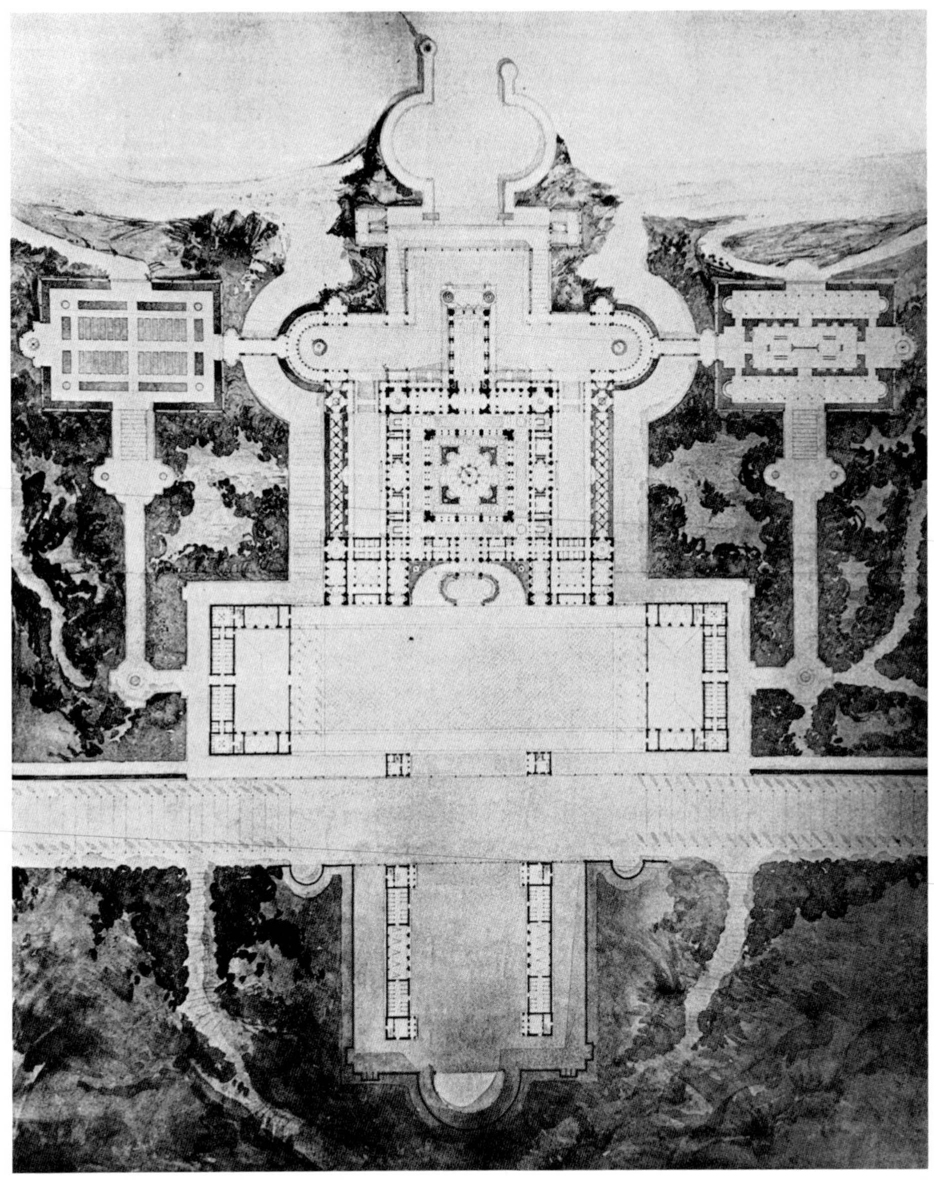

173 Design for "Une Vaste Hôtellerie pour des Voyageurs," by Louis Noguet, 1865. Awarded first prize, that year, in the Prix de Rome competition of the Ecole des Beaux-Arts.
(Ecole Nationale des Beaux-Arts, *Les Grands Prix de Rome d'Architecture, de 1850 à 1900*, Paris, n.d., pl. 78)

selves, and thus they tended to favor the unified architectural grandeur and monumentality typical of the Beaux-Arts.

Ironically, the opposite effect—disunity—also could result from philanthropy. A donor who paid for the erection of a single building on a campus often purposely encouraged its disharmony with its surroundings, a phenomenon noted by an architect in 1912 who described "that curious desire on the part of each donor to build an individual memorial which should be architecturally as different as possible from all neighboring buildings."[14] (This no doubt was the reasoning of the philanthropist who reportedly offered Harvard a million dollars for a dormitory if they would build it in "the Turkish style." Harvard declined.)[15] But when an institution had a single great benefactor, as happened in the late nineteenth century more than ever before, the effect was always greater architectural unity. Just as the Medicis and their class had patronized ecclesiastical art in the Renaissance, wealthy Americans now chose higher education and its architectural planning as principal objects of their munificence—and as a means to immortality.

The two most extravagant university founders of the late nineteenth century were Leland Stanford and John D. Rockefeller. Of their two creations, Rockefeller's University of Chicago perhaps embodied more fully the educational ideals of the new American universities, with large sums of money allotted for ambitious academic programs, research facilities, and eminent faculty. Stanford University, however, represented more dramatically the personal role of the philanthropist in the physical planning of his school. Both institutions produced campus designs which, although not fully Beaux-Arts in nature, were harbingers of the new directions in campus planning.

Probably more than any other school, Stanford University (or Leland Stanford, Jr. University) was shaped by the personal motive for its founding. Leland Stanford, president of the Central Pacific Railroad and ex-governor of California, was one of the wealthiest men in America when in 1884 his only child died while the family was touring Europe. Stanford and his wife resolved to create a university in their son's memory and decided to locate it on their country estate, Palo Alto, south of San Francisco.[16] In 1886 they hired Frederick Law Olmsted to produce a master plan for the campus; to design the buildings, they chose the architect Charles A. Coolidge of the Boston firm of Shepley, Rutan & Coolidge (successors to Henry Hobson Richardson, whom the Stanfords originally wished to hire, but who had died that year).

From the beginning, however, Leland Stanford himself took a controlling hand in the planning, and even announced publicly that he intended to "be his own architect."[17] The experience was naturally frustrating for the designers, and especially for Olmsted, whose principles of planning conflicted in certain respects with Stanford's intentions. In September 1886, Olmsted came to California to inspect the site, along with Francis A. Walker, the president of M.I.T., whom Stanford had engaged as educational consultant. Olmsted first proposed a scheme that reflected the college plans he had developed twenty years earlier for the land-grant schools—a design with modest buildings nestled informally in the hills that formed part of Stanford's 8,000-acre estate (Fig. 174).[18] But Stanford insisted on a flat site that would allow a formal arrangement of buildings, fitting the image he and his wife had of a suitable memorial to their son.

At this time, a decision also was made to link the buildings with arcades, forming enclosed quadrangles, a notion apparently conceived by Leland Stanford himself, although Olmsted found it agreeably suited to the California climate.[19] In the following months, Olmsted and Coolidge in Boston explored a variety of possible arrangements of the university buildings, as Stanford directed. In April 1887, Coolidge took drawings and models of their design to Palo Alto and presented them to the Stanfords, who demanded further changes.[20] A letter from Coolidge to Olmsted reveals the conflict between the architects' more naturalistic concepts and the clients' desire for greater monumentality:

> We had the surveyors stake out [the buildings,] and when it was completed we went over the ground with [the Stanfords] and they said it faced the wrong way and that they . . . wished the main drive and tomb vista to be on the long side. We showed them how by this change they lost the vista from the tomb to the back hills through the trees because the church would cut

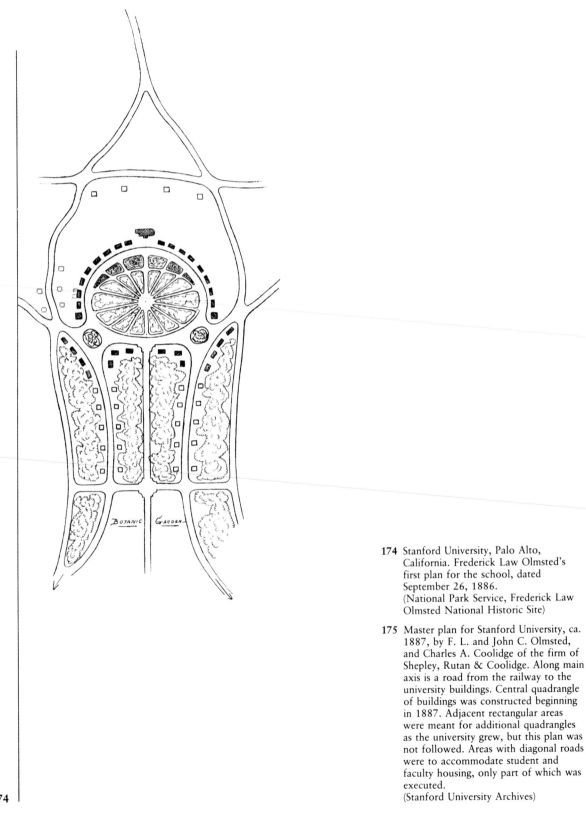

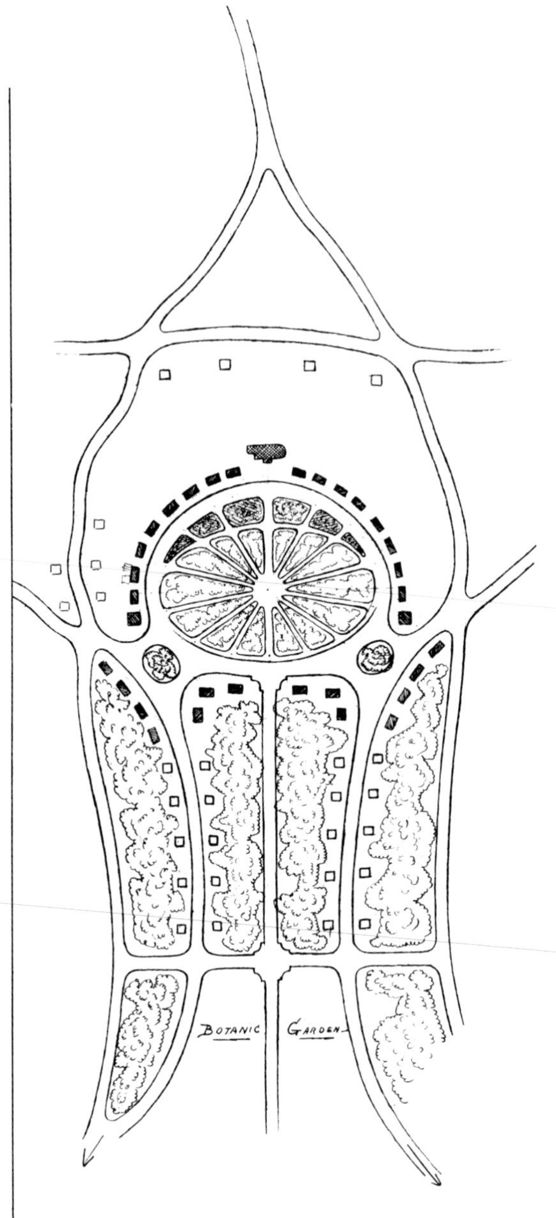

174

174 Stanford University, Palo Alto, California. Frederick Law Olmsted's first plan for the school, dated September 26, 1886.
(National Park Service, Frederick Law Olmsted National Historic Site)

175 Master plan for Stanford University, ca. 1887, by F. L. and John C. Olmsted, and Charles A. Coolidge of the firm of Shepley, Rutan & Coolidge. Along main axis is a road from the railway to the university buildings. Central quadrangle of buildings was constructed beginning in 1887. Adjacent rectangular areas were meant for additional quadrangles as the university grew, but this plan was not followed. Areas with diagonal roads were to accommodate student and faculty housing, only part of which was executed.
(Stanford University Archives)

175

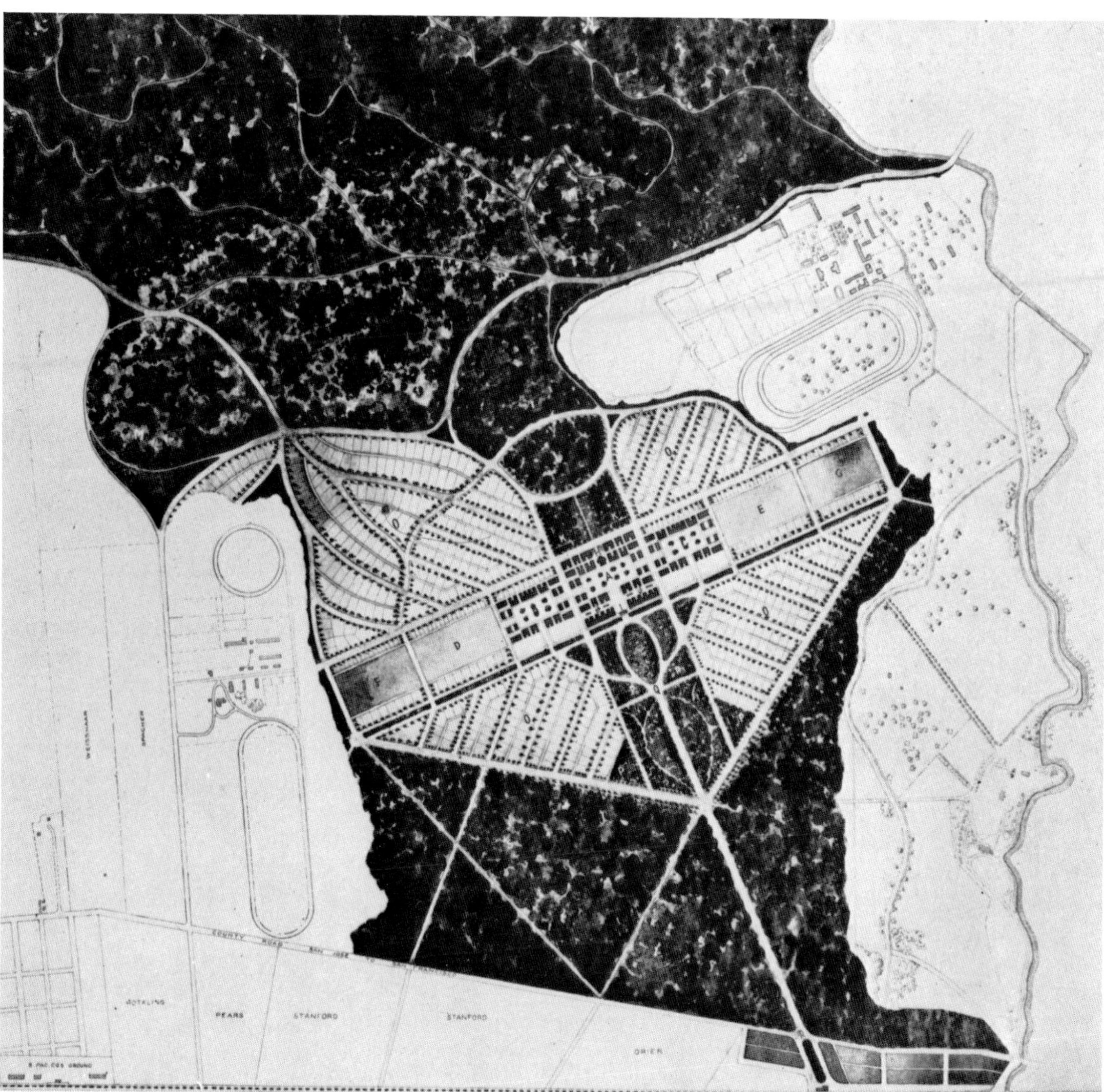

it off, but they thought the vista . . . would end more appropriately at the church. . . . Finally we told them that this would change the grade and upset your work, to which the Gov. replied, a Landscape Arch't and an Arch't might be disappointed but he was going to have the buildings the way he wanted them. . . . Both Mr. and Mrs. S. think the main entrance should be a large memorial arch with an enormously long approach, and in fact the very quietness and reserve which we like so much in it is what they want to get rid of.[21]

Coolidge stayed at Palo Alto, to revise the plan and to begin designing the buildings and supervising their construction. Master plans and drawings produced in 1887 and 1888 show the strongly unified character of the design, which was innovative in several ways (Figs. 175, 176).[22] The courtyards, formed of Richardsonian-Romanesque buildings linked by open arcades, suggestive of Spanish missions and other Mediterranean building types, comprise one of the earliest uses of the fully enclosed quadrangle in American campus planning (a subject examined in the next chapter). But most striking was the monumental formality of the whole scheme, with a major north-south axis defined by a mile-long approach to the campus, lined with palm trees, this axis passing through the Memorial Arch and a sequence of spaces, and culminating at the centrally placed Memorial Church (whose tower fell in the great earthquake of 1906, along with the Memorial Arch) (Figs. 177, 178). The main quadrangle defined a secondary, east-west axis, which was to be extended in both directions by additional quadrangles to be built as the university expanded, a plan that was never actually executed at Stanford but which probably influenced other American college plans.[23] Men's and women's dormitories were placed to the east and west in the design (the Stanfords having vetoed Olmsted's "cottage system" of student housing), and in the four angles between the intersecting axes, diagonal streets were to accommodate faculty housing, making the whole complex a self-sufficient university city.[24]

This design possessed a degree of formality and grandeur unknown to earlier colleges, although somewhat reminiscent of Jefferson's University of Virginia and Ramée's Union College—in which regard it is noteworthy that Leland Stanford's boyhood home in New York State was only a couple of miles from the Union campus, where buildings also were connected by arcades (Fig. 65). But the Stanford design probably also had European sources, including urban spaces that had impressed the Stanfords on their travels abroad, such as the succession of arcaded streets leading into the Place Vendôme, which was Leland Stanford's favorite spot in Paris.[25] Despite this combination of unlikely sources and the difficult collaboration between the Stanfords and their architects, the resulting design had a clarity and axial monumentality that foreshadowed the coming era of Beaux-Arts formalism.

Several decades later, an observer of Olmsted's work remarked that at Stanford he had "abandoned" his theories of informal design and "produced a thoroughly formal plan."[26] This oversimplified the facts and ignored the major role of Leland Stanford in the design. But it is true that this design was a turning point for the Olmsted firm. After the retirement of the senior Olmsted in about 1895, his sons and successors began producing campus plans and proposals that recalled, in certain respects, the Stanford design—examples being their recommendations for Washington University in St. Louis and the University of Rochester.[27] The ordered monumentality of the Stanford plan was well suited to the new type of American university that emerged at the end of the nineteenth century. For their own personal reasons, Leland Stanford and his wife had conceived a university plan that foretold the spirit of things to come.

John D. Rockefeller's endowment of the University of Chicago, beginning in 1890, was very different from that of Stanford. Rather than take personal control of the school's planning, Rockefeller simply provided the funds for the president and trustees to create the ideal American university.[28] The character of the institution was shaped by its first president, William Rainey Harper, who combined a zeal for the Germanic emphasis on research and graduate study with a reaffirmation of the Anglo-American collegiate tradition, which Harper promoted by insisting that dormitories be provided on campus, and that they be organized in a "house system" to foster social interaction. Harper also believed that the university had a re-

176 Rendering of Olmsted and Coolidge's master plan for Stanford University, 1888. Central group of buildings was constructed 1887–ca. 1903, but additional quadrangles to east and west never were executed. Drawing by D. A. Gregg.
(Stanford University Archives)

177

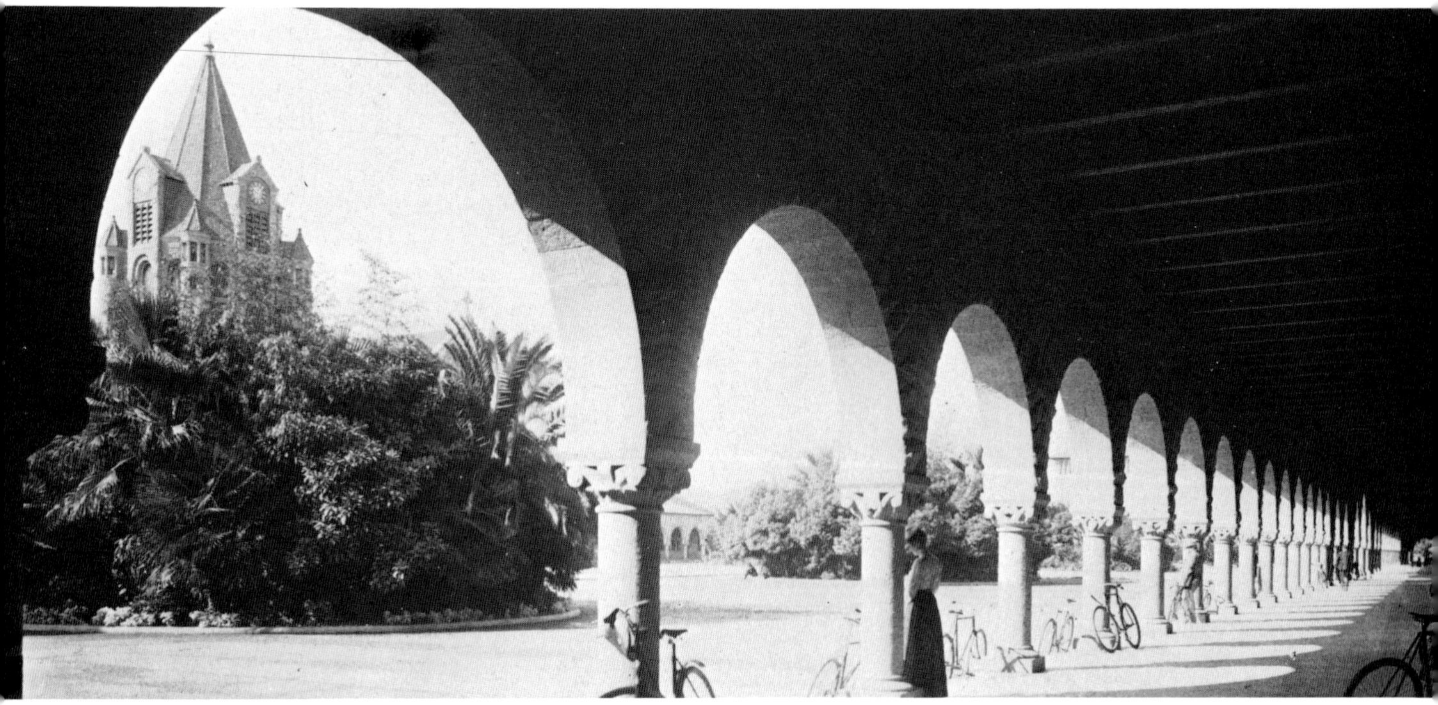

178

sponsibility to the larger community outside, and advocated that it provide extension courses and other community services. These considerations contributed to the trustees' decision to locate the institution in Chicago and to emphasize its urban character. But unlike earlier urban universities such as Johns Hopkins, the trustees felt the need for a strong master plan to give cohesion to the institution, and they announced from the beginning that "the buildings are to stand as the expression of a great University."[29]

The location chosen was a four-block site facing the thin strip of parkland that became the "Midway" of the Columbian Exposition, which was being planned in adjacent Jackson Park at the same time as the university. The grand "White City" of the exposition, which had such an influence on American architecture and planning, no doubt stimulated the university trustees to think in ambitious terms, although the resulting plan was not exactly Beaux-Arts in character. Its author was the Chicago architect Henry Ives Cobb, who drew on a number of sources for the design, following suggestions of the trustees. As early as 1890 they spoke of "our quadrangle plan," an idea probably inspired in part by Stanford's highly publicized design, as well as by Trinity College in Hartford and the English colleges of Oxford and Cambridge.[30] A practical consideration was the desire of the trustees to include as many facilities as possible on the relatively small urban site.

The resulting design, presented by Cobb in 1893, crowded seven quadrangles onto the site, each one composed rather awkwardly of buildings with various picturesque configurations (Fig. 179). Cobb's plan, in fact, shows more structures than could possibly have been fitted into the space.[31] The crowdedness of the plan also produced difficulties such as the blockage of the main entrance into the university by the chapel, which prevented the kind of axial vista into the complex that would have characterized a true Beaux-Arts plan. These problems resulted in large part from the complexity of the program, something the trustees probably had not been fully aware of when they acquired the site. Unlike the traditional American college, the new university required a great diversity of academic buildings and laboratories, separate dormitory areas for undergraduates and graduates (male and female), plus such facilities as a museum,

177 Stanford University, seen from the southwest, ca. 1905.
(Stanford University Archives)

178 Inner Quadrangle, Stanford University, ca. 1905. This large space is surrounded by arcades, onto which classrooms and offices open.
(Stanford University Archives)

179

179 University of Chicago. Rendering of master plan for the university by Henry Ives Cobb, 1893. Area shown is bounded (*foreground and background*) by Lexington and Ellis avenues (*right and left*), and by 57th and 59th streets. The Women's Quadrangle occupies corner in left foreground. In other corners are the Graduate Quadrangle and two Undergraduate Quadrangles. In center are the chapel and a building housing the University Hall and Library. (*Architectural Record*, October-December 1894, p. 230)

research library, and gymnasium. Accommodating these functions in a unified design was not easy, and became one of the major problems in campus planning in the following years.

At the same time as the Chicago design, Columbia University in New York City was creating a master plan that was a clearer expression of Beaux-Arts principles. By 1890 Columbia College had outgrown its site on 49th Street (to which it had moved, in 1859, from its original location in lower Manhattan), and decided to migrate even farther uptown.[32] A four-block site on upper Broadway was purchased in 1892, and the college proclaimed itself a university, officially recognizing its growing diversity of schools and departments, as well as the prevailing trends of American education. The trustees' committee on building, headed by President Seth Low, hired three architects to produce a master plan, but each of the three presented his own design.[33] Charles C. Haight, the architect of Columbia's Victorian Gothic buildings at the previous campus, produced a scheme with numerous small courtyards, somewhat similar to Cobb's plan for Chicago. The other two architects, Richard Morris Hunt and Charles Follen McKim (of the firm of McKim, Mead & White), had both studied at the Ecole des Beaux-Arts and produced plans reflecting French principles of planning. Hunt's scheme used a *parti* common in French institutions such as hospitals, with courtyards formed by pavilions set at right angles to the street.[34]

McKim, whom the trustees eventually chose as campus architect, formulated a design whose success was based on its consummately urban character (Figs. 180, 181). He recognized the civic-oriented stance that Columbia was taking (reflected, for example, in its decision not to have dormitories but to remain a commuter school), and in a description of his design he emphasized the "wholly municipal character of the problem, identical in this respect to the Sorbonne in Paris."[35] His plan, as revised in late 1894, concentrated the university on the southern part of the site (the rest to be used for later expansion), with buildings flanking the streets like any other urban structures, an exception being the main entrance area on 116th Street, where a quadrangle opened off the street—the *cour d'honneur*, in Beaux-Arts parlance—leading up to the central building, the library.

In McKim's earlier plan this library was treated like the other university buildings, but in the revised design he gave it a distinctive form, a domed, colonnaded structure raised on a podium (Fig. 5). Besides providing a strong focal point for the university, this change may have been prompted by President Low (who donated the money to erect the library) in order to enhance its role as a civic monument. Low, a businessman and civic leader rather than an academician, was about to declare himself a candidate for mayor of New York, and the transformation of Low Library into the domed focus of the whole university gave it increased value as a memorial to the philanthropist.[36]

The Low Library at Columbia is often compared with Jefferson's Rotunda at the University of Virginia. The evolution of McKim's design suggests that this was probably not a principal source.[37] But Jefferson's design, which soon became a popular model in American college planning, nevertheless played a prominent role in the work of McKim, Mead & White. In 1895, the Rotunda of the University of Virginia was severely damaged by fire, and Stanford White was hired to remodel the building and to design additional academic structures for the southern end of Jefferson's Lawn (Fig. 182).[38] And beginning in 1892, White had designed a new campus for New York University, which also featured a domed library and recalled Jefferson's Virginia plan (as well as Ramée's design for Union College) (Fig. 183).[39] This design by White, and McKim's plan for Columbia, with their monumental compositions of urban buildings culminating in the focal point of the library—the heart of a research institution—were probably the first truly successful applications of Beaux-Arts principles to the problem of the new American university. And they became models for numerous schools.

At the close of the nineteenth century, architectural competitions became a common method of choosing designs for universities. This procedure itself was a reflection of the Beaux-Arts tradition, with its emphasis on design contests like the Prix de Rome, and the practice played an important role in introducing Beaux-Arts attitudes to American schools. Colleges and universities that held

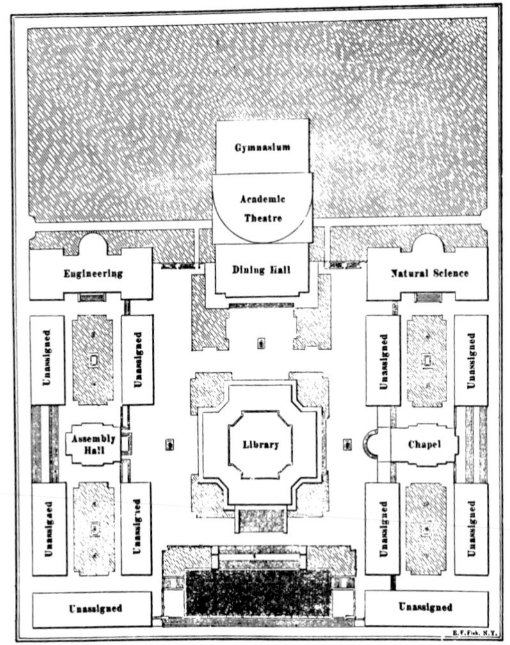

180

181

180 Columbia University, New York City. Master plan, as revised in 1894, by Charles F. McKim of McKim, Mead & White. Area is bounded (*bottom and top*) by 116th and 120th streets, and (*left and right*) by Broadway and Amsterdam Avenue.
(*Harper's Weekly*, November 3, 1894, p. 1036)

181 Columbia University. Rendering of master plan by McKim, of 1895, looking north toward the Hudson River.
(*King's New York Views*, 1905. Courtesy of Francesco Passanti)

182 Plan of the University of Virginia, showing additions proposed by McKim, Mead & White, ca. 1898. At top is Jefferson's Rotunda, which was damaged by fire in 1895 and rebuilt by Stanford White. At bottom, closing southern end of the Lawn, are proposed academic buildings.
(*A Monograph of the Work of McKim Mead and White, 1879–1915*, vol. 2, New York, 1915, pl. 110. Courtesy Architectural Book Publishing Co.)

183 New York University. Rendering of master plan for the new University Heights campus of the school, by Stanford White, ca. 1893. Principal, domed structure is the library. Semicircular colonnade is Hall of Fame, intended to commemorate notable Americans.
(Joshua L. Chamberlain, *New York University*, vol. 1, Boston, 1901, p. 187)

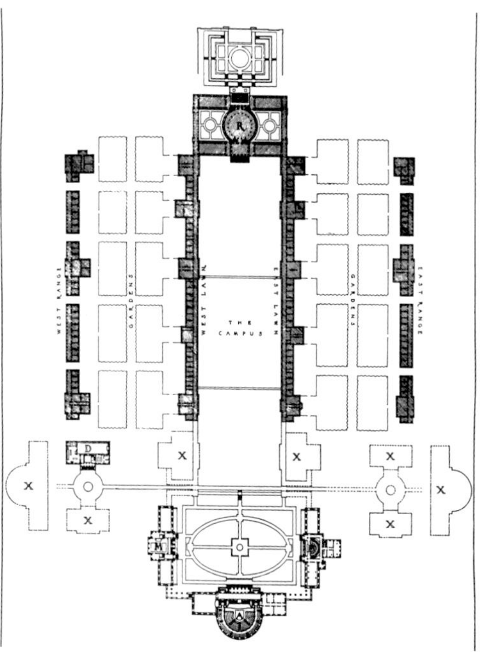

182

183

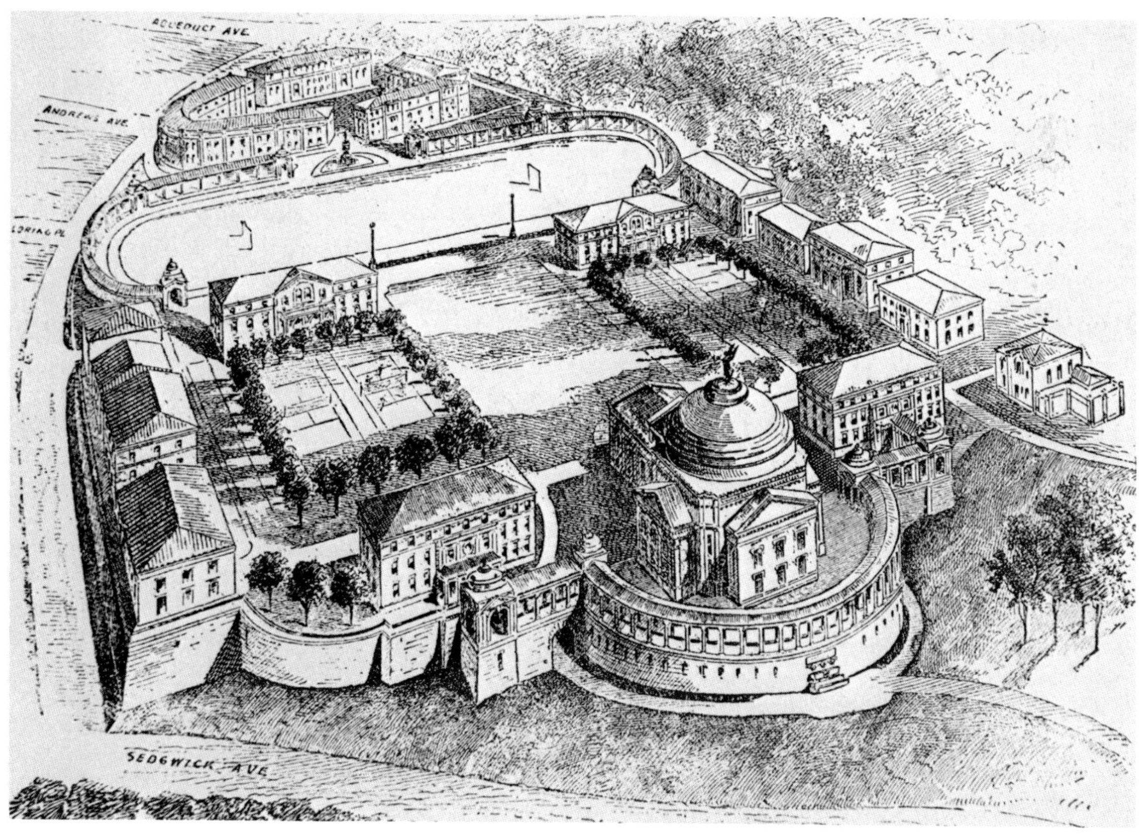

competitions for master plans during this period included the University of California at Berkeley, Washington University in St. Louis, the United States Military Academy at West Point, the Carnegie Schools in Pittsburgh (now Carnegie-Mellon University), the University of Minnesota, and the Western University of Pennsylvania (now the University of Pittsburgh).[40]

The designs for the University of California at Berkeley, probably more than any others, epitomized the new Beaux-Arts attitudes toward university planning, and suggested both their potential and their dangers. Olmsted's park-like plan for the Berkeley campus, of the 1860s (Fig. 144), never was executed, and by the 1890s the school consisted of several widely spaced structures dotting the dramatic site that sloped down toward the San Francisco Bay. The university was growing rapidly, reflecting not only the general trends in American education but more specifically the growth of California. As the state university, it saw itself as embodying the seemingly unlimited potential of California and the American West, and it was eager to express this vision in physical form.[41] In 1895 the local architect Bernard Maybeck, who had studied at the Ecole des Beaux-Arts, began promoting the idea of a master plan worthy of the university, and the notion was enthusiastically endorsed by the university trustees, one of whom described his vision of "an architectural pile of stately and glorious buildings which shall rival the dreams of the builders of the Columbian Exposition, and shall do honor and justice to a superb Republic and to its most favored State."[42]

Maybeck himself produced sketches of a proposed plan, a bold and sweeping composition of semicircular colonnades and domed structures crowning the vistas (Fig. 184).[43] But then he suggested the idea of an international competition for a master plan, an enterprise which Phoebe Apperson Hearst (wife of the publisher and benefactress of the university) offered to finance. She eventually lavished $200,000 on the affair, which, besides being one of the grandest architectural competitions in American history, had a major influence on university planning by focusing attention on its architectural possibilities and by "bringing about a sweeping victory for formal design," as the planner Werner Hegemann wrote two decades later.[44] From the beginning, the competition and its program strongly reflected Beaux-Arts principles (its consultants even included Professor Julien Guadet from the Ecole in Paris), and the prospectus that was sent to architects around the world in 1897 revealed the extraordinary scope and idealism of the project. Large numbers of buildings and facilities were called for, but most remarkable was the visionary tone of the prospectus and its emphasis on the aesthetic nature of the enterprise:

> It is seldom in any age that an artist has had a chance to express his thought so freely, on so large a scale, and with such entire exemption from the influence of discordant surroundings. Here there will be at least twenty-eight buildings, all mutually related and, at the same time, entirely cut off from anything that could mar the effect of the picture. In fact, it is a city that is to be created—a City of Learning—in which there is to be no sordid or inharmonious feature. There are to be no definite limitations of cost, materials or style. All is to be left to the unfettered discretion of the designer. He is asked to record his conception of an ideal home for a University, assuming time and resources to be unlimited. He is to plan for centuries to come. . . . The architect will simply design; others must provide the cost.[45]

The university was not as wealthy as this suggested. But in their unbounded enthusiasm the promoters of the competition believed that an inspiring master plan would elicit the needed funds from the state legislature and private benefactors (a belief shared by countless other college administrators and planners before and since, usually in vain). The University of California's vaunted largesse attracted worldwide attention, and even prompted an orator at Oxford University to proclaim wistfully: "To us Oxonians, who bear uncomplainingly our poverty and lessened revenues, is brought a report that in California there is already established a university furnished with so great resources that even to the architects (a lavish kind of men) full permission has been given to spare no expense."[46]

The Hearst competition in 1899 attracted a wide range of ambitious entries from America and abroad, from which the jury chose the winning designs—nearly all of them by Beaux-Arts-trained

184

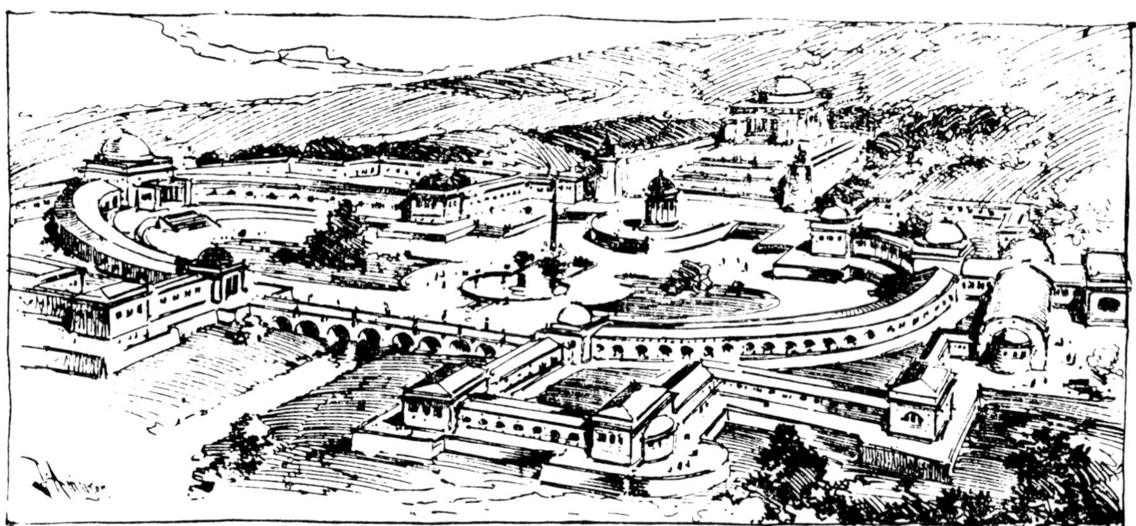

184 Rendering of design for the University of California, Berkeley, by Bernard Maybeck, 1896.
(*San Francisco Examiner*, April 30, 1896. Courtesy of Kenneth Cardwell)

architects—which were then exhibited and published.[47] Despite their common adherence to Beaux-Arts principles, the successful designs fell into two groups, the American entries being generally more open and spacious, the European entries more compact and urban. Typical of the latter was the design awarded first prize, by Emile Bénard of France, a beautifully worked-out scheme whose mastery of Beaux-Arts principles and techniques evidently dazzled the jury (Figs. 185–187).

Bénard took very literally the program's reference to a "City of Learning" and created a classic Beaux-Arts urban plan, with the buildings arranged along axial boulevards and around city squares devoted to the various academic disciplines, and linked to the community outside by continuous streets and trolley-car lines. The principal entrance to the university, from the south, would lead into a "College Square" by way of a tremendously ornate Baroque rotunda in the university gymnasium (Fig. 187). This incongruity of form and function probably reflected Bénard's ignorance of American education. To him, the gymnasium and adjacent stadium were apparently potential settings for academic festivities and pomp, as his renderings of these spaces suggested, and had little to do with the realities of American collegiate athletics (Fig. 186). In this and other ways, the University of California trustees got the "artistic" plan they had asked for in the competition, but it was not fully appropriate for an American school. Nor was it very suitable to the steep and rugged site at Berkeley. Bénard went to California to revise his plan, but when he refused to stay on as supervising architect, the university hired a runner-up in the competition, John Galen Howard, to assume this post, and Bénard's plan eventually was modified beyond recognition.[48]

The designs for the Berkeley campus submitted by American architects were more influential. The second-prize winner, the firm of Howells, Stokes & Hornbostel, and the fourth-place winners, John Galen Howard and S. M. Cauldwell, were typical of several of the American entrants in their use of a pattern reminiscent of Jefferson's design for the University of Virginia, with a central mall flanked by academic buildings and terminating in a domed structure, although superimposed on this were cross-axes and subsidiary spaces (Fig. 188). After Howard was chosen as the university architect, he produced a master plan for the campus that followed this basic concept, typifying a pattern common in campus planning by that time.[49]

185 University of California, Berkeley. Rendering of design awarded first prize in the Hearst competition, 1899, by Emile Bénard. View from the west, looking toward the Berkeley hills. In foreground, at western end of the plan's main axis, is a square dominated by the Library. A larger square, at the center of plan, was closed at its southern end by the monumental Gymnasium (on the right in this drawing). Dormitories and other facilities were to be located at the eastern end of the main axis, ascending the hills.
(*The International Competition for the Phoebe Hearst Architectural Plan for the University of California*, 1899, p. 45)

186 Design by Bénard for the stadium, University of California, Berkeley, 1899. (*The International Competition for the Phoebe Hearst Architectural Plan for the University of California*, 1899, p. 52)

185

186

188

187 Design by Bénard for "Entrance Vestibule of Gymnasium," University of California, Berkeley, 1899.
(College of Environmental Design Documents Collection, University of California, Berkeley)

188 University of California, Berkeley. Rendering of fourth-prize design in the Hearst competition, by John Galen Howard and S. M. Cauldwell, 1899. Howard later was chosen as campus architect, and oversaw transformation of Bénard's plan and execution of the university buildings, from 1901 to 1924.
(College of Environmental Design Documents Collection, University of California, Berkeley)

The Appearance of College Planning Theory

Around 1900, numerous articles appeared in American magazines on the subject of college and university planning, the first examples of a substantial literature in this field. Their authors generally took a Beaux-Arts approach to campus design, which tended to color their views of the physical characteristics of the American school. In an article published in 1897, the art critic Ashton Willard criticized the traditional American campus for being simply a group of independent buildings, unrelated to one another in any unified way.[50] This idea was elaborated in 1903 by the architect and educator A. D. F. Hamlin.[51] He too complained that older American college buildings were "wholly unrelated architecturally" to one another, but he found hopeful signs in current developments. He stated that "a nation that has many new buildings to erect and plenty of money to spend upon them is sure to develop a characteristic architecture," which will be "an index of its artistic taste," and he found that collegiate architecture was beginning to make a contribution in this area. New college buildings were generally "more artistic in design, more monumental in effect," and often conformed to a unifying master plan.

A good master plan was especially important now, Hamlin noted, because of the complexity of the modern university, which, in contrast to the two or three simple buildings adequate for an earlier college, now required libraries, laboratories, lecture halls, gymnasia, administration buildings, dining halls, and clubhouses. The main task facing the planner was to create a "general unity of effect" out of all these disparate elements, and to produce visual harmony and order. Successful examples cited by Hamlin included McKim's Columbia, the new buildings of New York University and the City College of New York, the master plan for Stanford, and the "unexampled magnificence" of the Hearst competition designs for Berkeley. He claimed that these efforts disproved the charge that Americans devoted themselves solely to commerce and materialism and that they showed the country's equal dedication to culture and learning.

A similar call for "art" and "unity" was made in 1909 by the architect Claude Bragdon, in an article on "The Growth of Taste" in American architecture. Bragdon pointed proudly to "the newly acquired architectural beauty and dignity of many of our schools and colleges," and sug-

189 United States Naval Academy, Annapolis, Maryland. Master plan for development of the campus, by Ernest Flagg, ca. 1900.
(*The American Architect and Building News*, July 1, 1908, p. 2)

190 Rendering of Flagg's design for the United States Naval Academy, looking to the southwest from the Severn River. In center is the Chapel, flanked by Cadet Quarters (*left*) and Academy Group (*right*).
(*The American Architect and Building News*, July 1, 1908, p. 2)

187

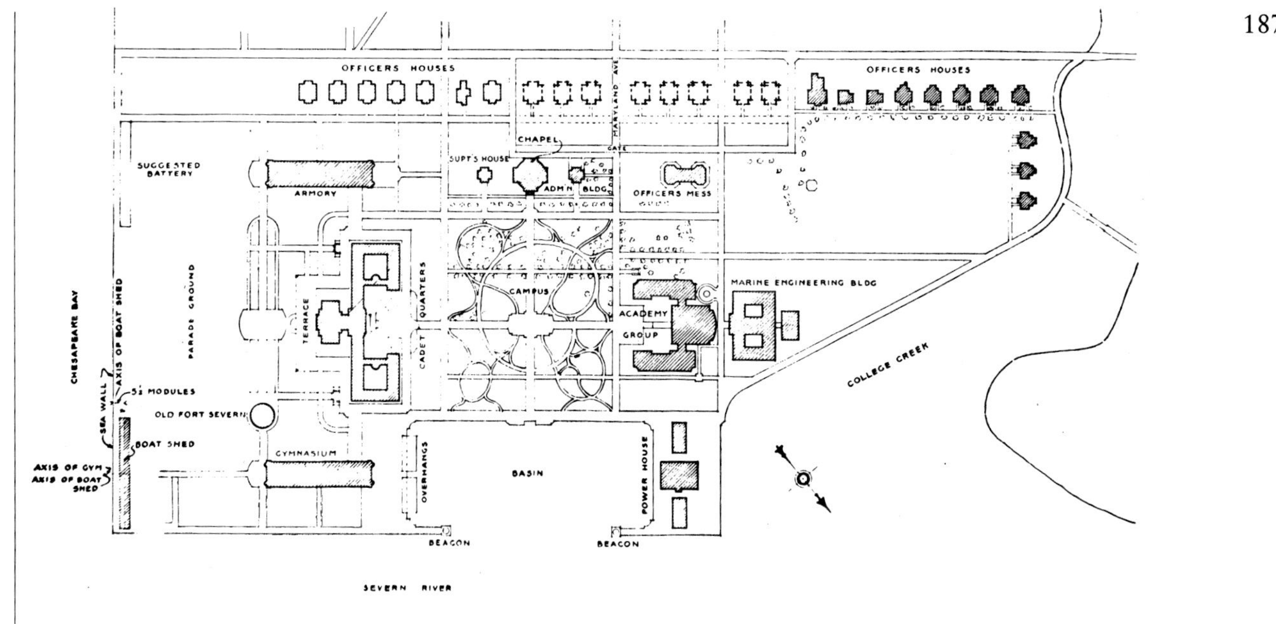
OFFICERS HOUSES
OFFICERS HOUSES
CHAPEL
SUPT'S HOUSE
ADMN BLDG
GATE
MARYLAND AVE
OFFICERS MESS
SUGGESTED BATTERY
ARMORY
PARADE GROUND
TERRACE
CADET QUARTERS
CAMPUS
ACADEMY GROUP
MARINE ENGINEERING BLDG
COLLEGE CREEK
CHESAPEAKE BAY
SEA WALL
AXIS OF BOAT SHED
5½ MODULES
OLD FORT SEVERN
BOAT SHED
AXIS OF GYM
AXIS OF BOAT SHED
GYMNASIUM
OVERHANGS
BASIN
POWER HOUSE
BEACON
BEACON
SEVERN RIVER

189

190

gested that the question of what style to build in was less important than the achievement of "harmony and coherence," with all the buildings on a campus conforming to the same style.[52]

In 1906–7 the Ecole-trained Alfred Morton Githens published a series of articles on "group plans," or the design of ensembles of buildings.[53] Githens presented a classically Beaux-Arts analysis, by dividing plans into categories based on their overall shapes or *partis*—such as the "closed court," the "open court," the "line," the "avenue," and the "unsymmetrical composition on two axes." Many of the examples he used to illustrate these categories were recent American campus plans (Fig. 197).[54] Githens pointed out that choosing between such plan-types was more than a simply aesthetic matter, involving as it did many functional and topographic considerations. But like the other writers of the period, his analysis of college planning was predominantly formalistic and visual, with emphasis on "unity of composition," "central vistas," and the like.

Implicit in these calls for unified and artistic campus plans was the assumption that the master plan drawn by an architect would be executed faithfully by a school. The danger of such an assumption was soon pointed out by several writers, including the architectural critic Montgomery Schuyler, who recalled in 1910 that

> the history of American collegiate architecture [shows] that the original architect, essaying to set a point of departure for his successors, is commonly found to have done so in the sense only that they depart from his work as speedily and as widely as possible.[55]

But even college officials fully aware of the dangers of master plans usually favored their use. A trustee of Columbia University wrote in 1914:

> While the adoption of a comprehensive plan does not insure its realization, it is none the less essential for an intelligent beginning, and it has often proved that the mere existence of such a plan has done much to further its realization.[56]

Around 1900, architects working within the Beaux-Arts context began coming to a consensus about the most suitable plan-types or *partis* for the American college or university. First of all, it was recognized by most that the campus, or large open space, was an essential part of the American tradition—"distinctly an American feature," as Githens said, and "the natural center for an American scholastic group."[57] Buildings could be arranged around a campus in various ways. They could form roughly a square, as in Cornell's main quadrangle, although this had the disadvantage, to Beaux-Arts eyes, of creating no dominant axis. Preferable was an elongated campus, open at one end or partially at one side, but within this formula there were endless possible variations.

Another early Beaux-Arts campus plan was produced in the late 1890s by the Ecole-trained Ernest Flagg for the United States Naval Academy at Annapolis (Figs. 189, 190). Flagg kept the existing campus as the center of his scheme, with one side of the square open to the water and the opposite end dominated by his high-domed chapel based on the church of Les Invalides in Paris.[58] On the other two sides, Flagg created monumental groupings, one for the academic center and the other for cadet quarters, each with an open courtyard and in a grand style that was more authentically French Baroque than anything else on an American campus (Fig. 191). With their evocation of the courts of Louis XIV and his successors, these lavish and urbane structures suggested something about America's imperial power and prestige, but they were somewhat incongruous with the less formal (and more American) tree-filled, spacious campus around which they were placed—and they thus suggested a potential conflict between the Beaux-Arts system and the traditional American campus.

191

191 United States Naval Academy. Central pavilion of Cadet Quarters, designed by Ernest Flagg.
(*The American Architect and Building News*, July 8, 1908, pl. 19)

192 Harvard Medical School, Boston, Massachusetts, designed by Shepley, Rutan & Coolidge, and constructed in 1906. Redrawn from a plan by A. A. Shurtleff.

193 American University, Washington, D.C. Rendering of master plan for the campus by Henry Ives Cobb, ca. 1898. In the early 1890s, Frederick Law Olmsted and his firm had suggested an informal, park-like plan for the new institution; but its founder, Bishop John Fletcher Hurst, favored a classical plan; in 1896 architects Van Brunt & Howe proposed a scheme with two formal malls, which was revised by Cobb as shown here.
(Office of University Relations, The American University)

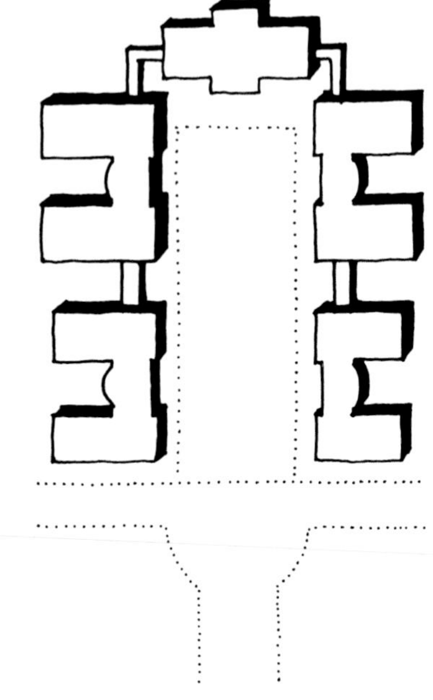

192

193

The Jeffersonian Revival

The most popular pattern for a campus that emerged at this time, within the Beaux-Arts context, was based on the form of Jefferson's University of Virginia: an extended rectangular space, defining a longitudinal axis, with a dominant structure as focal point at one end and subsidiary buildings ranged along the sides (Fig. 71). The University of Virginia had exerted little influence on American college design in the nineteenth century. But around 1900, Jefferson's plan was in a sense rediscovered, no doubt for a number of reasons, including the new classical taste inspired by the Chicago World's Fair, and a surge of interest in America's architectural heritage. Moreover, the fire that damaged Jefferson's Rotunda in 1895, followed by Stanford White's remodeling of it, brought the Virginia campus into the national news and also helped popularize it.

But while Beaux-Arts architects generally approved of Jefferson's design, they were not totally satisfied with it, and subjected it to transformations in their own plans. Some were embarrassed by Jefferson's unorthodox handling of classical forms—"childlike and naive," said one writer in 1897, and another sniffed that the stark Rotunda "slightly suggests a gas tank."[59] But some also found fault with the overall plan of Jefferson's campus. The Beaux-Arts system was at its best in creating unity out of variety, and Jefferson's plan did not have quite the right kind of variety. Cross-axes and secondary spaces were needed to create a hierarchy of parts and to support the principal forms. There was also a practical problem with the Virginia *parti*. The modern college or university needed many more buildings and facilities than were required in Jefferson's day, and to arrange them all around a single space produced an awkwardly large scale. This danger was apparent in McKim, Mead & White's 1903 plan for the War College in Washington, D.C., which for topographic reasons had to assume this simple, elongated rectangular form.[60] Of the few institutions that used the pure, single-axis Jeffersonian plan during this period, most were specialized schools that did not have to accommodate the full panoply of university functions—such as the Harvard Medical School in Boston, designed by Shepley, Rutan & Coolidge in about 1905 (Fig. 192).[61]

Architects modified the Jeffersonian pattern in various ways, principally with the Beaux-Arts device of creating secondary axes and subsidiary groupings of buildings. A perpendicular axis could be added at the open end of the campus, a solution used by Stanford White at the University of Virginia itself in his additions of the late 1890s, and by Henry Ives Cobb in his master plan of about 1899 for the American University in Washington, D.C. (Figs. 182, 193).[62] A variation of this was used by Henry Hornbostel—who had studied at the Ecole des Beaux-Arts—in his competition-winning design for the Carnegie Schools in Pittsburgh of 1900, now the Carnegie-Mellon University (Fig. 194). (In 1908, Hornbostel's firm won another competition in the same city, for the new campus of the University of Pittsburgh; it was an unusual plan in which several rows of buildings formed a kind of procession up the hilly site, crowned by a temple-like structure and other buildings, suggesting an academic acropolis [Figs. 195, 196].)[63]

In 1904, the Johns Hopkins University, rejecting the policies of its early days, decided to move from its urban buildings in Baltimore and to create a master-planned campus outside the city. A competition was held, and the winning design, by the firm of Parker, Thomas & Rice, devised another variation on the theme of intersecting cross-axes (Figs. 197, 198).[64] In both the Carnegie and the Johns Hopkins plans, topographic considerations also led to the inclusion of extra groups of buildings placed diagonally to the main axes, a practical expediency allowed in the Beaux-Arts system, which made the axial *partis* easier to apply to hilly or irregular sites.

Another variation on the Virginia pattern rotated the axis of the space so that it was perpendicular to the axis of the principal building. McKim, Mead & White did this in their design for New York University in the 1890s; and in 1902 Ralph Adams Cram combined this pattern with another axial space, creating three intersecting axes, in his design for Sweet Briar College in Virginia, which was praised several years later in a book on American architecture as being "more pleasing, lighter and freer" than Jefferson's design (Figs. 183, 199, 200).[65]

Cass Gilbert, in his competition-winning master plan for the University of Minnesota in Minneapolis, of 1908, combined a Jeffersonian mall with a large space resembling a city square, and flanked them with subsidiary courtyards and groups of

194

194 Carnegie Technical Schools (now Carnegie-Mellon University), Pittsburgh, Pennsylvania. Master plan for campus, by Palmer & Hornbostel, ca. 1900. Most of the buildings around the main space (housing primarily classrooms and workshops) were executed, but structures shown at upper right were not built. (*The American Architect and Building News*, February 25, 1905, no. 1522)

195 Western University of Pennsylvania, Pittsburgh (now the University of Pittsburgh). Master plan by Palmer & Hornbostel, 1908. Only a portion of this competition-winning plan for a hilly site in Pittsburgh was executed, principally several buildings toward the bottom (east) of this plan, along Bayard Street. In succeeding years the university developed more toward the east. (*Architectural Review*, July 1908, p. 117)

196 Elevation drawing of Palmer & Hornbostel's master plan for the University of Pittsburgh, 1908. (*Architectural Review*, July 1908, p. 117)

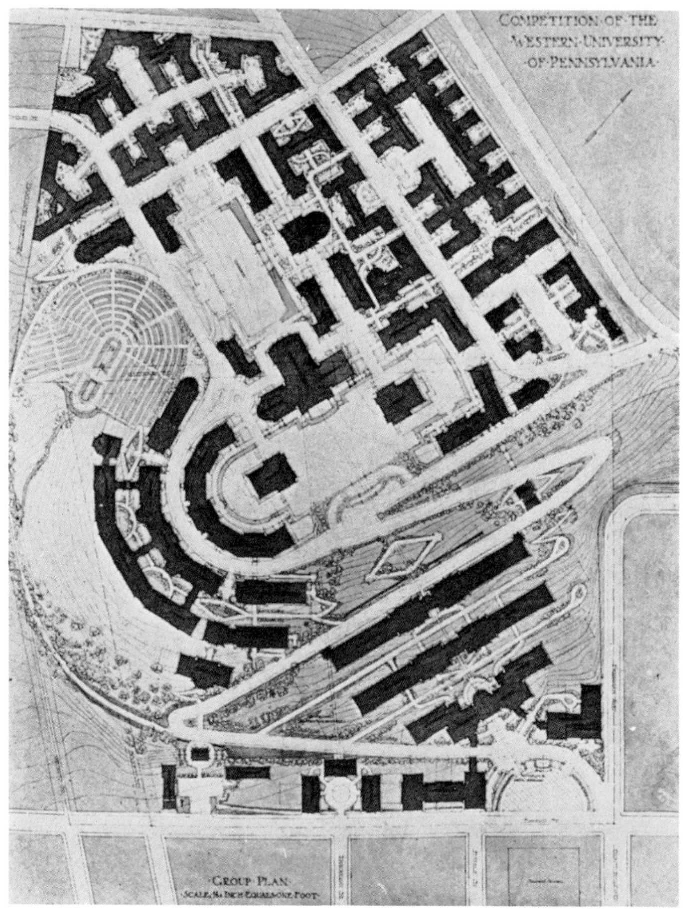
COMPETITION OF THE WESTERN UNIVERSITY OF PENNSYLVANIA
GROUP PLAN

195

196

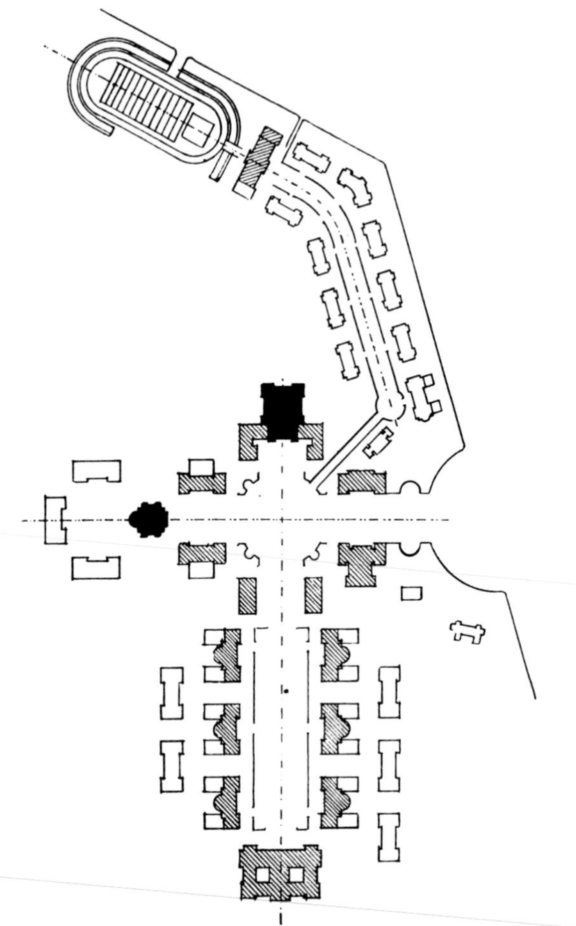

197

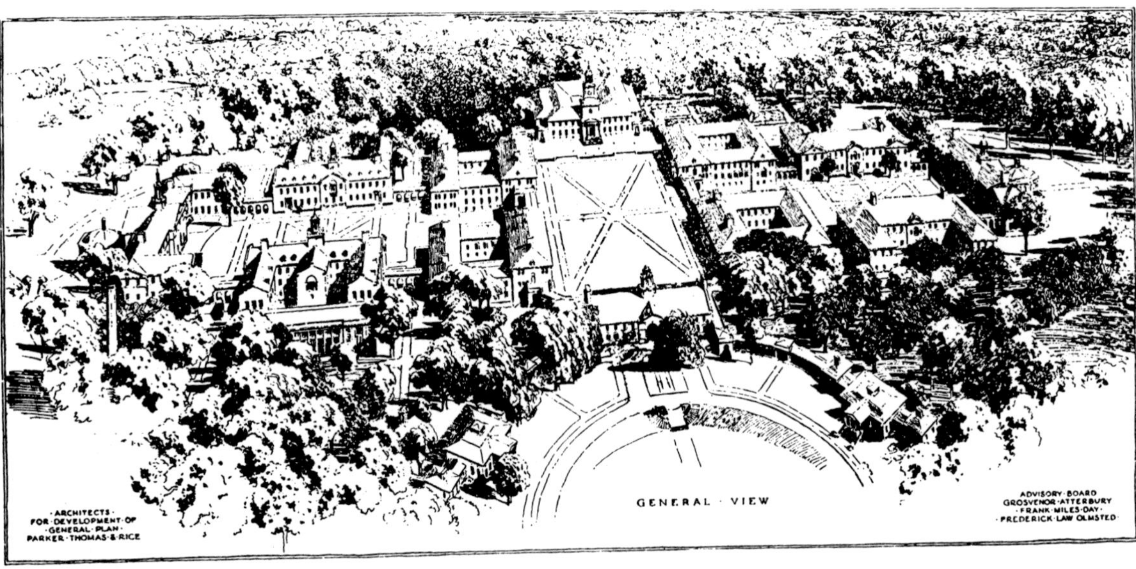

198

197 Johns Hopkins University. Master plan for new campus, outside Baltimore, Maryland, by Parker, Thomas & Rice, 1904. This schematic drawing was published in 1907 in an article by Alfred M. Githens advocating Beaux-Arts principles of design, and categorizing various types of campus plans. Githens used this plan to illustrate the "Unsymmetrical Composition on Two Axes." (*The Brickbuilder*, December 1907, p. 224)

198 Rendering of master plan for Johns Hopkins University, by Parker, Thomas & Rice, 1904. Serving as planning consultants were Grosvenor Atterbury, Frank Miles Day, and Frederick Law Olmsted, Jr. (*Architectural Record*, June 1915, p. 482)

199 Sweet Briar College, Sweet Briar, Virginia. Rendering of master plan by Cram, Goodhue & Ferguson, ca. 1901. To left is main campus space, formed by academic buildings and dominated by domed Commencement Hall. To right is a secondary courtyard, formed by dormitories, Refectory, and Chapel. (*The American Architect and Building News*, August 23, 1902, no. 1391)

200 Design for Commencement Hall, Sweet Briar College. Drawing by Bertram Goodhue, ca. 1901.
(*The American Architect and Building News*, August 30, 1902)

buildings in a dense pattern appropriate to the urban location (Figs. 201, 202).[66] Yet Gilbert also provided an area of parkland (in the formal, French manner) where the central axis met the Mississippi river. Next to Bénard's design for Berkeley, this was perhaps the most authentically French Beaux-Arts plan for an American campus. Moreover, as the university was constructed in succeeding years, the plan was largely followed—except for the area closest to the river, where Gilbert's Versailles-like vision gave way to a jumble of miscellaneous structures and parking lots (always a danger when an architect designates an area as "park" or "garden").

Another type of urban solution was devised by the Ecole-trained Welles Bosworth in his 1913 design for the new Massachusetts Institute of Technology, which was moved across the Charles River from Boston to Cambridge (Figs. 203, 204).[67] Bosworth rejected the American tradition of separate buildings in favor of one great structure, with wings extending from the central dome to embrace a large courtyard open to the river, thus uniting two traditions, the French *cour d'honneur* and the Jeffersonian rotunda.

In succeeding years, the University of Virginia pattern and related Beaux-Arts *partis* were used in master plans for countless schools around the country, including Rice University in Houston, Emory University in Atlanta, Southern Methodist University in Dallas, the University of Delaware, the University of Rochester, the University of California at Los Angeles, the women's campus of Duke University, the Yale Divinity School, the Harvard Business School, the University of Southern California, and the University of Maryland (Figs. 205–207).[68]

In describing the Beaux-Arts campus, a distinction should be made between the overall pattern of a plan and the architectural "style" in which it was executed. The actual styles of the buildings at Beaux-Arts campuses varied widely, and included not only all the standard classical modes but medieval styles as well. This reflected the Beaux-Arts premise that the ground plan was supreme, and that once a good plan was drawn it could be executed in almost any style, although the classical styles generally were preferred. In reality, the more opulent Renaissance and Baroque styles commonly associated with the French Beaux-

201

201 University of Minnesota, on the Mississippi River, Minneapolis. Rendering of master plan by Cass Gilbert, 1910. At end of main axis is library. In front of it, mall and departmental buildings flanking it constitute the Upper Campus; three-sided quadrangle of structures below is the Lower Campus. The essential form of this plan was carried out, although with modifications. (University of Minnesota)

202

202 Rendering of design for buildings at the University of Minnesota, by Cass Gilbert, 1910.
(University of Minnesota)

203 Massachusetts Institute of Technology, on Charles River, Cambridge. Rendering of main group of buildings in master plan by William Welles Bosworth, ca. 1913.
(The M.I.T. Museum and Historical Collections)

204 Central building, M.I.T., designed by W. W. Bosworth, completed in 1916.
(The M.I.T. Museum and Historical Collections)

203

204

205

206

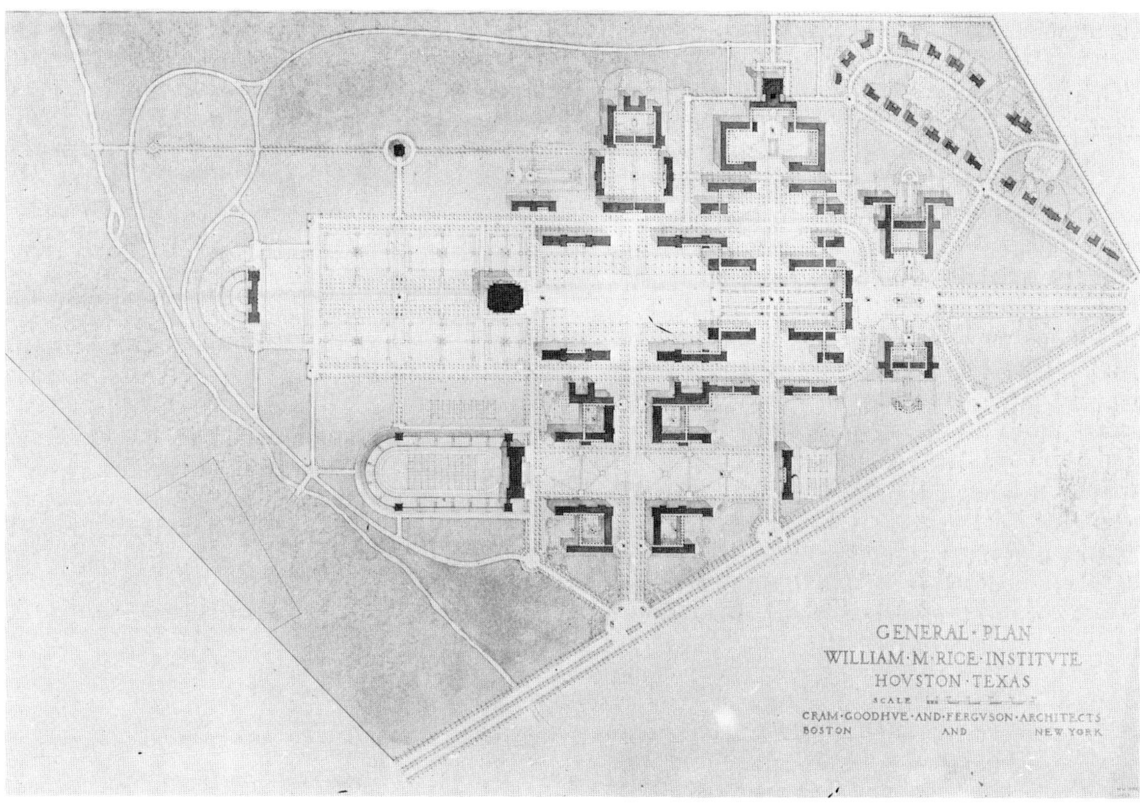

207

205 Emory University, Atlanta, Georgia. Rendering of master plan for school by Henry Hornbostel, 1915. (Emory University, Special Collections)

206 University of California, Los Angeles. Rendering of master plan by George W. Kelham, 1926. (University of California, Los Angeles)

207 Master plan for the William M. Rice Institute (now Rice University), Houston, Texas, by Cram, Goodhue & Ferguson, 1910. (University Archives, Woodson Research Center, Rice University Library)

Arts tradition were seldom used for the American campus (Flagg's work at Annapolis was an exception), more austere styles being considered better suited to an atmosphere of learning, as well as being cheaper to build.

The monumental Roman manner used by McKim for the library at Columbia became relatively common (Fig. 5), but more popular were the various styles called "Colonial" or "Georgian," because of their American associations. Some schools chose "Colonial" to stress their antiquity or their adherence to traditional American virtues, or to conform with existing structures. The architecture at the new campus of Johns Hopkins was fashioned to echo the style of an eighteenth-century mansion located on the university's new site.[69] Sometimes a particular style was considered appropriate to a school's orientation or curriculum, as when Bosworth's stark interpretation of classicism at M.I.T. was described as having "an austerity that suggests steel and concrete" (Fig. 204).[70]

Other schools chose styles thought to be expressive of their geographical locations. Cram's design for Sweet Briar contained allusions to the work of Jefferson and other Virginian architecture, and Hornbostel proposed an Italian Renaissance mode for Emory University because of supposed similarities in flora and topography between Northern Italy and the area around Atlanta (Figs. 199, 200, 205).[71] When hired to make a master plan for the Rice Institute in Houston (now Rice University), Cram found, as he later recalled, "no possible *point d'appui*, . . . no historical or stylistic precedent, and no ideas imposed by the President or Trustees," so he invented a style he considered suitable to a Mediterranean-like climate, combining "all the elements I could from Southern France and Italy, Dalmatia, the Peloponnesus, Byzantium, Anatolia, Syria, Sicily, Spain" (Figs. 208, 209).[72] But despite such imaginative eclecticism in the architectural style of the individual buildings, Cram's overall plan for Rice followed standard Beaux-Arts principles, with groups of buildings forming open and closed courtyards, arranged hierarchically along major and minor axes (Fig. 207). The scale of the plan was tremendously ambitious, and was never fully executed. But despite this, and the inevitable alterations to the design over the years, the spirit of Cram's concept was effectively maintained as the campus developed.

The case of the Gothic style was somewhat different, since it was considered by some architects to be antithetical to the Beaux-Arts spirit, and it inspired its own aesthetic of campus planning. But the use of the Gothic in a classical context was defended by some planners, such as Werner Hegemann, who shared the Beaux-Arts tolerance and flexibility in the matter of style:

> The use of the forms of the Gothic [or other medieval styles] upon plans of Renaissance character is not necessarily contradictory, [since the] sinuosity of old Gothic plans was caused by conditions of crowding and lack of space which should not prevail on the American campus. It is therefore not surprising that modern designers in Gothic have produced plans for college grounds . . . perfectly balanced and axiated according to the best modern ideas.[73]

208

209

208 Design for Administration Building, Rice Institute, by Cram, Goodhue & Ferguson, ca. 1910. (University Archives, Woodson Research Center, Rice University Library)

209 Central part of Administration Building, Rice Institute, constructed 1910–1912. (University Archives, Woodson Research Center, Rice University Library)

The Problem of the Existing Campus

Most of the campus plans mentioned so far were either for new schools, or for schools that were moving to new sites and therefore able to start with a clean slate. This was the ideal condition for the Beaux-Arts architect, with his overriding concern for the unity and harmony of the whole. For an architect like Githens, older colleges that had "grown up haphazard," with buildings of different ages and "incongruous styles," were "less fortunate" than new schools, for the older ones possessed "no unity of effect in the ensemble, no group plan."[74] The English architect Charles R. Ashbee, surveying American universities, remarked that the newer ones "have an immense advantage over the older," although he conceded that Harvard's plan possessed a "pleasant sense of medieval muddle" (Fig. 210).[75] By the early years of the twentieth century, planners were beginning to address this problem, by persuading colleges to city-beautify their existing campuses.

At first this was done in rather timid ways. In 1903, A. D. F. Hamlin wrote, "It is . . . impossible to correct the chaos of an existing group of heterogeneous buildings, but it is at least possible to establish a definite plan and scheme to which all future additions shall conform."[76] Remedies like the planting of ivy were advocated to camouflage the disparate styles of existing buildings; and Montgomery Schuyler, writing about the older structures at Harvard, said, "to such raw and bald brick edifices as these, the parasitic vegetation does great good in its season."[77] But soon the planners were tackling the problem more boldly. In a 1912 article on the subject, Githens described the chaos of existing campuses, and the new interest in correcting it:

> Lately the colleges have sickened of their haphazard buildings and trustees have come to architectural advisors, "landscape" and otherwise, and each received something in the nature of a comprehensive plan, ingeniously contrived so that by moving a building here, tearing down a building there, building a new yonder, taking up the old meandering drives and paths and setting out straight ones, and so forth, their predecessors' sins might no longer be in evidence. . . .[78]

The idea was to transform an existing campus so that it would conform as closely as possible to the Beaux-Arts principles of planning: symmetry, axiality, focal points, and an overall geometric clarity. To achieve this, and yet retain most of the existing "haphazard" structures, was often a formidable challenge. The Olmsted firm (headed by Frederick Law Olmsted's two sons) and the landscape architect Warren H. Manning were among the professionals specializing in this procedure at the beginning of the twentieth century. As early as 1896, the Olmsted office had drawn up a plan for Harvard, which proposed new structures positioned so as to produce as much symmetry and axiality as possible in the existing arrangement of buildings (Fig. 211).[79] More drastic were Manning's proposals for Guilford College in North Carolina and Lake Forest University in Illinois, both of about 1909, which demonstrated the transformation of campus character that could be produced by this method (Fig. 212).[80]

One of the ironies of this procedure is that it was precisely the opposite of what had occurred at colleges about forty years earlier. At that time, when the fashion was informal planning and park-like settings, many schools had transformed their campuses by purposely destroying geometric patterns in the landscaping, roadways, and relationships of buildings—as happened at Hamilton College (Fig. 162).[81] Now architects were calling for the transformation back to geometric order, although the type of order they wanted was somewhat different, with the Beaux-Arts principles stressed now, rather than the earlier, simpler patterns such as that of the Yale Row. Some schools actually went through both transformations, from formality to informality to formality. Something like this happened at Princeton: In the early nineteenth century the school had located new buildings in a carefully symmetrical way; toward the end of the century President McCosh transformed it into an informal campus of asymmetrically placed structures; and at the beginning of the twentieth century the architect Ralph Adams Cram attempted to give it a new axial order (Figs. 85, 164, 235).

Even the architectural critic Montgomery Schuyler, although not strictly a partisan of the Beaux-Arts, was caught up in this new attitude about replanning campuses. In a series of articles on college architecture beginning in 1909, he savaged a number of existing schools for their chaotic

210 

210 View of Harvard Yard, ca. 1875. In foreground (*left*) is Appleton Chapel, built 1856, demolished 1931. In middle ground are University Hall, built 1813, and Thayer Hall, built 1869. Beyond these, obscured by trees, are colonial buildings of Harvard. Prominent tower in background is Unitarian Church of Cambridge.
(*Harper's New Monthly Magazine* January 1876, p. 197)

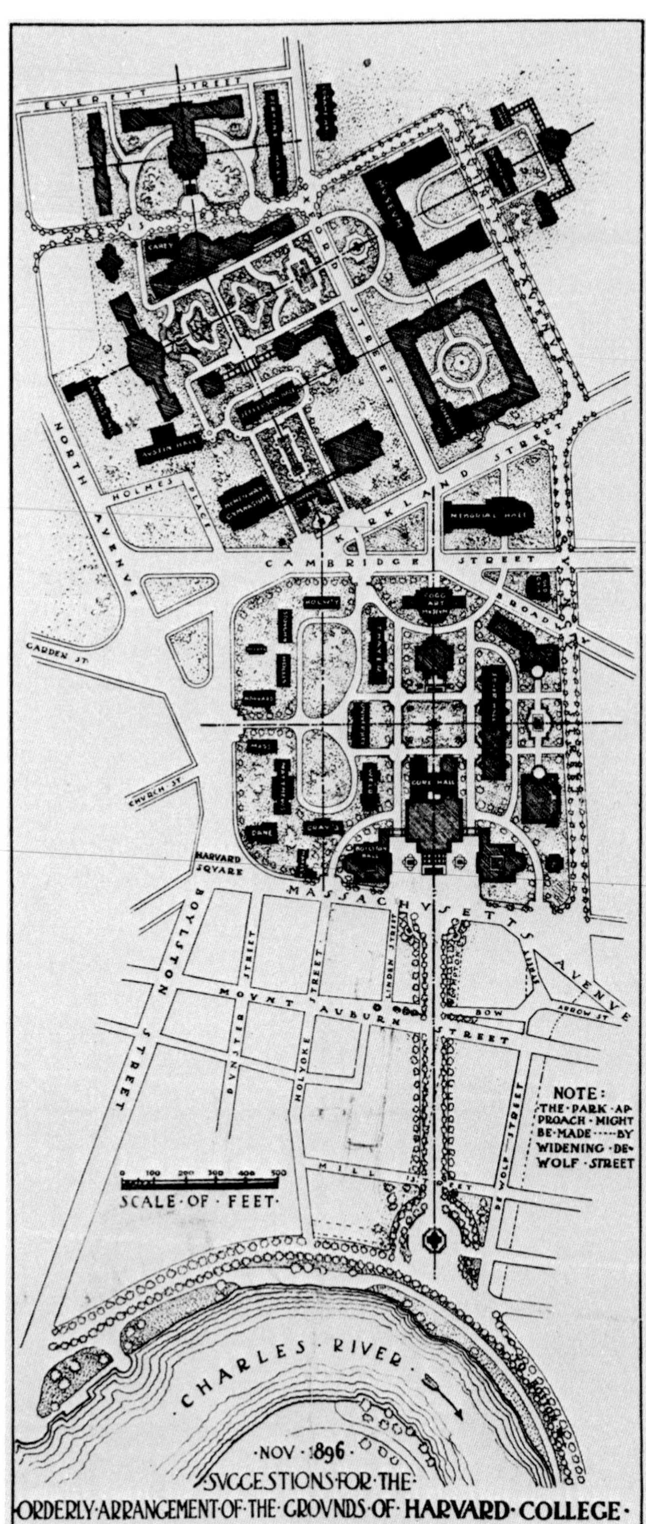

211 "Suggestions for the Orderly Arrangement of the Grounds of Harvard College." Development plan prepared by the Olmsted firm, 1896. New buildings were proposed in order to increase the symmetry and axiality of the campus, and a tree-lined avenue (or "Park Approach") was suggested, extending one of the axes from the Yard to the Charles River. None of this was executed.
(National Park Service, Frederick Law Olmsted National Historic Site)

212 Guilford College, Greensboro, North Carolina. Existing and proposed plans, drawn by Warren H. Manning, ca. 1909. In proposed plan (*right*) dark buildings are existing structures (minus several that Manning wished to demolish), while diagonally shaded buildings are new.
(*The Brickbuilder*, December 1912, p. 314)

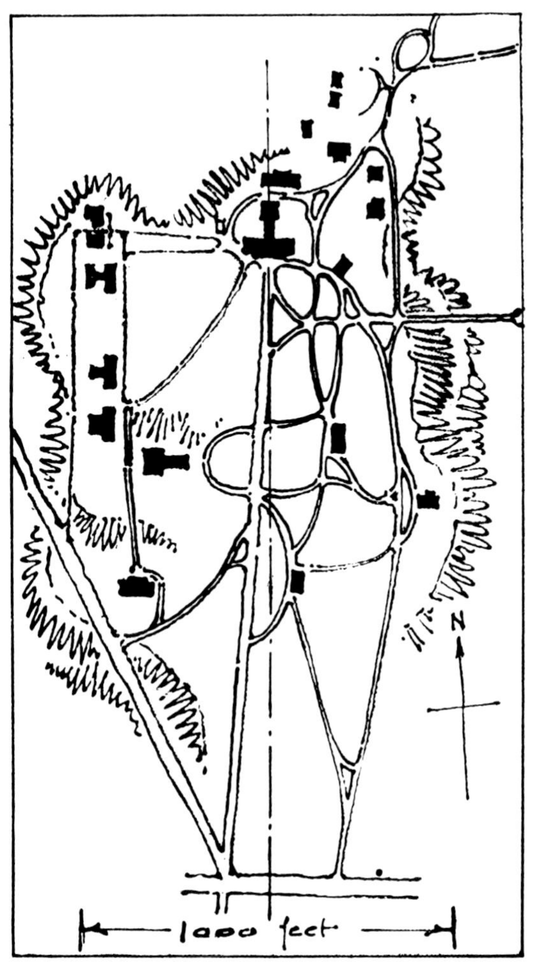

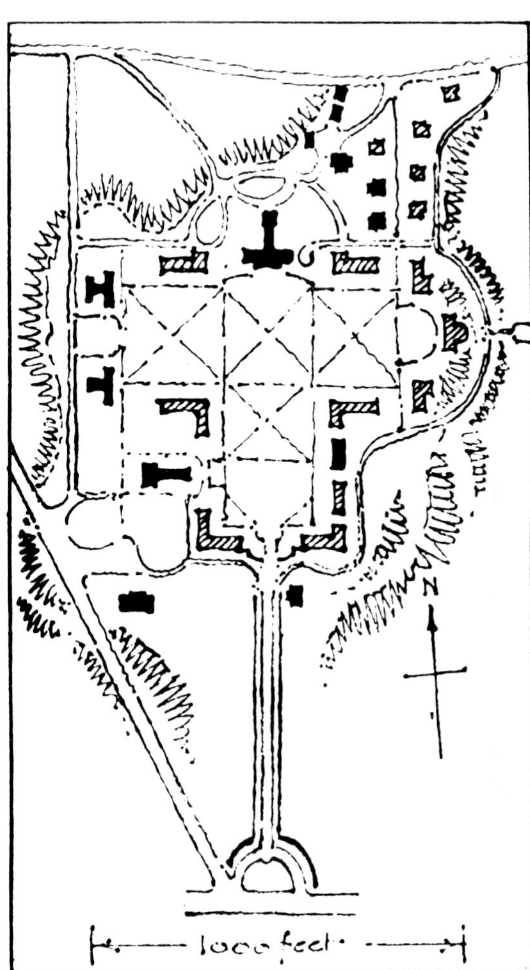

212

213

213 University of Wisconsin, Madison. "General Design for Future Constructional Development," by Paul Philippe Cret, Warren Powers Laird, and Arthur Peabody, 1908. (University of Wisconsin Archives)

plans and their lack of order.[82] In discussing Harvard, he stated that what it needed most (besides ivy) was "axes," with buildings arranged symmetrically around them, so that one would get "vistas" through the Yard to buildings serving as focal points. To achieve this, Schuyler went much further than the Olmsted plan for Harvard of 1896, and made an astounding proposal:

> It could be attained without any demolition, by the simple expedient of moving the buildings about. . . . Such a rearrangement might readily enable the visitor to see through, on the central line, from gate to gate, from Massachusetts Avenue to Cambridge Street, from gate to gate from Quincy Street to Peabody Street, to the enormous advantage of the general impression.[83]

Lest the reader not take him seriously, Schuyler later in his article argued again for "a mere moving about of the existing buildings" at Harvard, and included H. H. Richardson's massive Sever Hall among those to be relocated, in order to gain "an effective vista."

Few architects had the temerity to make such a proposal to their college clients. Typically, they recommended that a school demolish just a few of its structures that were "obsolete" or "impractical" (often meaning they were in the wrong place), and slowly add new buildings in an ordered geometric pattern. This was called a "comprehensive plan" or a "development plan," and it became one of the basic components of college planning in the twentieth century.

A notable early example of this type of design was the master plan for the University of Wisconsin at Madison, of 1908, by the French-born and Ecole-trained architect Paul Philippe Cret (Fig. 213). This design extended the rather modest mall of the existing campus, making it the central axis of a complex pattern of cross-axes, radiating vistas, and domed buildings serving as focal points in a classically Beaux-Arts organization.[84] Two years later, Cass Gilbert (who had produced the master plan for the University of Minnesota) was hired by the University of Texas at Austin, and created an ingenious development plan that managed to incorporate the irregularly sited existing buildings into a new, unified pattern, with two intersecting axes, four quadrangles of buildings at the corners of the site, and a dominating focal structure at the center.[85] The basic outlines of this plan were followed as construction proceeded in subsequent years. From 1930 to 1942, Paul Philippe Cret served as consulting architect for the university, producing a revised version of the master plan in 1933, and executing a number of structures, including the central library with its great tower (now Main Building), which replaced the school's original Old Main and symbolized the Beaux-Arts transformation of the campus.[86]

In 1912, Cass Gilbert was named campus architect for Oberlin College in Ohio, and produced a comprehensive plan whose fate illustrates a number of the problems of remodeling a campus in the Beaux-Arts manner (Figs. 214, 215).[87] Gilbert did not conceal his dislike for most of the existing buildings at Oberlin, which he characterized as "fussy or stupid, and not of a style that would be well to continue."[88] His master plan required the demolition of several of them, including the massive Romanesque Peters Hall, which Gilbert proposed replacing by a 300-foot-tall bell tower, to be the focal point of the new order (Fig. 216). The president of Oberlin supported Gilbert, but others did not and the uncompromising nature of the master plan effectively doomed it. Except for a couple of buildings that Gilbert did erect—notably the elegant Allen Memorial Art Gallery of 1917—his master plan had little impact on the Oberlin campus, which largely retained its nineteenth-century informality. The most significant change it underwent in this period was the removal of the few remaining structures from the area that had originally constituted the campus, in order to create a large open space (now called Tappan Square)—an idea that the Olmsted brothers had proposed in 1903.[89] This is one of the rare cases of a college transforming part of its built-upon campus into open space, in contrast to the normal filling-up of open areas with buildings.

As with Beaux-Arts planning in general, the principles of these types of campus replanning were not linked to any particular style of architecture. Theoretically, the buildings could be clothed in any brand of classical or medieval style, with little change in the overall plan. Despite the apparent advantage in continuing to build in a style already dominant on a campus, some architects attempted to impose their preferred styles of architecture in their development plans. The successful college

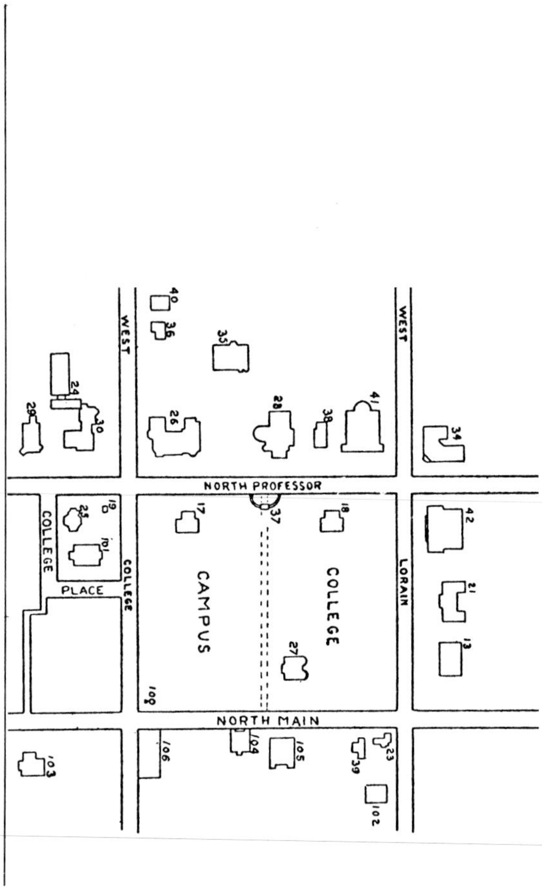

214

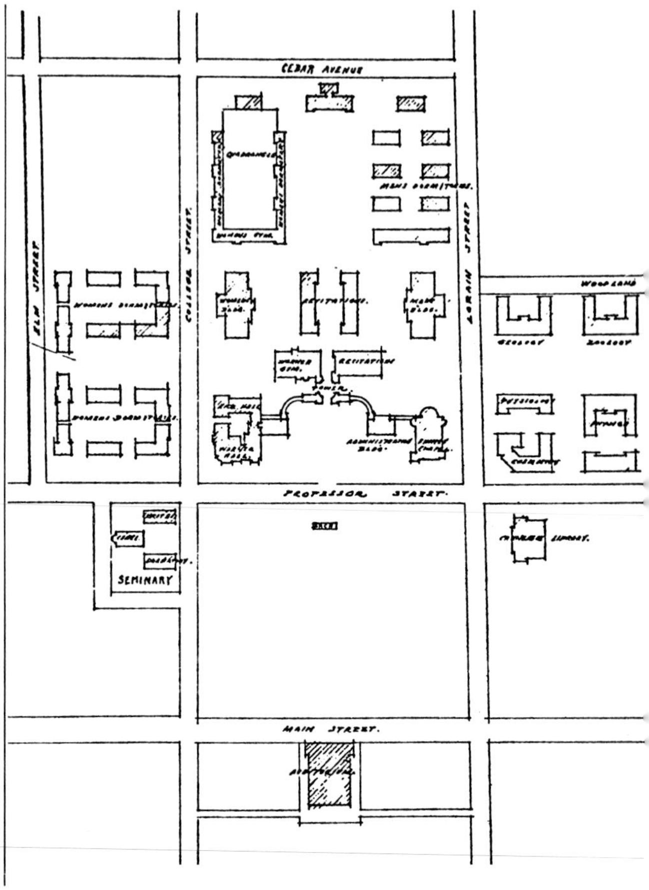

215

214 Oberlin College, Oberlin, Ohio. Plan of college buildings, 1908. North is to the right.
(*Oberlin College Alumni Catalogue*, 1936)

215 Development plan for Oberlin College, by Cass Gilbert, ca. 1914. Gilbert's proposal required demolition of several existing Oberlin buildings.
(*Hi-O-Hi*, Oberlin College, 1914)

216 Study for proposed tower, to serve as focal point of new Oberlin campus, by Cass Gilbert, 1916.
(*Oberlin College Observer*, February 18, 1982, p. 6)

216

planner Jens Frederick Larson, in a book on the subject published in 1933, revealed his prejudice for the colonial American "Georgian" styles, which he used in practically all of his designs.[90] Typical of his development plans was that for Wabash College in Indiana, in which he not only transformed the informal existing campus into a symmetrical and axial pattern, but also proposed that the main building, an impressive Italianate-style structure erected in 1853, be remodeled *à la* Independence Hall—a suggestion the school happily declined to follow.[91] Other colleges for which Larson produced development plans were Marietta in Ohio and Colby in Maine, the latter planned by him in 1931 for a site a couple of miles from the old campus.[92]

The development of the University of Washington, in Seattle, in the early twentieth century, epitomized in several ways the ideals of the Beaux-Arts campus. In 1904 the Olmsted firm produced a development plan incorporating the school's existing buildings on its hillside campus overlooking Lake Washington.[93] In 1909, the university played host to the Alaska-Yukon-Pacific Exposition, whose structures produced a monumental Beaux-Arts ensemble, organized along an axis aligned with the vista of Mount Rainier (Fig. 217). After the fair, only a few of the exposition buildings were permanent enough to be used by the school, but the underlying axial plan of the fair formed the basis of the development plan designed in 1915 by the firm of Bebb & Gould (Fig. 218).[94] Thus, two traditions were united symbolically—that of the campus development plan, and the heritage of the Columbian Exposition of 1893 that had inspired the City Beautiful movement in America.

217 Alaska-Yukon-Pacific Exposition, on University of Washington campus, Seattle, 1909.
(Charles M. Gates, *The First Century at the University of Washington*, Seattle, 1961, following p. 74)

218 Development plan for University of Washington, by Charles H. Bebb and Carl F. Gould, 1915.
(*Architectural Record*, August 1917, p. 175)

217

218

VI. The Monastic Quadrangle and Collegiate Ideals

In the early years of the twentieth century, as the large university came to dominate American higher education, a reaction against it appeared, which soon led to a renaissance of collegiate values. As the university became larger and increasingly complex, many educators regretted the changes and promoted a return to the ideals of the traditional American college—an intimate community of undergraduate students and teachers, with shared intellectual and social values, and emphasizing the development of character or culture more than the learning of trades. The motives for this movement ranged from a desire for improved intellectual standards to a nostalgia for gentlemanly elitism. The results included not only changes in educational practices, but a new concept of the ideal campus.

Some colleges, reacting against specialization, put restraints on the elective system and attempted to reformulate a classical curriculum shared by all educated citizens, a trend that produced the "general education" movement begun at Columbia in 1919.[1] Concerned about the depersonalization of university life, some schools looked to English traditions for ways to regain close student-teacher relationships, resulting in the "preceptor" system begun by Woodrow Wilson at Princeton, and the "tutorial" system at Harvard. One consequence of these concerns was the creation of smaller educational units within the large university. Alexander Meikeljohn's experimental college at the University of Wisconsin epitomized the movement in the 1920s, with its students and teachers living together in "a community of liberal learning."[2] Similar in intent was the creation of the "house system" at Harvard in 1928 and the "college system" at Yale two years later, in which the large undergraduate populations were divided into several groups whose members lived and dined together, had some of their instruction in their own "house" or "college," and shared a sense of social community. This recalled the traditional English system of colleges within a university; and, in general, English education—or at least American notions of English education—had a major influence on the revival of collegiate ideals during this period.

The appropriate architectural expression of these ideals seemed obvious to most people: the quadrangle, and especially the enclosed quadrangle typical of the medieval English college (Figs. 6–11).

Besides its English associations, the small, enclosed quadrangle seemed to provide a natural setting for a college community that valued intimacy and fellowship. Even the monastic connotations of the medieval quadrangle were well suited to a new mood of introversion and elitism in higher education. Princeton's Woodrow Wilson in the 1890s argued that collegiate studies ideally were "ascetic" in nature and required a "secluded" environment in order to flourish.[3] The architectural critic Montgomery Schuyler, in his series of articles on campus architecture beginning in 1909, repeatedly stated that a college should be like a "cloister."[4] And the ring of brick walls and wrought-iron gates erected around Harvard Yard in about 1900 was praised by Henry James as being "emblematic of cloistrality and restriction and exclusion."[5]

The mood was very different from that of the earlier university promoters, such as Cornell's Andrew D. White, who had ridiculed the conservative American college by calling it "as stagnant as a Spanish convent."[6] The monastic metaphor was now considered a compliment rather than an insult.

At this time there was also a strong reaffirmation of the Anglo-American collegiate principle that students should live together, in dormitories, at the college. Montgomery Schuyler reflected this view in 1911 when he said of the University of Rochester that "it has apparently never maintained any dormitories and thus could in no case have . . . the complete collegiate character."[7] (The University of Rochester had already recognized this deficiency, when it noted in its catalogue of 1895, "Although the University owns no dormitories, several of the chapter-houses of the Greek-letter fraternities are not far removed from the university grounds, and there is a growing tendency to multiply them in close proximity to the Campus."[8] This points out, incidentally, one of the important roles that fraternities have played at American schools, and helps explain why the Greek-letter societies experienced great popularity and growth during this period around 1900, when the collegiate ideal was in resurgence but many of the new or expanding institutions lacked facilities for residence on campus. In 1931, the author of a book on American college fraternities claimed that "one of the most practical things the fraternities have done . . . is materially to help in taking care of the problems of housing students.")[9]

The English quadrangle came to be regarded by many people as the most appropriate embodiment of the principle of the residential college. The historical fact that the American college, despite its adherence to the residential principle, had almost never used the closed quadrangle was ignored by most of those who promoted this form. One historian who recognized this fact nevertheless lamented it. A. Bailey Cutts, writing in 1935 about the early days of the College of William and Mary in Virginia, claimed that disciplinary problems at the school could have been prevented "had the original plans for a closed quadrangle been carried out" (Figs. 26–30).[10] For Cutts, the power of the monastic quadrangle was so great that its rejection in colonial America was a major catastrophe for subsequent education in the country, producing a "breakdown of discipline and ritual within the college precincts."

Ralph Adams Cram

The architect Ralph Adams Cram was probably the most fervent and vocal advocate of the revival of the medieval English quadrangle as an expression of collegiate traditionalism. A devout Anglican, a political conservative, and a Gothicist in architecture (despite his willingness to experiment with other styles), Cram believed strongly in the traditional values that were reemerging in American education. Speaking to the Royal Institute of British Architects in 1912 on the subject of American university architecture, Cram stressed the importance of the Anglo-American "residential college" to the development of "personal honour, clean living, . . . good fellowship, obedience to law, reverence and the fear of God—all those elements that are implied in the word 'Character.' " And he rejoiced that American education was returning to these principles after a lapse into Germanic specialization and "insane secularism."[11]

To Cram, the physical proof of this collegiate resurgence in America was the fact that "everywhere residential quads are coming into existence," built in the late Gothic style of Oxford and Cambridge—"the only style that absolutely expresses [the] ideals of an education that makes for culture and . . . character." Cram did not explain why the traditional American college, even before corruption by Germanic influences, had never favored the quadrangle, although he gave halfhearted approval to the "honest and sincere" buildings of colonial American colleges. According to him, the real decline of collegiate architecture began with the "pompous style President Jefferson did so much to advance," after which the remainder of the nineteenth century was a chaos of architectural "anarchy" at the American college, until the revival of the English quadrangle by himself (notably at Princeton) and a few other right-minded architects. Several years after his speech to the British architects, Cram summed up his philosophy succinctly with the remark that a school should be "half college and half monastery."[12]

Early Quadrangular Plans

Although the English enclosed quadrangle had never played an important role in American college planning before this period, there were some earlier premonitions of its appearance. Renwick's plan for Columbia College of 1813, Bishop Chase's Jubilee College, and several of Davis's college designs were quadrangular or nearly quadrangular, although they were never fully executed (Figs. 110, 117, 128).[13] But in the late nineteenth century, there were several more substantial indications of the movement that was to come.

Beginning in the late 1860s, Yale College erected a series of dormitories and other buildings that by 1900 resulted in a more or less quadrangular enclosure around its "Old Campus" (Figs. 219, 220). An interest in English colleges was perhaps one of the motives for this construction; but more important were the practical problem of Yale's crowded position in the middle of New Haven and the fact that building around the perimeter of the campus allowed a more intensive use of its land than was possible with the existing row of buildings set back from the street. Moreover, the old buildings, slated for demolition, could be kept up during the erection of the new structures to allow the school's uninterrupted operation during construction. The president of Yale during most of this period, Noah Porter, was a strong advocate of the traditional collegiate principles, including the necessity of dormitories centrally located and easily supervised—a subject to which he devoted a chapter in a book on American college education in 1870.[14] These concerns also favored a compact campus that was closed off from the city outside. But Porter also approved the quadrangular arrangement on aesthetic grounds, and predicted that

> when the contemplated quadrangle shall be completed, no university or college now existing will be able to show a larger or more beautiful inner court, with two nobler rows of elms, than Yale College.[15]

A very different type of quadrangular plan was proposed for Trinity College in Hartford, Connecticut. In 1872, the Episcopal school sold its campus to the state (for the location of a new state capitol), and acquired a new site outside of town.[16] The president of Trinity, Reverend Abner Jackson, spent a summer in England and Scotland looking at college buildings. In London he con-

218

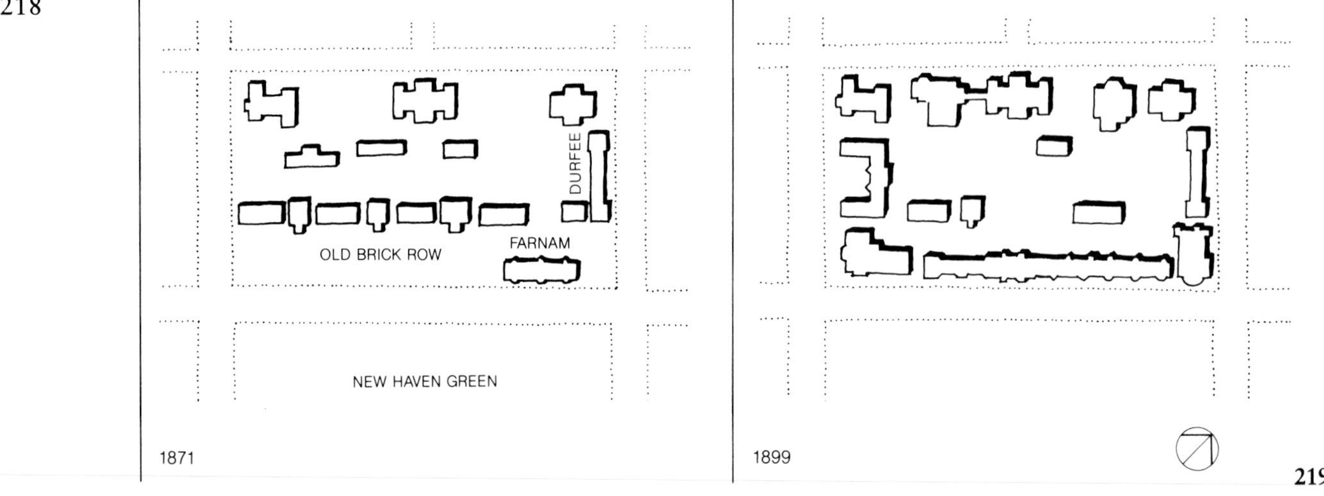

219

220

ferred with the architect William Burges, who in 1874 produced a master plan for the new campus that was unlike anything seen in America before (Fig. 221). It consisted of a series of four quadrangles, each one enclosed on all sides by structures combining late-Romanesque and early-Gothic forms, with only small arched gateways opening into the adjacent quads and the country outside.

In its axial alignment of courtyards, the Trinity scheme recalled St. John's College at Cambridge, but it was grander than the plan of any English college (if fully executed, the buildings would have extended more than 1,000 feet), and it greatly exceeded the resources of Trinity College. In 1875, the college directed the local architect Francis Kimball, who had worked with Burges on the design, to modify it by removing one of the interior ranges of buildings (producing a three-quadrangle plan), and construction began.[17] But it is significant that instead of erecting even one of the smaller quadrangles entirely, Trinity began by building the western sides of two of Burges's quads—the only part of the scheme to be executed, as it turned out (Fig. 222). Thus, ironically, the school found itself with a long row of structures (the Long Walk, as it appropriately came to be called), not very different in character from the Yale-like alignment of buildings at the original Trinity campus (Fig. 42). This underscored the foreignness of the enclosed quadrangle in America at this time, and the persistent strength of the earlier American patterns of campus planning.

Even though largely unbuilt, the Burges plan for Trinity impressed many American architects and began to influence other college designs toward the end of the century. The master plan for Stanford University, a decade after Burges's design, had a somewhat similar arrangement of quadrangles in a row, although its axial organization was very different (Fig. 175).[18] And it is known that the University of Chicago trustees were interested in the Trinity design when they began planning their own campus in 1890 (Fig. 179).[19] Montgomery Schuyler called Burges's design "the most impressive embodiment in the Western world of the spirit and the charm of Oxford."[20] But another architectural critic, Ashton Willard, pointed out a difference between the Trinity design and English colleges:

219 Plans showing development of the Old Campus at Yale between 1871 and 1899. In 1871, the seven buildings of Old Brick Row still dominated the campus, but the just-completed Farnam and Durfee halls (both designed by Russell Sturgis, Jr.) began a new pattern of construction around the periphery of the campus. By 1899, new buildings virtually enclosed the area, and Old Brick Row was being demolished.

220 Yale College. Photograph of College Street, ca. 1908, with New Haven Green to left. In foreground is Farnam Hall, constructed in 1869. This, and buildings subsequently erected along the street, enclosed the Old Campus. (*The Yale Banner and Pot Pourri*, 1908–1909, p. 166)

There is nothing at Oxford which can be compared with it. Everything there is irregular and casual compared with the superb symmetry of this great mass.[21]

Willard typified a surge of interest in the enclosed quadrangle that occurred in the 1890s. His praise of the Trinity plan appeared in an article entitled "The Development of College Architecture in America," in which he stated his love of quadrangles in the very first sentence:

I think we all occasionally feel a certain regret that our Puritan ancestors should have carried their Puritanism into their ideas of art and architecture and so rigidly excluded from their first attempts at making a home for their higher school of learning the severe, calm and tranquil idea of the cloistered college built around its quadrangles.

Willard's theory was that the traditional American college plan of separate buildings was an expression of Puritan or "Congregational" beliefs—such as individualism—whereas the enclosed quadrangle was "Anglican" in its emphasis on unity. He surveyed approvingly the recent appearance of quadrangles at a few American colleges (such as Trinity, Stanford, and the University of Pennsylvania), and he expressed his preference for order over irregularity in the form of these spaces (Figs. 221, 176, 226). He pointed out that the English quadrangles had "the irregularity of all wholes which are produced by gradual accretion," whereas the order of the Trinity design was found "only in masses created by fiat," and it seemed obvious to him that the latter was more suitable to America. This was similar to the position of the Beaux-Arts planner Werner Hegemann when he stated that Gothic college plans were acceptable as long as they were "perfectly balanced and axiated according to the best modern ideas."[22]

This view was soon to be challenged by a younger generation of neo-Gothic enthusiasts. But the symmetrical, ordered quadrangle nevertheless remained popular for many years among American campus planners, as a kind of compromise between medievalism and classicism. A good example is the ambitious master plan that Albert E. Doyle prepared in 1911–12 for the newly founded Reed College in Portland, Oregon (too ambitious, as it turned out, for only a small portion of it was constructed, as was often the case with such plans) (Fig. 223).[23] Doyle designed a series of Tudor-Gothic quadrangles, whose architectural forms reportedly were drawn from St. John's College at Oxford, but whose overall organization was essentially Beaux-Arts, with open and closed spaces arranged along axes and cross-axes, culminating in towers and other focal points. However, at certain places around the edges of the plan, this formal order gave way to a meandering architectural irregularity—a concession to new concepts of Gothic campus design that had emerged by this time.

221 Trinity College, Hartford, Connecticut. Master plan for the school's new campus, by William Burges, 1873. (*New England Magazine*, 1897, p. 517)

222 Trinity College. The "Long Walk," during construction in 1878. Structures correspond to the western sides of two of the quadrangles in Burges's plan, and are the only parts of it that were constructed. They contained classrooms, dormitories, library, museum, refectory, and chapel. (Trinity College Archives)

221

222

223

223 Reed College, Portland, Oregon. Rendering of master plan for the campus, by Albert Doyle of Doyle, Patterson & Beach, ca. 1912. (Reed College)

The Work of Cope & Stewardson

A new phase in the use of the collegiate quadrangle was inaugurated by the Philadelphia architects Walter Cope and John Stewardson, at Bryn Mawr, Princeton, and the University of Pennsylvania in the 1890s. Both still in their twenties when they did this work, and by temperament more "poetic" than most architects (as Ralph Adams Cram put it), Cope and Stewardson had a love of the picturesque qualities of late medieval architecture, based in part on studying the English colleges in person.[24] In 1886 they found a compatible client in Bryn Mawr College for women outside Philadelphia, whose trustees directed the young architects to "create here counterparts of the Oxford and Cambridge buildings."[25] Their first two buildings for the school were essentially traditional, but in Pembroke Hall of 1894 and Rockefeller Hall of 1897, Walter Cope (who apparently had the major role in the Bryn Mawr work) created an unprecedented form: a meandering, linear series of structures along the southern edge of the campus, with two towered gateways serving as entrances into the school (Figs. 224, 225). Although inspired partly by the English colleges, this concept had its own special character, which did not depend on the subsequent completion of a whole enclosed quadrangle. In fact, the architects may have been inspired partly by a landscaping proposal that Calvert Vaux (Frederick Law Olmsted's former partner) had made to Bryn Mawr in 1884, that the college create a "screening out" of its southern boundary by a close planting of trees and shrubs.[26] By substituting buildings for trees, they created a more effective closure, and nicely defined the boundaries of the campus.

At about the same time, Cope & Stewardson designed a group of dormitories for the University of Pennsylvania, which in 1872 had moved from its old location in Philadelphia to a site that was farther from the center of the city but still largely urban in character. Here, the architects used their new device of linear construction to create fully enclosed quadrangles (Figs. 226, 227). But their approach was very different from that of a Beaux-Arts architect, for they made no attempt to create symmetry or axes. Instead, they took advantage of the awkwardly angled site to create a picturesque progression of irregular spaces and forms—which Cram in 1904 praised as being "altogether wonderful in mass and in composition."[27]

The fertile collaboration of Cope and Stewardson ended when Stewardson died in 1896, after the start of their next major collegiate commission, at Princeton (Fig. 230). Cope himself lived for only six more years, but during that time (in partnership with Stewardson's brother Emlyn) he produced a master plan for Washington University in Missouri (Fig. 228). This institution had decided to move from its location in downtown St. Louis to a long and narrow site on a promontory outside town, and it had hired the Olmsted firm to draw a preliminary plan, which was similar to the plan for Stanford University in consisting of an aligned series of enclosed and arcaded quadrangles.[28] In 1899 the university held a competition for a master plan, advising the entrants that a quadrangular scheme was preferred, although it did not have to follow the pattern of the Olmsted proposal.[29]

Of the six architectural firms invited to compete, five submitted typically Beaux-Arts designs, with classical buildings arranged symmetrically around axial courtyards.[30] The sixth participating firm, Cope & Stewardson, submitted a much less conventional design, which won and was ultimately executed with some modifications. Cope's design imaginatively combined various styles of architecture and planning (Figs. 228, 229). The eastern end of the design, serving as an entrance to the campus, was largely Beaux-Arts in character, with a strong axis and symmetrical structures forming a quadrangle which one entered through a centrally placed portal. To the west of this, however, the plan became progressively less formal, with a series of quadrangles and ranges of buildings creating an irregular, meandering space of changing vistas. It was a bold solution to the problem of an elongated site, with its danger of tiresomely similar spaces. Together with Cope's work at Princeton, the design for Washington University concluded one of the most inventive careers in American college planning.

224

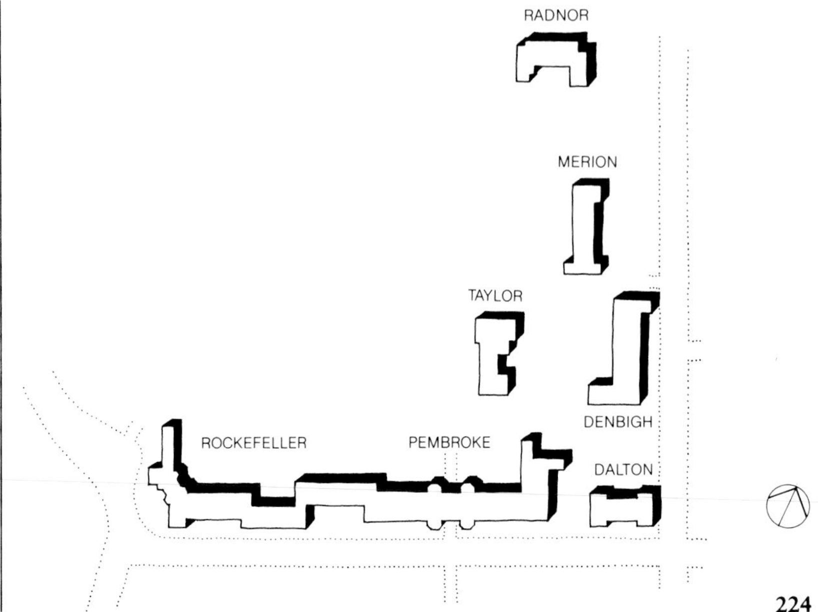
RADNOR
MERION
TAYLOR
DENBIGH
ROCKEFELLER
PEMBROKE
DALTON

224

225

226

227

224 Bryn Mawr College, Bryn Mawr, Pennsylvania. Plan of part of the campus, ca. 1905. The school's first two buildings were Taylor and Merion halls, erected 1880–1885. Buildings designed by Cope & Stewardson included Radnor Hall, 1886; Denbigh Hall, 1890; Pembroke Hall, 1894; and Rockefeller Hall, 1897–1904.

225 Rockefeller Hall, Bryn Mawr College, designed by Cope & Stewardson, 1897. (*Architectural Record*, September 1910, p. 208)

226 University of Pennsylvania, Philadelphia. Drawing of design for residence halls, by Cope & Stewardson, 1895. As executed, the design was modified somewhat, and part of the complex was not completed until the 1950s. (*The Brickbuilder*, December 1907, p. 223)

227 University of Pennsylvania. Memorial Gateway Tower, in residence hall complex designed by Cope & Stewardson. (Photograph by Buford Pickens)

228 Washington University, St. Louis, Missouri. Master plan by Cope & Stewardson, awarded first prize in competition of 1899. (Washington University)

229 Rendering of plan for Washington University, by Cope & Stewardson, ca. 1900. Building in foreground is Brookings Hall, whose central section serves as principal entrance to the university. Behind it, forming far side of first quadrangle, is the library. Beyond are further academic buildings, chapel, student residences, and other facilities. (Washington University)

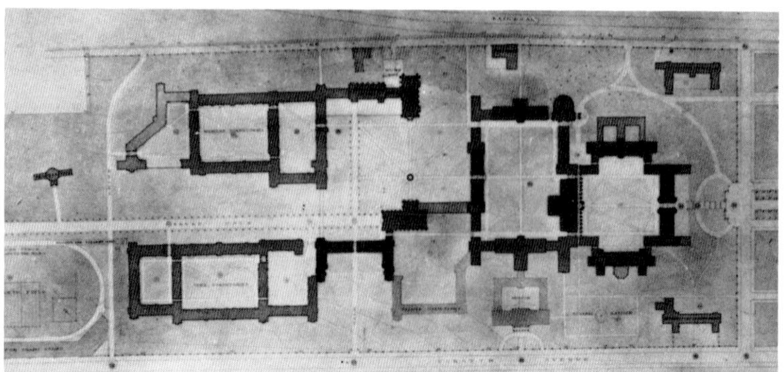

228

229

The Remaking of Princeton

In 1896 the College of New Jersey at Princeton proclaimed itself Princeton University, and began a period of tremendous growth and construction. At the same time, it resolved to use the Gothic style of architecture exclusively for its new buildings, and it chose Cope & Stewardson to design a series of new dormitories. Princeton embodied many of the conservative trends in college education during this period, and the architecture it erected expressed these ideals more fully than probably any other collegiate design of the period.

In the 1890s and the first decades of the twentieth century, Princeton was characterized increasingly by its wealthy and socially prominent student body, aristocratic in outlook, and more Anglican than Presbyterian in religious orientation.[31] Club values tended to be encouraged as much as those of scholarship, and the school's president at this time, Francis Patton, defended this fact in a speech to alumni in 1888—although he added, "I am not prepared to say that it is better to have gone and loafed than never to have gone at all."[32] Woodrow Wilson, a professor and major force at the college in the 1890s, before assuming its presidency in 1902, had more rigorous academic standards, but his view of education was also essentially conservative and collegiate. Harvard's President Eliot called his views "a little archaic."[33] Wilson's ideal college was a place of seclusion and separation from the world, a view that attracted him strongly to the quadrangles of Oxford and Cambridge, which he visited in 1896 and 1899. On the latter occasion, he described Cambridge as

> a place full of quiet chambers, secluded ancient courts, and gardens shut away from intrusion—a town full of coverts, for those who would learn and be with their own thoughts. I bring away from it a very keen sense of what we lack in our democratic colleges, where no one has privacy or claims to have his own thoughts.[34]

Cope & Stewardson's work at Princeton was the first step toward the creation of a collegiate environment appropriate both to Wilson's ideal of scholarly introspection and to a clubby elitism. Following the Bryn Mawr pattern, Cope & Stewardson created a meandering and thoroughly un-Beaux-Arts line of buildings, composed of two dormitories, Blair and Stafford Little halls (built starting in 1897) and a gymnasium (1903), along the southwest boundary of the campus, to serve as a screen separating the college from the railroad tracks that approached the school on that side (Figs. 230, 231). A massive tower in Blair Hall, recalling the Tudor gate towers of English colleges, served as an entryway into the campus from the railway station. Thus the design neatly served several functions at once: habitable space, entry gate, and barrier against unwanted sights and sounds. Most of all, it created a symbolic or psychological boundary between the college and the world outside, and it did this more effectively than the fences that many colleges were erecting at this time, such as those at Harvard, which Henry James hailed, or those at Bowdoin College in Maine, which Montgomery Schuyler, reflecting the new elitist attitudes, said would serve "visibly to exclude the *profanum vulgus* . . . and thus to promote the expression which college grounds should take of seclusion and cloistrality" (Fig. 232).[35]

Upon assuming the presidency of Princeton in 1902, Woodrow Wilson praised the new buildings by Cope, saying that they were the first stage in the formation of "a sort of circle and quadrangle, . . . girt about with buildings in the style that is historic," and creating "a little town" unto itself.[36] The specific style of Cope's buildings, a picturesque interpretation of Tudor or Jacobean collegiate architecture, appealed for several reasons. It was consummately English, and thus, according to Ralph Adams Cram, it evoked "racial memories."[37] And it had aristocratic connotations, which were emphasized by the carving of heraldic shields on the facades of the new structures, in line with Princeton's adoption of a coat of arms in 1896. Wilson praised this Tudor architecture with the observation that

> by the very simple device of building our new buildings in the Tudor Gothic Style we seem to have added to Princeton the age of Oxford and Cambridge; we have added a thousand years to the history of Princeton by merely putting those lines in our buildings which point every man's imagination to the historic traditions of learning in the English-speaking race.[38]

Further construction at Princeton was needed not only for new academic buildings, but more importantly for extra dormitories. Even after Blair and Stafford Little halls were erected, the college

228

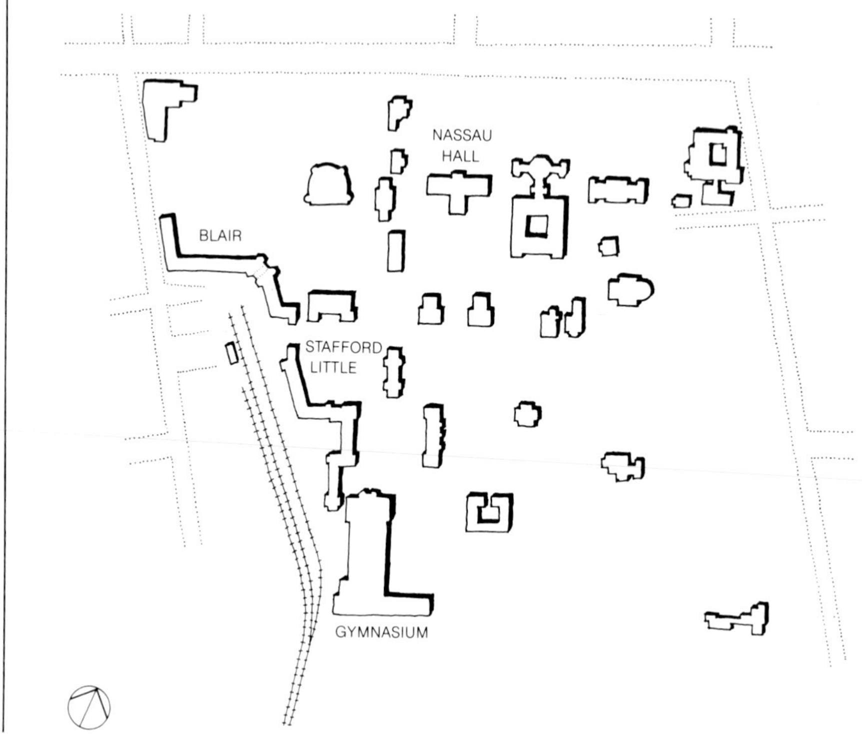

230

231

232

230 Plan of Princeton University, ca. 1909, showing the enclosure of campus at its southwest edge, by Blair Hall, Stafford Little Hall, and Gymnasium, designed by Cope & Stewardson, 1897–1903.

231 Princeton University. Stafford Little and Blair halls, seen from railroad tracks on west side of campus. Photograph taken shortly after construction of the buildings.
(Princeton University Archives)

232 Memorial Gateway, Bowdoin College, Brunswick, Maine. Drawing by Charles W. Furlong, ca. 1902.
(*The Outlook*, August 1, 1903, p. 794)

could not accommodate all its students on campus, as strict adherence to the collegiate ideal now demanded. The residential principle was so strong at Princeton that even its newly created graduate school was planned from the beginning—by Wilson and the graduate dean, Andrew Fleming West—to be a perfectly self-contained "college," with students living and eating together, in contrast to nearly all other American graduate schools (Fig. 237). Moreover, Wilson wanted to create a "quadrangle system of residential colleges" within the undergraduate body, partly in order to counteract the influence of the "eating clubs" that had replaced the Greek-letter fraternities previously outlawed at Princeton.[39]

To accomplish all of these goals in a unified way, Princeton in 1906 hired Ralph Adams Cram to prepare a "general plan" for the development of the campus, and to act as Supervising Architect for the university—meaning that Cram would determine the location and overall form and character of all new buildings, not that his firm would design all of them.[40] As we have seen, the general plan, or "development plan," was common at this time for institutions building from scratch. Princeton was one of the first schools with an existing campus to create the post of supervising architect to coordinate a major physical replanning. This reflected the importance of architecture to Wilson and the Princeton community, and their desire to make the campus more uniformly Gothic and quadrangular.

Cram, whose views on architecture and education have already been summarized, was widely recognized by this time as a foremost proponent of collegiate Gothic architecture.[41] In 1900, he and his partner Bertram Goodhue had entered the competition for a master plan for the United States Military Academy at West Point, and had bucked the Beaux-Arts tide by producing an uncompromisingly Gothic and picturesque design, which won the competition.[42] Cram and Goodhue's design for West Point took full advantage of the Academy's spectacular mountainside site along the Hudson River by creating a complex of rugged structures that in places clung to the cliffs, and over which the looming chapel looked down from above—the whole ensemble evoking romantic images of medieval fortresses or monastic strongholds (Figs. 233, 234). In 1903, Cram produced a classical design for Sweet Briar College in Virginia, in accord with his notion that different architectural styles were appropriate to different geographical regions (Fig. 199). But for another Virginia school, Richmond College, he produced a Gothic design similar to West Point's in its irregular plan adapted to a hilly topography.[43]

The general plan that Cram produced for Princeton starting in 1906 reflected not only his own principles of design, but the wishes and needs of his client (Fig. 235).[44] All new construction was to be Gothic in style, and the campus eventually would assume the character of an enclosed and compact community, with a preponderance of quadrangular or near-quadrangular spaces. Cram wrote of his master plan:

> Certain psychological principles were laid down at once. . . . First of all, a university was conceived as a place where the community life and spirit were supreme, . . . a citadel of learning and culture, . . . containing within itself all necessary influences towards the making of character, repelling all those that work against the same: a walled city against materialism and all its works.[45]

A peculiarity of Cram's general plan is that it embodied certain Beaux-Arts principles in its overall form, but rejected them in the individual parts. Cram took pains to position new groups of buildings so that the whole campus would take on a roughly symmetrical form, composed around axes. This strengthened the axis that already existed with Nassau Hall as its focus, by adding new buildings to define it more clearly, and extending it along a vista toward the newly created Lake Carnegie. But within this framework of axes and vistas, Cram designed smaller spaces that were thoroughly unclassical in form. He held the work of Cope & Stewardson in high esteem and followed their lead in proposing ranges of buildings that either served as barriers along the campus edges or formed enclosed quadrangles. In designing these smaller spaces, Cram purposely avoided symmetry and axiality, following instead the picturesque principle that the design

> should not reveal itself at once and from any spot, but gradually, through narrowed and intensified vistas, the unforeseen opening out of

233

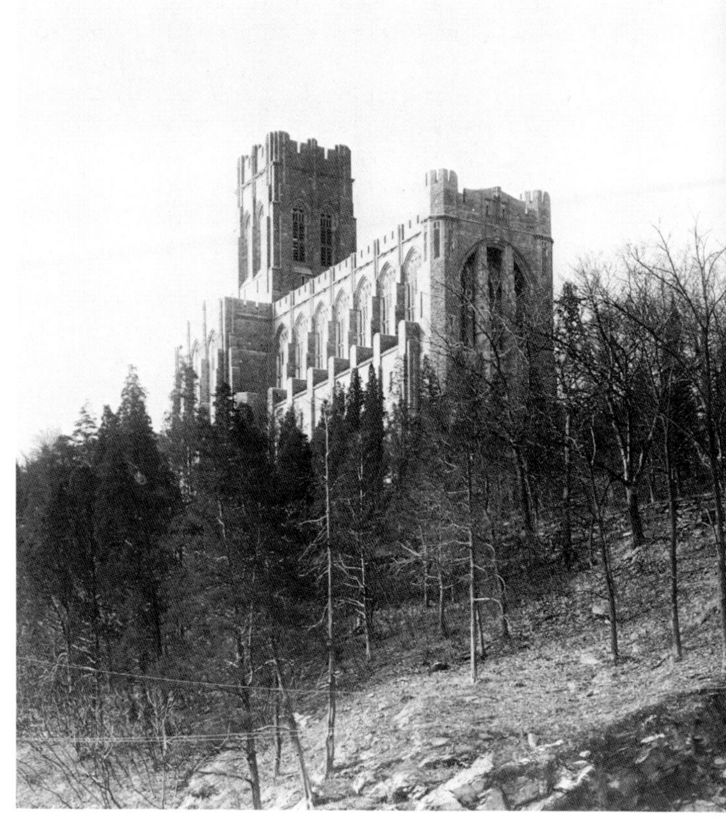

234

233 United States Military Academy, West Point, New York. Post Headquarters, designed by Cram, Goodhue & Ferguson, following their development plan of 1900; constructed 1908. (United States Military Academy Archives)

234 United States Military Academy. Chapel, designed by Cram, Goodhue & Ferguson; constructed 1910. (United States Military Academy Archives)

232

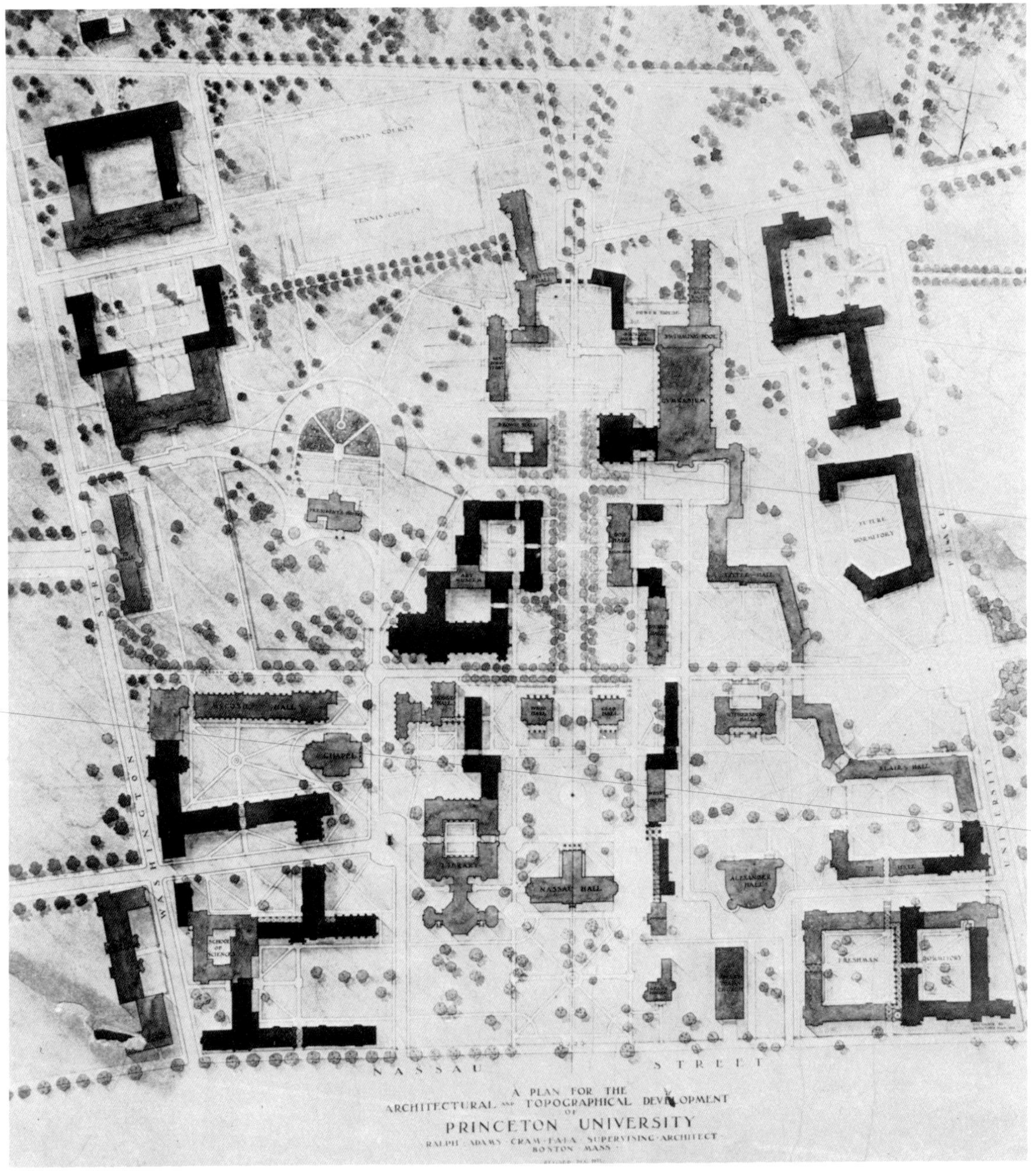
TENNIS COURTS
TENNIS COURTS
GYMNASIUM
BROWN HALL
FUTURE DORMITORY
CHAPEL
LIBRARY
NASSAU HALL
ALEXANDER HALL
BLAIR HALL
FRESHMAN DORMITORY
WASHINGTON STREET
UNIVERSITY PLACE
NASSAU STREET
A PLAN FOR THE
ARCHITECTURAL AND TOPOGRAPHICAL DEVELOPMENT
OF
PRINCETON UNIVERSITY
RALPH ADAMS CRAM F.A.I.A. SUPERVISING ARCHITECT
BOSTON MASS

> unanticipated paths and quadrangles, the surprise of retirement, the revelation of the unexpected.[46]

This attitude is exemplified in Cram's designs for the Princeton Graduate College (Fig. 236). In the earlier stages of the planning, the complex was to consist of adjoining quadrangles made up of irregularly angled parts, precisely as if the college had evolved over a period of centuries in a constricted medieval town. As finally built, the quadrangles were straightened out a bit, and they were located farther from the center of the campus than originally intended (Fig. 237). But their character remained unchanged, with the monastic quadrangles under the shadow of the memorial tower, a perfect reflection of the views not only of Woodrow Wilson but of the graduate dean, Andrew Fleming West.[47] West's romantic vision of the ideal community of graduate scholars was one in which all lived together in cloistered seclusion, dined in their academic gowns in the Great Hall (after saying grace in Latin), and regulated their daily activities by the chimes in the towering belfry (Fig. 238). In his words, the perfect college had

> quadrangles shadowing sunny lawns, towers and gateways opening into quiet retreats, ivy-grown walls looking on sheltered gardens, vistas through avenues of arching elms, . . . these are the places where the affections linger and where memories cling like the ivies themselves, and these are the answers in architecture and scenic setting to the immemorial longings of academic generations.[48]

235 Development plan for Princeton University, by Ralph Adams Cram, 1906–1911. Lighter-shaded buildings were existing structures; darker ones are those proposed by Cram—in many cases to increase the regularity and symmetry of the campus—around the central axis passing through Nassau Hall (in lower middle of plan). This revised version of Cram's plan, of 1911, does not show the Graduate College, whose intended location had been moved to a more distant part of the campus.
(Princeton University Archives)

234

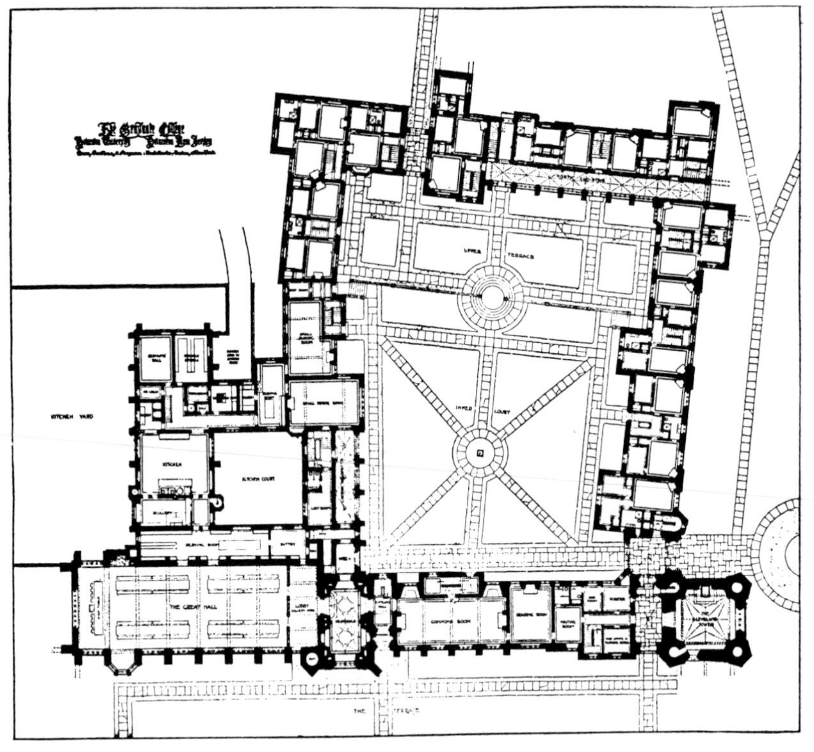
KITCHEN YARD
KITCHEN COURT
UPPER TERRACE
INNER COURT
THE GREAT HALL
COMMONS ROOM
THE TERRACE

236

237

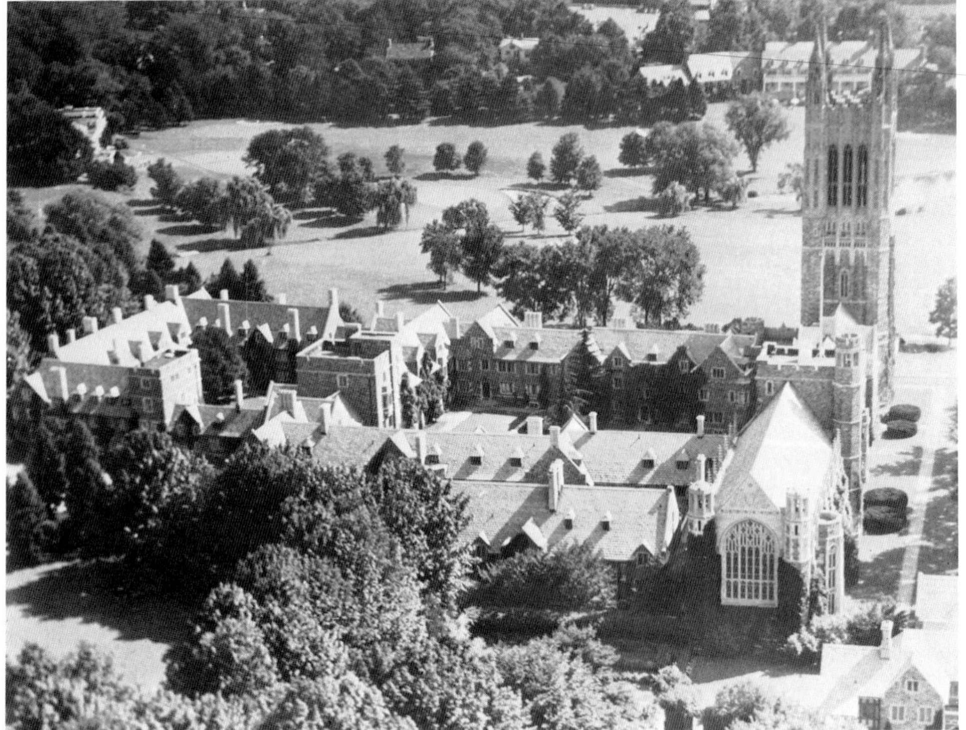

238

236 Plan of the Graduate College, Princeton, by Cram, Goodhue & Ferguson, ca. 1910. Plan was modified somewhat before the complex was executed.
(*The American Architect*, October 25, 1911, p. 167)

237 Graduate College, Princeton.
(Princeton University Archives)

238 Graduate College, Princeton. Proctor Hall, the dining hall.
(Photograph courtesy of Robert J. Clark)

Charles Klauder's Collegiate Designs

The group of dormitories at the northwest corner of the Princeton campus, whose overall form was indicated in Cram's master plan of 1907, was designed in the next couple of years by the architect Frank Miles Day and his young associate Charles Zeller Klauder, soon to become one of the most successful proponents of Gothic collegiate architecture.[49] This group of buildings, consisting of Holder and Hamilton halls (dormitories) and Madison Hall (dining rooms), formed two enclosed quadrangles, dominated by a high tower (Fig. 239).[50] The overall plan was similar to Cram's Graduate College, but Day & Klauder's design had its own individual character, distinguished by such features as the picturesque rhythm of gables along the facades. The monastic imagery, as strong here as in Cram's work, extended even to the inclusion of a "Cloister" in the complex (Fig. 240); and the desire for authenticity of detail impelled the architects to import stonecutters from Europe to do the carving.[51]

Klauder, first in partnership with Day and then alone after 1918, continued to design dormitory buildings for Princeton.[52] His Gothic designs at other colleges included several buildings at Wellesley beginning in about 1914, several at Cornell, and the master plan for Concordia Seminary in St. Louis of about 1925, in which he used again Cram's formula of a tall tower contrasting with low buildings arranged around quadrangles (Fig. 300).[53]

The tower assumed preeminence in Klauder's most extraordinary educational building, the Cathedral of Learning at the University of Pittsburgh, a forty-two-story Gothic structure erected beginning in 1926 (Fig. 241).[54] The university was landpoor in the midst of the city, and its chancellor, John G. Bowman, faced with rapidly increasing enrollments and the need for new facilities, had made the bold decision to create, in effect, a skyscraper-university. But, significantly, he and Klauder chose to call the structure a "cathedral," not a "skyscraper," thereby giving it a spiritual, rather than a technological or mercantile identity. This reflected Bowman's essentially conservative views on education, typical of the revived collegianism of the period—as expressed in one of his first chancellor's reports, which called on the university to "perpetuate the most precious and sound traditions, . . . faith in God, spiritual responsibility,

239

240

241

239 Aerial view of part of Princeton campus, showing Holder, Hamilton, and Madison halls (undergraduate dormitories and dining halls). Cram indicated these buildings in his development plan for the campus, but they were designed by Day & Klauder, and constructed from 1910 to 1916. (Princeton University Archives)

240 "Cloister" of Holder Hall, Princeton. (Princeton University Archives)

241 University of Pittsburgh, Pittsburgh, Pennsylvania. Drawing of the Cathedral of Learning, designed by Charles Z. Klauder, ca. 1925. (University of Pittsburgh)

the power and the will to create."[55] Moreover, the designation "cathedral of learning" facilitated a rousing and inspirational fund-raising campaign, which was reported by a contemporary as follows:

> The picture of the building was everywhere, in store windows, in people's homes, in schoolhouses. It appeared on banquet tables and in advertisements. Seldom had Pittsburghers allowed their enthusiasm to reach so high a pitch. Never had they contributed so much money toward one cause. Phrases from booklets, describing the building, were heard everywhere: "Our University"; "Sincerity like the ring of steel." . . . Seventeen thousand men and women and ninety-seven thousand school children gave toward the Cathedral of Learning in the campaign of 1925.[56]

Thus was Klauder's Cathedral of Learning an ingenious and effective resolution of ostensibly conflicting goals: the high-density requirements of a large urban university, and the assertion of traditional ideals of collegiate education.

Even though known especially for his Gothic designs, Klauder also used other styles for his collegiate buildings. Like Cram, he felt that various types of architecture were appropriate to different circumstances, and in his prolific career as college planner he experimented with classical as well as medieval styles, for example at Brown University in Rhode Island, Franklin and Marshall College in Pennsylvania, and the University of Delaware, where he produced a master plan in 1917 and designed numerous buildings in succeeding years.[57] Klauder's most innovative stylistic experiment occurred at the University of Colorado at Boulder, for which he produced a master plan in 1919. His preliminary designs for the buildings were Gothic in style, but then he decided this was inappropriate to the school's physical environment, with its vast plains set against the backdrop of rugged mountains. In response to this setting, Klauder devised a style that he called "Rural Italian," an imaginative combination of various historical elements, with towers, robust stone walls, shed roofs, and arcaded cloister-like spaces (Fig. 242).[58] Klauder's site plan was essentially Beaux-Arts, with the buildings arranged symmetrically around intersecting axes, another example of the persistence of the Beaux-Arts system in twentieth-century American college planning regardless of the architectural style of the buildings.

In 1929 Klauder published a book on college planning, commissioned by the Association of American Colleges—a demonstration of the growing acceptance among educational institutions of the usefulness of master plans, development plans, and the college planner in general.[59] (He mentioned in his introduction that out of two hundred colleges surveyed, fifty were currently involved in master planning.) Klauder's tone in the book was generally pragmatic, as he analyzed the practical considerations that influenced the design of master plans and individual buildings for colleges. He pointed out that different architectural styles and types of plans were appropriate to different locations and kinds of schools, and suggested that "the individuality of each institution should be sought" and emphasized in its design.[60] But Klauder also revealed his personal preferences and prejudices, in particular a dislike of the traditional American pattern of spaciously separated buildings, to which he contrasted the medieval quadrangle:

> The habit has been to make the college grounds . . . park-like, to spread the buildings about in a nothing-to-conceal manner. . . . This park-like manner may answer some demands, . . . but the best architectural effect is gained by a more compact grouping. Notably in the case of dormitories, scattered buildings afford no recompense for the loss of those beautiful and tranquil enclosed or partly enclosed spaces, or quads as they are found at Oxford, Cambridge, Princeton and Yale.[61]

Klauder's inclusion of Yale among the exemplary quadrangular designs was an acknowledgment of the Harkness Quadrangle, which was built on the west side of Yale's Old Campus starting in 1917, and which inaugurated a creative new phase of planning at the school (Fig. 243). Designed by the New York architect James Gamble Rogers, this extensive complex of residence halls for over six hundred students (which now constitute Branford and Saybrook colleges) largely followed the principles established by Cram's and Klauder's work at Princeton; it was a group of enclosed courtyards entered by fortress-like gates and presided over by a lofty Gothic tower.[62] But the

242 University of Colorado, Boulder. Rendering of design for Social Center Building, by Charles Z. Klauder, ca. 1919.
(*Architectural Forum*, September 1919)

243 Harkness Memorial Quadrangle and Tower, Yale. Designed by James Gamble Rogers, 1917. This complex of dormitory buildings, which includes several smaller courtyards as well as the one shown here, is now occupied by Branford and Saybrook colleges.

242

243

Harkness complex had its own distinctive character, reflecting Rogers's special abilities and concerns as a designer: a fascination with architectural scale, producing unexpected juxtapositions of forms and spaces of differing sizes; a picturesque combination of allusions to medieval domestic, defensive, and ecclesiastical, as well as collegiate, architecture; and the creation of a rich and often whimsical pattern of urban streetscapes.

Rogers's style of campus planning was perfectly suited to the spirit of the times at Yale, but also to the need for dense accommodations within the relatively small areas available for university expansion in the city of New Haven. In the next two decades, Rogers put his stamp firmly on the physical character of Yale by designing a large number of important facilities, including several new student residences, the main library, the law school, and the center of graduate studies.[63] In varying ways, all of these shared the richness of form and romantic historical allusions found in Harkness Quadrangle. And most of them shared another of its features: an abundance of memorial tablets, shields, inscriptions, and other carved devices set into the walls and gateways, serving not only to honor financial benefactors of the college, but also to display its history and the accomplishments of its alumni (Fig. 244). Even the architectural history of the school was commemorated in representations of the latest buildings' predecessors (above an entrance to the library was a complete visual record of the buildings that had housed Yale's library since the colonial period). This programmatic use of architecture, of which John Ruskin no doubt would have approved heartily, was turned to whimsy in places by Rogers, as in the law building, where the carved heads of policemen and masked burglars can be seen, pursuing and fleeing in the window frames.

Not everyone approved Rogers's romanticism or, more generally, the use of the medieval enclosed quadrangle. In a book on the nineteenth-century architect A. J. Davis, one observer defended Davis's simple, foursquare Gothic designs, and stated that the old library at Yale "still manages to look askance at Harkness Quadrangle nearby and other specimens of the pseudo-supercram style in monasticism."[64] But such dissent was rare. In the 1920s and 1930s, the medieval quadrangle was widely regarded as the ideal form of a college. And the buildings by Rogers at Yale exemplified the era's desire for collegiate intimacy, clubby good humor, and the confirmation of an ancient and noble institutional heritage.

244

244 Harkness Memorial Quadrangle (now Branford College), Yale. Doorway with inscription commemorating "James Fenimore Cooper, Novelist, Class of 1806."
(Yale University Library)

The Collegiate Residential Unit

Starting in 1930, Harkness Quadrangle was remodeled to accommodate the first two "colleges" of Yale's new system of residential units within the undergraduate student body. Harvard's similar "house system" also was inaugurated at this time. These were major victories for the movement to divide the large university into smaller entities more compatible with the collegiate ideal of a community of students, residing, dining, and socializing together. After creating Branford and Saybrook colleges in Harkness Quadrangle, Yale added eight more such colleges in the 1930s, whose styles represented several varieties of Gothic or classical architecture, each one planned in such a way as to give it an individual identity.[65] A particularly remarkable architectural character was created by James Gamble Rogers at Davenport College, the interior courtyard of which he made Georgian in style, but the facade on York Street was Gothic to match the buildings across the street; the range along the street is perhaps the only building ever designed, all at once, to be Gothic on one side and classical on the other (Figs. 245, 246).

Harvard's "houses," seven of which were created around 1930, were located either in remodeled existing structures, or in new complexes built for the purpose along the banks of the Charles River (Fig. 247).[66] Mostly designed by the firm of Coolidge, Shepley, Bulfinch & Abbott, these buildings exhibited variations of Georgian or colonial styles of architecture that alluded in a general way to the eighteenth-century buildings in Harvard Yard—a stylistic choice which the university had made at the beginning of the century, just as Princeton had committed itself to the Gothic.[67] But regardless of external style, the character of the Harvard "houses" was similar to that of the Yale colleges and the dormitory complexes at Princeton: compact arrangements of linked structures forming enclosed or nearly enclosed courtyards, inward-turning and reclusive in nature, quite different from the traditional American pattern of separate buildings placed on an open campus (Fig. 248).

Besides making better use of the limited urban space, these forms reflected a new interpretation of the collegiate tradition, in reaction partly to the perceived threats posed by the modern university and the contemporary world. The new attitude was represented at Harvard by President

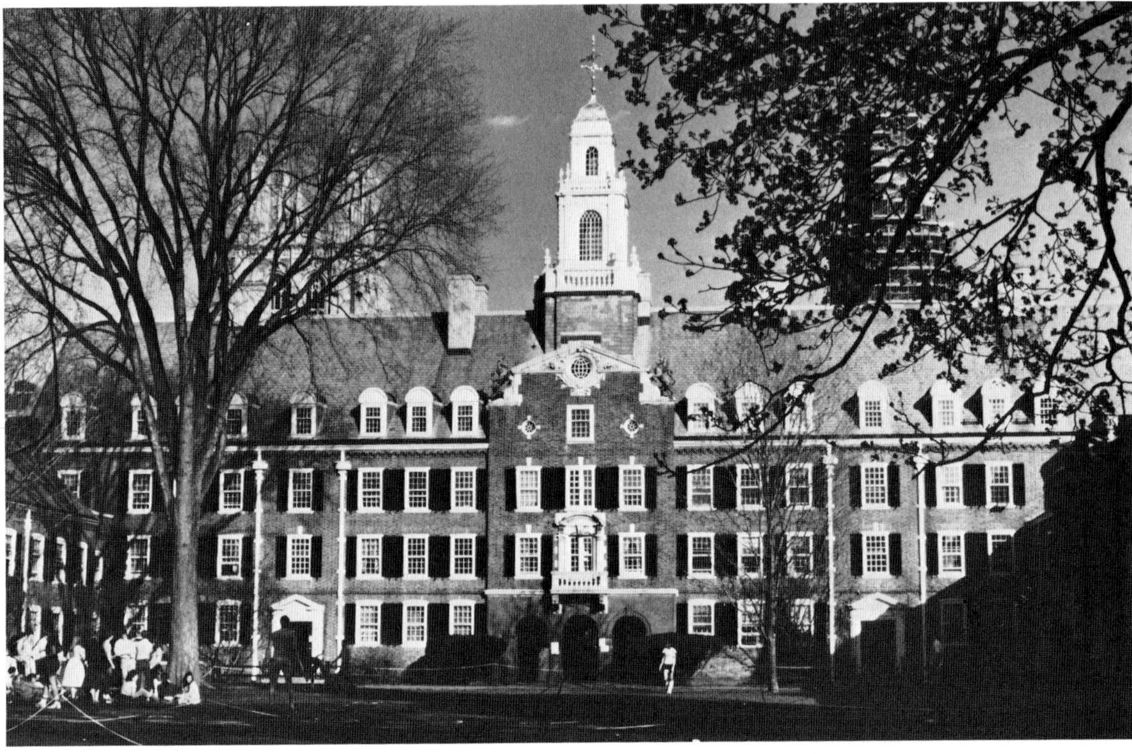

245

246

245 Davenport College, Yale, designed by James Gamble Rogers, 1930. Georgian-style interior court. The center of this facade is patterned on eighteenth-century Old State House in Boston.

246 Davenport College, Yale. Gothic-style facade on York Street. Georgian tower candidly reveals the two-faced architectural character of the building.

247 Harvard "houses," seen from across Charles River. Designed principally by Coolidge, Shepley, Bulfinch & Abbott, ca. 1930.
(Harvard University Archives)

248 Plan of Lowell House, Harvard, designed by Coolidge, Shepley, Bulfinch & Abbott, 1929.
(*Architectural Forum*, June 1931, p. 658)

247

248

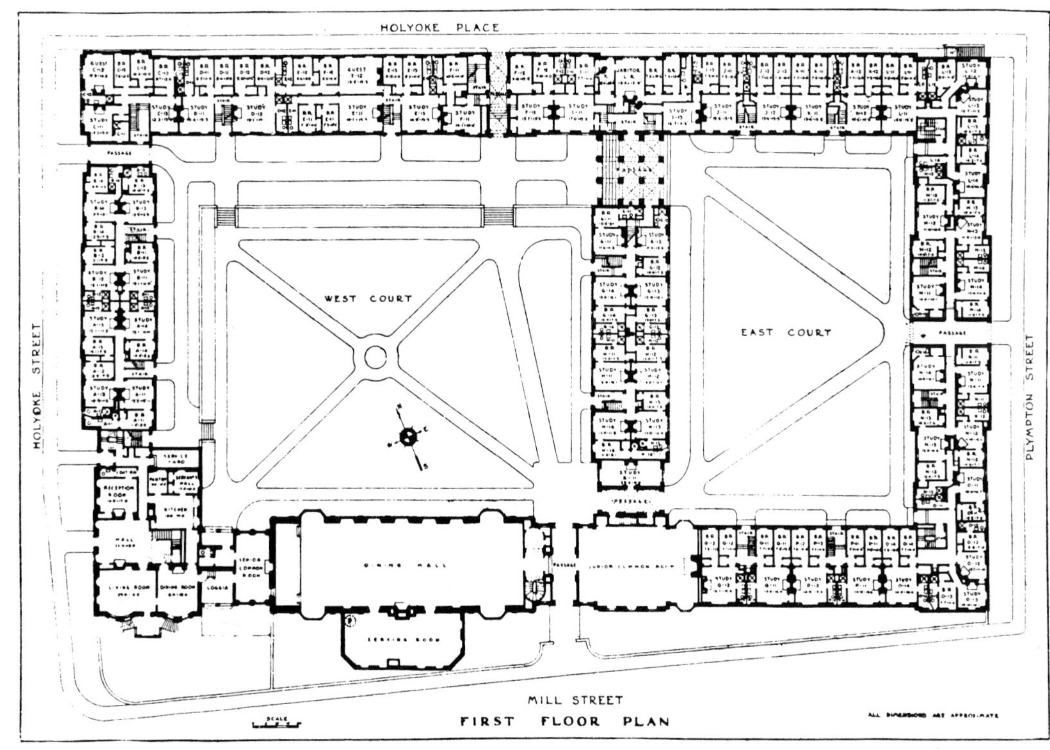
HOLYOKE PLACE
WEST COURT
EAST COURT
HOLYOKE STREET
PLYMPTON STREET
MILL STREET
FIRST FLOOR PLAN

Abbott Lawrence Lowell, who during his long tenure from 1904 to 1933 reversed or tempered many of the anticollegiate measures taken in the late nineteenth century by President Eliot. Lowell wrote in 1929: "The policy in the past . . . has been very vocational and materialistic. We are now striving to make it more cultural and spiritual."[68] Lowell's values were expressed not only in the new "houses" at Harvard, but in several other architectural enterprises. During the 1920s he led the campaign for a new Memorial Church, which was erected in 1932 and, with its tall Georgian tower, became the focal point of Harvard Yard—or at least shared dominance with the massive Widener Library, built in 1913.[69] And from 1924 to 1938, Lowell presided over the construction of a series of seven narrow dormitories along two sides of the Yard, creating a continuous barrier between the inner college and the city outside. This wall of buildings served the practical function of screening the Yard from the noise and activity of the growing city of Cambridge, but it also embodied the new desire for cloistered collegiality.[70]

The central importance of the residential principle to the collegiate ideal in American higher education at this time led to a greater emphasis on the architectural problems of designing dormitories. In the 1920s and 1930s, nearly every book and article that appeared on the subject of college planning gave considerable attention to dormitory design; and at least one book was devoted wholly to dormitory planning.[71] An issue of *Architectural Forum* of 1925 devoted to college architecture was dominated by articles on the subject.[72] Among the issues debated was the relative merit of different types of dormitory plans, such as the common American type in which rooms opened off of long corridors (criticized by Cram and others as barrack-like), and the "separate entry" system, in which many stairways each served only a small number of rooms, with each stairway having its own entrance from the exterior (Fig. 249). This system, typical of the English colleges, had been used at Harvard and Yale in the colonial period, but was effectively replaced in the nineteenth century by the corridor plan. It now reappeared in America, at least at those schools that could afford the extra expense of multiple stairways and the increased space they required.

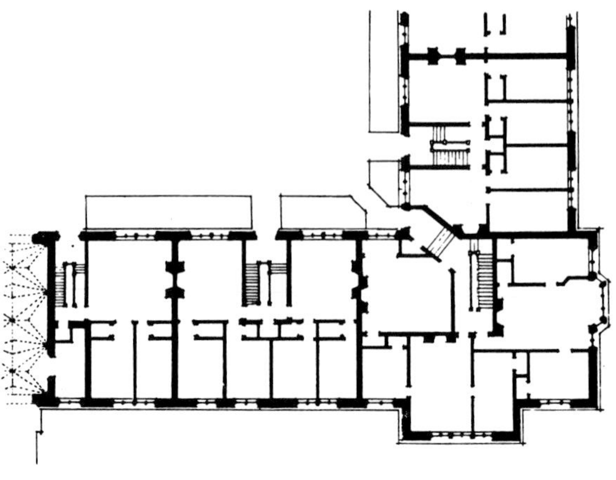

249

249 Plan of portion of Holder Hall, Princeton, designed by Day & Klauder, 1910, using "separate entry" dormitory system.
(*Architectural Forum*, December 1925, p. 332)

Several different forms for the overall plans of dormitories also were proposed and used at this time. Besides the monastic quadrangular form, and the traditional American form of rectangular "barracks," other plans began appearing that had a more domestic character. A group of dormitories at Swarthmore College in Pennsylvania, designed in the 1920s by Walter Karcher and Livingston Smith, had a small scale and an informality that suggested domestic more than collegiate prototypes (Figs. 250, 251).[73] The strong emphasis on the residential character of the American campus was reflected in G. H. Edgell's *The American Architecture of Today*, published in 1928, in which collegiate and domestic architecture were treated together as one category.[74] Edgell, who was the dean of architecture at Harvard, represented both the Beaux-Arts tradition and the reaffirmation of collegiate values. He supported President Lowell's erection of buildings around Harvard's periphery (in order to "cloister the Yard" from the "bustling city," as he put it); but somewhat incongruously, he also echoed Montgomery Schuyler's earlier call for Beaux-Arts order at Harvard:

> What a nightmare confronts the future planner of Harvard. Our admirable forebears had little idea of planning an architectural ensemble. As they acquired means, they added buildings, putting each where they happened to find room for it. There is not a building really on axis with anything else.[75]

The most popular type of architecture for colleges during this period was still a blend of medieval or Georgian forms and Beaux-Arts principles of planning. Probably the most ambitious college-planning project of the 1920s was the master plan for the new campus of Duke University in North Carolina, designed by the Philadelphia firm of Horace Trumbauer (Fig. 252). The plan was composed around two intersecting axes, with the tower of the chapel serving as focal point of the grand approach to the university, reminiscent of the plan for Stanford in the 1880s. But the individual groups of buildings took the form of Gothic quadrangles, irregular and asymmetrical, and as authentic in their details as the Gothic designs of Cram or Klauder (Fig. 253). The incongruity between the parts and the whole was pointed out in the 1930s by William Blackburn, a professor at Duke, who noted that "irregular buildings face upon a regular court . . . as if a Gothic village had been put down in a Renaissance garden."[76]

Each of the two modes served important functions. The Beaux-Arts system allowed the fullest expression of the principles of the American university: grand in scale, clearly organized, and open to the world outside. The Gothic quadrangles, on the other hand, reflected the reaffirmation of the collegiate ideals of intimacy and introspection, and a nostalgia for the elitism of the past. As Blackburn candidly observed, "this architectural conservatism [of the 'Collegiate Gothic' at Duke] expresses the desire, perhaps subconscious, to establish in stone or brick some token of our intellectual and racial heritage."[77]

250

251

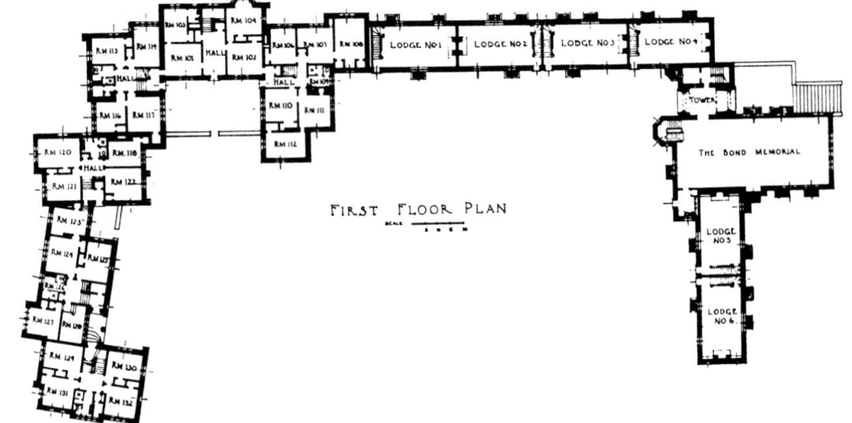

250 Swarthmore College, Swarthmore, Pennsylvania. Women's residential complex (Worth Hall and Bond Memorial and Lodges), designed by Karcher & Smith, 1922; constructed 1924–1927. (*Architectural Forum*, June 1931, p. 674)

251 Plan of women's residential complex, Swarthmore College. (*Architectural Forum*, June 1931, p. 674)

252 Duke University, Durham, North Carolina. Rendering of master plan for the campus, by Horace Trumbauer, ca. 1925. (Duke University)

253 Duke University. Chapel and adjacent structures at center of campus. Designed by Horace Trumbauer; constructed ca. 1927–1930. (Duke University Archives)

252

253

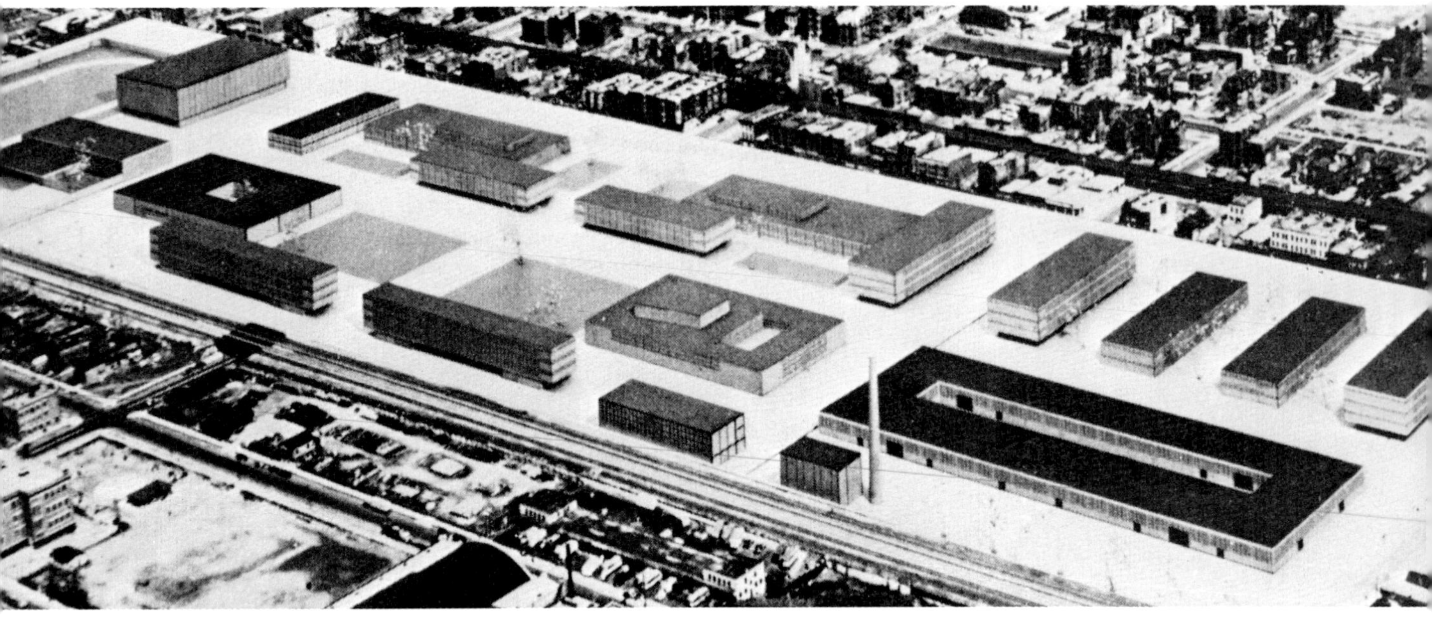

254

254 Illinois Institute of Technology, Chicago. Master plan for the campus by Ludwig Mies van der Rohe, 1940. Model superimposed on photograph of neighborhood.
(Philip Johnson, *Mies van der Rohe*, New York, 1947, p. 135)

VII. Dynamism, Change, and Renewal

After World War II, American higher education underwent transformations that drastically affected campus planning. Increasing enrollments and changing patterns of education made the planner's task more difficult and complex than ever before, and rendered the traditional forms of campus design obsolete in many respects. Collegiate plans by several progressive modern architects (some as early as the 1930s) suggested new approaches to planning, which produced a type of design concerned more with growth and change than with traditional concepts of campus form. But at the same time that the postwar educational institution became more complicated, the need was also felt to break it down into smaller units, and in other ways to regain the positive qualities of the traditional college. In recent years, this trend has been reinforced by a reawakened interest in the historical forms of the American campus, inspired by the architectural preservation movement, and necessitated at many schools by declining resources and slowed growth. These diverse, and often conflicting, developments have made the postwar years one of the most complex periods of American campus design.

The most striking change in American higher education after World War II was a rapid increase in student enrollments, caused first by war veterans taking advantage of the G.I. bill for education, and in succeeding years by a steadily greater proportion of the population attending college and by the "baby boom" generation that came of college age in the 1960s. In 1947, a presidential commission on higher education described the "phenomenal" expansion of enrollments that had already begun, with over two million students in American colleges.[1] By 1951 the increases had leveled off a bit, but in the following decade enrollments jumped to over four million, as greater proportions of the population went to college (from 24 percent in 1951 to 37 percent in 1961).[2] The words "desperate," "unprecedented," and "terrifying" were commonly used to describe this "educational explosion," and projections of future enrollments became a major preoccupation of educators and college planners.[3]

By 1962 it was reported that nearly all of the roughly two thousand institutions of higher education in America had plans for expansion and that two hundred entirely new campuses were being planned or were under construction.[4] The following year, an observer called higher education "one of the most spectacular growth industries."[5] A national organization of campus planners was founded, the Society for College and University Planning, which held annual meetings and later began publishing its own journal—a sure sign of the arrival of campus planning as a distinct profession.[6] Significantly, however, this society encouraged university administrators and other nonarchitects to join, in recognition of the increasing complexity of the physical planning of a large institution, requiring the collaboration of many different professionals, both inside and outside the school.

The problems of planning for the new growth of higher education were complicated by the uncertainty about how great the increasing enrollments would get and when they would level off. Moreover, the very nature and functions of the university were changing in unpredictable ways. The diversity of departments and academic offerings that characterized the American university as it had developed around the turn of the century became much greater, with a multiplication of undergraduate and graduate programs, as well as nontraditional services such as adult education and extension courses. Furthermore, universities began assuming functions that were not strictly educational in nature, such as grant-supported "research and development," which became increasingly important at major universities and often required special facilities.[7]

In striking contrast to the old-time American college that had a relatively unified program and purpose, the new university—or "multiversity," as some called it—was a collection of widely divergent components, with varying aims and often conflicting interests. Harvard in the 1960s was described jokingly as "a loose confederation of departments held together by allegiance to the central heating plant." Moreover, the student population at most schools became increasingly heterogeneous, with students of widely differing backgrounds and ages—some of them married and with families—and at many schools a high proportion of commuting students, factors that intensified the invasion of the campus by the automobile.

Thus, many universities took on the scale and complexity of actual cities. Earlier in the century, when universities like that at Berkeley called themselves "cities of learning," it was largely meant metaphorically. But now the typical university faced very real urban problems, such as high population densities, conflicting land-use patterns, traffic congestion, and opposing interests in different segments of its population. These and other developments made the task of campus planning more difficult than ever before, and necessitated new approaches to the planning process. The complex, fluid, and unpredictable nature of many schools required a type of planning that was itself fluid and flexible, unhampered by formal preconceptions of what a campus should look like.

The Impact of Modern Architecture on Campus Planning

Modern architecture, with its rejection of historical tradition and its frequent emphasis on functionalism and flexibility of planning, was well qualified to tackle many of these new problems of campus planning. But most colleges and universities resisted the advent of modern design, no doubt due to an inherent conservatism in regard to their physical environment, and thus the impact of modern architecture tended to be felt later in campus planning than in other fields.

In the 1930s, when the International Style and other modern movements in architecture were becoming accepted in America, the instances of their use at colleges and universities were rare and surrounded by controversy. To the modernists, all traditional collegiate forms were bankrupt, and the erection of any "modern" building on the campus was a victory. To the traditionalists, the goal was just as simply to keep the American school free of the alien International Style.

Reflecting these polarized positions, the architectural journals often ignored more complex issues of campus planning in their preoccupation with choosing sides in the battle of the ancients versus the moderns. *Architectural Forum* was one of the first strong voices for the modernists, and for many years it used its reporting of college architecture primarily as a vehicle for advancing its views. As early as 1931 it printed an article by a crusading Yale student condemning the "heavily Gothic, or deadly Classical" architecture of American colleges, and praising Walter Gropius's Bauhaus buildings in Germany.[8] In 1938 the magazine joined the New York Museum of Modern Art in cosponsoring a competition for an Art Center at Wheaton College in Massachusetts, with the prize going to an International Style design, which was, however, never built.[9] (After the war, a new president at Wheaton announced that all future construction would be traditional in style, a decision that provoked heated debate at the school, which *Architectural Forum* reported with stories such as "Campus Controversy: Students Unite for Modern Architecture, as Prexy Plugs for Georgian.")[10]

In 1942 the magazine praised the new International Style structure for Hunter College in New York City, defending it against "the more sentimental section of the public and profession decrying the omission of the customary collegiate trimmings."[11] Later in the 1940s the magazine reported another modern-versus-traditional controversy at Wake Forest College in North Carolina with the headline "Down With Georgian," and it celebrated a series of new buildings at the University of Oklahoma in an article entitled "Oklahoma University Goes Modern," which took jabs at the previous styles of "Cherokee Gothic" and "sterile Classic, pompous, inhuman and awkward."[12]

The debate over whether colleges should "go modern" was still strong even after World War II. Walter Gropius, by then chairman of the architecture department at Harvard, wrote an article for the *New York Times* in 1949 entitled "Not Gothic But Modern For Our Colleges."[13] And the following year, the planner Walter Creese rebutted the detractors of campus modernism in an article called "Architecture and Learning: A Collegiate Quandary"—the "quandary" still being the choice between traditional and modern architecture.[14]

This preoccupation with architectural style tended to divert attention from questions of campus planning in the larger sense. Thus, Ludwig Mies van der Rohe's design for the Illinois Institute of Technology in Chicago, of 1938–40, was widely publicized in the following decade as the epitome of modernism because of the uncompromising purity of its International Style buildings, which used an exposed steel-frame structural system.[15] But its overall plan was actually conventional in many respects (Fig. 254). The symmetrical and axial arrangement of buildings, forming a central quadrangle and subsidiary groups of structures, was not very different from Beaux-Arts collegiate designs, except for the absence of a dominating focal point. In fact, Mies's original site plans, of 1938–39, were even more clearly classical than the final scheme, for they consisted simply of the central portion of the final plan. (In 1940, the school decided to expand the site, and Mies elongated his scheme by adding the secondary groups of buildings, somewhat less formal in character, to the ends of the original composition.) The overall plan of I.I.T. belonged essentially to a classical tradition of planning, which soon came to be considered too rigid and inflexible by most campus planners. Even the notion of a master plan that predetermined the position and forms of buildings was a convention that soon was challenged.

However, hints of new attitudes toward campus planning did appear in the late 1930s and 1940s, in designs for several small or progressive colleges. In 1938 Goucher College, a women's school in Baltimore, held a competition for the master plan of a new campus on a hilly site outside the city.[16] The competition program described the informal and intimate character of the college, and stated that the new plan "should reflect these progressive principles in education," as well as "preserve the natural loveliness of the landscape," and that "the emphasis should be upon the informal rather than the institutional or monumental."[17]

Many of the competitors ignored these suggestions, submitting more or less standard, axial, Beaux-Arts plans—an indication of the ingrained traditions of campus design at this time.[18] But the first prize went to a design by John C. B. Moore and Robert S. Hutchins, which showed simple, rubble-stone buildings arranged irregularly to conform with the topography, in a manner the architects described as embodying "flexibility, convenience, and efficiency" (Fig. 255).[19] (Moore and Hutchins also stated that their plan allowed "the construction of one building after another through a period of years, without injury to the effectiveness of the group during this natural process of growth"—exactly the same claim that John Trumbull had made for his master plan for Yale in 1792.)[20] The sketches that Moore and Hutchins made in the process of their design reveal that they, too, began with a standard Beaux-Arts scheme of buildings placed symmetrically along an axis, but then modified it beyond recognition in response to a more careful reading of the programmatic requirements and topographical features.[21] After the first building, a residence hall, was erected, World War II interrupted execution of the Moore and Hutchins master plan, but subsequent construction largely adhered to it (Fig. 256).

Another departure from campus-planning tradition occurred in Frank Lloyd Wright's designs for Florida Southern College, also begun in 1938. This project, which was Wright's first commission for an entire college, was brought to him by the school's president, Ludd M. Spivey, who was an admirer of the architect's work and who gave him full freedom of design as well as an agreeable site in a citrus grove next to a lake.[22] Wright's exper-

255 Goucher College, Towson, Maryland. Master plan by Moore and Hutchins, 1938. Toward top of plan (north), academic buildings form an irregular three-sided courtyard; extending southeast are the residential "house-groups."
(Goucher College)

256 Goucher College. Mary Fisher Hall, designed by Moore and Hutchins; constructed ca. 1943.
(Goucher College)

LAKE
FACULTY
PRESIDENT
ACADEMIC GROUP
CHAPEL
PARKING
AUDITORIUM
UNION
HOUSE GROUPS
SPORTS
SERVICE
POND
ENTRANCE DRIVE

255

256

iments in the 1930s with nonrectilinear geometries led him to create a campus of irregular spaces and casual movement from building to building, along paths forming thirty-, sixty-, and ninety-degree angles (Figs. 257–259). The flexibility of this scheme allowed Wright to give the individual buildings a wide range of shapes—hexagonal in the chapel and theater, circular in the library, rectangular in some of the other buildings, and a combination of hexagonal and rectangular in the music building.

Wright's motives in creating this variety had more to do with his own architectural interests during this phase of his career than with any specific concern for college-planning issues. But in the process, he dealt with a problem that was to become increasingly troublesome to college planners in succeeding years: the difficulty of accommodating within traditional campus formats the bulky or irregularly shaped buildings required by a modern institution. The Gothic quadrangle or the neat Beaux-Arts grid, even if executed in the International Style, demanded a high degree of uniformity or consistency in its parts, preferably with buildings of similar forms or unified by a common modular system. In contrast, Wright's design for Florida Southern implied a kind of looseness of planning that could admit the most idiosyncratic components. In this regard, Wright's background was significant. His executed works had nearly all been individual buildings, usually domestic houses in suburban settings, and he had little interest in the problems of planning large groups of buildings in which the freedom of the part had to be subordinated to a greater order. Even in his one venture into "urban" planning, the Utopian "Broadacre City," his plans were conceived in a context of rural spaciousness in which all the buildings could have their own character and individuality.

At Florida Southern, Wright applied the same kind of thinking, creating a kind of Broadacre College, in which the separate buildings were more important than an overall system of order. Wright did make a gesture of unifying the diverse parts, by connecting the buildings with walkways covered by concrete canopies or arcades (which may have been inspired by the arcades at Stanford University, which Wright had visited the year before and had praised highly).[23] But Wright's design remained es-

257 Florida Southern College, Lakeland. Rendering of master plan for campus, by Frank Lloyd Wright, begun 1938. Covered walkways, or "esplanades," connect buildings. At left is "water dome" that Wright intended as a focal point of campus.
(© The Frank Lloyd Wright Foundation, 1962. Courtesy of The Frank Lloyd Wright Memorial Foundation)

258 Florida Southern College. Three main structures in foreground (*from left*) are: Administration Building, 1946–1950; Library, 1941; and Ann Pfeiffer Chapel, 1940.
(Photograph by Harold Sanborn. Provided by The Frank Lloyd Wright Memorial Foundation)

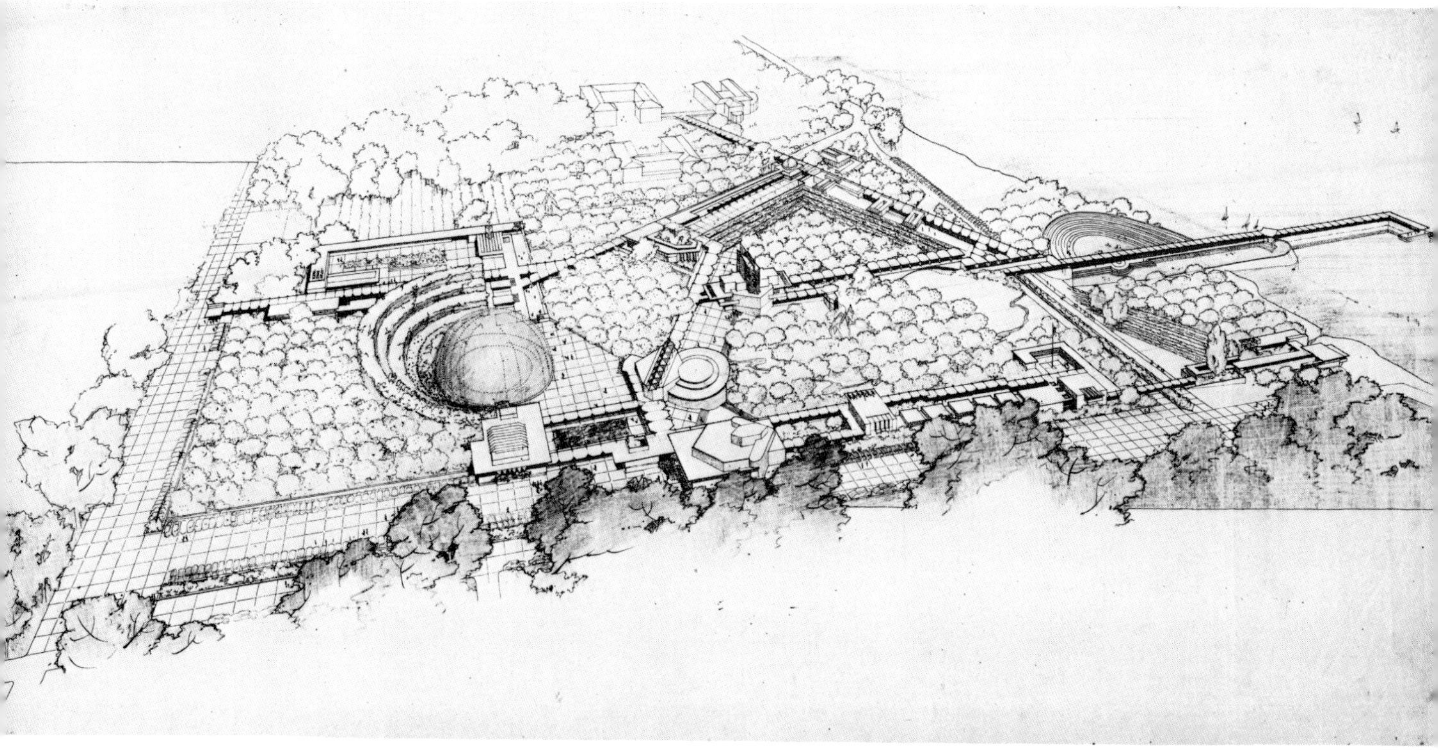

257

258

259

260

259 Ann Pfeiffer Chapel, Florida Southern College. In foreground, portion of covered walkway that connects Chapel to Library.
(Photograph by Harold Sanborn. Provided by The Frank Lloyd Wright Memorial Foundation)

260 Tuskegee Institute, Alabama. Rendering of design for chapel, by Paul Rudolph, 1960.
(Paul Rudolph, Architect)

sentially informal, and stressed the individuality of the parts.

The Florida Southern campus was widely publicized in architectural journals and the popular press as its buildings were gradually executed in the 1940s and 1950s, and in a general way it no doubt encouraged the rejection of Beaux-Arts principles of planning. But its nonrectilinear geometries and complex building shapes, largely out of step with the increasingly accepted International Style, seem to have had little effect on campus architects. One exception may be Paul Rudolph, who began his architectural practice in Florida as Wright's campus was still under construction, and several of whose designs recall its dynamic forms—such as his master plan for Tuskegee Institute in Alabama, of 1960 (Fig. 260).[24]

Another early experiment in campus design was made at Black Mountain College in North Carolina, an avant-garde school dedicated to new ideals of informal education, communal social values, and modernism in the arts.[25] Housed at first in borrowed quarters, the school in 1937 purchased land for a permanent campus, a hilly, rural site with a small lake. Among Black Mountain's distinguished faculty was Josef Albers, who arranged for his former Bauhaus teacher and colleague Walter Gropius to design the buildings for the new campus. The plan that Gropius and his associate Marcel Breuer prepared, for the modest fee of $400, called for several structures, of varying shapes according to their functions (classrooms, living quarters, and communal spaces), sited irregularly along the shore of the lake—parts of the buildings actually to be placed over the water, on columns (Figs. 261, 262).[26]

The school attempted to raise the funds required to execute the plan (estimated at $500,000), but the outbreak of war made the task nearly impossible. Faced with eviction from the temporary quarters, the school hired the architect A. Lawrence Kocher to produce a reduced plan. This design retained the general character of Gropius's scheme, with four structures or wings of different lengths extending from a central hub at irregular angles.[27] The major part of Kocher's design, called the Studies Building, was constructed in the early 1940s—largely by the students and faculty themselves—and housed the college until it was forced to close in the 1950s (Fig. 263). Black Mountain College may have been destroyed by its increasingly unstructured experimentation, for which even Kocher's building no doubt seemed confining. But the designs of Gropius and Kocher were appropriate expressions of the school's original goals of breaking the conventional bonds of higher education and creating a new communal model of a college.

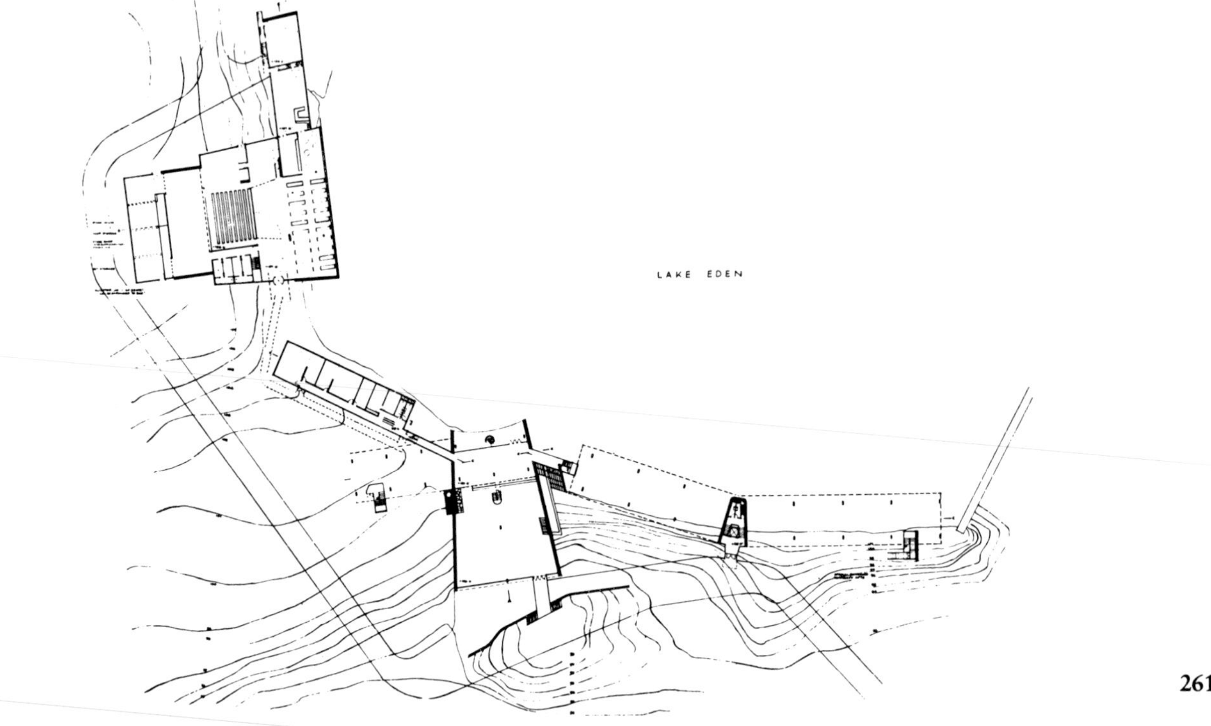

261

261 Black Mountain College, Black Mountain, North Carolina. Master plan for the school, by Walter Gropius and Marcel Breuer, 1939. (The Architects Collaborative)

262 Model of design for Black Mountain College, by Gropius and Breuer. (The Architects Collaborative)

263 Studies Building, Black Mountain College, designed by A. Lawrence Kocher, ca. 1941. (Photograph by F. S. Lincoln. *Architectural Forum*, June 1945, p. 129)

262

263

Campus Planning as Process

Traditional college planning in the twentieth century, whether a conception for an entirely new campus or a "development plan" for an existing campus, usually produced a unified design, specific in its overall form and architectural character. After World War II, college planners began to abandon this tradition of ambitious master plans, in favor of an approach that emphasized establishing principles for future growth. In a sense, the process of planning became more important than the final form. This shift was motivated not only by the complexity and unpredictability of the modern institution, but also by the disenchantment of the college administrators toward formal master plans, which they found were often unrealistic and almost always impossible to execute fully. In response to a questionnaire that asked, "Have master plans for your campus ever been made?" one college respondent replied, "Several, by professionals at considerable expense—usually discarded."[28] And the head of Harvard's planning office stated in 1964 that his policy was "guided, organic growth" rather than a master plan.[29]

An early statement of this new approach was made in 1947 by Joseph Hudnut, who introduced modern architecture into the School of Design at Harvard. In an article on college planning in *Architectural Forum*, Hudnut outlined the tradition of American campus plans, from Jefferson's University of Virginia to Mies's I.I.T., in which architects created "grand compositions, . . . corseting the body of a live and unpredictable creature," and he claimed that "in every instance the live creature has refused the mould."[30] Hudnut went on to describe his view of the proper kind of campus planning, in tune with modern principles of change and growth:

> Every attempt to bind [universities] to a pattern laid out in advance has failed—and ought to have failed. . . . We must set them free to develop their environment in whatever way may best suit their existing needs. . . . The task to be performed in university buildings and the methods by which they are built constantly change. Their nature tomorrow cannot be predicted. No program is possible which extends beyond a dozen years. . . . Let's imagine the university, as the city planners imagine the city, as a growing organism whose form lies partly in the past, partly in the future. Our university will never be completed. . . . If we make a master plan then, it must be in such general terms as will admit of new interpretations and unexpected development. We can take nothing for granted. Those facilities which have endured the longest may be the first to disappear.[31]

Hudnut's rejection of permanence and stability—qualities that colleges and universities traditionally had held sacred—and his embrace of obsolescence and flexibility, had far-reaching practical implications that soon became evident at American schools. One was the liberation of the individual building—as in Wright's Florida Southern College, but more completely. If it was impossible or undesirable to conceive the whole campus as a unified "grand composition," then each component could be given its own character, with little or no responsibility to the whole. Hudnut himself recommended precisely this, saying, "Let no building depend for its character upon its relation to another, nor let any of the open spaces be of such absolute proportions that new construction built into them will destroy them."[32]

This statement no doubt infuriated the traditional campus planners who read it and saw in it an open invitation to aesthetic chaos and expediency. Hudnut may not have meant it that way; but the fact is that the concept was convenient for institutions that needed to erect new buildings, often in limited space, and for whom visual considerations of campus unity or spatial composition were merely annoying obstacles. Across America, colleges and universities were filling the open spaces on their campuses. And the new permissiveness justified the erection of large and unconventional structures (huge lecture halls, student unions, or dormitories for large numbers of students), without having to try to disguise them or make them conform to an existing campus style. New forms of architecture could be embraced with no apologies.

The Massachusetts Institute of Technology was among the first schools to take positive advantage of this new approach to planning, when it built Alvar Aalto's serpentine-shaped dormitory in 1949, and about four years later had Eero Saarinen design a thin-shell, domical auditorium resting on three points, and a cylindrical chapel nearby (Fig.

264

264 Kresge Auditorium and Chapel, Massachusetts Institute of Technology, Cambridge. Designed by Eero Saarinen; constructed 1955.
(Balthazar Korab, Ltd., Photography)

264).[33] These buildings, like art objects, were conceived as individual shapes, each standing alone and producing its visual effect precisely by its dramatic contrast to, rather than conformity with, the other buildings and the environment around it.

A rather similar attitude emerged in the planning that took place at Yale in the 1950s, under the presidency of A. Whitney Griswold. Griswold had a strong personal interest in contemporary architecture, and took full advantage of the growth of Yale during this period to hire eminent architects to design new buildings. In contrast to Cram's supervision of the development of Princeton at the beginning of the century, Griswold felt no need for a strong unifying hand, and gave the architect of each building full freedom to create in his own manner. The result was an "architectural laboratory," as one observer put it, with many individual buildings of distinction, such as Louis Kahn's Art Gallery, Eero Saarinen's Hockey Rink and Morse and Stiles colleges, Gordon Bunshaft's Beinecke Rare Book Library, Paul Rudolph's Art and Architecture Building, and Philip Johnson's Kline Science Center (Figs. 302, 265, 266).[34]

The coherence of the campus as a whole was not a primary concern, for Griswold believed in the validity of each university building as a separate creation, having little dependence on its surroundings. Answering a critic who charged that Yale was allowing architects to "compete for effects," he admitted that this might be true, but defended it as an expression of the modern university's diversity. And asked if the work of the many architects he had hired shared a common denominator, Griswold replied, "No common denominator. Just quality."[35] In another interview toward the end of his presidency, Griswold described his close friendships with Saarinen and other architects, his successful efforts to bring the Yale Corporation (the school's governing board) around to his views on architecture, and his reasons for not having an official campus architect:

> We were opposed to it, because we felt that it would impose too great a uniformity on the campus. Buildings, like people, ought to be different from one another.[36]

Similar attitudes were apparent at other schools during this period, even in designs for groups of

265 Art and Architecture Building, Yale University. Designed by Paul Rudolph, 1958.
(Paul Rudolph, Architect)

266 Beinecke Rare Book and Manuscript Library, Yale University. Designed by Gordon Bunshaft of Skidmore, Owings & Merrill, 1961. At right is portion of the Bicentennial Buildings, designed by Carrère & Hastings and others, beginning in 1901.
(Yale University Library)

263

265

266

buildings or whole campuses. Harrison & Abramovitz's three chapels—Jewish, Catholic, and Protestant—built at Brandeis University in Massachusetts in 1955, were conceived rather like pieces of sculpture, arranged for display in an open field that was declared off limits to future construction (the only part of the campus so designated) in order to preserve the chapels' distinctiveness (Fig. 267).[37] The United States Air Force Academy in Colorado, designed by Skidmore, Owings & Merrill, was one of the most publicized new campuses in the mid-1950s (Fig. 268). Although its design was highly unified in certain respects, with most of the buildings adhering to a standard structural format and a grid plan, several of the buildings were given distinctive forms that set them apart—notably the impressive chapel, placed on a podium above the rest of the campus, with a dramatic folded-plate structural form (Fig. 269).[38]

In a sense, the new attitude of freedom in campus planning, with each building standing on its own, was a return to the old American pattern—from the days before Beaux-Arts master planning—of separate buildings in large open spaces. But to the extent that the buildings on the traditional American campus were markedly different from one another in shape or style, it was normally because they dated from different eras. Given a chance, earlier colleges usually chose architectural unity over disparity. Only in the 1950s and 1960s did architectural variety on the American campus become a fully acceptable, even desirable, phenomenon. This change not only reflected the importance that modern architecture attached to originality (and its disdain of conformity), but it also expressed, as Yale's President Griswold suggested, the diversity of the postwar university. For an institution in flux, and made up of conflicting individual constituencies, held together only by "allegiance to the central heating plant," neither a unified master plan nor stylistic conformity made sense.

The new attitude toward planning was presented most fully in Richard P. Dober's *Campus Planning*, published in 1963.[39] The first thorough work on the subject since the books of Klauder and Larson of 1929 and 1933, its approach was totally different from theirs. Whereas Klauder and Larson had a great deal to say about architectural styles,

267

267 Brandeis University, Waltham, Massachusetts. The Three Chapels (Jewish, Catholic, and Protestant), designed by Harrison & Abramovitz, ca. 1954.
(Brandeis University)

268 United States Air Force Academy, Colorado Springs, Colorado. Campus designed by Skidmore, Owings & Merrill, 1954; constructed 1956–1962. At left (east), main group of buildings includes Cadet Quarters, dining hall, and academic structures. To right, around the Court of Honor, are Administration Building, Social Center, and Chapel.
(Skidmore, Owings & Merrill)

269 Chapel, United States Air Force Academy, Colorado.
(Skidmore, Owings & Merrill)

268

269

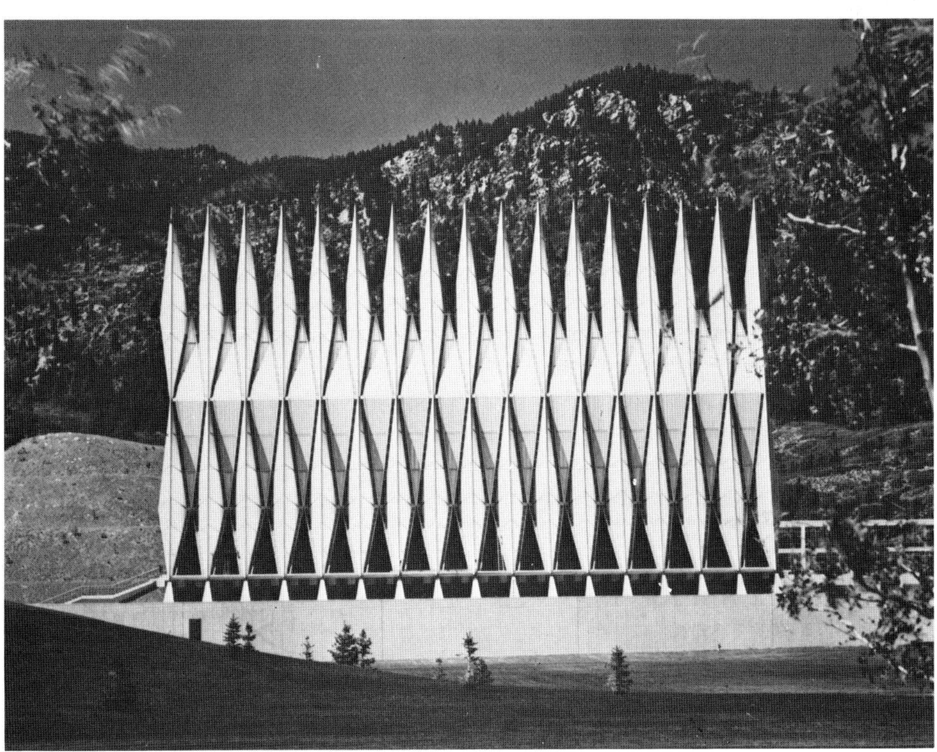

and about the role of master plans in bringing unity and order to the overall visual pattern of a campus, Dober concentrated on the process of planning rather than on the ultimate form. Projections of future enrollments and educational needs were basic tools for Dober; but even with these it was impossible to know for certain how an institution would grow and change, so flexibility was essential, and the planner could do no more than establish guidelines for growth, with little or no preconceived formal bias. More immediate decisions, such as where to locate a new building, were based on the analysis of existing facilities, traffic patterns, densities, and other conditions both on the campus and in the surrounding environment. As proposed by Hudnut in 1947, each building or campus component was thought of as an independent unit, not as a fixed element in a predetermined pattern. Dober called these units "planning modules," and said, "the planning module is a chess piece, the campus a chessboard."[40] He devoted separate chapters to the different types of these "modules," categorized as Instructional Facilities; Libraries and Museums; Research; Centers of Extracurricular Life; Institutional Services; Housing; Sports, Recreation and Physical Education; Circulation and Parking; and Utilities. (Significantly, classrooms and dormitories, the core of the traditional college, were only two of the many parts of the new institution.) Carrying the chess analogy further, Dober wrote:

> Each move has consequences for all other pieces, and there are several strategies in planning which can be pursued with equal success. For this reason, through constant testing, adjustment, and feedback, the program from which the module is derived will itself be refined as preliminary agreements are reached on such decisions as the location of roads, the connections between one building and another, or the order in which the long-range planning is to be accomplished.[41]

The complexity of the modern educational institution, in a state of constant change, thus required an equally complex and fluid process of planning. The physical results of this process were inevitably different from earlier campus designs, with their strong formal clarity. To have such clarity would have falsified the nature of the American university of the postwar period—an institution complex, dynamic, and unpredictable.

Movement and the Urban Model

The Harvard Graduate Center, a dining and dormitory complex for graduate students, designed by Walter Gropius and The Architects' Collaborative in 1949, was one of the first large groups of International Style buildings on an American campus (Figs. 270, 271).[42] Gropius arranged the eight buildings to form spaces reminiscent of collegiate quadrangles, but these spaces were irregular, flowed into one another with ambiguous boundaries, were nonrectilinear in places, and created patterns of open and closed forms—all of which Gropius described as embodying "motion or the illusion of motion."[43]

This concept of "motion" in architecture was part of the aesthetic theory developed at the Bauhaus in the 1920s. But it was especially appropriate to the dynamic and changing nature of the American university after World War II. And in the following years, real movement—both pedestrian and vehicular—began to influence campus planning in significant ways, and inspired a whole new approach to campus design.

The automobile became a principal factor in postwar campus planning, especially at schools with a high proportion of commuting students. For the first time, problems of vehicular access, parking, and traffic congestion became serious concerns of the planner, as indicated by Dober's devoting a chapter in his book to the subject. At many schools parking lots began to claim immense areas of land (providing the comedian Bob Hope with the line, "U.C.L.A. is a four-year university—or five years if you park in Lot 32").[44] Increasingly, new campuses were laid out in patterns determined largely by vehicular considerations, such as the proximity of access roads to campus facilities, or the optimum relationship of parking areas to buildings. The kinds of campus plans that resulted from these considerations included a linear arrangement of buildings along a road and parking lots, and a "ring road" type of plan, in which vehicles were kept mainly on the outside of a central campus area.[45] The University of California at Irvine was a new campus laid out roughly in this pattern (Fig. 286).[46] Many existing schools, such as Stanford University, redesigned their traffic routes in the 1950s and 1960s to create ring roads and parking areas, within which the heart of the campus could theoretically be safe for pedestrians, while retaining the traditional scale that was threatened by automobiles.

Pedestrian circulation, too, began to be seen by planners as a potential shaper of campus form. Le Corbusier, when he came to Harvard in 1959 to design a visual arts center, was fascinated with the movement of students between classes along the diagonal paths crisscrossing Harvard Yard, and was inspired to create a building organized around a ramp that cut through it diagonally to connect two streets, and also to advertise the building's activities to passing students (Fig. 272).[47] As executed, the ramp was not fully successful as a circulation route (especially in the icy Cambridge winters). But the concept of a building—or even a whole campus—designed around pedestrian movement appealed to architects, and soon became a major force in campus planning.

I. M. Pei & Partners, commissioned in the mid-1960s to design several new structures for the State University College at Fredonia, New York, transformed the existing campus with a bold plan structured principally around a "pedestrian spine" that linked the new buildings (student union, lecture center, library, administration building, fine arts center, and academic buildings) along two diagonal lines—reminiscent of the typical American campus paths that had impressed Le Corbusier (Figs. 273, 274).[48] In its long course across the Fredonia campus, this "spine" variously took the form of bridges or ground-level paths, opened into terraces or courtyards between buildings, was above grade or below, and generally functioned as a focus of student movement and activity. Significantly, the other major component of the Fredonia design, according to the architects, was a roadway they created to encircle a large part of the campus—another evidence of the fascination with vehicular and pedestrian movement during this period.

By the mid-1960s, many architects and planners were talking about circulation as a primary shaper of campus form, along with flexibility and growth. These three concerns were exemplified in a master plan for Tougaloo College in Mississippi by Gunnar Birkerts & Associates, which was described in 1966 as "a design for a process, not for a final result" (Fig. 275).[49] The plan proposed a dense "matrix" of components on several superimposed

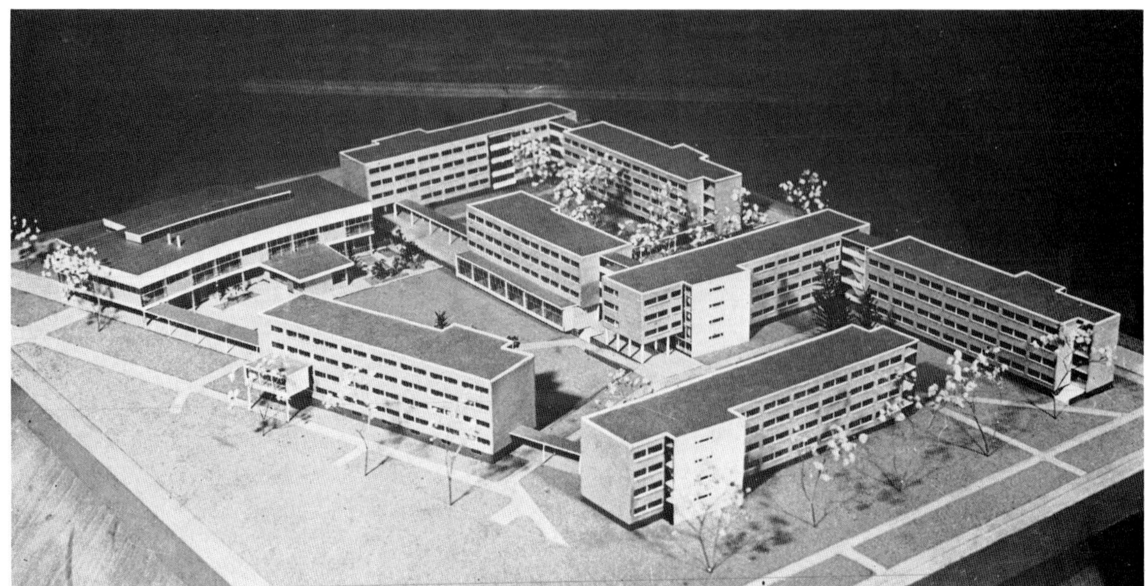
270

271

272 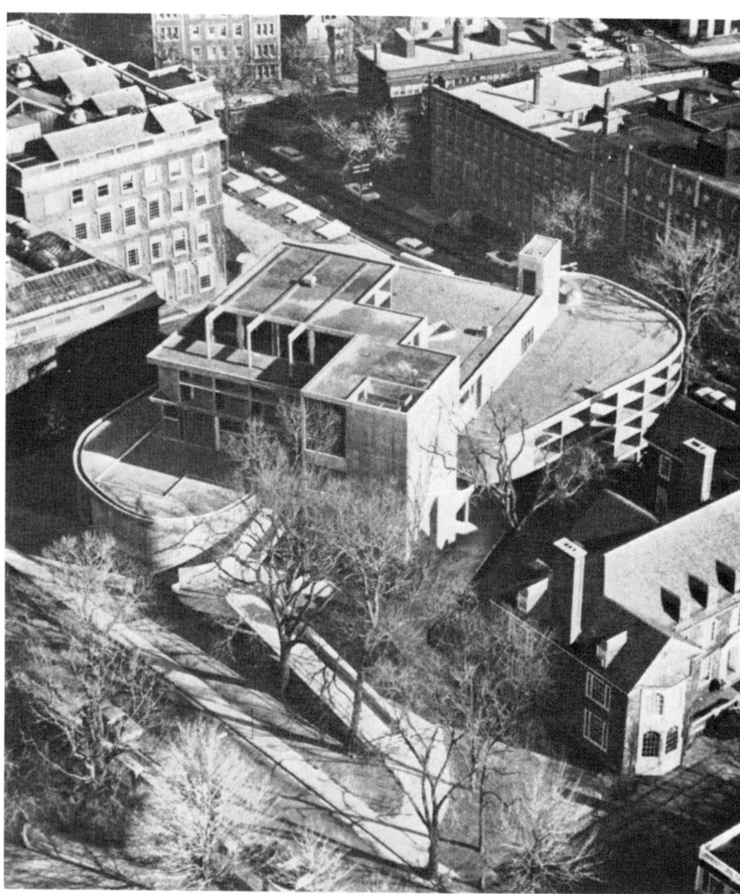

270 Graduate Center, Harvard University. Model of design by Walter Gropius and The Architects Collaborative, 1949. (The Architects Collaborative)

271 Graduate Center, Harvard. At left is dining hall; in background, two of the dormitories.
(Photograph by Fred Stone, provided by the Cambridge Historical Commission)

272 Carpenter Center for the Visual Arts, Harvard. Designed by Le Corbusier, 1960. In foreground is part of ramp that leads from street and passes diagonally through the building.
(Photograph by Laurence Lowry. *Architectural Forum*, March 1963, p. 81)

273 State University College of Fredonia, Fredonia, New York. Development plan for campus, by I. M. Pei & Partners (Henry N. Cobb, partner in charge), ca. 1964. Preexisting structures included the physical education, music, science, and classroom buildings. Situated along the diagonal circulation route are the new Student Union, Lecture Center, Library, Administration Building, and Fine Arts Building. (*Architectural Forum*, May 1969, p. 39)

274 State University College at Fredonia. Pedestrian bridge from Student Union to Lecture Center (*right*). In background are Administration Building and Library. (Photograph by Daniel Reiff)

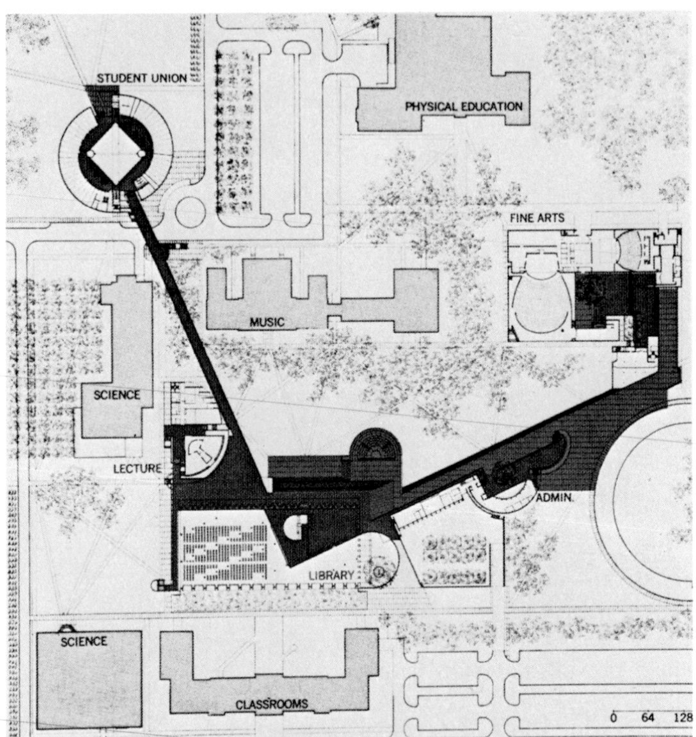

273

274

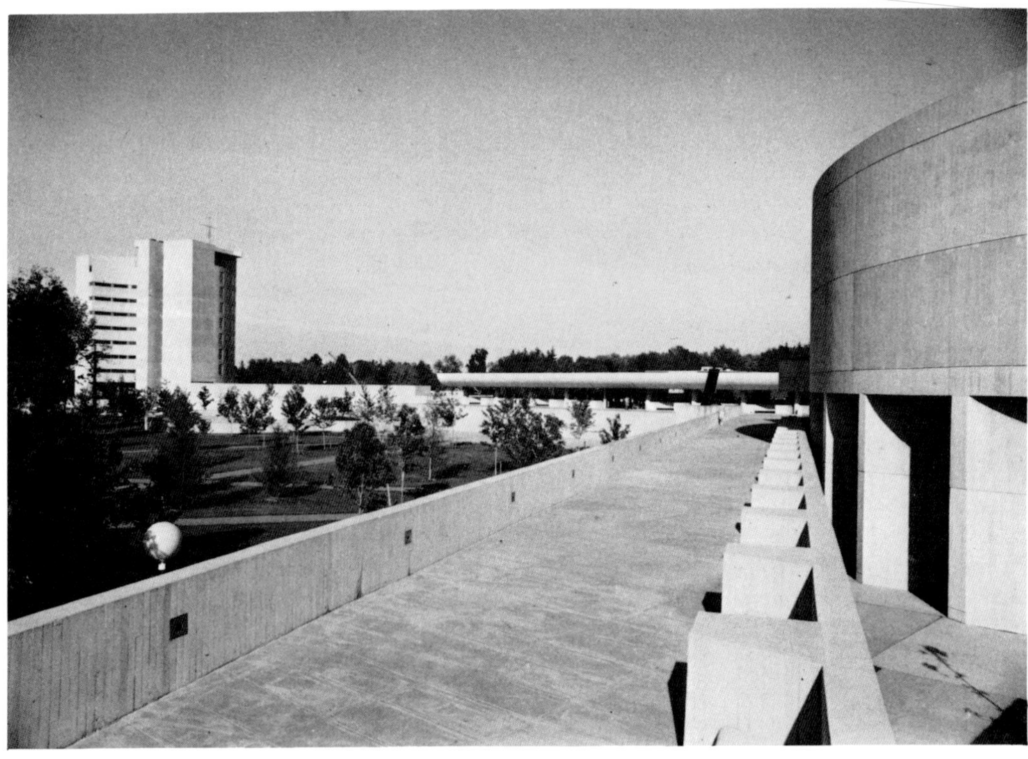

levels, to be built in stages. The ground level was to be devoted to vehicular traffic, the next level to the "academic matrix," and above that would be the dormitories, connected to the lower levels by stairs and walkways (Fig. 276). The concept was described as an attempt to "promote the kind of close social contacts characteristic of urban life"—a remarkable reversal of the traditional American ideal of the nonurban college.[50] As it happened, only part of the Tougaloo plan was built, so that instead of the densely "urban" complex envisioned, the result was dormitories stranded somewhat awkwardly on stilts. But the design epitomized the fascination of planners, during this period, with patterns of movement as shapers of architectural form, and with the notion that campus planning could be a model for city planning.

Josep Lluis Sert, of Harvard's school of design, stated this view in 1963 when he said that "a university campus is a laboratory for urban design."[51] But in contrast to the plan for Tougaloo, where an essentially rural campus was made a metaphor for urbanism, Sert was involved in the problems of truly urban universities, such as Harvard and Boston University, which were desperate to expand but had little room to do so.[52] Many universities in cities were forced to construct large, bulky structures that filled up whole city blocks or previously open areas of a campus, or high-rise buildings that introduced a dimension previously alien to the American college and university. An article in *Architectural Forum* in 1964 described this phenomenon at several of the universities in the Boston area.[53] At many institutions, dormitories were built that recalled Le Corbusier's "Unité d'Habitation" experiments in high-rise housing, but often without the large surrounding areas of parkland that Le Corbusier had stipulated.[54] At Harvard, Sert attempted to deal with these problems in his design for a large married-student housing complex, sited on the Charles River adjacent to the Georgian-style undergraduate "houses" of the 1930s. The complex consisted of three tall towers at the center of the site, forming an open space that functioned more like a city square than a traditional "campus," with the rest of the structures stepping down gradually to mediate with the smaller scale of the college and neighborhood buildings on the periphery (Fig. 277).[55]

A 1966 article by Oscar Newman summarized current trends in campus planning.[56] Newman praised several designs for new campuses that had a dense urban character and were organized in terms of circulation patterns and "hierarchies of activity." These included Scarborough College in Ontario, designed by John Andrews; Forest Park Community College in St. Louis, by Harry Weese & Associates; and the Chicago Circle campus of the University of Illinois, by Skidmore, Owings & Merrill. Newman noted that the traditional division of the campus into areas devoted to the various departments or academic disciplines often was replaced in these designs by an organization based on "functional activities" (that is, putting all classrooms together, and all faculty offices together), to increase efficiency and flexibility. Newman acknowledged that this might contribute to a "lack of identity" among students. But he suggested:

> Since one of the university's major functions is to prepare the student for a leading role in society, this separation of professional identity from spacial identity is [perhaps] in fact readying him to face our unstructured world.[57]

Thus the new campus—urban in its scale, density, complexity, and even in its potential for alientation—could be justified as a mirror not only of the current state of higher education, but of modern society in general.

Probably the most ambitious university plan of the 1960s was for the "Chicago Circle" campus of the University of Illinois, which exemplified many of the new ideas in planning, as well as the political complexities involved in creating a new public institution. After World War II, the University of Illinois, with its main campus at Urbana-Champaign, opened a two-year undergraduate branch in Chicago, primarily to accommodate war veterans. The site was an old Navy pier on Lake Michigan, and the facility was meant to be temporary, but by the early 1950s increased public demand for higher education spurred the university to study the feasibility of a permanent branch in the Chicago area. For nearly a decade, heated controversy surrounded the questions of whether to create such a school, and if so, where to locate it.[58] Partisans of the main campus at Urbana-Champaign feared that its resources would be di-

272

275

276

277

275 Tougaloo College, Tougaloo, Mississippi. Model of design for new buildings, by Gunnar Birkerts & Associates, ca. 1965. (Balthazar Korab, Ltd., Photography)

276 Tougaloo College. In foreground is one of the dormitory structures; in background, the library. (Balthazar Korab, Ltd., Photography)

277 Harvard University. Peabody Terrace (married students' housing), seen from Charles River. Designed by Sert, Jackson & Gourley, 1962–1964. (Harvard University News Office)

luted by a rival branch. Support for the new institution was strong in Chicago, but even there it had opponents, notably at the city's private universities.

The Illinois state legislature, which reflected all the differing positions, voted in 1957 to allocate funds for a new campus. Most of the members of the university's Board of Trustees favored the creation of a traditional campus, with ample land and greenery, and they attempted to acquire a suburban Chicago site. This effort was unsuccessful, however, and the university was forced to negotiate with the powerful mayor of Chicago, Richard J. Daley, who eventually offered a site in an economically depressed part of the city, at the intersection of two major highways—a site that had been slated for urban renewal. Neighborhood groups opposed the change in plans for this site, but without avail, and in 1961 the university formally accepted the site and proceeded to plan the new campus, which opened in 1965. It quickly became known as the Chicago Circle campus, in recognition of its central, urban location at a nexus of traffic interchange, appropriate to an institution for commuting students.

The principal architect of the Chicago Circle campus, Walter Netsch of Skidmore, Owings & Merrill, responded to the constricted site and the character of the school by creating what he called a "micro-environment" of a twentieth-century city (Figs. 278, 279).[59] His plans were complex, with buildings of diverse heights, shapes, and relationships to one another. Circulation played a key role in the design, with elevated pedestrian corridors leading from the peripheral parking lots to the center of the campus, forming a second level of traffic above the ground (Fig. 280). Instead of having a separate building or area for each academic department, the campus was organized by functions, with one tall structure for faculty offices and other buildings for the library, student union, laboratories, and classrooms that could be assigned flexibly to any department.

Whereas this system forced the faculty often to walk long distances to their classes, and tended to weaken the identity of the individual departments, it was argued that this would stimulate wider communication within the university. According to Netsch, the campus would "provide the meeting-in-the-corridor on a grand scale," and

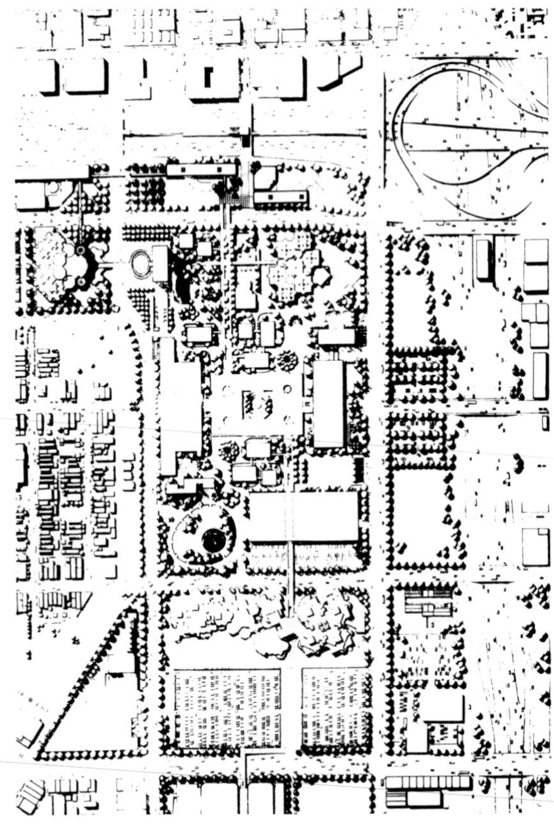

278

278 University of Illinois at Chicago Circle. Master plan by Skidmore, Owings & Merrill (Walter Netsch, partner in charge), ca. 1963. At intersection of two expressways, campus is a dense grouping of buildings of various heights, linked by pedestrian corridors and bridges to adjacent parking lots and public transportation. (Skidmore, Owings & Merrill)

279 Central area of the University of Illinois at Chicago Circle. (Skidmore, Owings & Merrill)

280 University of Illinois at Chicago Circle. Detail of pedestrian bridge. (Photograph by Orlando R. Cabanban)

279

280

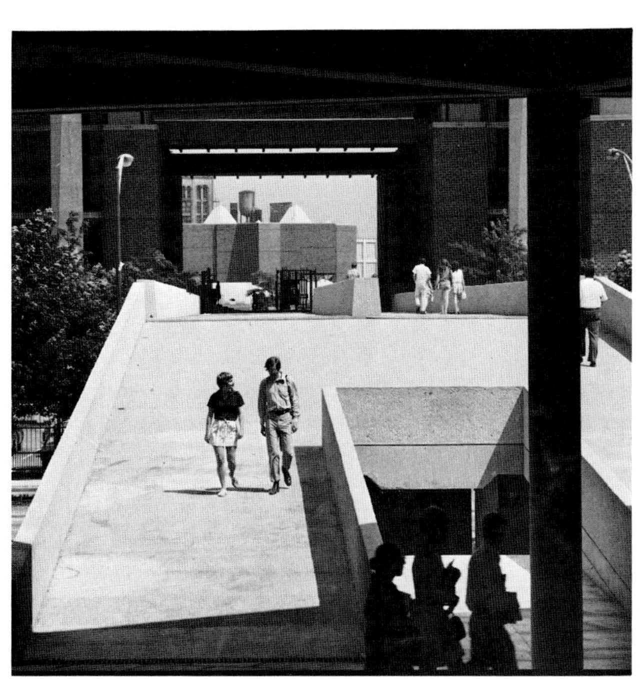

he created many spaces for informal social contact as an antidote to the problem of isolation at a commuter school. The central focal point of the campus was a large area, the "Great Court," with stepped "exedras" where students and faculty could relax and meet. But unlike the traditional college quadrangle, this space was actually the roof of a massive structure of lecture halls, and thus part of the multilevel organization of the whole plan. The bold and stark architectural forms, of reinforced concrete, were rather similar in character to the adjacent elevated highways, and expressed the forthrightly urban nature of the school—as well, perhaps, as a certain enclave mentality due to the school's location on a bulldozed urban-renewal site in a potentially hostile neighborhood.

The design of the Chicago Circle campus was widely publicized in the 1960s and elicited varied reactions from architects and planners. Oscar Newman approved the design's "organization by function" and its two-level circulation system, but felt it did not fully "explore the organizational freedom implied in these concepts."[60] He added that the design was shaped more by traditional architectural "monumentality" than by the dynamic planning processes that interested him. At the other extreme, a critic argued that the design departed too much from traditional campus patterns, especially in its downgrading of academic departments:

> For the students, Chicago Circle would seem to offer little to allay the sense of alienation that is an inherent danger in a large university. The buildings belong to everyone, and therefore to no one. The environment is hard, unyielding, vast in scale.[61]

In contrast to the battles of the 1930s and 1940s over whether campus architecture should "go modern," the major controversy among college planners in this period was the suitability of the urban model—large, complex, and structured around movement and change. An extreme statement of the role of movement and change in campus planning was made by an English architect, Ian Brown, in a 1972 article in *Architectural Forum* entitled "Irrelevance of University Architecture," which was a critique of recent British planning but was presented by the magazine as having "an important message for American campuses."[62] Brown rejected all interest in permanence or "the static values of the past," and stated that the college or university, like any urban entity, should be structured solely by the "laws of rapid access, rapid change, rapid obsolescence." The school was to be "revisualized, with its access ways as the primary configurator and growth definer," and be

> reconceived as a skeleton or network of horizontal, vertical, oblique access ways on various scales and with a versatility in which, in the most temporary way compatible with a decent environment, should be located the various units of accommodation it requires. There should be the least possible fixity about these, the least possible nostalgia.[63]

This call for impermanence and obsolescence struck at the heart of the American tradition of the campus as a physical place that is meaningful precisely because of its enduring embodiment of values. Not surprisingly, it had little effect on American college planning. But the concept of circulation shaping the campus was further explored in various ways by planners in the 1970s. In an article entitled "Movement Systems as Generators of Built Form," the architects Gerhard M. Kallmann and Noel M. McKinnell described various forms such systems could take, with single or multiple "spines" of circulation, which they had investigated in several designs for campus structures, such as gymnasium facilities at Phillips Exeter Academy and Harvard.[64]

A number of designs for entire campuses were based on concepts of this sort, often taking the form of "megastructures"—large buildings or linked structures, incorporating diverse parts, and frequently organized along linear circulation spines. An early example was the design for Governors State University in Illinois, planned in 1969 by the firm of Caudill Rowlett Scott (Fig. 281). Its design for the school created several structures for the various departments or "colleges," each shaped by its individual needs, and linked together by an enclosed circulation corridor, or mall (Fig. 282). One of the architects described the reasoning behind this plan:

> Each college required some highly specialized areas—like sculpture or painting studios, music

281 Governors State University, Park Forest South, Illinois. Site plan, designed by Caudill Rowlett Scott in association with Orme Evans Associates, 1969. (Caudill Rowlett Scott)

282 Governors State University. Rendering of central concourse, or "academic street." (Caudill Rowlett Scott)

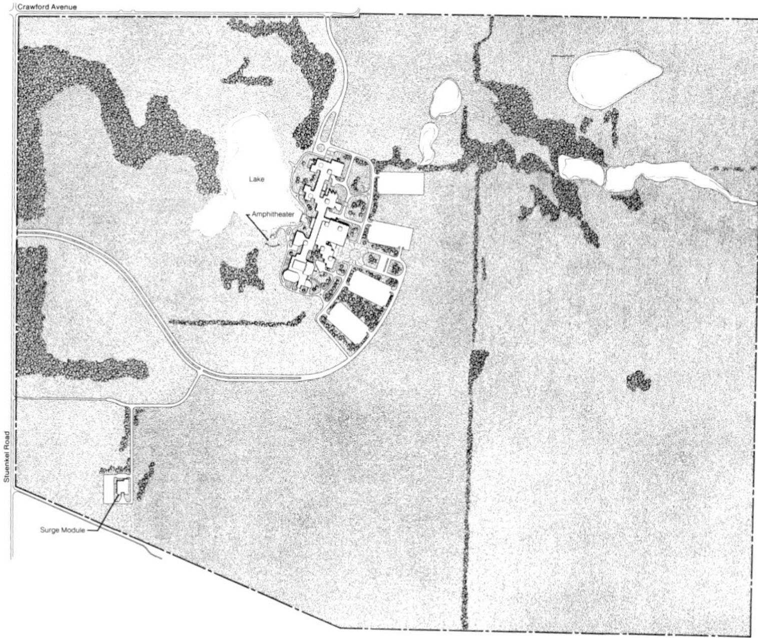

281

282

rooms, or research labs. But we also needed a central concourse which was everyone's domain where things would happen that would be relevant to everyone. The program goals of openness and mix of people and activities evolved into the academic street concept. It's an educational shopping center mall where you can walk along and find the things you need.[65]

This concept was clearly appropriate to the "open university" philosophy of the school when it was founded, reflecting the liberal educational views of the period—that higher education should be available to almost everyone, and that students should be able to choose nearly any type of course or program they wanted. For such an ideal, the American shopping center was a perfect architectural model.

A similar plan was executed for Stockton State College in New Jersey by the architects Geddes, Brecher, Qualls, and Cunningham, in the early 1970s (Figs. 283–285). The academic structures, built in stages, were arranged along an enclosed, street-like "gallery," bent in places to conform with the topography of the site next to a small lake, and paralleling an access road and parking areas. The architects conceived this "gallery" as a stimulus to "interaction and participation by the faculty and students" (half of whom were residential, the other half commuting), and saw the plan as an expression of "egalitarianism because of its non-hierarchic organization."[66]

Other schools structured in similar ways included the Southeastern Massachusetts University, Allegheny Community College in Pennsylvania, Holyoke Community College in Massachusetts, and Kingsborough Community College in Brooklyn, New York (Fig. 306).[67] Significantly, many of these were community colleges or other relatively small institutions which, despite their compact and circulation-oriented plans, did not have a truly urban scale or complexity. The "megastructure" was being used to make schools appear larger, more complex, or more urban than they actually were. But ironically, at the same time, a movement to do exactly the opposite was gathering momentum in university planning.

283 Stockton State College, Pomona, New Jersey. Campus designed by Geddes Brecher Qualls Cunningham, ca. 1970. (Geddes Brecher Qualls Cunningham)

284 Stockton State College, site plan. Buildings shown in black are academic facilities, arranged along a circulation "gallery," and with adjacent parking lots for commuting students. On opposite shore of the lake are clusters of student residences. (Geddes Brecher Qualls Cunningham)

283

284

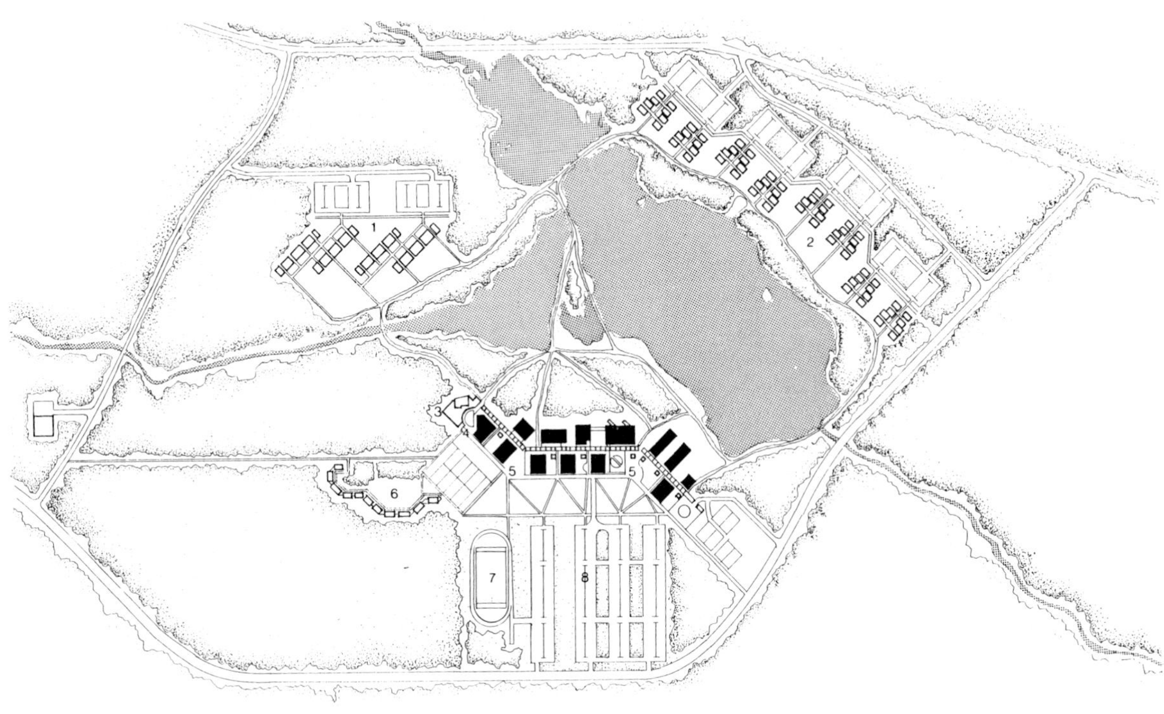

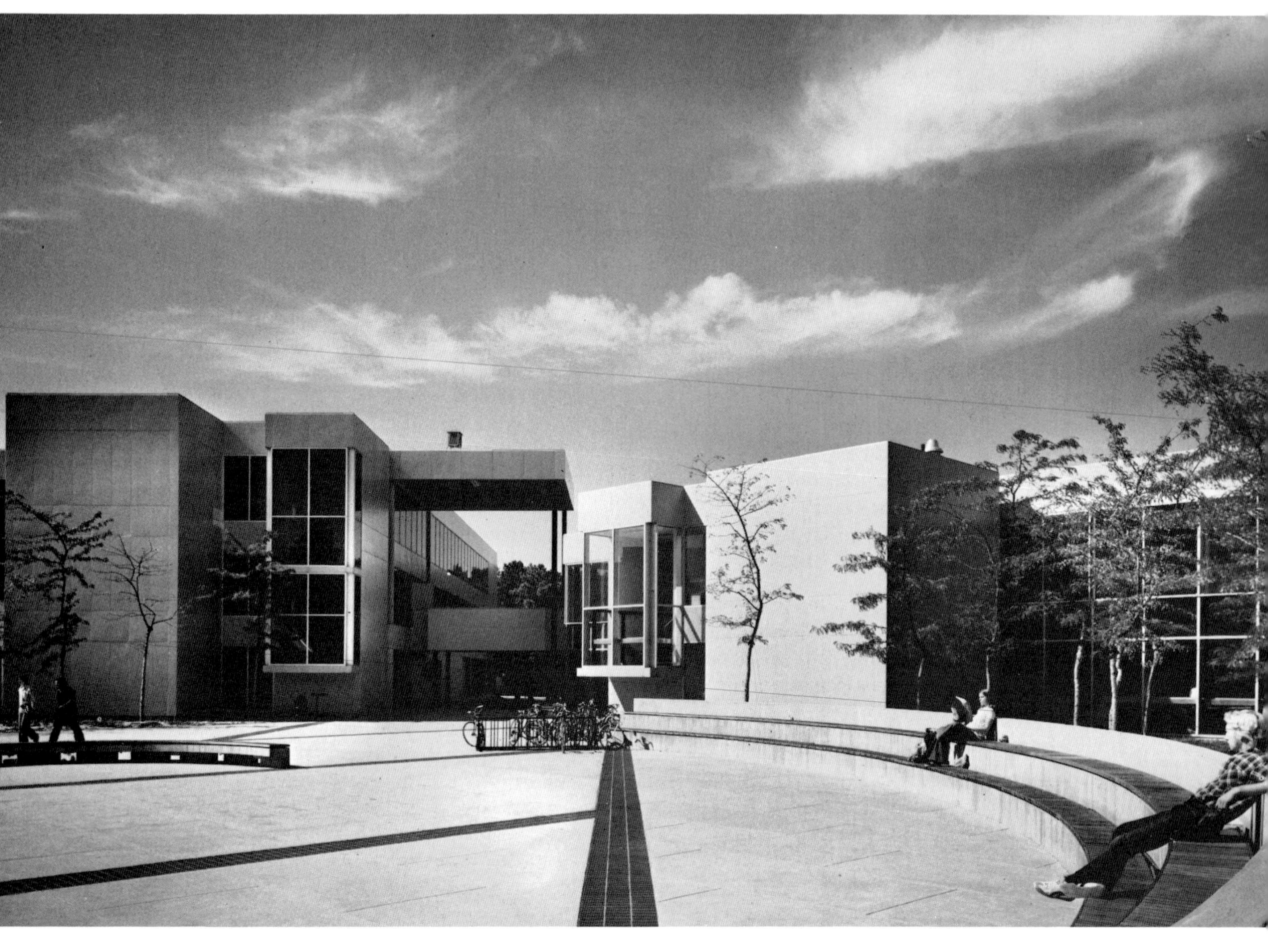

285

285 Stockton State College. View of academic buildings. (Photograph by Norman McGrath)

Making the Big Small

The education explosion of the 1950s and 1960s produced perhaps the most dramatic results in California, with its growing population and its strong tradition of state universities and colleges. In 1957, the state legislature, in response to a projection of future needs, voted to create four new state colleges and three new branches of the state university—each of the latter planned to accommodate 27,500 students. By 1965, the state's university, college, and junior college system had a combined enrollment of almost 350,000 and it was predicted that the figure would practically double in ten years.[68] In contrast to the earlier euphoria of many administrators about the growth of education, more of them now became concerned about the quality of instruction and life at the new megauniversities, and tried to find ways to mitigate the dangers of size. In 1964, Clark Kerr, president of California's state university system, listed the benefits of a large school, but then added:

> the big campus lacks the inestimable virtue which the small liberal arts college counts as its hallmark: the emphasis on the individual which small classes, a residential environment and a strong sense of relationship to others on the campus . . . give.[69]

Kerr reported that attempts to solve this problem had motivated the designs for the three new state university campuses then under construction—at San Diego, Santa Cruz, and Irvine. "Each of the university's new campuses is an experiment in combining the advantages of the large and the small," he said. The master plan for the Irvine campus, by William L. Pereira & Associates, created six groups of buildings around the perimeter of a "university park," with each group devoted to a different academic discipline and separated from its neighbors by radiating strips of parkland (Fig. 286).[70] Beyond the academic areas were clusters of student housing, and then parking lots and a ring road that circled the campus. The concentric pattern of the overall plan, the park in the center, and the separation of groups of buildings by planted areas, were all reminiscent of Ebenezer Howard's "Garden City" of the 1890s. Just as Howard had attempted to control and humanize the cancerously growing industrial city of the late nineteenth century, campus planners were now trying to do the same with the university.

The plans for the Santa Cruz campus, begun in the early 1960s, were the most dramatic expression of Clark Kerr's educational goals. Kerr and his friend Dean McHenry, who became the school's first chancellor, set out to create a truly collegiate environment, with students and teachers studying and living together in intimate communities. They devised a system of "cluster colleges," semiautonomous educational units to be established one by one as the school grew. Each of these colleges would have several hundred students, most of whom would reside, dine, and take some of their classes there. Several professors also would live in the college, "eating with the students and engaging in informal discussion."[71]

These colleges, rather than the academic departments or other university components, would be the focus of the intellectual and social life of the school. The concept recalled the English system of colleges at Oxford and Cambridge, but its execution was thoroughly American. To emphasize the independence of the colleges, they were located in isolation from one another, in the great redwood forest next to grazing land on a hill above the Pacific Ocean, which the school had acquired as its site. The physical setting epitomized the romantic American tradition of the college isolated in sublime wilderness. And the importance of the natural environment at Santa Cruz was suggested by a university regulation that no building be taller than two-thirds the height of the redwood trees.[72]

The colleges at Santa Cruz also were motivated and shaped by an idealism that was characteristic of the 1960s, and of American utopianism in general (the subject of a course Chancellor McHenry himself taught at the school).[73] The principal ideal was of a cohesive, caring, and noncompetitive community, in which each person could explore his own individual needs with the greatest possible freedom. The curriculum and organization of the school reflected this ideal in many ways, for example, by having each student structure his own course of study, and by a pass-fail system of grading. But the residential college was the heart of the concept and shaped the physical form of the campus plan. McHenry stated that "the architectural character of this campus is overwhelmingly important," and that the design of each college must "convey to its members, both students and

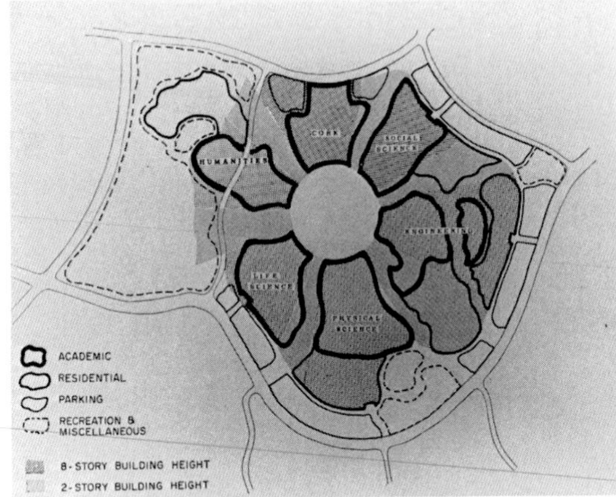

286

286 University of California, Irvine. Diagram of central part of master plan for the campus, by William L. Pereira & Associates, ca. 1963. (*Architectural Record*, November 1964, p. 187)

faculty, a sense of the place which will enhance the educational experience and deepen the cultural implications."[74]

The master plan for the Santa Cruz campus, prepared in 1963 by a team of architects headed by John Carl Warnecke, sited the colleges and the facilities shared by them (such as the main library) in such a way as to make them as isolated as possible from one another and least disruptive of the natural character of the environment (Fig. 287). The result was a plan of meandering roads and clusters of buildings, determined principally by the site's topography and by a desire to make the human presence almost invisible. Indeed, Thomas Church, the landscape architect who worked with Warnecke on the master plan, stated, "the buildings are less important in the visual composition than the trees," and stressed that the architecture should complement the natural landscape.[75] General guidelines were established for the design of all buildings (suggesting types of material, colors, and overall forms), but different architects were chosen for the colleges in order that each would have its own special character. The first opened in 1965, and there were annual additions until eight colleges were operating in 1972.

Kresge College, planned in two stages in 1965 and 1970, exemplified the qualities and ideals of the Santa Cruz campus. Each college had its own theme or focus, and Kresge's theme, "Man and the Environment," was especially appropriate to the principles of the whole university. The college's first provost and assistant provost, Robert Edgar and Michael Kahn, were involved in the human-potential and group-interaction movements that were becoming popular at the time, and they conceived Kresge as an intimate community of "kin groups" that would function like families, the whole college to be run as a "participatory democracy," making each person "freely responsible" for himself and using encounter groups "to help people explore and extend their communication skills," as Edgar stated.[76]

The architects chosen to design Kresge College, William Turnbull and Charles W. Moore, worked closely with the provosts and others at Santa Cruz to create a physical setting supportive of these ideals. There was even a course, entitled "Creating Kresge College," in which students contributed ideas about the design. The site selected by the

287

287 University of California, Santa Cruz. Master plan for the campus, by John Carl Warnecke & Associates, ca. 1963. Vehicular roads are mostly on periphery of the heavily wooded site. "Colleges," constructed in sequence, are isolated visually from one another, but are within easy walking distance of the library and other common facilities. (*Architectural Record*, November 1964, p. 177)

architects was along a steep ridge in a particularly hilly part of the forest, a site Thomas Church described as "a landscape out of scale with the conventional academic one."[77] Moore and Turnbull took literally the idea that the college should be a "community," by conceiving a compact village of buildings and spaces along a street winding its way up the ridge (Figs. 3, 288–290). All of the dormitory rooms, classrooms, and other facilities opened directly onto this street, and the street facades were painted white, enlivened by splashes of bright supergraphics—in contrast to the earth tones of the backs of the buildings, facing the forest. At several places—near the post office, laundry, library, and dining hall—the street widened to create "plazas" as focal points for communal activity. Moore and Turnbull's whimsical style of architecture, with thin cutout walls creating a "triumphal arch," "public rostrum," and "fountain court," was well suited to the founding spirit of the college, with its interest in symbolism, ritual, and other academically unconventional modes of thought. When the buildings were ready for occupancy, the students devised a solemn ritual for the event, in which "each of the kin groups stood in a circle around a bonfire while they burned their unwanted possessions," and then "walked single file, holding hands, up through the woods to their new home."[78]

The architects created a variety of dormitory accommodations, ranging from more or less conventional rooms to "octet" units, in which eight students would eat, sleep, and interact in communal intimacy. Like a number of the unusual features of Kresge College, these "octets" ultimately proved not very popular with students, and were modified for more conventional use. But their architectural design was a fitting embodiment of the ideals that originally inspired the college.

Kresge College was in many ways an expression of countercultural ideas current in the late 1960s, but its essential qualities, far from being radical or new, were deeply rooted in traditions of American educational utopianism. The concept of the college as a village was part of the heritage of Jefferson's "academical village." The emphasis on creating a family-like environment recalled idealistic nineteenth-century educators such as Union College's Eliphalet Nott, with his plan that the students would be part of "the family of the officer

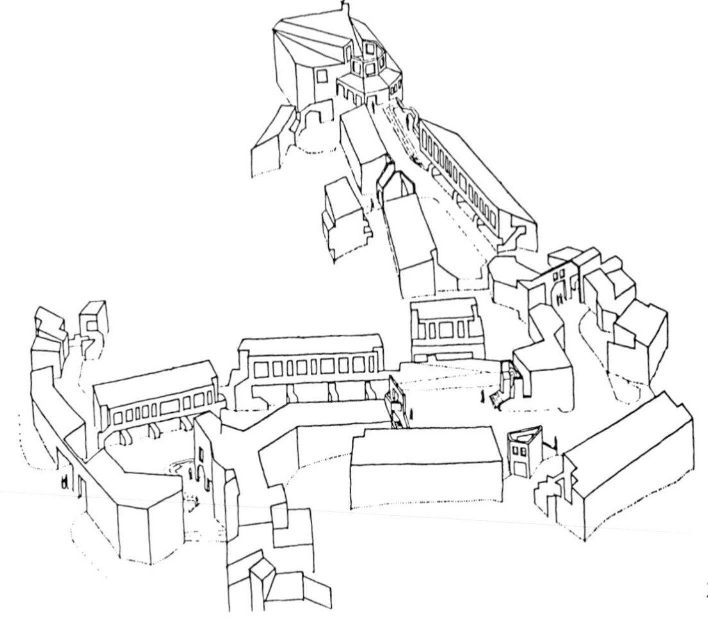

288

289

290

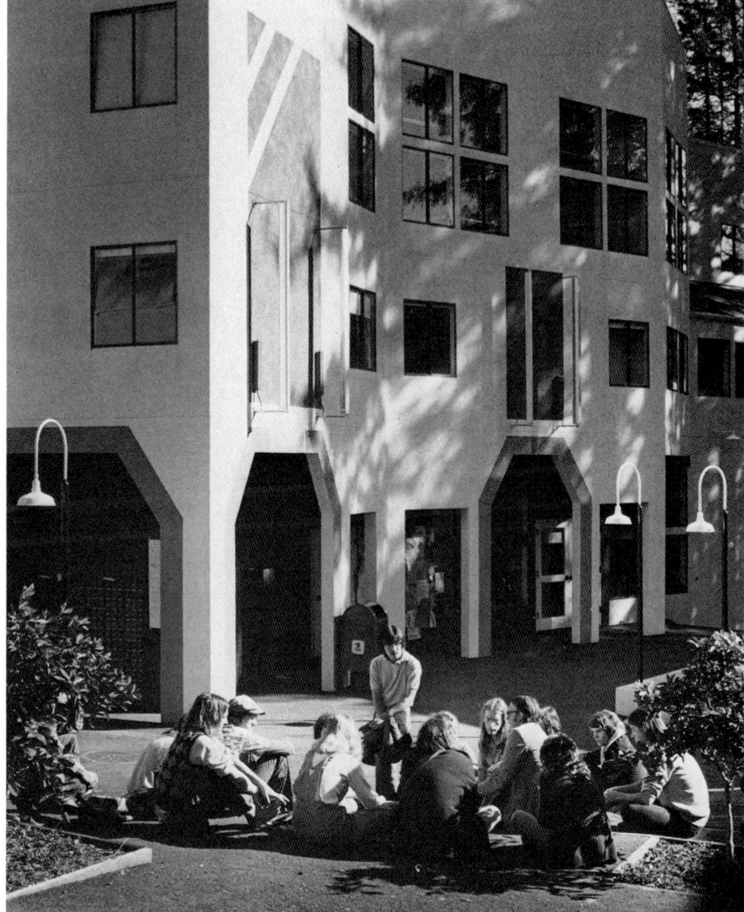

288 Kresge College, University of California, Santa Cruz. Diagram of design by Charles W. Moore and William Turnbull (Moore Lyndon Turnbull Whitaker), 1965–1972; constructed 1974. Residences and common buildings are arranged along a "street" that winds up the steep hillside, passing through gateways and forming public squares along its route. (Courtesy of Charles W. Moore)

289 Kresge College, University of California, Santa Cruz. Street lined by student residences. (Photograph © Morley Baer)

290 Kresge College, University of California, Santa Cruz. (Photograph © Morley Baer)

who instructs them," all living and dining together.[79] The reverence toward the forest in which Kresge was set was typical of the American romanticism of the college in nature. And the overriding concern that Kresge be a vital "community" was a reaffirmation of the whole collegiate tradition. The architectural design of Kresge College was an inventive embodiment of distinctively American educational principles.

Commuters' Colleges

The junior college, or community college (as it is now more often called), was probably the fastest growing part of American higher education in the 1960s and 1970s. These schools, providing the first two years of a college education and serving a relatively small regional area, first appeared at the beginning of the twentieth century; they began proliferating in the late 1950s, and by 1977 there were at least six hundred of them, with several dozen new ones being founded each year.[80] The success of the community college resulted from its appeal to specific local needs and interests: the desire that any high school graduate be able to receive some college education, the economy of being able to do this while living at home, and the offering of a wide range of "adult education" courses to local residents. In this way, such schools functioned as community centers, and often became the scene of local activities and organizations of all sorts. In many ways the community college was part of the American populist tradition, its ideals similar to those of the land-grant colleges of the mid-nineteenth century—especially the desire to make education available to everyone. Like the land-grant schools, the community colleges developed their own distinctive campus forms, while also reflecting general trends in postwar college planning.

In 1959, *Architectural Forum* reported on the emerging community college phenomenon, and suggested how its distinctive traits could influence its physical planning.[81] The fact that the students were commuters had many ramifications, including the obvious absence of dormitories, and the need for easy vehicular access, which meant that the traditional preference of the American college for an isolated location was replaced by a need to be close to the center of population, or near a major highway, like "any shopping center" (a decade later one of the architects of Governors State University in Illinois would describe the core of the school as "an educational shopping center mall").[82] What concerned educators and planners most was the danger that a nonresidential school would have none of the "collegiate" spirit that had always been so important in American education. It therefore became important to "create a sense of educational community," to stimulate "contact between students and instructors," and to provide substitutions for the social life of the residential college.[83]

Foothill College on the San Francisco Peninsula in California, designed in 1959 by Ernest Kump and Masten & Hurd, was widely publicized and praised for its response to these challenges. Kump reportedly was dissatisfied with the typical designs of junior colleges at that time, which often resembled high schools in their alignment of classrooms along a corridor in one large building.[84] On the hilly 120-acre site chosen for Foothill College—picturesquely rural, but next to a major highway for easy access—Kump created clusters of buildings on a plateau, with automobiles segregated below (Fig. 291). The buildings, featuring prominent shingled roofs which recalled San Francisco Bay Area architectural traditions, combined classrooms, instructors' offices, and the other college facilities in informal patterns that created numerous small outdoor spaces meant to encourage social interaction (Fig. 292). Kump's first plans had been more monumental and included a campanile. But reflecting the desire of the school authorities, the design was made less formal and the individual parts as small in scale as possible.

The Foothill design was praised by nearly all observers for its sympathetic embodiment of the goals of the community college. The architectural critic Allan Temko, who reviewed the newly built campus in 1962, described the many civic functions that it served (such as presenting symphony concerts and theater productions), called it "a multipurpose cultural resource," and noted the diversity of outdoor spaces that "range from intimate planted patios . . . to a spacious assembly area before the library which has the mood and dimensions of a village square."[85] The village metaphor, so common throughout American collegiate history, again was used to describe a successful campus, despite the fact that in this case it was a commuter school and no one really lived in this "village."

In the following decade, many of the junior colleges founded around the country created campuses that, like Foothill's, were shaped by a desire to encourage communality and sociability as substitutes for the traditional collegiate life. At Pima County Community College in Arizona in the late 1960s, the architectural firms of Caudill Rowlett Scott and Friedman Jobusch Wilde created a system of structures arranged to form numerous courtyards and other spaces conducive to social interaction (Fig. 293). Among the "precepts" that guided the master planning was a contrast between an academic zone that would be "a quiet place" with informal "intimate spaces," and a more public zone, having "a formal grand scale with paved areas to accommodate a large number of people."[86] (The architects called this the "central business district.") The desire to simulate the life of a residential college even led to the creation of a system of six "houses" to which all students and faculty would be assigned, and where they would meet regularly for informal camaraderie and "student-faculty mingling."[87] These "houses" were located next to the classrooms and opened onto the most intimate of the courtyard spaces.

Several years later, Caudill Rowlett Scott, in collaboration with William Blurock & Partners, used the house concept in their master plan for Cypress College in California, projecting an eventual eight houses to accommodate 12,500 students—thereby "breaking up bigness into intimate units that individuals can relate to" (Fig. 294).[88] But the Cypress campus plan was less directly shaped by the "house" concept than at Pima College, for here the "houses" were attached to the various functional facilities of the school (one "house" being in the Fine Arts Building, another in the Science Building, and so forth)—perhaps a recognition of the difficulty of structuring a commuter school along this pattern. A more important force in shaping the Cypress College plan was the problem of parking and the relationship between vehicular and pedestrian traffic. The architects forthrightly accepted the automobile-oriented reality of the community college and surrounded the structures with parking lots on all sides, rather than try to hide them or relegate them to one side of the campus. In fact, they allowed autos to pass through the very heart of the campus, by creating two levels of circulation, the upper one a pedestrian "piazza" connecting all the buildings (Fig. 295).

Other community colleges were planned around one large space reminiscent of the traditional college quadrangle. These included Mountain View Junior College near Dallas, and Kingsborough Community College on Coney Island in Brooklyn, whose academic buildings were designed "to integrate classroom space with activity areas of a

291

292

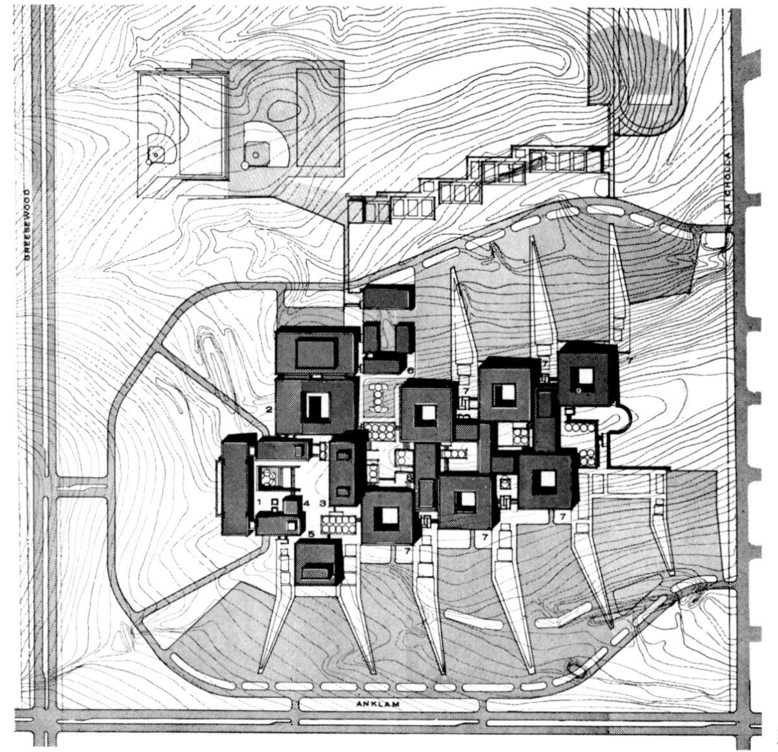

293

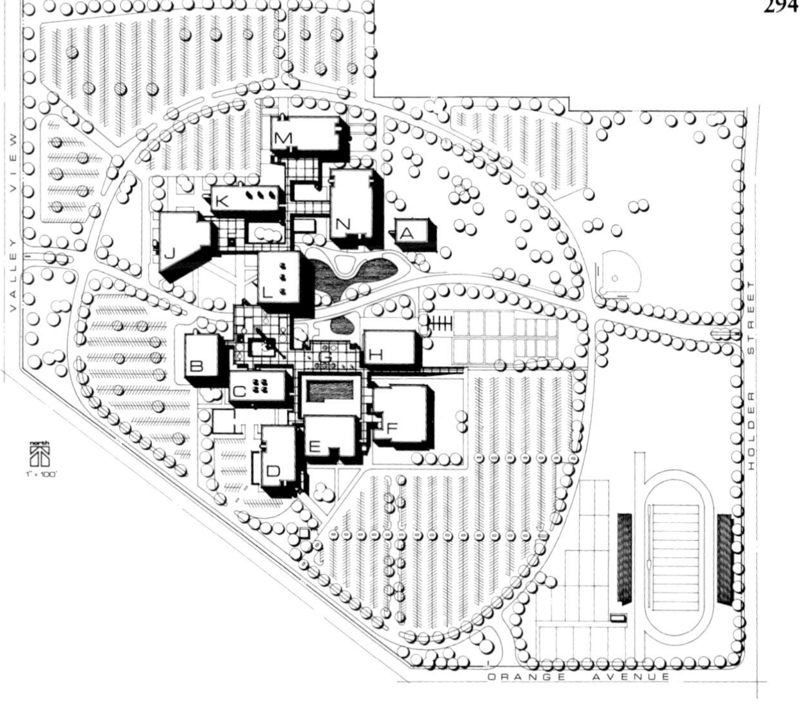

294

291 Foothill College, Los Altos Hills, California, designed by Ernest Kump and Masten & Hurd, 1959. Freeway that connects San Jose and San Francisco is seen at upper right. (Foothill College)

292 Foothill College. (Photograph © Morley Baer; provided by Sprankle, Lynd, & Sprague, Architects)

293 Pima County Community College, Tucson, Arizona. Master plan, by Caudill Rowlett Scott and Friedman Jobusch Wilde, 1967. Six "houses" at right constitute the academic portion of the school. To left is "central business district" of public spaces and facilities. Buildings are sited along the ridge of a hill, with parking lots on lower ground. (Caudill Rowlett Scott)

294 Cypress College, Cypress, California. Master plan by Caudill Rowlett Scott and William Blurock & Partners, ca. 1967. Surrounding elevated "Piazza" at center of plan are: Library (L), Business Education Building (B), Technical Education Building (C), and Women's Gymnasium (H). Parking lots surround the structures. (Caudill Rowlett Scott)

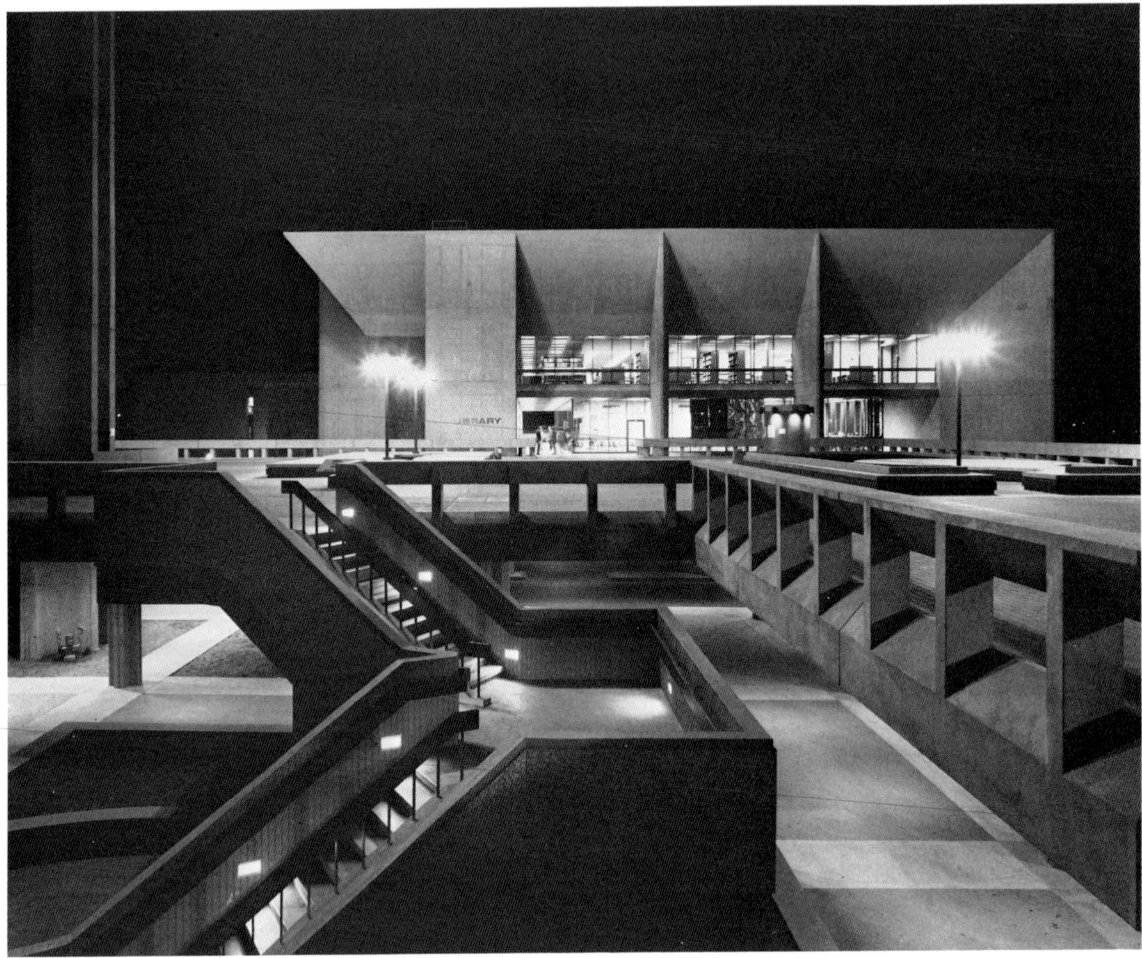

295

295 Cypress College. View across piazza to library.
(MPS Photographic Services, Costa Mesa, Calif.)

more sociable function," and "to enhance student interaction"—again, the preoccupation with making the commuter school as truly collegiate as possible.[89] Even schools designed as one large building were often generously provided with spaces meant to facilitate a college-like spirit. Northlake Community College in Texas was conceived as a linear structure in which "the spine of the campus is an outdoor terraced garden accessible at all levels . . . adjacent [to which] are various spaces which encourage casual meetings and social activity."[90] Schools based on similar concepts included Florida Community College, the Harbor Campus of the Community College of Baltimore, and Holyoke Community College in Massachusetts, organized along a "multi-level mall" that served both as a circulation spine and as "people spaces."[91]

Urban community colleges, with less area to build on, sometimes structured their buildings around vertical rather than horizontal social space. The Downtown Campus of Miami-Dade Community College in Florida was designed around a seven-story-high "atrium," onto which all of the circulation and public spaces of the college opened.[92]

Like the community colleges, many urban institutions with a largely commuting student population also attempted to create a sense of collegiality in their campuses. In 1974, Hunter College in New York City (which in 1945 had constructed a large International Style building that made no concession to collegiate traditions) hired the architect Ulrich Franzen to provide extra facilities for the school, and also to create a "sense of campus" (Figs. 296, 297). At the base of the new buildings, Franzen designed a sunken plaza intended to be "the active heart" of the school; and the new and old structures were linked by bridges over the streets, which were described not only as being practical but as uniting the college visually and "defining a campus gateway."[93]

Cleveland State University in Ohio, with more land at its disposal than Hunter, although still thoroughly urban, was able to create more extensive open space for student gatherings and the feeling of a campus. But the real focal point of the school was provided in the University Center, designed by Don Hisaka & Associates, a structure housing various student services and activities, and dominated by a tremendous six-story-high space that functions as a kind of indoor "campus" in winter and at all times of the year as a focus of the school's activity and identity (Fig. 298).[94]

296 Hunter College, New York City. Plan for new buildings, by Ulrich Franzen, ca. 1974, connecting with the school's existing structure.
(Ulrich Franzen)

297 Hunter College. Rendering of new buildings and "plaza" at corner of Lexington Avenue and 68th Street.
(Ulrich Franzen)

298 Cleveland State University, Ohio. University Center, designed by Don M. Hisaka & Associates, constructed 1971–1974.
(Photograph by George Cserna)

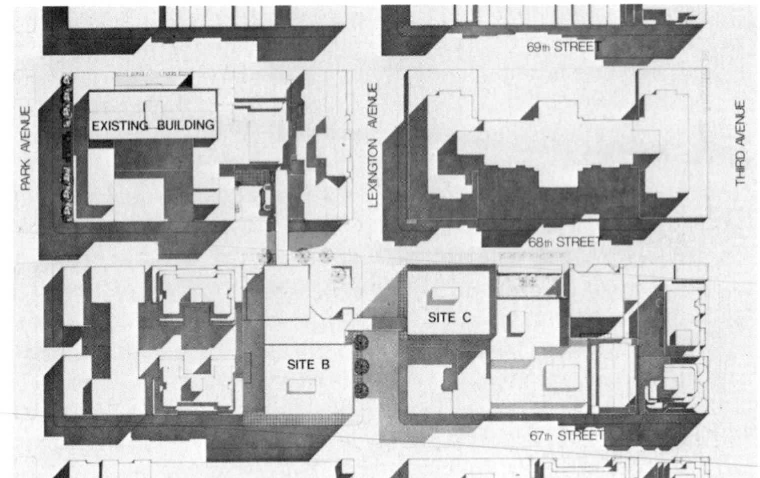

296

297

Reinterpreting the Past

By 1960, it was clear that the battle between the architectural traditionalists and modernists, which had been waged on the American campus for at least three decades, had been won firmly by the moderns. The few "Gothic" or "classical" buildings still being constructed were so unauthentic (due either to economic constraints or ineptitude) that they only advertised the demise of the traditions they aped. Nearly as defunct were the Beaux-Arts and other systems of "master-planning" for campuses, victims mainly of the practical expediencies of explosive growth. But at the same time, a few architects with modernist credentials began to look more sympathetically at the traditions of American campus planning. In the following years this attitude became increasingly common, and has affected collegiate planning in many ways.

An early expression of the new thinking was voiced by Paul Rudolph, in his design for the Jewett Arts Center at Wellesley, begun in 1955 (Figs. 299, 300). The program required a large structure to house several functions, located at the heart of the Gothic Revival campus. Rudolph first attempted to define the formal and spatial qualities of the campus in statements such as: "Buildings are grouped in rather close clusters . . . but the distance between these clusters is great," and "the buildings have elaborate silhouettes; they are constructed with facings of brick or limestone; and the vertical line is emphasized."[95] Rudolph incorporated some of these qualities into his design for the arts center, by the choice of shapes and materials and by making the complex a "cluster" of parts through which one walked.

But in particular it was Eero Saarinen's design for Morse and Stiles colleges at Yale that focused attention on the neotraditionalist approach and made it controversial in architectural circles. Saarinen, whose youthful work had been properly International Style, flirted with historicism as early as the mid-1950s in his design for Concordia College, a Lutheran seminary in Indiana, whose site plan and pitch-roofed buildings he freely admitted were inspired by "medieval hill-towns and . . . the silhouette . . . of Danish villages with the church dominating" (Fig. 301).[96] When commissioned around 1960 to design two new undergraduate "colleges" at Yale, Saarinen looked specifically at the historical environment in which he was building

299 Wellesley College, Wellesley, Massachusetts. Rendering of design for Jewett Arts Center, by Paul Rudolph, 1955.
(Paul Rudolph, Architect)

300 Wellesley College. Aerial view of Academic Quadrangle with Jewett Arts Center at bottom. Other buildings (*clockwise*) are: Pendleton Hall, 1935; Green Hall and Galen Stone Tower, 1931; and Founder Hall, 1919—all designed by Day & Klauder, as part of development plan for campus supervised by Cram & Ferguson, beginning in 1915.
(Wellesley College)

299

300

301

301 Concordia College, Fort Wayne, Indiana. Model of master plan for the campus, by Eero Saarinen, ca. 1954. (*Architectural Forum*, December 1954, p. 132)

and shamelessly emulated it. The site of the new dormitory and dining hall complexes was within view of several of Yale's neo-Gothic structures, notably the fortress-like gymnasium built in 1930. For Morse and Stiles colleges, Saarinen created an arrangement of tower-like forms, constructed of rough stone and concrete walls, and grouped around narrow passageways through which one glimpsed views of the old Gothic Yale (Figs. 302–304).[97] Saarinen was encouraged in this endeavor by the president of Yale, A. Whitney Griswold, an architectural enthusiast who later recalled:

> I urged Eero to go to Oxford and look at the walls, particularly the rubble ones. In my imagination they had a quality that was close to that of surrounding Yale buildings, such as the gym. Eero said, "I'm going to do this. I'm also going to San Gimignano. I think we can do something here in the way of a little Italian village." He felt that he could produce an atmosphere akin to that of the existing colleges using the elements of the building itself—courts, walls, towers—rather than the superficial decoration.[98]

The interior plans of Morse and Stiles colleges were made just as irregular as the exterior shapes, with winding corridors and odd-sized dormitory rooms, lit by narrow window slits that reinforced the medieval castle effect. There was nothing literally Gothic about the design, but it was clearly intended to echo the overall forms, spaces, and textures of the picturesque Gothic Revival. Much publicized in the architectural press in the early 1960s, the design caused a furor of controversy, and was widely attacked as a betrayal of modernism—one critic going so far as to report that its picturesqueness "disgusted me at sight," and represented a "creeping malady" suggesting that "Yale is a very sick place."[99]

The "malady" was in fact contagious. Colleges and universities gradually became concerned with making new construction "compatible" with existing campus traditions. The virtue of continuity was rediscovered. It could be achieved in various ways, the most obvious being to give new structures some of the formal characteristics of existing buildings. A new library at the University of Nevada in Reno was provided with a folded-plate roof in order to "echo the pediments and gables of the university's traditional skyline."[100] Stanford University in California insisted that all new buildings, regardless of their shape or scale, have red-tile roofs like the architecture of its original quadrangles. The University of New Mexico at Albuquerque continued to give its new buildings forms considered compatible with its traditional "neo-pueblo" style of architecture.[101] The University of Colorado tried to be faithful to the spirit of the "Rural Italian" style of architecture created for it by Charles Klauder in the 1930s. And the design for a new complex of buildings at Washington University in St. Louis of 1966, although unconventional in its plan, was described as having a "silhouette echoing that of the Collegiate Gothic campus."[102]

Another approach toward compatibility focused more on the spatial and circulation patterns of a campus than on its specific architectural forms. Harvard, faced in the 1960s with a shortage of land but also the need to grow, was forced to build tall new structures that clearly could not imitate the older buildings. But an attempt was made to perpetuate the existing "character and scale of open space and the system of paths"—described in 1960 as typified by complex, "interpenetrating" spaces and "circuitous" routes.[103] These qualities that only a few years earlier would have been considered lamentable were now identified as principles for future planning.

In the case of totally new campuses, traditional patterns of planning began to reappear, and even the Beaux-Arts system of design made a comeback of sorts—as in Edward Durell Stone's plan for the Albany campus of the State University of New York (Fig. 305).[104] With four dormitory towers in quadrangles placed symmetrically at the corners of a vast, raised Academic Podium where a fountain and campanile provided the central focus, the plan was rigidly formal and violated most of the precepts of postwar campus planning theory, especially in its resistance to change or revision. In contrast to the preoccupation with "process" and "flexibility" among most campus planners of the period, Stone's Albany design spoke nostalgically of collegiate permanence and order.

A rather different expression of the new sympathy for campus planning traditions appeared in Paul Rudolph's design for Southeastern Massachusetts University, begun in 1963 (Fig. 306). Al-

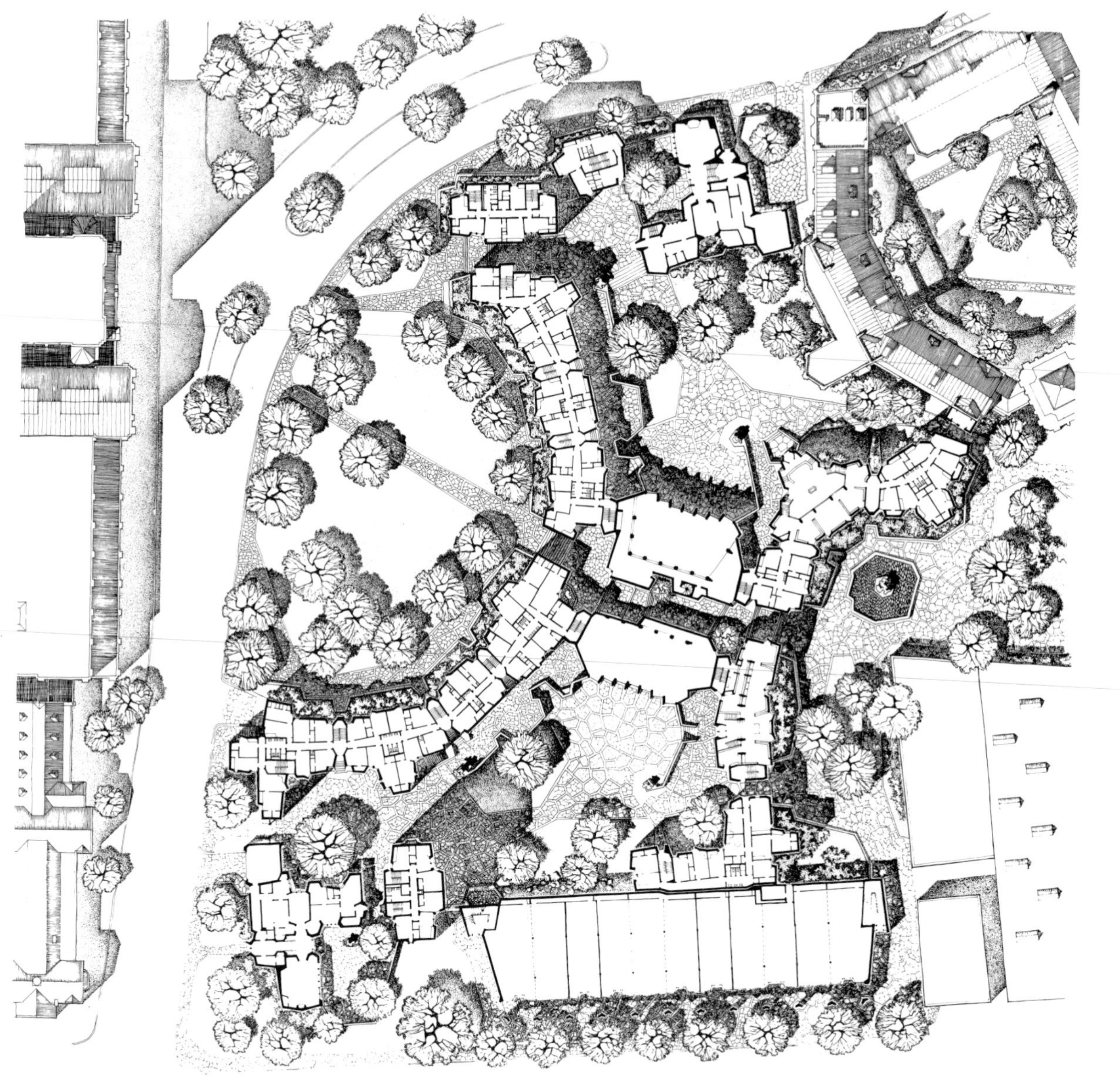

302

302 Yale University. Plan of Morse and Stiles colleges, by Eero Saarinen, ca. 1960; constructed 1962. (Courtesy of Kevin Roche)

303 Morse and Stiles colleges, Yale. (Photograph by George Cserna)

303

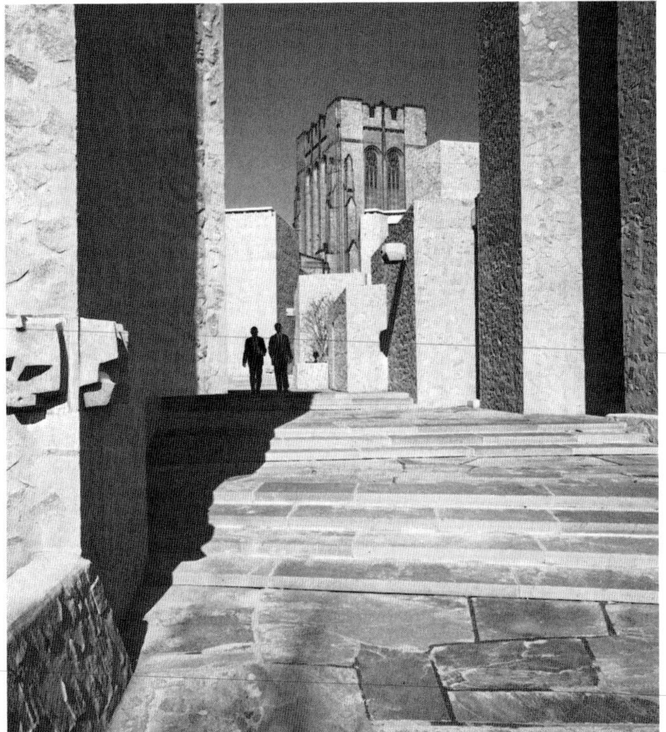

304

305

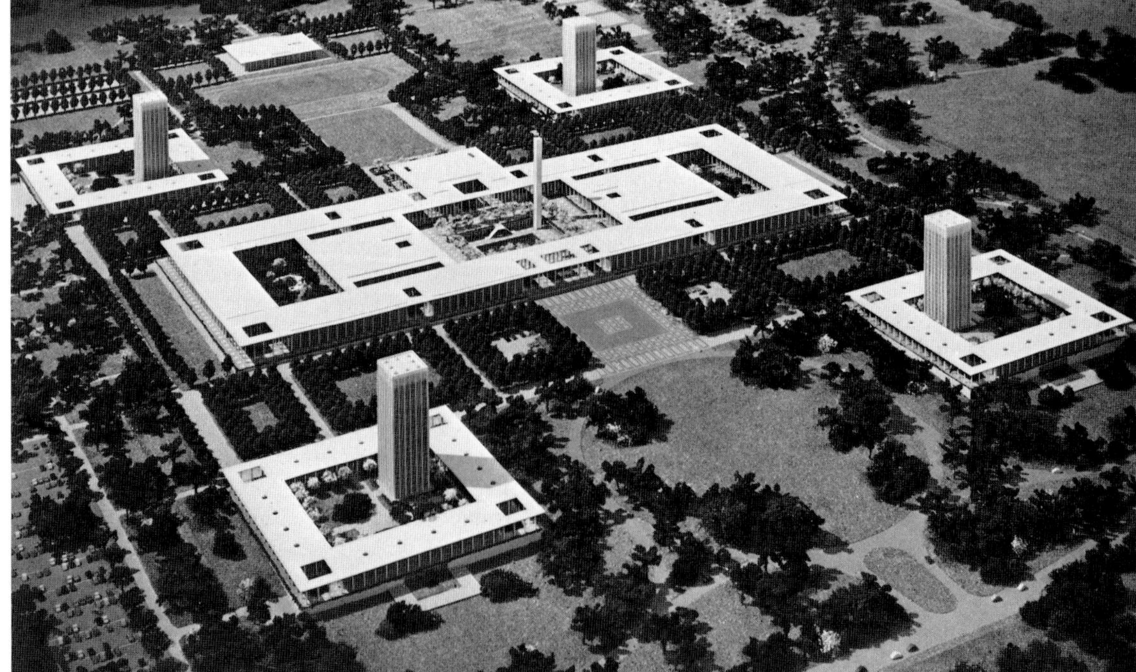

304 Morse and Stiles colleges, Yale. In background is Payne Whitney Gymnasium (designed by John Russell Pope, 1930), whose neo-Gothic forms and textures are echoed in Saarinen's buildings.
(Photograph by George Cserna)

305 State University of New York at Albany. Model of master plan by Edward Durell Stone, 1961. In center are the academic facilities. At four corners are dormitory complexes, each with a quadrangle surrounding a twenty-two-story tower.
(Edward Durell Stone Associates)

though fluid and informal in many respects, the design was full of references to earlier campus forms—notably in its organization along a mall formed of stepped terraces (as in the University of Virginia) and flanked by rows of connected "pavilions" (which also recalled Jefferson's campus).[105]

The spirit of Jefferson's University of Virginia subsequently appeared in other campus designs, such as Edward Larrabee Barnes's master plan for the new arts college of the State University of New York at Purchase (Fig. 307). The main buildings were again arranged along a mall, and were partially connected by "colonnades," although the scale was much greater than at Charlottesville, the parts less unified, and the overall plan with its hierarchy of axial spaces more akin to Beaux-Arts campus plans of the early twentieth century.[106]

Traditional campus forms inspired other college designs by Barnes as well, a fact that he freely admitted. At the State University College of Potsdam, New York, he linked together several existing buildings with new structures, to create a series of aligned quadrangles, the main one fully enclosed and having at its four corners massive "gates" that reinforced the historical associations of the collegiate quadrangle. Commissioned to design a Fine Arts Building for Bowdoin College in Maine, Barnes created another "gateway" with the building itself, positioning it as an entrance into the college quadrangle, on axis with the school's nineteenth-century Gothic Revival chapel (Figs. 308, 309). In describing this design for Bowdoin, Barnes revealed a sympathetic appreciation of the college's earlier architecture, and for the distinctively American campus formed by separate buildings:

> I love this campus. The buildings make the quadrangle seem like a great room, but because so much space [is between the buildings], you can look through it in all directions. Originally I was expected to hook the new building onto the McKim, Mead and White structure. I insisted that it had to be one more separate building and not a wing, to respect the open-close, open-close perimeter of the quadrangle.[107]

Barnes exemplifies a new attitude among college planners, concerned with identifying and preserving the spatial and formal character of an historically significant campus to which additions are being made. This contrasts not only with the earlier generation of modernists, but also with earlier "traditionalists," such as Klauder and Larson, who usually attempted to impose their own eclectic preferences on existing campuses.

The new interest in historical traditions of campus planning reflected the growth of the architectural preservation movement in America during this period. But it also coincided with, and was fostered by, some basic changes in the state of higher education in the 1970s, especially the end of the explosive growth of enrollments that had dominated the postwar years, and the financial difficulties that became a serious threat at many schools. Suddenly, colleges and universities were forced to cut back drastically from the levels of expansion and building activity to which they had become accustomed. Even when new facilities were needed, funding was much less readily available than before, and schools had to find alternatives to large-scale construction.

The Society for College and University Planning, founded in the mid-1960s when the excitement about educational growth and ambitious planning was still strong, began publishing a journal in 1972, *Planning for Higher Education*, which quickly reflected the new trends. An article on the subject in 1973 was entitled "For Planners, That Shrinking Feeling."[108] (Not surprisingly, the article argued that even in a period of declining growth, full-scale professional planning activities were essential for colleges and universities.) Reports on ambitious plans for physical development, which would have dominated a journal like this ten years earlier, became rare and were replaced by articles on how to cope with hard times.

A series of articles in 1974 explored alternatives to constructing new buildings, such as sharing facilities with neighboring schools, and using non-campus structures (a former tire factory at Hostos Community College in the Bronx, a church-turned-library at Westbrook College in Maine, and a department store acquired by El Centro Community College in Dallas).[109] But most of the attention of the series was given to a fuller exploitation of existing campus facilities. Illustrations included the remodeling of old dormitories (at M.I.T.) to create apartment-like suites that would woo students

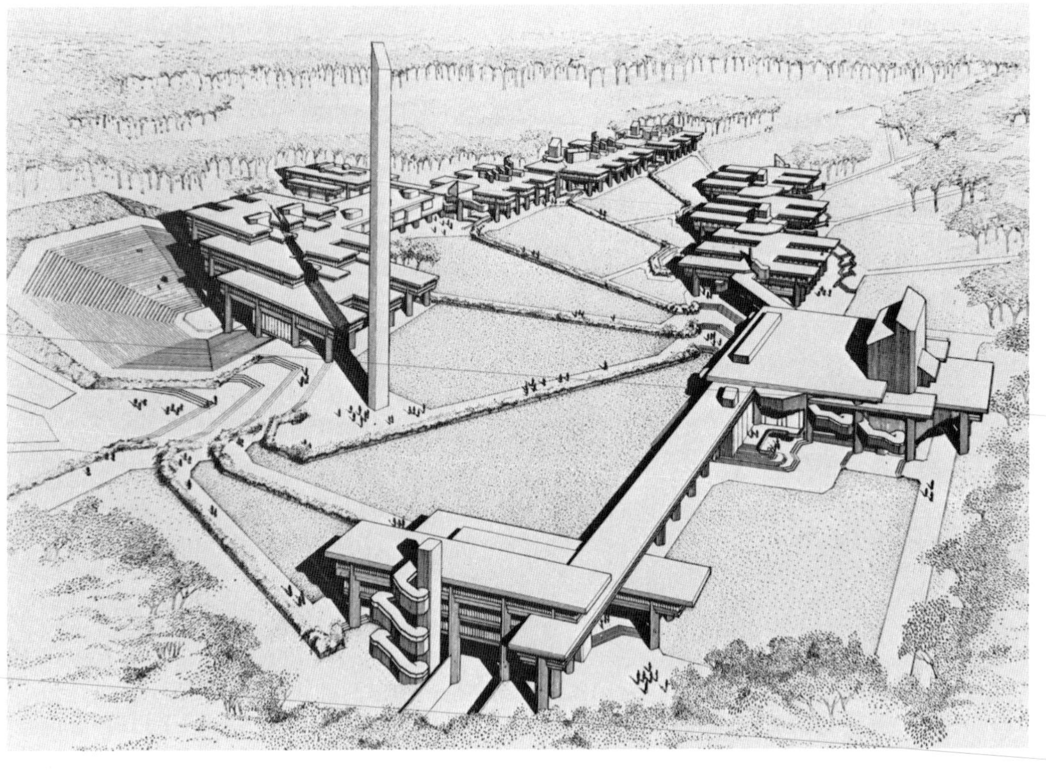

306

307

306 Southeastern Massachusetts University, North Dartmouth, Massachusetts. Rendering of master plan by Paul Rudolph, 1963.
(Paul Rudolph, Architect)

307 State University of New York at Purchase. Designed by Edward Larrabee Barnes Associates, beginning in 1967; constructed 1970–1979.
(Edward Larrabee Barnes Associates)

308 Bowdoin College, Brunswick, Maine. Plan of campus, showing Fine Arts Building (*top center*), designed by Edward Larrabee Barnes Associates, 1973, which serves as a gateway into quadrangle. At bottom of plan is the original row of college buildings, with Richard Upjohn's chapel of ca. 1850 in center.
(Edward Larrabee Barnes Associates)

309 Fine Arts Building, Bowdoin College, seen from inside the quadrangle.
(Photograph by Nick Wheeler)

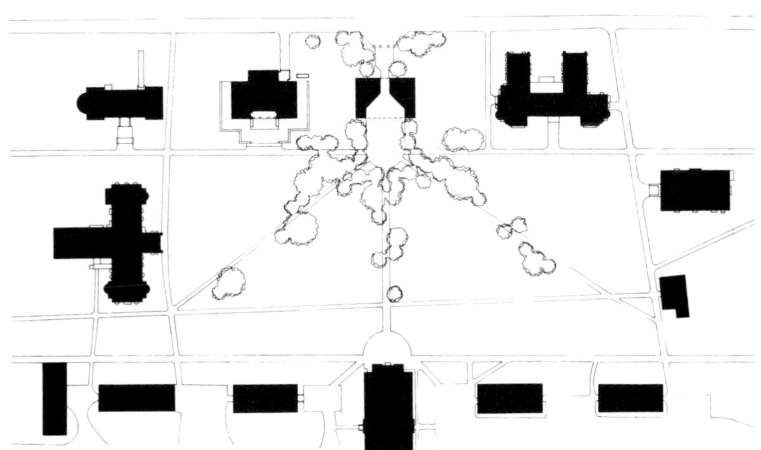

308

309

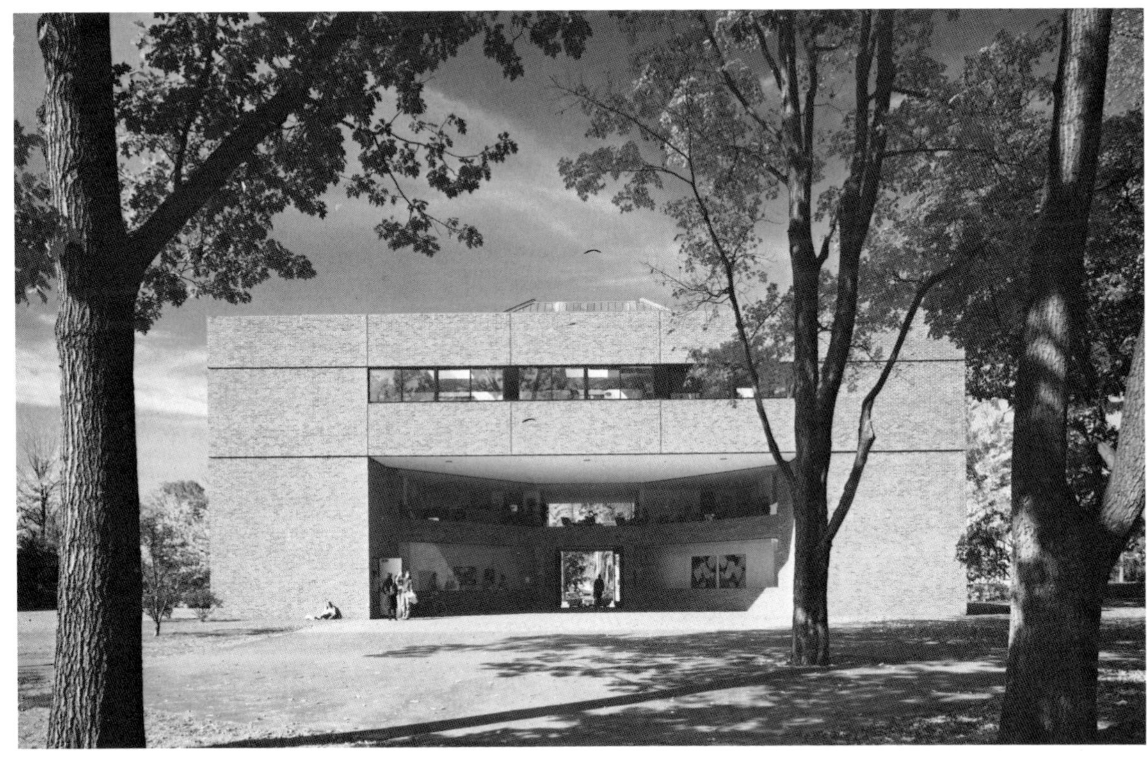

back from off-campus housing, and the transformation of little-used buildings to serve other functions.

The most radical type of transformation (radical, at least, in light of the history of the American college) involved the campus chapel, that indispensable core of the old-time sectarian college, but now virtually abandoned at many institutions. A separate article on this problem reported that the planner Richard P. Dober estimated there were nearly four hundred college chapels in America that were unused and ripe for recycling.[110] Dober held a conference on the subject at Oberlin College in Ohio (whose Cass Gilbert-designed chapel was one of the four hundred), which focused on the conversion of these relics to performing-arts centers or audiovisual-communications facilities. Significantly, the planners did not recommend demolishing these outmoded buildings, as they probably would have done ten or twenty years earlier. The new economic realities, and preservation consciousness, now conspired to save the physical structures, even if their original use was abandoned.

More than at any earlier time, college planners are presently involved in problems of restoring campus landmarks, remodeling existing buildings for new uses, and making modest additions compatible with a school's traditions. At Yale, after decades of bold new construction, the architectural news in the early 1980s is about remodeling and preserving the Old Campus.[111] At Stanford, nearly as much money is being spent on rebuilding the original buildings of Olmsted and Coolidge's quandrangles (to meet new earthquake-safety standards), as on new construction (Fig. 176). At Union College in New York, controversy centers on how best to preserve and use the remarkable sixteen-sided Victorian Gothic memorial building erected in the mid-nineteenth century as the focal point of Ramée's campus (Fig. 67).[112] And at Princeton, the architect of new Butler College, Robert Venturi, proudly claims that he is "returning to the Gothic tradition" and has incorporated into his design the "picturesqueness" of old Princeton.[113]

The Character of the American Campus

The present time—the 1980s—provides a good opportunity to survey the history of the American campus and identify its distinctive traits. As the educational growth of the postwar decades slows down, colleges and universities are able to assess their goals and plans in a calmer atmosphere. And the new sympathy for traditional campus forms encourages schools to see the planning process as an integral part of their historical development.

The American campus possesses qualities and functions different from those of any other type of architecture or built environment. One of its most important qualities is a peculiar state of equilibrium between change and continuity. As a community, it is like a city—complex and inevitably subject to growth and change—and it therefore cannot be viewed as a static architectural monument. But it is not exactly a city; it requires a special kind of physical coherence and continuity. The planners of recent decades who advocated treating the campus like any urban entity—epitomized by Ian Brown's call for obsolescence planning and "the least possible nostalgia"—ignored the special nature of the college and university. As institutions, they have purposes and ideals, whether explicit and specific (such as the doctrinal creeds of early American colleges), or more general (the search for truth, the training of people for careers, or the fostering of "college spirit"). The campus serves the institution not only by satisfying physical needs, but by expressing and reinforcing these ideals or goals.

The history of the American campus reveals the varied and innovative forms this expression can take. These have included the open quadrangles of colonial Harvard or the College of William and Mary, forthrightly part of the towns they were in and of the society whose values they represented; the nineteenth-century college in nature, often poised on a hill, surveying the "New Zion," as Union's President Nott called his vision of America; the informal, park-like campus plans of the early land-grant schools, reflecting populist values in reaction against the elitist formality of the classical college; the Beaux-Arts organization of the new American university, with its complex and orderly system of parts; the revival of the English medieval enclosed quadrangle, expressing the resurgence of conservative collegiate values; and the recent campus plans generated by circulation patterns, reflecting the fluid and unpredictable nature of contemporary education.

The historical succession of these and other planning patterns often can be seen even at a single college. The Princeton campus has undergone many changes of this sort over the centuries, including the imposition of rigid classical symmetry in Joseph Henry's plan of the 1830s, President McCosh's destruction of this order a half-century later to create an informal landscape, and Ralph Adams Cram's transformation of the school into his vision of an English medieval college at the beginning of the twentieth century (Figs. 85, 164, 235). Another example is Lake Erie College in Ohio, which began in the mid-nineteenth century as a large all-inclusive building typical of women's schools of the period, then in the 1920s embraced an orderly Beaux-Arts master plan, and after World War II constructed modern buildings in a free-form plan that gave each component of the growing college its own character and individuality.[114]

Despite growth and change, most campuses have a special individual character that endures over time. This may be associated with a distinctive pattern of buildings—around a quadrangle or along a mall; or with an individual structure—such as a campanile or Old Main; or with a style of architecture—such as the Gothic of Duke University or the "Pueblo" of the University of New Mexico; or a topographical feature or dramatic site. Or it may be a less easily defined quality in the overall form of the campus. These characteristics often originated as expressions of the educational ideals or character of the school, and acquired special significance that endured for successive generations of students and faculty as a physical embodiment of the school's spirit. They are among the most valuable assets of an institution, and their preservation ought to be a prime goal of the planning process.

Beyond the special traits of individual schools, and the changes in patterns of planning over time, there are fundamental characteristics that distinguish the American campus. Most of all, it has typically been open and extroverted, with buildings set in a landscape—in contrast to the inward-turning quadrangles or courts of traditional European institutions. There have been exceptions to this American pattern, as in the case of urban schools with a scarcity of land, or those institutions that were caught up in the early-twentieth-century enthusiasm for the medieval English quadrangle. This revivalist movement produced much collegiate architecture of high quality. But it is significant that even at those schools where enclosed quadrangular plans were executed, subsequent construction has typically reverted to the American pattern of separate buildings in open space.[115] Some people may agree with the Gothicist Ralph Adams Cram that this rejection of the European monastic quadrangle is regrettable. But the fact remains that from the earliest days at the colonial colleges, Americans normally have preferred open and expansive schools that look confidently outward to the world.

The result is that uniquely American place, the campus. As a kind of city in microcosm, it has been shaped by the desire to create an ideal community, and has often been a vehicle for expressing the utopian social visions of the American imagination. Above all, the campus reveals the power that a physical environment can possess as the embodiment of an institution's character.

Notes

Abbreviations:
A.I.A. Journal—American Institute of Architects Journal
J.S.A.H.—Journal of the Society of Architectural Historians

Preface

1. Jefferson used this term many times, beginning in about 1810—for example, in a letter to Benjamin Latrobe in August 1817. See Chapter II.
2. Charles Dickens, *American Notes*, London, 1908, p. 75 (originally published in 1842).
3. Charles R. Ashbee, *Exhibition of University Planning and Building*, The University of London, 1912, p. 5. This catalogue, in which Ashbee described the plans of colleges and universities in Britain, the United States, and elsewhere, was brought to my attention by Professor Peter Stansky of Stanford University.
4. Le Corbusier, *When the Cathedrals Were White*, New York, 1964, p. 135 (original French edition, 1937).
5. The early use of the word *campus* to designate collegiate grounds in America is discussed in the section on Princeton in Chapter I.
6. "Ein Gelände, das mit den Gebäuden einer amerikanischen Universität bedeckt ist, wird 'Campus' genannt." Werner Hegemann, *Amerikanische Architektur und Stadtbaukunst*, Berlin, 1925, p. 87.
7. H. J. Van Dyke, Jr., in *The Princeton Book*, 1879, p. 375; quoted in Albert Matthews, "The Term 'Campus' in American Colleges," *Publications of the Colonial Society of Massachusetts*, vol. 3, 1900, p. 436. The word *campus* seems to have taken on these additional connotations earlier at Princeton (where it had originated) than at other schools.
8. The principal books by campus planners, on the practice of their profession, are: Charles Z. Klauder and Herbert C. Wise, *College Architecture in America and Its Part in the Development of the Campus*, New York, 1929; Jens F. Larson and Archie M. Palmer, *Architectural Planning of the American College*, New York, 1933; and Richard P. Dober, *Campus Planning*, New York, 1963, which contains a chapter on the history of the subject. The appearance of articles on college planning, starting around 1900, will be discussed in Chapter V. A few regional studies have been made, notably Eric Johannesen, *Ohio College Architecture Before 1870*, Cleveland, 1969. Also: Bryant Franklin Tolles, "College Architecture in Northern New England Before 1860, A Social and Cultural History," Ph.D. dissertation, Boston University, 1970. General histories of American architecture have only rarely treated collegiate architecture as a distinct subject. Hugh Morrison did this, to some extent, in *Early American Architecture*, New York, 1952, pp. 463–71.
9. Albert Bush-Brown, "Image of a University: A Study of Architecture as an Expression of Education at Colleges and Universities in the United States Between 1800 and 1900," Ph.D. dissertation, Princeton University, 1958. Bush-Brown focused mainly on East Coast institutions and gave principal attention to the architectural design of their individual buildings rather than to the overall patterns of campus development. Bush-Brown's documentation of the buildings he examined is extensive, and helped me considerably in my own investigation of the institutions he covered.
10. In determining what constitutes an institution of higher education, I have been guided, in a general way, by the criteria in Donald G. Tewksbury's *The Founding of American Colleges and Universities Before the Civil War*, New York, 1932, republished 1965.
11. An architectural plan (quadrangular in form) for Codrington College, of 1713, is illustrated in Marcus Whiffen, *The Public Buildings of Williamsburg*, Williamsburg, Virginia, 1958, p. 104.
12. The degree to which individual schools or plans are examined in detail here varies from chapter to chapter, due to the special character of the various periods and issues examined. For example, several of the colleges of colonial America are studied closely, because of their crucial importance in establishing patterns of planning for the later development of American colleges, whereas in some of the more recent periods, in which no single institutions have played comparable roles, a wider but less detailed survey was adopted.

Introduction

1. For the English universities during this period, see: Mark Curtis, *Oxford and Cambridge in Transition, 1558–1642*, Oxford, 1959; and portions of V.H.H. Green, *A History of Oxford University*, London, 1974; Charles Edward Mallet, *A History of the University of Oxford*, 2 vols., London, 1924; and S. C. Roberts, *British Universities*, London, 1947. For the architecture of the universities of Oxford and Cambridge, see: Nikolaus Pevsner, *The Buildings of England: Cambridgeshire*, Harmondsworth, 1954, and *The Buildings of England: Oxfordshire*, Harmondsworth, 1974; John Summerson, *Architecture in Britain, 1530–1830*, Harmondsworth, 1953, chapter 11; Robert Willis and John Willis Clark, *The Architectural History of the University of Cambridge*, 3 vols., Cambridge, 1886; and Thomas D. Atkinson, *Cambridge Described and Illustrated*, London, 1897. For other aspects of English educational architecture of the period, see Malcolm Seaborne, *The English School: Its Architecture and Organization, 1370–1870*, Toronto, 1971. The general subject of European collegiate architecture is treated in Konrad Rückbrod, *Universität und Kollegium, Baugeschichte und Bautyp*, Darmstadt, 1977.
2. See Gervase Jackson-Stops, "The Architecture of the College," in John Buxton and Penry Williams, eds., *New College Oxford, 1379–1979*, Oxford, 1979.
3. See "The Collegiate Plan," in Willis and Clark, *Architectural History of Cambridge*, vol. 3, pp. 247–82. Willis and Clark described the complex development of the English collegiate plan, in opposition to the previously common belief that it was simply an imitation of the monastic cloister.
4. Green, *History of Oxford*, p. 19.
5. David Loggan's engravings of Oxford and Cambridge and their colleges, the most complete visual record of the buildings up to that time, were published as *Oxonia Illustrata*, 1675, and *Cantabrigia Illustrata*, 1688.
6. Willis and Clark, *Architectural History of Cambridge*, vol. 1, p. 176.
7. Pevsner, *Cambridgeshire*, p. 77.
8. Pevsner, *Oxfordshire*, pp. 32ff; Green, *History of Oxford*, pp. 69ff.
9. See T. G. Jackson, *Wadham College Oxford, Its Foundation, Architecture and History*, Oxford, 1893.
10. Green, *History of Oxford*, pp. 40ff.
11. *Ibid.*, p. 49.
12. See: Douglas Sloan, *The Scottish Enlightenment and the American College Ideal*, New York, 1971; George S. Pryde, *The Scottish Universities and the Colleges of Colonial America*, Glasgow, 1957; and A. Bailey Cutts, "The Educational Influence of Aberdeen in Seventeenth-Century Virginia," *William and Mary Quarterly*, July 1935, pp. 229–48.
13. Pryde, *Scottish Universities*, p. 3.
14. See: P. J. Anderson, ed., *Studies in the History and Development of the University of Aberdeen*, Aberdeen, 1906; Anne Ross, *"A New and Splendid Edifice": The Architecture of the University of Glasgow*, Glasgow, 1975; and Ronald G. Cant, *The University of St. Andrews, A Short History*, Edinburgh, 1946.
15. See John W. Stubbs, *The History of the University of Dublin*, Dublin, 1889.

Chapter I

1. Samuel Eliot Morison, *The Founding of Harvard College*, Cambridge, 1935, p. 361.
2. For the colonial college, see: Lawrence A. Cremin, *American Education: The Colonial Experience, 1607–1783*, New York, 1970; Richard Hofstadter and Wilson Smith, eds., *American Higher Education, A Documentary History*, Chicago, 1961, vol. 1; Frederick Rudolph, *The American College and University*, New York, 1962, chapters 1 and 2; and other works cited in this chapter.
3. The founding dates of these colleges are as determined by Donald G. Tewksbury, in *The Founding of American Colleges and Universities Before the Civil War*, New York, 1932, reprinted 1965.
4. Samuel Eliot Morison, "A Conjectural Restoration of the 'Old College' at Harvard," *Old-Time New England*, April 1933, p. 158. Hugh Morrison, *Early American Architecture*, New York, 1952, p. 84. The building was about 50′ by 90′, according to Morison's reconstruction.
5. Morrison, *Early American Architecture*, p. 85. This building measured 42′ by 99′, according to Hamilton V. Bail, *Views of Harvard, A Pictorial Record to 1860*, Cambridge, Mass., 1949, p. 25.
6. Morrison, *Early American Architecture*, p. 322. The building measured 138′ by 46′ and had a 64′-by-32′ ell (Marcus Whiffen, *The Public Buildings of Williamsburg*, Williamsburg, 1958, p. 24).
7. Rudolph, *The American College*, p. 33. Nassau Hall's dimensions are about 175′ by 55′ (Thomas J. Wertenbaker, *Princeton, 1746–1896*, Princeton, 1946, pp. 37ff).
8. Well into the nineteenth century, many American colleges erected buildings of remarkable size—examples being the main building of Bucknell University in Lewisburg, Pennsylvania, constructed in 1848; Antioch Hall at Antioch College in Yellow Springs, Ohio, which was reputedly the largest building west of the Alleghenies when built in 1852; and the main building of Vassar College in Poughkeepsie, New York, which was said to be the largest structure in the United States for a time in the 1860s, before the completion of the U.S. Capitol. (Richard P.

Dober, *Campus Planning*, New York, 1963, p. 30; Eric Johannesen, *Ohio College Architecture Before 1870*, Cleveland, 1969, p. 34; information from Vassar College.)

9. R. H. Land, "Henrico and Its College," *William and Mary Quarterly*, October 1938, pp. 453ff.
10. According to J. E. Morpurgo (*Their Majesties' Royall Colledge*, Williamsburg, 1976, p. 6), "it is probable that two buildings were begun, one for the Rector of the college and one to house a school for the settlers' children."
11. Ralph N. Hill, *The College on the Hill: A Dartmouth Chronicle*, Hanover, N. H., 1964. In the nineteenth century, as the frontier moved west, many other colleges were founded with the idea of training Indians, or were associated with or grew out of Indian mission schools. An example is the University of Tulsa in Oklahoma. (Guy W. Logsdon, *The University of Tulsa*, Norman, Okla., 1977. This book illustrates photographs of several Indian mission schools in Oklahoma in the late nineteenth century.)
12. Cremin, *American Education*, pp. 322ff. A reconstructed view of the "Log College" at Neshaminy is illustrated in Wheaton J. Lane, ed., *Pictorial History of Princeton*, Princeton, 1947, p. 5.
13. Another building specifically called "The Log College" was at Union Academy, the predecessor of Maryville College in Tennessee, built in about 1802 (Samuel T. Wilson, *A Century of Maryville College, 1819–1919*, Maryville, Tenn., 1916, p. 23). Several "log schools" in western Pennsylvania are mentioned in Charles M. Stotz, *Architectural Heritage of Early Western Pennsylvania*, Pittsburgh, 1966, p. 214. At the University of Notre Dame in Indiana, the "Log Chapel" that was the school's first building in 1842, and which burned in the 1850s, was reconstructed in 1906 and is maintained as a revered symbol of the humble origins of the institution (Thomas J. Schlereth, *The University of Notre Dame: A Portrait of Its History and Campus*, Notre Dame, Ind., 1976, pp. 10–13). Similarly, the original log building of Concordia Seminary in Perry County, Missouri, built in 1839, has been replicated on the school's present campus in St. Louis (information from Concordia Seminary).
14. Samuel Eliot Morison, *Harvard in the Seventeenth Century*, Cambridge, Mass., 1936, vol. 2, p. 400.
15. William Smith, *A General Idea of the College of Mirania*, New York, 1753, reprinted 1969.
16. *Ibid.*, pp. 61–64.
17. The University of Pennsylvania's first buildings, an academic structure and a dormitory, were on Fourth Street near Arch Street in Philadelphia. The main building was constructed in 1740 and first housed a charity school and the academy out of which the university developed. See George B. Wood, *Early History of the University of Pennsylvania*, Philadelphia, 1896, pp. 10ff; and Martin Meyerson and D. P. Winegrad, *Gladly Learn and Gladly Teach: Franklin and His Heirs at the University of Pennsylvania*, Philadelphia, 1978, pp. 15–18.
18. A reconstruction of this compound of buildings is illustrated in Hill, *College on the Hill*, pp. 40–41.
19. Milton Halsey Thomas, "The King's College Building," *New-York Historical Society Quarterly*, January 1955, pp. 23–61. This article was brought to my attention by Francesco Passanti. The King's College building (ca. 180′ by 30′ in dimension) was bounded by Barclay, Chapel, Murray, and Church streets, on the west side of lower Manhattan; it was demolished in 1857, when the college moved uptown to 49th Street and Madison Avenue. The building is shown in an engraving, published in *The New York Magazine*, May 1790, and in other representations illustrated in Thomas's article, and in *A History of Columbia University*, New York, 1904. Plans to remodel or expand the building, in the 1810s, are described in Franklin Toker, "James O'Donnell: An Irish Georgian in America," *J.S.A.H.*, May 1970, pp. 135–37, and in a note by Adolf K. Placzek in the same journal, May 1952, p. 23. Another plan, of 1792, to complete the originally intended quadrangle, is preserved at Columbia University in the Office of Columbiana at Low Library.
20. See Morrison, *Early American Architecture*, pp. 468–71. For University Hall at Brown, see Reuben A. Guild, *Early History of Brown University*, Providence, R.I., 1897. (Professor William H. Jordy of Brown informs me that the university preserves extensive documentation of the construction of University Hall. A study of the building, unpublished, was made by Lawrence Wroth.) For Queen's Building at Rutgers, see Richard McCormick, *Rutgers, A Bicentennial History*, New Brunswick, N.J., 1966. For Dartmouth Hall, see: Frederick Chase, *A History of Dartmouth College*, Cambridge, Mass., 1891; and Hill, *College on the Hill*. The preeminent architect in eighteenth-century New England, Peter Harrison, was approached in 1773 about designing a main building for Dartmouth, but he was not hired, and the structure ultimately was built by a designer-carpenter, as were most of the college buildings of the period (Carl Bridenbaugh, *Peter Harrison, American Architect*, Chapel Hill, 1949, pp. 150–53). It is interesting that University Hall at Brown and Old Queen's at Rutgers were both originally flanked by president's houses, as was Nassau Hall at Princeton. Also see Eldon L. Dean, "Early College and Educational Buildings in New England," *Pencil Points*, December 1934, pp. 597–602.
21. Rudolph, *The American College*, p. 3.
22. Samuel Eliot Morison, *The Founding of Harvard College* and *Harvard in the Seventeenth Century*. For the architecture of early Harvard, see also: Bainbridge Bunting and Robert Nylander, *Survey of Architectural History in Cambridge*, vol. 4, Cambridge, Mass., 1973, pp. 148–203; and Hamilton V. Bail, *Views of Harvard, A Pictorial Record to 1860*, Cambridge, Mass., 1949. A history of Harvard architecture, by the late Bainbridge Bunting, is presently being prepared for publication.
23. Morison, *Seventeenth Century*, vol. 1, p. 49.
24. Hofstadter and Smith, *American Higher Education*, vol. 1, p. 15.
25. Morison, *Seventeenth Century*, vol. 1, pp. 75–76.
26. Morison, *Founding of Harvard*, p. 252.

27. Samuel Eliot Morison, "A Conjectural Restoration," pp. 130–58. The reconstruction was made by Harold R. Shurtleff.
28. Captain Edward Johnson, *A History of New England*, London, 1654; quoted in Bail, *Views of Harvard*, p. 2.
29. Morison, *Founding of Harvard*, pp. 229–30. For the use of the word *campus*, see the discussion of Princeton in this chapter.
30. Johnson, *History of New England*, quoted in Bail, *Views of Harvard*, p. 2.
31. Morison compared the Harvard chambers to those in the Perse and Legge buildings at Gonville and Caius College, Cambridge ("A Conjectural Restoration," pp. 146–48).
32. Morison, "A Conjectural Restoration," pp. 143ff.
33. Morison (*Seventeenth Century*, vol. 1, pp. 340ff) presented a hypothetical reconstruction of this building.
34. *Ibid.*, p. 343, n. 3.
35. Ashton R. Willard, "The Development of College Architecture in America," *The New England Magazine*, July 1897, pp. 513–35. Willard's preference for the "Anglican" pattern was typical of the revival of interest in the enclosed quadrangle at the end of the nineteenth century in America—which is examined in Chapter VI.
36. Another reason that has been suggested for the American abandonment of the enclosed quadrangle is "the poverty of American resources" in the colonial period (John S. Brubacher and Willis Rudy, *Higher Education in Transition, An American History, 1636–1956*, New York, 1958, p. 41). Perhaps this was a contributing factor, but it does not explain the new American pattern of widely spaced structures, which could have been constructed next to one another, to form an enclosed quadrangle over a period of time, as the English colleges themselves had evolved.
37. The *Oxford English Dictionary* gives examples of the use of the word *college* in England to designate generally the architecture of a college, but no example of its specific designation of one or more of several buildings at a college—as the word was used at Harvard and other American schools. This uniquely American sense of the term was discussed by Oliver Farrar Emerson in a series of letters published in *The Nation* in 1895 (November 7 and 28, pp. 327, 387–88). See also *A Dictionary of Americanisms, on Historical Principles*, Chicago, 1951, vol. 1, p. 357; and Morison, *Seventeenth Century*, vol. 1, pp. 43–44.
38. Morison (*Seventeenth Century*, vol. 1, p. 71) suggested that the main reason Harvard did not "promptly declare itself a university" was that this would have drawn attention to the dubious powers it was exercising. But he did not make a connection between this fact and the physical form of the college.
39. Examples of buildings called "colleges" are: West, East, and South colleges at Williams College (erected 1790–1842); Old West College at Dickinson College in Pennsylvania (1803); Rutledge, De Saussure, Pinckney, Elliott, Lieber, Harper, and Legare colleges at South Carolina College (ca. 1803–1848); North and South colleges at Union College in New York (1813); similarly named buildings at Wesleyan University in Connecticut, Colby College in Maine, Amherst College in Massachusetts, Western Reserve College in Ohio, and the University of Vermont (1820s); Morrison College at Transylvania College in Kentucky (1830); and West, Middle, and East colleges at Ripon College in Wisconsin (1850s). Most—but not all—of these structures were built as dormitories.
40. Morison, "A Conjectural Restoration," p. 131.
41. Morison, *Seventeenth Century*, vol. 2, p. 405. The dimensions of this building were 42′ by 99′.
42. Bunting and Nylander, *Architectural History in Cambridge*, pp. 150–51.
43. Morison stated that the work on Harvard Hall "was entrusted by the Overseers to a committee of their own number, headed by Deputy-Governor Leverett" (*Seventeenth Century*, vol. 2, p. 423).
44. Morison, *Founding of Harvard*, Appendix B and elsewhere.
45. For the early history of the College of William and Mary and its architecture, see: J. E. Morpurgo, *Their Majesties' Royall Colledge*, Williamsburg, 1976; Marcus Whiffen, *The Public Buildings of Williamsburg*, Williamsburg, 1958; John W. Reps, *Tidewater Towns: City Planning in Colonial Virginia and Maryland*, Williamsburg, 1972, pp. 141ff; and other works cited below. I am indebted to Professor James D. Kornwolf, of the College of William and Mary, who supplied me with additional information on the early architecture of the school.
46. Morpurgo, *Their Majesties' Colledge*, p. 36.
47. For the drawing, see Whiffen, *Public Buildings of Williamsburg*, pp. 26–28. The map is called the "Bland Map." Its legend says of the college: "The black lines Represent the Buildings already Erected, the prickt lines that part which is to be built."
48. Rudolph, *The American College*, p. 24.
49. Whiffen, *Public Buildings of Williamsburg*, pp. 23–25.
50. Hugh Jones, *The Present State of Virginia*, London, 1724; quoted in Morpurgo, *Their Majesties' Colledge*, pp. 64 and 36.
51. Moreover, it is known that in 1694 an employee of the Court was sent to Virginia with plans for a garden, "designed for the new Colledge," making it likely that plans for the building itself also were provided by the appropriate royal officials (letter from John Evelyn to John Walker, May 1694; *Virginia Magazine of History and Biography*, January 1970, p. 27). This and other information pertinent to Wren's involvement in the design of William and Mary was given to me by Professor Kornwolf of the college.
52. Letter from Wren to the president of Trinity College, Oxford, in 1665; quoted in Martin S. Briggs, *Wren the Incomparable*, London, 1953, p. 36.
53. The Williamson Building, constructed in 1671, has recently been attributed at least in part to Wren (Nikolaus Pevsner, *The Buildings of England: Oxfordshire*, Harmondsworth, 1974, p. 185). Professor Kornwolf has brought to my attention two other buildings associated with Wren that are similar in certain respects to the William and Mary building: Bromley College, Kent (1672), and Morden College, Blackheath (1695).

54. Wren's work at Oxford included the Sheldonian Theatre, a building for Trinity College, and Tom Tower of Christ Church College; at Cambridge, the Pembroke College Chapel and the library of Trinity College.
55. See Reps, *Tidewater Towns*, pp. 117–70, for Nicholson's work at Annapolis and Williamsburg.
56. Both structures probably were designed by the builder Henry Cary, Jr. They are not precisely parallel to one another, due to the fact that the main building was not exactly perpendicular to the Duke of Gloucester Street, and one of the flanking buildings was made parallel to the street while the other was made perpendicular to the main building.
57. Whiffen, *Public Buildings of Williamsburg*, p. 112.
58. It has also been suggested that the William and Mary pattern of buildings was influenced by the plan of King's College, Aberdeen (A. Bailey Cutts, "The Educational Influence of Aberdeen in Seventeenth-Century Virginia," *William and Mary Quarterly*, July 1935, p. 248).
59. See: G. M. Dodge et al., *Norwich University, 1819–1911*, Montpelier, Vt., 1911, p. 8; Eric Johannesen, *Ohio College Architecture Before 1870*, Cleveland, 1969, pp. 5–8, 31–34; and H. M. Klein, *History of Franklin and Marshall College*, Lancaster, Pa., 1952, p. 33. The pattern also was created at Princeton, with the erection of two buildings flanking Nassau Hall, in 1803 (see discussion of Latrobe's work, in Chapter II). A mid-nineteenth-century engraving of Christian College, in Columbia, Missouri, also shows a main structure flanked symmetrically by two small buildings, in the William and Mary manner.
60. Glenn Patton, "The College of William and Mary, Williamsburg, and the Enlightenment," *J.S.A.H.*, March 1970, pp. 24–32.
61. *Ibid.*, p. 27.
62. For the early architecture of Yale, see: Anthony H. B. Garvan, *Architecture and Town-Planning in Colonial Connecticut*, New Haven, 1951; Reuben A. Holden, *Yale: A Pictorial History*, New Haven, 1967; Elizabeth Mills Brown, *New Haven, A Guide to Architecture and Urban Design*, New Haven, 1976; and other works cited below. The Manuscripts and Archives Department of the Sterling Library at Yale has several files of information on the school's early architecture.
63. Garvan, *Architecture in Colonial Connecticut*, pp. 145–46.
64. John Archer, "Puritan Town Planning in New Haven," *J.S.A.H.*, May 1975, pp. 140–49.
65. This building, demolished in 1782, was reconstructed by Norman M. Isham, in "The Original College House at Yale," *Yale Alumni Weekly*, October 20, 1916, pp. 114–20. Also see Garvan, *Architecture in Colonial Connecticut*, p. 146.
66. It is possible that the buildings at Harvard served as a model for the Row at Yale. As pointed out earlier, the Harvard buildings by the 1760s constituted a kind of row, even though they were not exactly aligned. And at both schools, the row was characterized by an alternation of long facades with the gabled ends of buildings.
67. Thomas Clap, *Annals or History of Yale College*, New Haven, 1766, p. 55; quoted by Garvan, *Architecture in Colonial Connecticut*, p. 146. Garvan argues that Clap's construction of a separate college chapel was motivated by the desire to remove his students from the influence of the minister of the meetinghouse on the Green, with whose religious views he disagreed.
68. Anne S. Pratt, "John Trumbull and the Old Brick Row," *Yale University Library Gazette*, July 1934, pp. 11–20.
69. These drawings are in the Beinecke Library at Yale. See: Pratt, "John Trumbull," and Theodore Sizer, "John Trumbull, Amateur Architect," *J.S.A.H.*, July–December 1949, pp. 1–6.
70. One of the indications of Hillhouse's role is a letter from him to President Stiles, of December 24, 1792, in which he described the new plan with phrases very similar to those written on the drawings themselves (Beinecke Library, Yale).
71. Notes by Trumbull on his sheet of floor plans and elevation drawings of the proposed buildings.
72. Notes on Trumbull's site plan of the design for the new buildings.
73. Notes on the sheet of floor plans and elevation drawings.
74. At Dartmouth, the row was created by buildings flanking Dartmouth Hall that were erected 1828–29 (see Osmund Overby, "Ammi B. Young in the Connecticut Valley," *J.S.A.H.*, October 1960, and Lawrence Wodehouse, "Ammi Burnham Young, 1798–1874," *J.S.A.H.*, December 1966). The buildings at Brown, flanking University Hall, were begun in 1823; the row at Amherst was constructed 1820–27; that at Bowdoin, 1806–55; that at Colby, 1821–37; that at Hamilton, 1793–1827; that at Hobart (now Hobart and William Smith Colleges), 1822–77; that at Washington (later Trinity College), 1824–45; that at Wesleyan, 1824–69; that at St. John's, 1837–58; that at Washington College in Maryland, 1844–54; that at Middlebury, 1814–59; that at the University of Vermont, 1825–28; that at Ohio Wesleyan, in the 1840s; that at Western Reserve, 1826–37. Views of several of these groups of buildings are illustrated in Bryant Franklin Tolles, Jr., "College Architecture in New England Before 1860 in Printed and Sketched Views," *Antiques*, March 1973.
75. For example, Andrew D. White, the first president of Cornell University, who had been a student at Yale, wrote that "the long line of brick barracks . . . repelled me" (quoted in Albert Bush-Brown, "Image of a University: A Study of Architecture as an Expression of Education at Colleges and Universities in the United States between 1800 and 1900," Ph.D. dissertation, Princeton, 1958, p. 89). More recently, the historian Albert Bush-Brown himself expressed a similar dissatisfaction, calling the Yale Row a "harsh, impenetrable wall of brick," lacking "focus, variety, or a dominant accent" ("Image of a University," p. 42).
76. See: Thomas J. Wertenbaker, *Princeton, 1746–1896*, Princeton, 1946; Wheaton J. Lane, ed., *Pictorial History of Princeton*, Princeton, 1947; Henry L. Savage, ed., *Nassau Hall, 1756–1956*, Princeton, 1956; Montgomery Schuyler, "Architecture of American Colleges: Princeton," *Architectural Record*, February 1910, pp. 129–60; and other works cited below.

77. Quoted in Alexander Leitch, *A Princeton Companion*, Princeton, 1978, p. 75. The author of this remark is not identified.
78. Letter from Charles C. Beatty to Enoch Green, January 31, 1774; quoted in Leitch, *A Princeton Companion*, p. 74.
79. Albert Matthews, "The Term 'Campus' in American Colleges," paper presented March 1897, *Publications of the Colonial Society of Massachusetts*, Boston, vol. 3, 1900, pp. 431–37. The word was used at South Carolina College as early as 1821, which was the earliest use of it Matthews could find at a school other than Princeton.
80. *Ibid.*, p. 434. Matthews found that several Roman Catholic colleges used *campus* to designate their athletic fields, but not their entire college grounds, as most American schools did by this time.
81. For Nassau Hall, see: Robert C. Smith, "John Notman's Nassau Hall," *Princeton Library Chronicle*, vol. 14, 1953; Henry L. Savage, ed., *Nassau Hall, 1756–1956*.
82. See: Bunting and Nylander, *Architectural History in Cambridge*, pp. 152–53; Morrison, *Early American Architecture*, pp. 466–71; Daniel Reiff, *Washington Architecture, 1791–1861*, Washington, D.C., 1971, p. 24; John Morrill Bryan, *An Architectural History of the South Carolina College, 1801–1855*, Columbia, S.C., 1976; Richard P. McCormick, *Rutgers: A Bicentennial History*; Rexford Newcomb, *Architecture in Old Kentucky*, Urbana, Ill., 1953, p. 80; John D. Wright, Jr., *Transylvania, Tutor to the West*, Lexington, Ky., 1975, pp. 58–59; L. W. Spring, *History of Williams College*, Boston, 1917.

Chapter II

1. For the educational history of this period, see: Frederick Rudolph, *The American College and University*, New York, 1962; Frederick Rudolph, ed., *Essays on Education in the Early Republic*, Cambridge, Mass., 1965; John S. Brubacher and Willis Rudy, *Higher Education in Transition*, New York, 1958, Part II; and other studies cited below.
2. Donald G. Tewksbury, *The Founding of American Colleges and Universities Before the Civil War*, New York, 1932, reprinted 1965.
3. *Ibid.*, p. 1.
4. Richard Hofstadter and Wilson Smith, eds., *American Higher Education: A Documentary History*, Chicago, 1961, vol. 1, pp. 233–34.
5. *Ibid.*, Part 4, "Quest for an Adequate Educational System."
6. *Ibid.*, pp. 275–91. This report was published in *The American Journal of Science and Arts*, January 1829, and in 1830 as "Report on the Course of Instruction in Yale College."
7. William P. and J. P. Cutler, *Life, Journals and Correspondence of Rev. M. Cutler*, Cincinnati, 1888, vol. 2, p. 31; quoted in Brubacher and Rudy, *Higher Education*, p. 41. Cutler's remark regarded a proposed college in Ohio.
8. Rudolph, *The American College*, p. 90; Francis Wayland, *Thoughts on the Present Collegiate System in the United States*, Boston, 1842, pp. 112–31.
9. "Report on the Course of Instruction in Yale College," quoted in Albert Bush-Brown, "Image of a University: A Study of Architecture as an Expression of Education at Colleges and Universities in the United States Between 1800 and 1900," Ph.D. dissertation, Princeton University, 1958, p. 52.
10. Elmer D. Johnson, *History of Libraries in the Western World*, Metuchen, N.J., 1970, chapter 16.
11. See Chapter I for examples of schools using these patterns of planning. For Bentley Hall at Allegheny College in Pennsylvania, see C. M. Stotz, *Architectural History of Early Western Pennsylvania*, Pittsburgh, 1966, pp. 215–21.
12. See: E. L Kayser, *Bricks Without Straw: The Evolution of George Washington University*, New York, 1970; Eric Johannesen, *Ohio College Architecture Before 1870*, Cleveland, 1969, pp. 6–10; W. Havighurst, *The Miami Years, 1809–69*, New York, 1958; Charles H. Rammelkamp, *Illinois College, A Centennial History*, New Haven, 1928; Frederick Koeper, *Illinois Architecture*, Chicago, 1968, p. 154.
13. See: Archibald Henderson, *The Campus of the First State University*, Chapel Hill, N.C., 1949; William S. Powell, *The First State University: A Pictorial History of the University of North Carolina*, Chapel Hill, 1972.
14. Henderson, *The Campus*, figure opposite p. 56.
15. *Ibid.*, p. 13 and elsewhere.
16. John Morrill Bryan, *An Architectural History of the South Carolina College*, Columbia, S.C., 1976, p. 12.
17. See: H. M. Pierce Gallagher, *Robert Mills, Architect of the Washington Monument*, New York, 1935; Paul V. Turner, review of Bryan, *An Architectural History*, in *J.S.A.H.*, May 1978, pp. 112–13.
18. Mills's competition drawings, rendered in watercolor, are illustrated in Bryan, *An Architectural History*.
19. David Madsen, *The National University, Enduring Dream of the United States of America*, Detroit, 1966, pp. 16ff.
20. Samuel Knox, "An Essay on the Best System of Liberal Education," Philadelphia, 1799; reprinted in Rudolph, *Essays on Education*, pp. 271ff.
21. This design was published in Piranesi's *Opere Varie di Architettura* of ca. 1750. See: J. Wilton-Ely, *The Mind and Art of Giovanni Battista Piranesi*, London, 1978, fig. 19; Konrad Rückbrod, *Universität und Kollegium: Baugeschichte und Bautyp*, Darmstadt, 1977, figs. 32, 33.
22. Knox, "An Essay," in Rudolph, *Essays on Education*, p. 360.
23. *Ibid.*, pp. 360–61.
24. See: H. V. Bail, *Views of Harvard*, Cambridge, Mass., 1949, p. 141; Harold Kirker, *The Architecture of Charles Bulfinch*, Cambridge, Mass., 1969.
25. Harvard University Archives. These drawings have the numbers 3451-A/5, 3451-A/6, and UA-I-15-740-PF. None of them is dated or signed by Bulfinch, but all three can be associated with his 1812 work for Harvard, by internal evi-

dence. I am indebted to Professor John P. Coolidge of Harvard, who examined these drawings with me in October 1977.

26. Bulfinch's earlier Tontine Crescent in Boston also probably was inspired by the Royal Crescent in Bath. See Kirker, *The Architecture of Bulfinch*.
27. See Talbot Hamlin, *Benjamin Henry Latrobe*, New York, 1935. I am grateful to Charles Brownell, of the Maryland Historical Society, for various observations on Latrobe's work, in conversation in 1977.
28. For the military academy, see below. For Latrobe's work at the University of Pennsylvania, see Hamlin, *Latrobe*, pp. 194ff.
29. Wheaton J. Lane, ed., *Pictorial History of Princeton*, Princeton, 1947, p. 31.
30. According to Professor Robert J. Clark of Princeton, the school's trustees' minutes of July 11, 1803, and other evidence, confirm the attribution of Stanhope and Philosophical halls to Latrobe. The pattern created by Nassau Hall and these two flanking buildings is similar to the William and Mary pattern, which Latrobe saw on a visit to Williamsburg in 1796.
31. Bryan, *An Architectural History*, pp. 123–25. Paul F. Norton, "Latrobe and Old West at Dickinson College," *The Art Bulletin*, June 1951, pp. 125–32; Charles C. Sellers, *Dickinson College*, Middletown, Conn., 1973; Hamlin, *Latrobe*, p. 188.
32. Rexford Newcomb, *Architecture in Old Kentucky*, Urbana, Ill., 1953, pp. 79–81.
33. John W. Reps, *Monumental Washington*, Princeton, 1967, p. 35. Latrobe's plan is in the Library of Congress, Maps Division.
34. See the discussion of the University of Virginia later in this chapter.
35. Norton, "Latrobe and Old West," p. 130.
36. *Ibid*., p. 128.
37. The Library of Congress has seven sheets of drawings, inscribed "Sketches for a Design of a Military Academy, to accommodate seven Professors and fifty Students. By B. Henry Latrobe Archt & Eng. January 26 1800." Talbot Hamlin (*Latrobe*, p. 256) argued that this was a design for the national military academy later placed at West Point.
38. An exception was Roman Catholic colleges, which often were planned in a tighter, more linked manner than other schools. Examples include Georgetown University in the District of Columbia and St. Louis University in Missouri. See Chapter III.
39. Among the studies of Ramée's design are: Harold A. Larrabee, "Joseph-Jacques Ramée and America's First Unified College Plan," *Franco-American Pamphlet Series*, no. 1, New York, 1934; Codman Hislop and Harold A. Larrabee, "Joseph-Jacques Ramée and the Building of North and South Colleges," *Union Alumni Monthly*, vol. 27, 1938, pp. 1–16; and Roy Eugene Graham, "Joseph-Jacques Ramée and the French Emigré Architects in America," M.A. thesis, University of Virginia, 1968.
40. For the history of Union College, see: Andrew V. Raymond, *Union University, Its History, Influence, Characteristics, and Equipment*, New York, 1907; and Codman Hislop, *Eliphalet Nott*, Middletown, Conn., 1971.
41. Hislop, *Eliphalet Nott*, pp. 73, 95.
42. *Ibid*., pp. 83–84.
43. This building, which was designed by the architect Philip Hooker, in 1797, was demolished in the 1890s. It is described and illustrated in Edward W. Root, *Philip Hooker*, New York, 1929, pp. 66–71.
44. Treasurer's records and other documents, in the Union College Archives. I am grateful to Ellen Fladger, Union College Archivist, and other members of the college's staff, for assistance in my research at the college.
45. Codman Hislop, "The Ramée Plans," *Union Alumni Monthly*, vol. 22, no. 2, 1932, pp. 48–53. There are about thirty-five of these drawings, which are now in the Union College Archives. An inventory of them, made in 1856, lists ten more, which are now lost.
46. The plan was published in Joseph-Jacques Ramée, *Parcs et Jardins, Composés et Exécutés dans Différentes Contrées de l'Europe et des Etats Unis d'Amérique*, Paris, n.d., plate 13. The engraving, by J. Klein and V. Balch, is not dated, but probably was made in about 1820. A painting by William Givens, owned by Union College, shows a somewhat different version of Ramée's design, and may have been based on a separate drawing, now lost.
47. The 1856 inventory, accompanying Ramée's drawings, refers to plans (now lost) of "the Circular Chapel."
48. This structure, now called the Nott Memorial, was designed by Edward Tuckerman Potter in 1858, and was one of the first examples of the Ruskinian influence on American architecture. See: Sarah Bradford Landau, *Edward T. and William A. Potter: American Victorian Architects*, New York, 1979; and Mendel, Mesick & Cohen, *The Nott Memorial, A Historic Structure Report*, Schenectady, 1973. Potter was one of the grandchildren of Eliphalet Nott.
49. In the 1860s, a professor at Union College reported President Nott's recollection that construction began in 1812, and that when Ramée was hired, "the foundations and walls already built had to be adapted to the new plan" (Jonathan Pearson's Diaries, entry for June 25, 1861, Union College Archives).
50. The drawings are labeled simply "Union College."
51. Among the numerous studies of the University of Virginia campus are: Fiske Kimball, *Thomas Jefferson, Architect*, Boston, 1916, and "The Genesis of Jefferson's Plan for the University of Virginia," *Architecture*, December 1923, pp. 397–99; William B. O'Neal, *Jefferson's Buildings at the University of Virginia: The Rotunda*, Charlottesville, 1960, and *Pictorial History of the University of Virginia*, Charlottesville, 1968; William H. Pierson, *American Buildings and Their Architects: The Colonial and Neoclassical Styles*, New York, 1970, pp. 316–34; Frederick D. Nichols, "The University of Virginia," in William H. Adams, ed., *The Eye of Thomas Jefferson*, Washington, 1976, pp. 284–304. I am grateful for observations made to me personally by Professor Nichols, and for unpublished work on Jefferson by Harold Hellenbrand.
52. Talbot Hamlin, *Greek Revival Architecture in America*, Oxford, 1944, p. 42.

53. A. Lawrence Kocher and Howard Dearstyne, "Discovery of Foundations for Jefferson's Addition to the Wren Building," *J.S.A.H.*, October 1951, pp. 28–31.
54. A. A. Lipscomb, ed., *The Writings of Thomas Jefferson*, Washington, 1904, vol. 2, p. 212.
55. Roy J. Honeywell, *The Educational Work of Thomas Jefferson*, Cambridge, Mass., 1931, p. 9.
56. Adams, *Eye of Jefferson*, p. 293. Ledoux's building was the Pavillon Guimard, built in the 1770s.
57. The possible influence of the Hôtel-Dieu plans on Jefferson was suggested to me by Professor Robert Bruegmann of the University of Illinois, who wrote a dissertation on "Architecture of the Hospital, 1770–1870" (University of Pennsylvania, 1976). It is perhaps significant that one of the arguments in France for the pavilion type of plan for hospitals was its prevention of the spread of disease from one part of the institution to another—an argument that Jefferson used for avoiding large single collegiate buildings (see the quotation, in the text below, from Jefferson's letter to L. W. Tazewell of January 5, 1805).
58. See the earlier discussion of the South Carolina College.
59. Letter of January 5, 1805, to L. W. Tazewell, in the Jefferson Papers of the University of Virginia.
60. Letter to Benjamin Latrobe, of August 3, 1817; quoted in Kimball, *Thomas Jefferson*, p. 190.
61. The sketch is in the Massachusetts Historical Society. Kimball (*Thomas Jefferson*, p. 205) associates it with the letter to Tazewell, and thus dates it 1804–5.
62. Howard C. Rice, Jr., *Thomas Jefferson's Paris*, Princeton, 1976, pp. 18ff. For Trumbull's Yale plan, see Chapter I.
63. Letter of May 6, 1810, to Hugh L. White et al., "Trustees of the Lottery of East Tennessee College"; published in Lipscomb, *Writings of Jefferson*, pp. 386–88.
64. The ancient palestra and forum were proposed as influences on Jefferson by Kimball (*Thomas Jefferson*, p. 80). The lyceum was proposed by Karl Lehman, in *Thomas Jefferson, American Humanist*, New York, 1947, p. 186. The chateau of Marly was proposed by Kimball ("Genesis of Jefferson's Plan").
65. This original concept is seen, for example, in the site plan Jefferson presented to the university trustees in 1817 (see below).
66. This comparison was suggested to me by Peter Atherton.
67. Jefferson traveled in New England in the summer of 1784. He is known to have visited Yale at this time, and spent about two weeks in Boston, when he no doubt visited Harvard.
68. This drawing is in the University of Virginia library. See: William A. Lambeth and Warren H. Manning, *Thomas Jefferson as an Architect and a Designer of Landscapes*, Boston, 1913, plate IV; Kimball, *Thomas Jefferson*, p. 75; and O'Neal, *Pictorial History*, p. 12. Kimball dated the drawing 1814, and O'Neal dated it ca. 1815.
69. See Adams, *Eye of Jefferson*, p. 287.
70. Glenn Brown, "Letters from Thomas Jefferson and William Thornton, Architect, Relating to the University of Virginia," *A.I.A. Journal*, January 1913, pp. 21–27.
71. Bernhard von Saxe-Weimar (in *Reise . . . durch nord-America im Jahren 1825 und 1826*, Weimar, 1828) wrote that because of the irregularity, "kein ensemble im Ganzen ist, und deswegen keinen schoenen und grossen Anblick gewaehrt"; quoted in Kimball, p. 79.
72. Latrobe presented this idea in a letter to Jefferson, of July 24, 1817, which is now in the Jefferson Papers at the Library of Congress. See Kimball, *Thomas Jefferson*, pp. 187ff. There is evidence, however, that Jefferson thought of including a structure different from the pavilions, at the end of the Lawn, even before Latrobe wrote to him. Notes by Jefferson, of July 18, 1817, refer to the center point of the northern end of the campus as being "destined for some principal building." See Lambeth and Manning, *Thomas Jefferson as an Architect*, plate XIII, and Dumas Malone, *Jefferson and His Time*, vol. 6, Boston, 1981, p. 259. This was brought to my attention by John C. Van Horne, Associate Editor of the Papers of B. H. Latrobe.
73. Letter to James Breckinridge, July 18, 1819; quoted in Adams, *Eye of Jefferson*, p. 299.
74. Similarly, there was a discrepancy between Jefferson's desire that the students govern themselves and be given much responsibility, and the reality of American collegiate life of the period. Soon after the university opened, student disorder required a return to traditional discipline (O'Neal, *Pictorial History*, p. 48).
75. From conversation with Professor Frederick D. Nichols of the University of Virginia, December 1977.
76. J. B. Sellers, *History of the University of Alabama*, University, Ala., 1953. Information from C. Ford Peatross of the Library of Congress.
77. M. Curti and V. Carstensen, *The University of Wisconsin: A History*, Madison, 1949. Thomas J. Schlereth, *The University of Notre Dame, A Portrait of Its History and Campus*, Notre Dame, 1976. A lithograph of ca. 1856 (in the Library of Congress, Prints and Photographs Division), identified as "Wilberforce University, Xenia, Ohio, the colored people's college," shows a main building at the end of a mall lined on both sides by structures of a domestic character.

Chapter III

1. Frederick Rudolph, *The American College and University*, New York, 1962, p. 47.
2. Ralph Waldo Emerson, *The Young Americans*; quoted in Donald G. Tewksbury, *The Founding of American Colleges and Universities Before the Civil War*, New York, 1932, p. 1.
3. See the beginning of Chapter II.
4. Rudolph, *The American College*, p. 97.
5. John Morrill Bryan, *An Architectural History of the South Carolina College*, Columbia, S.C., 1976, pp. 15, 73.
6. This is suggested by the portfolios in which Davis compiled his designs (now kept in the Metropolitan Museum of Art, New York, Print Room), in which he juxtaposed these building types on the same sheets. For more on this, see the discussion later in this chapter of Davis's collegiate work.
7. Quoted in Tewksbury, *Founding of American Colleges*, p. 5. This was President W. S. Taylor of Amherst.
8. Talbot Hamlin, *Greek Revival Architecture in America*, Oxford, 1944. The index in this work has a category of "colleges, seminaries, and universities" possessing buildings that Hamlin considered significant Greek Revival structures.
9. Rudolph, *The American College*, pp. 49–50.
10. *Ibid.*, p. 138.
11. See: Charles R. Williams, *The Cliosophic Society*, Princeton, 1916; Jacob N. Beam, *The American Whig Society*, Princeton, 1933; H. M. Bullock, *History of Emory University*, Nashville, 1936. The symmetry of the two society halls at Princeton is especially remarkable, considering that each was paid for and erected independently by its membership (Beam, *Whig Society*, p. 89).
12. Joseph Henry's plan was printed, in 1836, as part of a fund-raising letter for the construction of the society halls. (I am grateful to Earle E. Coleman of the Princeton University Archives, for this and other information about Princeton architecture.) Joseph Henry joined the Princeton faculty in 1832, as professor of natural philosophy.
13. Reuben Holden, *Yale: A Pictorial History*, New Haven, 1967, text accompanying fig. 172.
14. See: George B. Wood, *Early History of the University of Pennsylvania*, Philadelphia, 1896; and Agnes Addison Gilchrist, *William Strickland, Architect and Engineer*, Philadelphia, 1950.
15. M. Curti and V. Carstensen, *The University of Wisconsin: A History*, Madison, 1949, p. 67; "A Summary of Campus Planning, The University of Wisconsin, 1850 to 1954," and other unpublished papers in the University of Wisconsin Archives. The design was by John F. Rague (who was also the architect of the territorial capitol of Iowa, in Iowa City, which became the central building of the University of Iowa).
16. See: E. Merton Coulter, *College Life in the Old South*, New York, 1928; K. F. Marsh and B. Marsh, *Athens: Georgia's Columned City*, Asheville, N.C., 1964; and J. H. Easterby, *A History of the College of Charleston*, Charleston, 1935.
17. For Girard College, see below. For the other schools mentioned, see: H. B. Eberlein et al., *Historic Buildings of Delaware*, Dover, 1963; M. M. Fisher, *History of Westminster College*, Columbia, Mo., 1903; John D. Wright, Jr., *Transylvania: Tutor to the West*, Lexington, Ky., 1975; Frederick D. Nichols, *Architecture of Georgia*, Savannah, 1976; Talbot Hamlin, *Greek Revival Architecture in America*, Oxford, 1944. Another school in a single temple-form structure was the Collegiate School in Poughkeepsie, New York (illustrated in Robert Sears, *Pictorial Description of the United States*, New York, 1855, p. 181).
18. See: Charles E. Peterson and E. Newbold Cooper, "The Girard College Architectural Competition, 1833," and Agnes A. Gilchrist, "Girard College: An Example of the Layman's Influence on Architecture," *J.S.A.H.*, May 1957, pp. 20–27; and John Baker Cutler, "The Girard College Architectural Competition, 1832–1848," Ph.D. dissertation, Yale University, 1969.
19. Walter's competition entry is illustrated in Gilchrist, "Girard College," p. 21. The drawings of seventeen entrants in the competition are preserved at the Historical Society of Pennsylvania, in Philadelphia. Among the competitors were William Strickland (who took second place), Isaiah Rogers (third place), John Haviland, and the firm of Town, Davis, & Dakin. Drawings from the entries of Walter and Haviland are illustrated in David Gebhard and Deborah Nevins, *Two Hundred Years of American Architectural Drawings*, New York, 1977, pp. 107, 123. Drawings for the competition by A. J. Davis are preserved at the Avery Library at Columbia University. William Strickland's entry is illustrated in Agnes A. Gilchrist, *William Strickland*, plate 29-A.
20. Gilchrist, "Girard College," p. 24.
21. John V. Allcott, "Scholarly Books and Frolicsome Blades: A. J. Davis Designs a Library-Ballroom," *J.S.A.H.*, May 1974, pp. 145–54.
22. *Ibid.*, p. 148.
23. *An Introduction: Williams College*, Williamstown, Mass., 1977, p. 3.
24. Frederick Rudolph, *Mark Hopkins and the Log*, New Haven, 1956, p. 227.
25. Charles Thwing, *American Colleges: Their Students and Work*, New York, 1878, p. 48.
26. Charles Dickens, *American Notes*, London, 1908, p. 75 (originally published in 1842).
27. Francis Wayland, *Thoughts on the Present Collegiate System in the United States*, Boston, 1842, pp. 121–22.
28. L. A. Dunn, *Review of the American College with Reference to the Question of Location*, Pella, Iowa, 1876.
29. *Catalogue of the Officers and Students of the St. Louis University*, St. Louis, 1861, frontispiece; Joseph W. Riordan, *The First Half Century of St. Ignatius Church and College*, San Francisco, 1905; Henry Howe, *Historical Collections of Ohio*, Cincinnati, 1847, p. 219 (engraving and description of St. Xavier's College, Cincinnati).
30. Thomas J. Schlereth, *The University of Notre Dame, A Portrait of Its History and Campus*, Notre Dame, Ind., 1976.
31. Hardy George, "Georgetown University's Healy Building," *J.S.A.H.*, October 1972, pp. 208–16. R. I. Gannon, *Up to the Present: The Story of Fordham*, Garden City, N.Y., 1967, fig. 4.
32. See: John Howard Hinton, *The History and Topography of the United States*, Boston, 1844, opposite p. 370 (view of West Point);

Sherman Day, *Historical Collections of the State of Pennsylvania*, Philadelphia, 1843, p. 59 (Gettysburg College); Charles Rammelkamp, *Illinois College, A Centennial History*, New Haven, 1928, p. 57; *Catalogue of the Officers and Students of Mount St. Mary's College*, 1856, frontispiece.

33. Henry Barnard, *School Architecture*, New York, 1848; 5th edition, 1854, p. 242. A more accurate view of the building (designed by James Renwick and built in 1849) was illustrated in *Valentine's Manuals*, 1849, opposite p. 224. See S. Willis Rudy, *The College of the City of New York: A History, 1847–1947*, New York, 1949.
34. See Warren H. Smith, *Hobart and William Smith Colleges: The History of Two Colleges*, Geneva, N. Y., 1972.
35. *A Catalogue of the Officers and Students of Georgetown College*, 1877, frontispiece; Henry Howe, *Historical Collections of Ohio*, Norwalk, Ohio, 1898, p. 398 (view of Wittenberg College); Alaric B. Start, ed., *History of Tufts College*, Medford, Mass., 1896, frontispiece; Robert Sears, *A Pictorial Description of the United States*, New York, 1855, p. 105 (view of Amherst College); *Register of the University of Tennessee*, 1891, opposite p. 21.
36. Information from Williams College, and from a plaque on the observatory at the original campus of Western Reserve College, Hudson, Ohio. See Rudolph, *The American College*, p. 225. As mentioned in Chapter I, William Smith's plans for a "College of Mirania," in 1753, had envisioned "a small but handsome Observatory" in the steeple of the central building. Thomas Jefferson, in 1825, designed an octagonal observatory for the University of Virginia, but it was never built (William B. O'Neal, *Pictorial History of the University of Virginia*, Charlottesville, 1968, p. 36).
37. Rudolph, *The American College*, p. 226.
38. *Catalogue of the Officers and Students of Georgetown College*, 1880, p. 17.
39. See: Rudolph, *The American College*, pp. 144–50; Henry D. Sheldon, *Student Life and Customs*, New York, 1901.
40. William Bodine, *The Kenyon Book*, Columbus, Ohio, 1890, pp. 281–85, and illustration, opposite p. 288. Bodine claims that this structure was "the first hall of a college fraternity built in the United States."
41. R. L. Alexander, *The Architecture of Maximilian Godefroy*, Baltimore, 1974, pp. 41–71.
42. Adolf K. Placzek, "Design for Columbia College, 1813," *J.S.A.H.*, May 1952, p. 23. Renwick's drawings for this design are in the Avery Library at Columbia University.
43. For other designs of the period for Columbia College, see Franklin Toker, "James O'Donnell: An Irish Georgian in America," *J.S.A.H.*, May 1970, pp. 135ff.
44. Eric Johannesen, *Ohio College Architecture Before 1870*, Cleveland, 1969, pp. 10–16; Albert Bush-Brown, "Image of a University: A Study of Architecture as an Expression of Education at Colleges and Universities in the United States Between 1800 and 1900," Ph.D. dissertation, Princeton University, 1958, pp. 81, 91. Nash's design for the Kenyon College building is shown in an engraving, dated December 14, 1826—an impression of which is in the Library of Congress, Prints and Photographs Division.
45. Frederick Koeper, *Illinois Architecture*, Chicago, 1968, p. 138 (the building at Knox College); H.M.J. Klein, *History of Franklin and Marshall College, 1787–1948*, Lancaster, Pa., 1952. Another early use of the Gothic was at the United States Military Academy at West Point, New York, where Gothic-style barracks and other structures were erected starting in about 1840.
46. Bush-Brown, "Image of a University," pp. 82–85; Bainbridge Bunting and Robert H. Nylander, *Survey of Architectural History in Cambridge*, vol. 4, Cambridge, Mass., 1973, pp. 157–58. Richard Bond was the architect of Gore Hall. The books in the library originally were arranged by donor's collections, rather than subject matter—a system that was inconvenient to users but encouraged gifts. In the 1870s, a wing was added to the building that included innovative steel book stacks which served as the structure for the tiers above them. Gore Hall was demolished in 1913.
47. Louis C. Hatch, *History of Bowdoin College*, Portland, Maine, 1927; *Memorial of the 100th Anniversary of the Incorporation of Bowdoin College*, Brunswick, Maine, 1894, illustration opposite p. lxxxiv.
48. Historic American Buildings Survey report on Jubilee College, in the Library of Congress; Koeper, *Illinois Architecture*, p. 158. The Jubilee College buildings now stand abandoned, in a state park, near Peoria, Illinois.
49. Historic American Buildings Survey report, pp. 4–5.
50. Anonymous, "College Edifices and Their Relations to Education," *American Literary Magazine*, November 1847, p. 271. The Yale library was designed by Henry Austin. See also William Morgan, *The Almighty Wall, the Architecture of Henry Vaughan*, New York, 1983.
51. "One Suggestion to College Architects," *The Yale Literary Magazine*, May 1853, pp. 240–44. The article is signed "W." Albert Bush-Brown ("Images of a University," p. 149 and n. 110) suggested that this was Andrew D. White, later the president of Cornell University.
52. *Ibid.*, p. 244.
53. This building, Antioch Hall, was designed by the building contractor A. M. Merrifield, who was one of the founders of the college. His design was evidently based on the main building of Worcester Academy in Massachusetts, which in turn was inspired by James Renwick's Smithsonian Institution in Washington, D.C. See: W. B. Alexander, "The Architectural Ancestry of Antioch Hall," *Antioch Alumni Bulletin*, February 1939, pp. 3–9; Johannesen, *Ohio College Architecture*, pp. 31–35; Robert L. Straker, *Horace Mann and Others: Chapters from the History of Antioch College*, Yellow Springs, Ohio, 1963, pp. 15–24; and W. C. Kidney, *Historic Buildings of Ohio*, Pittsburgh, Pa., 1972, pp. 70–73.
54. William G. Brown, ed., *Official Guide to Harvard University*, Cambridge, 1899, p. 11; quoted by Montgomery Schuyler, in an article on Harvard in *Architectural Record*, October 1909, p. 243.

55. Anonymous, "American Architecture," *North American Review*, October 1836, p. 362.
56. See: S. Willis Rudy, *The College of the City of New York*, New York, 1949; Montgomery Schuyler, article on Lehigh University, in *Architectural Record*, September 1910, pp. 201ff; Mildred McClary Tymeson, *Two Towers, The Story of Worcester Tech, 1865–1965*, Worcester, 1965. The building at Lehigh, Packer Hall (now University Center), was designed by Edward T. Potter in 1865 (see Sarah Bradford Landau, *Edward T. and William A. Potter: American Victorian Architects*, New York, 1979). The building at Worcester, Boynton Hall, was designed by Stephen Earle and James Fuller, at about the same time. Both buildings were constructed with funds provided by the schools' founders–Asa Packer at Lehigh, John Boynton at Worcester.
57. F. D. Powers, *The Life of William Kimbrough Pendleton*, St. Louis, 1902, p. 50. Pendleton was vice-president of the college during the design of the Gothic buildings, but he apparently played a leading role in the design and the choice of the Gothic style. See: Glenn Patton, "James Keys Wilson, 1828–1894," *J.S.A.H.*, December 1967; and W. K. Woolery, *Bethany Years*, Huntington, W.Va., 1941.
58. See: Robert B. Shaffer, "Ruskin, Norton, and Memorial Hall," *Harvard Library Bulletin*, vol. 3, 1949, pp. 213–31; and Bush-Brown, "Image of a University," pp. 120–26.
59. Richard Hofstadter and Wilson Smith, eds., *American Higher Education, A Documentary History*, Chicago, 1961, vol. 1, p. 233.
60. Rudolph, *The American College*, pp. 48–49.
61. Hofstadter and Smith, *American Higher Education*, vol. 1, p. 256.
62. Everard M. Upjohn, *Richard Upjohn*, New York, 1939, pp. 94–95, and fig. 51. The Avery Library of Columbia University, in its collection of Upjohn material, has a drawing and several other documents pertaining to Upjohn's design for Jubilee College.
63. George L. Hersey, "Thomas U. Walter and the University at Lewisburg," *J.S.A.H.*, March 1957, pp. 20–24. Richard P. Dober (*Campus Planning*, New York, 1963, p. 30) calls this "the largest college building constructed prior to the Civil War." The central portion of the building was 80′ square, and the two wings were each 125′ long, thus creating a facade 330′ long. The building was partially destroyed by fire in 1932, but was rebuilt and now serves as a dormitory.
64. George C. Mason, Jr., "Thomas Ustick Walter, F.A.I.A.," *A.I.A. Journal*, November 1947, p. 226.
65. See J. D. Forbes, *Victorian Architect: William Tinsley*, Bloomington, Ind., 1953.
66. G. P. Randall, *A Hand Book of Designs . . . of Court Houses, Universities, Academies, School Houses . . .*, Chicago, 1868. Included are views of Randall's designs for buildings at colleges in Illinois, Wisconsin, Minnesota, and Missouri. In the Pacific Northwest, William W. Piper seems to have been the foremost architect of educational buildings in the 1860s–1870s (Elizabeth Walton, "A Note on William W. Piper and Academy Architecture in Oregon in the Nineteenth Century," *J.S.A.H.*, October 1973, pp. 231–38).
67. Davis's office diary (in the Metropolitan Museum of Art, New York, Print Room, Davis Collection, vol. 1) indicates that besides the schools mentioned in the text, the architect did designs for a "Female Seminary at Albany" (1833), "a college at Buffalo" (1836), a "Library and Academy, Rome, N.Y." (1848), a "Methodist College, Greensboro, N.C." (1851), and work at the University of Virginia (1854). Also see: Roger Hale Newton, *Town and Davis, Architects*, New York, 1942; and Edna Donnell, "A. J. Davis and the Gothic Revival," *Metropolitan Museum Studies*, vol. 5, 1936, pp. 183–233.
68. Drawings and other documentation of these designs are preserved in the Print Room of the Metropolitan Museum of Art, New York, and in the Avery Library of Columbia University.
69. Classical and Gothic designs by Davis, for both of these schools, are in the Metropolitan Museum of Art, New York, Print Room.
70. Davis's office diary for 1845–46 refers to domestic designs as "Collegiate style," "Collegiate Gothic Villa style," and "English Collegiate style" (Metropolitan Museum of Art, New York, Print Room).
71. Newton, *Town and Davis*, pp. 230ff; Arthur Scully, *James Dakin*, Baton Rouge, La., 1973, pp. 17ff; Glenn Patton, "Chapel in the Sky," *Architectural Review*, March 1969, pp. 177–80; Donnell, "A. J. Davis," pp. 186ff. Scully argues that Davis's partner Dakin was more responsible for the design of the New York University building than Davis himself. The building was demolished in 1911.
72. Davis's office diary has an 1835 entry for "White Hall" at Bristol College, in "Collegiate Style," accompanied by a rough sketch similar to the Metropolitan Museum of Art, New York, drawing 24.66.21.
73. Davis's office diary, entry for September 1838 (Metropolitan Museum of Art, New York). See Newton, pp. 236ff. In the 1840s and 1850s the University of Michigan erected several buildings in a Yale-like alignment. See Ruth Bordin, *The University of Michigan, A Pictorial History*, Ann Arbor, 1967, pp. 16–17.
74. Newton (*Town and Davis*, p. 106) refers to a design by Davis for Davidson College of 1837. But Davis's office diary for 1856 indicates that his plans for the college date from that year. It also shows that he visited the college in July–August 1856 (Metropolitan Museum of Art, New York, Print Room).
75. Drawings and other documentation of this design are in the Metropolitan Museum of Art, New York, Print Room and Avery Library of Columbia University.
76. Drawing in the Avery Library.
77. Drawings in the Metropolitan Museum of Art, New York, Print Room. Buildings designed by Davis were constructed at the Virginia Military Institute from 1840 to 1860. They were burned in the Civil War, and were rebuilt under Davis's direction. In 1914 they were remodeled by Bertram G. Goodhue. (William B. O'Neal, *Architecture in Virginia*, New York, 1968, p. 29.)
78. See R. W. Liscombe, *William Wilkins, 1778–1839*, Cambridge, England, 1980, pp. 46–55, 156–69, and figs. 10–18, 84–86. Liscombe uses the term "campus plan" to de-

scribe these collegiate designs by Wilkins, and suggests they represent a synthesis of the medieval quadrangle and the ancient forum.

79. Metropolitan Museum of Art, New York, Print Room, 24.66.1403, leaf 24.
80. Hamlin, *Greek Revival Architecture*, p. 212. Called Chambers Hall, this building was destroyed by fire in 1921. I am grateful to Professor Chalmers G. Davidson, of Davidson College, for information about this structure and other buildings at the school.

Chapter IV

1. The architecture of agricultural, scientific, and women's colleges will be discussed later in this chapter. Among colleges for blacks, Jubilee Hall at Fisk University in Nashville, Tennessee, built 1873–76 and reputedly "the oldest permanent building for the higher education of Negroes in the United States," is described in Thomas B. Brumbaugh, *Architecture of Middle Tennessee*, Nashville, 1974, pp. 78–80. A lithograph of the 1850s, identified as "Wilberforce University, Xenia, Ohio, the colored people's college," shows a broad mall lined with domestic structures and with a main building at one end (Library of Congress, Prints and Photographs Division).
2. K. W. Pauli, "Evidence of Popular Support for the Land-Grant College Act of 1862 as Revealed in Selected Speeches in New England, 1850–1860," dissertation, Stanford University, 1959, p. 40.
3. Frederick Rudolph, *The American College and University*, New York, 1962, p. 237.
4. *The Variorem Walden*, New York, 1962, p. 59. Thoreau's *Walden* was originally published in 1854.
5. Quoted in Earle D. Ross, *Democracy's College: The Land-Grant Movement in the Formative Stage*, Ames, Iowa, 1942, p. 24. The People's College was in Elmira, New York.
6. For the Gothic Revival structure at Knox College in Galesburg, Illinois, see Chapter III. The impressive Italianate structure at Wabash College in Crawfordsville, Indiana, was begun in 1853, designed by the architect William Tinsley (see J. D. Forbes, *Victorian Architect: . . . William Tinsley*, Bloomington, Ind., 1953, plate XII). The buildings at both colleges still exist. For the Farmers' College in Hamilton County, Ohio, founded in 1846, see A. B. Huston, *Historical Sketch of Farmers' College*, n.p., n.d.
7. Samuel Rezneck, *Education for a Technical Society: The History of R.P.I.*, Troy, N. Y., 1968.
8. Albert Bush-Brown, "Image of a University: A Study of Architecture as an Expression of Education at Colleges and Universities in the United States Between 1800 and 1900," Ph.D. dissertation, Princeton University, 1958, pp. 96ff.
9. From a speech, reported in *Scientific American*, May 27, 1854, p. 294; quoted in Bush-Brown, "Image of a University," p. 105. Two decades earlier, in 1836, Joseph Henry had drawn a master plan of the buildings at Princeton that reflected a more formal notion of planning (see Chapter III).
10. Bainbridge Bunting and Robert H. Nylander, *Survey of Architectural History in Cambridge*, vol. 4, Cambridge, Mass., 1973, pp. 158–59. Lawrence Hall was designed in 1847 by Richard Bond, the architect of the Harvard library, Gore Hall (see Chapter III). Bond originally intended Lawrence Hall to have another wing balancing the professor's residence, but it was never built. Lawrence Hall was gutted by fire and demolished in 1970.
11. Correspondence between Davis and Downing, regarding this project, dated December 1849 and January 1850, is in volume 12 of the Davis material in the Print Room of the Metropolitan Museum of Art in New York. I was unable to find an indication, in these documents, of the proposed location of this institution. An undated nineteenth-century engraving (a copy of which is in the Library of Congress, Prints and Photographs Division) shows a building identified as "State Agricultural College, Ovid, Seneca County [New York]"; but this building is different from Davis's design.
12. Henry Barnard, *School Architecture; or Contributions to the Improvement of School-Houses in the United States*, New York, 1848.
13. *Ibid.* (5th edition, 1854), p. 82.
14. Edward Robert Robson, *School Architecture: Being Practical Remarks on the Planning, Designing, Building, and Furnishing of School-Houses*, London, 1874, p. 33.
15. Rudolph, *The American College*, p. 315. A history of American women's colleges, by Helen Lefkowitz Horowitz of Scripps College, is reportedly in preparation at the time of this writing.
16. See Robert S. Fletcher, *A History of Oberlin College*, Oberlin, Ohio, 1943. Useful maps showing the early development of the Oberlin campus were published in the *Oberlin Alumni Catalogue*, 1936.
17. See Robert L. Straker, *Horace Mann and Others: Chapters from*

the History of Antioch College, Antioch, Ohio, 1963.

18. Printed advertisement, in Library of Congress, Prints and Photographs Division.
19. W. Charles Barber, *Elmira College, The First Hundred Years*, New York, 1955, pp. 18, 40. The architect of the building was Ward B. Farrar. The college possesses the "Minutes of Building Committee and Executive Committee of Elmira Female College," of the period 1853–1863.
20. Information from the Director of Communications, Vassar College, June 1977. See Montgomery Schuyler, "Architecture of American Colleges: Vassar, Wellesley, Smith," *Architectural Record*, May 1912, pp. 512–37.
21. Quoted in Anna Brackett, "Vassar College," *Harper's New Monthly Magazine*, February 1876, p. 350.
22. Edward Abbott, "Wellesley College," *Harper's New Monthly Magazine*, August 1876, p. 326. Also see *Views of Wellesley College*, Gardner, Mass., 1889.
23. See: Jessie M. Pangburn, *The Evolution of the American Teachers College*, New York, 1932; and Charles A. Harper, *Development of the Teachers College in the United States, with Special Reference to the Illinois State Normal University*, Bloomington, Ill., 1935.
24. Brackett, "Vassar College," p. 359.
25. Rudolph, *The American College*, pp. 253ff.
26. *Ibid.*, p. 266.
27. Quoted in James Gray, *The University of Minnesota, 1851–1951*, Minneapolis, 1951, p. 39.
28. Drawings and records in the archives of the Olmsted office in Brookline, Massachusetts, which I examined in 1977 (as well as other sources of information) indicate that Frederick Law Olmsted was involved in the planning of at least the following schools. Beginning in the 1860s: the College of California at Berkeley, the University of Massachusetts at Amherst, Cornell University, the University of Maine at Orono, Gallaudet College in Washington, D.C., the Pennsylvania Agricultural College, Yale, Harvard, Vassar, and the Hampton Institute in Virginia. The 1870s: Amherst College, Trinity College in Hartford. The 1880s: Stanford University in California, Lawrenceville School in New Jersey. The early 1890s: the American University in Washington, D.C., Phillips Academy in Massachusetts, Smith College, Columbia University, Bryn Mawr College in Pennsylvania, and Cornell College in Iowa. After the retirement of Frederick Law Olmsted, Sr., in about 1895, his firm, headed by his sons and later by others, was extensively involved in collegiate planning. A list compiled by the Olmsted Associates office in the 1960s mentions over 150 colleges and universities for which the firm had done work over the years.
29. Letter from Frederick Law Olmsted to John Hull Olmsted, June 23, 1845; quoted in Elizabeth Stevenson, *Park Maker: A Life of Frederick Law Olmsted*, New York, 1977, p. 15.
30. Laura Wood Roper, *F L O, A Biography of Frederick Law Olmsted*, Baltimore, 1973, pp. 71, 75.
31. *Ibid.*, pp. 44, 54. See the discussion of this design, earlier in this chapter. Professor Charles McLaughlin, of the American University, has pointed out to me that Olmsted was also a personal friend of Senator Justin Morrill, the main proponent of the Land Grant bill.
32. Andrew Jackson Downing, *Rural Essays*, New York, 1856, chapter on "Agricultural Schools," pp. 410–15.
33. Roper, *F L O*, pp. 277, 305ff.
34. Olmsted, Vaux, & Co., *Report upon a Projected Improvement of the Estate of the College of California at Berkeley, near Oakland*, San Francisco and New York, 1866.
35. Roper, *F L O*, p. 277; Frederick Law Olmsted, Jr., and Theodora Kimball, *Frederick Law Olmsted, Landscape Architect, 1822–1903*, New York, 1970, p. 11.
36. Olmsted, *Report upon the College of California*, p. 25.
37. *Ibid.*, p. 25.
38. Olmsted had already expressed some of these ideas, as editorial contributor to *The Nation*. See Roper, *F L O*, p. 310.
39. Olmsted, Vaux, & Co., *A Few Things to be Thought of Before Proceeding to Plan Buildings for the National Agricultural Colleges*, New York, 1866. Olmsted's plan for the Massachusetts Agricultural College apparently no longer exists. But there is a plan in the Olmsted archives in Brookline, Massachusetts, identified as "Massachusetts Agricultural College, Design of Grounds by Frederick Law Olmsted—1866—Reconstructed by Frank A. Waugh, 1911, from Olmsted's Written Report."
40. *Ibid.*, p. 11.
41. Roper, *F L O*, p. 313.
42. "How Not to Establish an Agricultural College," *The Nation*, October 25, 1866, pp. 335–36.
43. Olmsted's Massachusetts Agricultural College report was reviewed in *The Nation*, December 27, 1866, p. 513.
44. Roper, *F L O*, pp. 314–21. Elizabeth Stevenson (in *Park Maker*, p. 280) states that Olmsted also received inquiries from the land-grant institution in Minnesota at about this time.
45. Letter from Peter Melendy to Olmsted, December 31, 1867; cited in Roper, *F L O*, p. 320. Apparently, Olmsted also was considered for the presidency of the College of California (*ibid.*, p. 320).
46. See: Kermit C. Parsons, "The Quad on the Hill: An Account of the First Buildings at Cornell," *J.S.A.H.*, December 1963, pp. 199–216, and *The Cornell Campus, A History of Its Planning and Development*, Ithaca, 1968. Parsons suggests that the projected 1,000-foot-square quadrangle at Cornell was inspired by plans for a "third university" in England, proposed by Charles Kelsall in 1814, in a book entitled *The Phantasm of an University*.
47. Letter from Olmsted to White, June 13, 1867; quoted by Parsons, *The Cornell Campus*, p. 48.
48. Parsons, *The Cornell Campus*, pp. 57–90. Sage Chapel and Sage College, both erected starting in 1872, were designed by Charles Babcock, professor of architecture at the university.
49. "Architect's Report," in *Annual Report of the State College of Agriculture and the Mechanic Arts*, Maine, 46th Legislature, 1867, pp. 15–29. I was not able to locate Olmsted's actual plan for the school, but examined a copy of it, in the Olmsted archives in Brookline, Mass. This plan is labeled "Olmsted, Vaux & Co., Landscape Architects, May 1st 1867," with the additional note, "Copied by L. S. Dickinson, Dec. 1909."

50. This arrangement is described in Olmsted's report ("Architect's Report"), and in notes written on his plan (as copied by Dickinson; see above).
51. Engravings of the campus are found in the school's early publications—e.g., *Sixth Annual Report of the Trustees of the Massachusetts Agricultural College*, Boston, 1869.
52. *Nineteenth Annual Catalogue of the Officers and Students of the State Agricultural College of Michigan, 1875*, Lansing, 1875, p. 42. The "professional landscape gardener" is not identified. Various plans and illustrations of the school are found in its catalogues of the 1860s and 1870s. The original part of the campus still retains much of its Olmstedian character.
53. Earle D. Ross, *The Land-Grant Idea at Iowa State College*, Ames, Iowa, 1959, p. 36.
54. Roper, *F L O*, p. 320.
55. The campus plan is illustrated in *Iowa State College of Agriculture and Mechanical Arts, Catalogue, 1891*, following p. 32.
56. The word "populist" is here applied to Anderson only in a general sense, for he was not a supporter of the Populist political party that later became an important force in Kansas.
57. *Hand-book of the Kansas State Agricultural College*, Manhattan, Kans., 1874, p. 65. This and other documents pertaining to the school were brought to my attention by Professor Richard Longstreth of Kansas State University.
58. *Ibid.*, pp. 67–69.
59. The campus is illustrated in *Biennial Catalogue of the Kansas State Agricultural College*, 1877.
60. Although its construction had just begun by 1880, this building was shown complete in an illustration in *Catalogue of the Officers and Students of the State Agricultural College of Kansas*, 1880.
61. For another land-grant school whose planning followed this pattern, see J. Meredith Neil, "Administrators, Architects, and Campus Development: Washington State University, 1890–1905," *J.S.A.H.*, May 1970, pp. 144–55.
62. Examples include: Old Main, at the University of Texas in Austin, built 1882–88, demolished 1934 (see Margaret C. Berry, *The University of Texas, A Pictorial Account of Its First Century*, Austin, 1980); Main Building at Howard University in Washington, D.C., built 1868 (see Rayford W. Logan, *Howard University, First 100 Years, 1867–1967*, New York, 1969); University Hall, at Illinois Industrial University (now University of Illinois), built 1874 (see Allen S. Weller, *One Hundred Years of Campus Architecture at the University of Illinois*, Illinois, 1968); Old Main, at the College of Wooster, in Wooster, Ohio (see Lucy L. Notestein, *Wooster of the Middle West*, New Haven, 1937); Old Main, at Case Institute of Technology, designed by John Eisenmann, 1883 (see M. P. Schofield, "The Cleveland Arcade," *J.S.A.H.*, December 1966); and College Hall, at the University of Pennsylvania, built 1871–72, designed by Thomas W. Richards (see Martin Meyerson and D. P. Winegrad, *Gladly Learn and Gladly Teach: Franklin and His Heirs at the University of Pennsylvania*, Philadelphia, 1978, pp. 204–5).
63. The *Historical Handbook of Smith College* (Northampton, Mass., 1932, p. 30) noted, "The College now houses practically all its undergraduate students; yet this has been brought about without loss of the original 'cottage plan' idea which the founders established." In the Olmsted archives in Brookline, Mass., I found plans of the Smith College campus prepared by the Olmsted firm in 1892–93.
64. For example, in 1895 the catalogue of the University of Rochester noted that "several of the chapter-houses of the Greek-letter fraternities are not far removed from the university grounds, and there is a growing tendency to multiply them in close proximity to the Campus" (*Forty-Sixth Annual Catalogue of the University of Rochester, 1895–96*, p. 13).
65. Plans of the Hamilton College campus, before and after this transformation, are illustrated in *Documentary History of Hamilton College*, Clinton, N. Y., 1922, following p. 254.
66. This is shown in a lithographic view of the University of Missouri campus, published in *Boone County, Missouri, Atlas*, 1875, p. 24.
67. Among the major buildings erected by McCosh were: Reunion and Witherspoon halls, both dormitories; Dickinson Hall, a classroom building; the Chancellor Green Library; the School of Science; and Marquand Chapel. (See Wheaton J. Lane, ed., *Pictorial History of Princeton*, Princeton, 1947, pp. 38–48.)
68. James McCosh, *Twenty Years of Princeton College*, New York, 1888, p. 14.
69. Rudolph, *The American College*, pp. 150–51.
70. William B. O'Neal, *Jefferson's Buildings at the University of Virginia: The Rotunda*, Charlottesville, 1960, p. 32. Similarly, in the mid-eighteenth century, William Smith's progressive collegiate plans included a colonnade that could serve as "an Ambulatory for the Youth to exercise themselves in" (William Smith, *A General Idea of the College of Mirania*, New York, 1753, pp. 61–64).
71. Rudolph, *The American College*, p. 151.
72. This lithographic view was produced by F. Sachse & Co. of Baltimore and published by C. Bohn of Washington and Richmond. See William B. O'Neal, *Pictorial History of the University of Virginia*, Charlottesville, 1968, p. 56.
73. *Harper's Weekly*, February 21, 1885, p. 125.
74. See Rudolph, *The American College*, chapter 18, "The Rise of Football."
75. *Ibid.*, p. 154.
76. *Ibid.*, p. 383.
77. This is Lake Carnegie, which was created in 1906, paid for by Andrew Carnegie. See Alexander Leitch, *A Princeton Companion*, Princeton, 1978, pp. 82–83.
78. Many articles on stadia appeared in architectural journals in the 1910s and 1920s. These include a series of five articles in *The American Architect*, July–August 1920; and articles in *Architectural Record*, November 1920, *The Architect and Engineer*, October 1921, and *Architectural Forum*, December 1925. Also see Richard P. Dober, *Campus Planning*, New York, 1963, pp. 148ff.
79. Le Corbusier, *When the Cathedrals Were White*, New York, 1964. First published in French in 1937.
80. *Ibid.*, p. 135.

Chapter V

1. See: Laurence R. Veysey, *The Emergence of the American University*, Chicago, 1965; and Richard Hofstadter and Wilson Smith, eds., *American Higher Education: A Documentary History*, vol. 2, Chicago, 1961.
2. Plans of the early Johns Hopkins buildings can be found in the school's catalogues and other publications of the period—such as *The Johns Hopkins Register*, of 1884–85.
3. *The Life of Daniel Coit Gilman*, New York, 1910, pp. 323f; quoted in Albert Bush-Brown, "Image of a University: A Study of Architecture as an Expression of Education at Colleges and Universities in the United States Between 1800 and 1900," Ph.D. dissertation, Princeton University, 1958, p. 191.
4. Daniel Coit Gilman, "The Dawn of a University," in *The Launching of a University, and Other Papers*, New York, 1906, pp. 255–77.
5. Bush-Brown, "Image of a University," pp. 254, 261. Bush-Brown states that Hall himself designed the building. But its cornerstone was laid in October 1887, while Hall (a professor at Johns Hopkins) was not offered the presidency of Clark University until April 1888. According to the university's *Register* of 1891, "Plans for the main building were submitted to the Board by Mr. Clark [Jonas Clark, the school's founder]" (p. 70).
6. See: Bush-Brown, "Image of a University," pp. 194ff, 261; and Samuel C. Prescott, *When M.I.T. was "Boston Tech," 1861–1916*, Cambridge, Mass., 1954.
7. E.g., *Massachusetts Institute of Technology, Ninth Annual Catalogue of the Officers and Students*, Boston, 1873, illustrations following p. 69.
8. Frederick Rudolph, *The American College and University*, New York, 1962, p. 329.
9. Princeton, *Trustees' Minutes*, vol. 8, June 11, 1894; quoted in Charles L. Dibble, "Architecture, Education, and Atmosphere: the Early Years of Princeton University, 1896–1916," thesis, Princeton University, 1974, p. 11.
10. Rudolph, *The American College*, p. 465.
11. John B. Pine, "Notes on the Building of a University," *The American Architect*, December 2, 1914, p. 333.
12. The term "City of Learning" was used, for example, in the prospectus of the 1899 competition for the design of the University of California at Berkeley (see below); and "Collegiate City" was used by A. M. Githens in an article in *The Brickbuilder*, December 1912, p. 316. John Fletcher Hurst, founder of the American University in Washington, D.C., in the 1890s, even referred to his envisioned campus as "the White City," an obvious allusion to the Chicago World's Fair of 1893, which was popularly known by that name. (Information from an unpublished paper on the planning of the American University, by Karin M. E. Alexis.)
13. John S. Brubacher and Willis Rudy, *Higher Education in Transition*, New York, 1976, p. 377.
14. Alfred Morton Githens, "Recent American Group Plans," Part III, *The Brickbuilder*, December 1912, p. 313.
15. Richard P. Dober, *Campus Planning*, New York, 1963, p. 34.
16. Orrin Leslie Elliott, *Stanford University, The First Twenty-Five Years*, Stanford, 1937.
17. Paul V. Turner, Marcia E. Vetrocq, and Karen Weitze, *The Founders and the Architects: The Design of Stanford University*, Stanford, 1976, p. 22.
18. This plan is in the Olmsted archives in Brookline, Mass. It is dated September 26, 1886, and inscribed "Leland Stanford, Jr. Univ., First Study & Sketch Map made in California." On the reverse side of the sheet is a topographic map, which reveals that the plan was meant for a hilly site south of the location that finally was chosen for the Stanford buildings. (See Turner et al., *The Founders and the Architects*, pp. 25–26.) This first plan by Olmsted for Stanford, with separate buildings placed around an oval area, is somewhat similar to the design that Olmsted produced for Lawrenceville School in New Jersey, also in 1886.
19. Turner et al., *The Founders and the Architects*, pp. 58, 69ff. Leland Stanford was evidently inspired to create arcaded quadrangles at least partly by the example of the Spanish missions of California—for he used the terms "Spanish," "Mission," and related words to describe his plans for the university. This is one of the earliest expressions of the interest that later produced the Mission Revival style of architecture in California. (See Karen Weitze, "Origins and Early Development of the Mission Revival in California," Ph.D. dissertation, Stanford University, 1977.)
20. Many of Olmsted and Coolidge's plans and sketches from this phase of the design survive, in the Olmsted archives and in the Stanford Museum (see Turner et al., *The Founders and the Architects*, pp. 30ff). Extensive correspondence concerning the design also survives, in the Stanford University Archives and in the Olmsted Papers at the Library of Congress.
21. Letter from Coolidge to Olmsted, May 3, 1887. Olmsted Papers, Library of Congress.
22. A "Plan of Central Premises—1888" exists in several lithographic copies, in the Stanford University Archives and elsewhere. A "General Plan," with descriptive legends, is known from photographs; and part of it was reproduced in *Garden and Forest*, December 19, 1888, p. 508. The large bird's-eye perspective rendering of the master plan, drawn by D. A. Gregg, is known to me only from photographs of it; I was not able to locate the original in the Olmsted archives.
23. Campus plans possibly influenced by that of Stanford include: Albert Doyle's master plan for Reed College in Oregon of ca. 1912; Horace Trumbauer's plan for Duke University in North Carolina of the 1920s.
24. Some of the earlier master plans even include additional housing, grade schools, and other facilities in close proximity to the university buildings; but these never were executed. See Turner et al., *The Founders and the Architects*, p. 31.
25. *Ibid.*, p. 18.
26. Werner Hegemann and Elbert Peets, *The American Vitruvius: An Architects' Handbook of Civic Art*, New York, 1922, p. 111. (This work was republished in 1925, in German, under Hegemann's name alone.)

27. For the Olmsteds' work at Washington University, see Chapter VI. For the firm's proposals at the University of Rochester, in collaboration with Charles Adams Platt and the firm of Gordon & Kaelber, see Jean R. France, "A Suitable and Worthy Architecture," *Rochester Review*, Fall 1980, pp. 8–9. The resulting master plan was illustrated in Charles Z. Klauder and Herbert C. Wise, *College Architecture in America*, New York, 1929, p. 41.
28. See: Thomas W. Goodspeed, *A History of the University of Chicago*, Chicago, 1916; R. J. Storr, *Harper's University . . . History of the University of Chicago*, Chicago, 1966; and Rudolph, *The American College*, pp. 349ff.
29. Letter from C. L. Hutchinson to President William Rainey Harper, March 2, 1891. President's Papers, Trustees, University of Chicago Archives. (Information from William T. Georgis.)
30. Letter from T. W. Goodspeed to President Harper, September 21, 1890. J. D. Rockefeller Papers, University of Chicago Archives. (Information from William T. Georgis.) Trinity College is examined in Chapter VI.
31. Julius Lewis, "Henry Ives Cobb, The Grand Design," *The University of Chicago Magazine*, Spring 1977, p. 9. Also see: C. E. Jenkins, "The University of Chicago," *Architectural Record*, October–December 1894, pp. 229–46; and *Dreams in Stone: The University of Chicago*, Chicago, 1976.
32. The Columbia campus at 49th Street and Madison Avenue had been designed by Charles C. Haight. Its plan is illustrated in *Harper's New Monthly Magazine*, November 1884, p. 826. Also see J. H. van Amrige et al., *A History of Columbia University, 1754–1904*, New York, 1904.
33. Francesco Passanti, "The Design of Columbia in the 1890s, McKim and His Client," *J.S.A.H.*, May 1977, pp. 69–84.
34. The plans of Haight and Hunt are illustrated in Passanti, "Design of Columbia," p. 71.
35. *Ibid.*, p. 72.
36. *Ibid.*, pp. 76–77.
37. *Ibid.*, p. 82.
38. Leland Roth, "McKim, Mead & White Reappraised," in *A Monograph of the Works of McKim, Mead & White, 1879–1915*, New York, 1973, pp. 32–33. Roth defends White's design of these new buildings at the University of Virginia, which often have been criticized for blocking the open end of Jefferson's Lawn.
39. *Ibid.*, pp. 31–32. Professor Roth, who pointed out to me the similarity between White's design for New York University and Ramée's plan for Union College, has recently found that White was working on the New York University plan as early as January 1892. Other collegiate work by McKim, Mead & White includes designs for Radcliffe College at Harvard, which are preserved in the firm's archives in the New-York Historical Society. Roth also has discovered correspondence between McKim and Bernard Maybeck (of 1897), concerning the Hearst competition for the design of the University of California campus at Berkeley.
40. See below, for information and bibliography on these competitions. In the 1920s, one of the most publicized architectural competitions was for the Harvard Graduate School of Business Administration; the resulting designs were described and illustrated in G. H. Edgell, *The American Architecture of To-day*, New York, 1928, pp. 162–69.
41. Loren W. Partridge, *John Galen Howard and the Berkeley Campus: Beaux-Arts Architecture in the "Athens of the West,"* Berkeley, 1978.
42. Newspaper article of December 1895; quoted in Partridge, *John Galen Howard*, p. 11. This trustee was Jacob Reinstein.
43. One of Maybeck's drawings was published in the *San Francisco Examiner*, April 30, 1896. For this drawing and Maybeck's role in the Hearst competition, see Kenneth Cardwell, *Bernard Maybeck, Artisan, Architect, Artist*, Santa Barbara, California, 1977, pp. 40–43.
44. Hegemann and Peets, *American Vitruvius*, p. 111.
45. *The International Competition for the Phoebe Hearst Architectural Plan for the University of California*, San Francisco, 1899, pp. 8–10. The competition prospectus is reproduced in this volume.
46. Quoted by Robert G. Sproul, in "The Architect and the University," *The Architect and Engineer*, October 1930, p. 35.
47. *The International Competition*. The designs of the following entrants were reproduced in this volume: E. Bénard (first prize); Howells, Stokes & Hornbostel (second prize); D. Despradelle and S. Codman (third prize); Howard & Cauldwell (fourth prize); Lord, Hewlett & Hull (fifth prize); and the designs of Whitney Warren, Rudolph Dick, J. H. Freedlander, Barbaud & Bauhain, Héraud & Eichmuller, and F. Bluntschli. Some of the competition drawings survive, and are kept in the university archives and the library of the School of Environmental Design at the University of California at Berkeley. I am grateful to Professor Peter Atherton of the University of Utah, for research he has conducted on Bénard's plan for Berkeley, and on Beaux-Arts campus planning in general.
48. See Partridge, *John Galen Howard*. I am also grateful to Sally Woodbridge of the University of California, for information on this phase of the development of the Berkeley campus.
49. Howard's master plan was reproduced widely, for example, in Hegemann and Peets, *American Vitruvius*, fig. 502.
50. Ashton R. Willard, "The Development of College Architecture in America," *New England Magazine*, July 1897, pp. 513–34. Among the schools discussed and illustrated are: Harvard, Columbia, Williams, Amherst, Trinity (in Hartford), Girard, Stanford, Princeton, the University of Pennsylvania, Yale, Bowdoin, and Brown.
51. A.D.F. Hamlin, "Recent American College Architecture," *The Outlook*, August 1, 1903, pp. 790–99. Hamlin also described recent work at the University of Pennsylvania, Bowdoin, Harvard, Yale, Oberlin, Berkeley, Washington University, and others.
52. Claude Bragdon, "Architecture in the United States, II, The Growth of Taste," *Architectural Record*, July 1909, pp. 38–45.
53. Alfred Morton Githens, "The Group Plan," five articles in *The Brickbuilder*, from July 1906 to December 1907. Article number V is entitled "Universities, Colleges and Schools," but numbers I and II also

deal principally with campus plans.

54. Among the campus plans Githens illustrated were those of the Carnegie Technical Schools in Pittsburgh, Washington University, Berkeley, Columbia, the College of the City of New York, the U.S. Naval Academy, the War College in Washington, the American College in Madoura, India, Canton Christian College in China, New York University, Sweet Briar College in Virginia, Stanford, the University of Pennsylvania, Johns Hopkins, the Lawrenceville School in New Jersey, Barnard College in New York, General Theological Seminary in New York, and Union Theological Seminary in New York.

55. Montgomery Schuyler, "Architecture of American Colleges. V " (article on Philadelphia-area schools), *Architectural Record*, September 1910, p. 187.

56. John B. Pine, "Notes on the Building of a University," *The American Architect*, December 2, 1914, p. 335.

57. Githens, "The Group Plan," article V, December 1907, p. 219. It is perhaps significant that the first serious interest in the use of the word *campus* in American education had just recently manifested itself–notably in an article by Albert Matthews (*Publications of the Colonial Society of Massachusetts*, Boston, 1900, pp. 431–37), but also in more popular publications. See the discussion of Princeton in Chapter I.

58. See: "The Works of Ernest Flagg," *Architectural Record*, April 1902, pp. 82ff; "New Buildings for the United States Naval Academy," *American Architect and Building News*, July 1, 1908 and July 8, 1908; and a forthcoming book on Flagg by Mardges Bacon.

59. Willard, "Development of College Architecture," p. 529; Hegemann and Peets, *American Vitruvius*, p. 114.

60. Githens, "The Group Plan," article V, December 1907, p. 220.

61. "The New Harvard Medical School Buildings, Boston, Mass.," *The American Architect*, December 21, 1907.

62. White's work at the University of Virginia was illustrated widely, for example in Githens, "The Group Plan," article V, p. 220, and in Hegemann and Peets, *American Vitruvius*, pp. 112–14. The early planning of the American University, in Washington, is described in Karin M. E. Alexis, "The American University: Classical Visions of the National University" (unpublished paper). Alexis summarizes Frederick Law Olmsted's park-like plans for the school, of about 1894, which were superseded by the more formal plans of Cobb, who was given the commission to design the campus in 1898.

63. Hornbostel's design for the Carnegie Schools was illustrated in *The American Architect*, February 25, 1905, and in *The Brickbuilder*, July 1906, pp. 134–38. Palmer and Hornbostel's design for the Western University of Pennsylvania (renamed University of Pittsburgh, at the cornerstone-laying ceremony for the new campus in 1908) was illustrated in *Architectural Review*, July 1906, p. 117. Also see Agnes Lynch Starrett, *Through One Hundred and Fifty Years, The University of Pittsburgh*, Pittsburgh, 1937, pp. 218–19. Another early Beaux-Arts plan was for Vanderbilt University in Nashville, Tennessee, by the firm of Hunt & Hunt, ca. 1902 (see Robert A. McGaw, *The Vanderbilt Campus, A Pictorial History*, Nashville, 1978, pp. 54–55).

64. John Martin Hammond, "The New Home of Johns Hopkins University," *Architectural Record*, June 1915, pp. 480–92.

65. Hegemann and Peets, *American Vitruvius*, p. 110. Several drawings of the design for Sweet Briar College were published in *The American Architect*, August 30, 1902.

66. See articles on the University of Minnesota plan in: *Architectural Review*, August 1908; *Town Planning Review*, vol. 1, 1910; and *The Western Architect*, August 1910.

67. *Survey of Architectural History in Cambridge*, vol. 3, Cambridge, Mass., 1971, pp. 127–132. Also see: "New Group for Massachusetts Institute of Technology," *The American Architect*, July 26, 1916, pp. 49–54; and "The New Buildings at Massachusetts Institute of Technology," *Architectural Forum*, December 1917, pp. 151–156.

68. See: Stephen Fox, *The General Plan of the William M. Rice Institute and Its Architectural Development*, Houston, 1980; Thomas H. English, *Emory University, 1915–1965, A Semicentennial History*, Atlanta, 1966; William Blackburn, *The Architecture of Duke University*, Durham, N.C., 1937; and plans illustrated in C. Z. Klauder and H. C. Wise, *College Architecture in America*, New York, 1929, and Jens F. Larson and Archie M. Palmer, *Architectural Planning of the American College*, New York, 1933.

69. John M. Hammond, "The New Home of Johns Hopkins University," *Architectural Record*, June 1915, pp. 481–92.

70. Hegemann and Peets, *American Vitruvius*, p. 114.

71. See: English, *Emory University*; and Elizabeth Lyon, "Atlanta Architecture," Ph.D. dissertation, Emory University.

72. Ralph Adams Cram, *My Life in Architecture*, Boston, 1937, pp. 124, 126. Other combinations of Byzantine and Romanesque forms were used at a number of schools in the early twentieth century, especially in the Southwest and California—such as the University of Southern California and the California State University at Chico. For Cram's design of Rice, see Stephen Fox, *The General Plan of the William M. Rice Institute, and Its Architectural Development.*

73. Hegemann and Peets, *American Vitruvius*, p. 115.

74. Githens, "The Group Plan," article V, December 1907, p. 219.

75. Charles R. Ashbee, *Exhibition of University Planning and Building*, The University of London, 1912, pp. 3, 18.

76. Hamlin, "Recent College Architecture," p. 792.

77. Montgomery Schuyler, "Architecture of American Colleges. I: Harvard," *Architectural Record*, October 1909, p. 249.

78. Alfred Morton Githens, "Recent American Group Plans, Part III, Colleges and Universities: Development of Existing Plans," *The Brickbuilder*, December 1912, p. 313.

79. Bainbridge Bunting and Robert Nylander, *Survey of Architectural History in Cambridge*, vol. 4, Cambridge, Mass., 1973, p. 176.

80. Manning's plans are illustrated in Githens, "Recent American Group Plans," p. 314. A collection of plans and other material pertaining to college design, put together by

Warren Manning, is kept in the library of the Harvard Graduate School of Design.

81. See Chapter IV.
82. Montgomery Schuyler, "Architecture of American Colleges," series of ten articles, *Architectural Record*, December 1909 to May 1912.
83. Schuyler, "Architecture of American Colleges. I: Harvard," p. 251.
84. Gordon D. Orr, "Paul P. Cret, Warren Powers Laird, and the University of Wisconsin Master Plan of 1906–1909," paper read at the annual meeting of the Society of Architectural Historians, 1980.
85. Gilbert's master plan was published in *The American Architect*, December 2, 1914, p. 336. See also Margaret C. Berry, *The University of Texas, A Pictorial Account of Its First Century*, Austin, 1980.
86. Cret's master plan of 1933 is illustrated in Berry, *University of Texas*, p. 42. At the time of this writing, an exhibition and publication is planned at the University of Texas at Austin, entitled *Paul Cret at Texas: Architectural Drawing and the Image of the University in the 1930s*.
87. Gilbert's master plan was published in the 1915 Oberlin College yearbook, the *Hi-O-Hi*, p. 8. See Geoffrey Blodgett, "President King and Cass Gilbert: The Grand Collaboration," *Oberlin College Observer*, February 4 and 18, 1982; and Geoffrey Blodgett, *Oberlin College Architecture, A Short History*, Oberlin, 1979.
88. Letter from Gilbert to Norman Patten, March 22, 1905. Cass Gilbert Papers, New-York Historical Society. Information from Professor Geoffrey Blodgett of Oberlin College.
89. Blodgett, "King and Gilbert," February 4, 1982, p. 4.
90. Larson and Palmer, *Architectural Planning*, pp. 19ff.
91. *Ibid.*, p. 52.
92. *Ibid.*, pp. 62–64.
93. John Paul Jones, "Campus Planning During the First Century," *The Washington Alumnus*, Winter 1963, pp. 4–13.
94. See: *Architectural Record*, August 1917, p. 175; and Carl F. Gould, "The American University and Its Library Problem," *Architectural Forum*, June 1926, pp. 361–62.

Chapter VI

1. See Frederick Rudolph, *The American College and University*, New York, 1962, pp. 455ff.
2. *Ibid.*, p. 477.
3. Address by Wilson, at Princeton, 1896; quoted in Charles L. Dibble, "Architecture, Education, and Atmosphere: The Early Years of Princeton University, 1896–1916," thesis, Princeton University, 1974, p. 19. Letter from Wilson to his wife, July 26, 1899, from Cambridge University; quoted in Ray S. Baker, *Woodrow Wilson, Life and Letters*, vol. 2, New York, 1927, p. 92.
4. Montgomery Schuyler, "The Architecture of American Colleges," series of ten articles, *Architectural Record*, December 1909 to May 1912. The schools examined by Schuyler include: Harvard, Yale, Princeton, Columbia, College of the City of New York, the University of Pennsylvania, Girard, Haverford, Lehigh, Bryn Mawr, Dartmouth, Williams, Amherst, Brown, Bowdoin, Trinity (in Hartford), Wesleyan, William and Mary, St. John's, the University of Georgia, the University of North Carolina, Davidson, Wake Forest, South Carolina College, the University of Virginia, Union, Hamilton, Hobart, Cornell, the University of Syracuse, Vassar, Wellesley, and Smith.
5. Quoted by Schuyler, "Architecture of American Colleges. I: Harvard," December 1909, p. 262.
6. Rudolph, *The American College*, p. 445.
7. Schuyler, "Architecture of American Colleges. IX," December 1911, p. 565.
8. *Forty-Sixth Annual Catalogue of the University of Rochester, 1895–96*, Rochester, 1895, p. 13. The campus referred to here was not the present University of Rochester campus, to which the school moved in about 1930, and where careful provision was made for dormitories in the plans by the Olmsted firm and others involved in the design. For the earlier campus, see J. L. Rosenberger, *Rochester, the Making of a University*, New York, 1927.
9. Thomas A. Clark, *The Fraternities and the College*, Wisconsin, 1931, p. 10. Clark was referring specifically to the University of Illinois in the period ca. 1915–30, but the point could be made about many institutions in the early twentieth century—and more recently.
10. A. Bailey Cutts, "The Educational Influence of Aberdeen in Seventeenth-Century Virginia," *William and Mary Quarterly*, July 1935, p. 248.
11. Ralph Adams Cram, "Recent University Architecture in the United States," *R.I.B.A. Journal*, May 25, 1912, pp. 497–98. Also see Cram's "College and University Chapels" (*Architectural Forum*, June 1926, pp. 367ff), in which he argued that "the right kind of service in the right kind of chapel would bring the students back with a rush, and the right sort of building is the start." In this article, Cram disapproved of most existing college chapels, such as Harvard's, which he called "morose"; Stanford's, which was "a neo-Byzantine effusion"; and Princeton's for its "cute affectation."
12. Ralph Adams Cram, *The Gothic Quest*, New York, 1918, p. 342. Cram's ideas soon were echoed by other American writers on college design. See, for example, C. Howard Walker, "The Inspirational Value of Collegiate Architecture," *Architectural Forum*, June 1926, pp. 345–48.
13. See Chapter III. Another plan that might be called quadrangular was John Haviland's entry in the Girard College competition of 1832. He proposed a large temple-form building, connected to additional structures on both sides by covered colonnades, producing two semi-enclosed courtyards. Haviland's perspective drawing of this scheme is illustrated in David Gebhard and Deborah Nevins, *Two Hundred Years of American Architectural Drawing*, New York, 1977, p. 107.
14. Noah Porter, *The American College and the American Public*, New Haven, 1870, chapter 8.
15. Quoted in Reuben A. Holden, *Yale: A Pictorial History*, New Haven, 1969, text accompanying figs. 52–54.
16. Schuyler, "Architecture of American Colleges. VII," February 1911; and Samuel Hart, "Trinity College, Hartford," *New England Magazine*, o.s., vol. 4, 1886. I am grateful to Peter J. Knapp, Trinity College Archivist, for further information about the school. Also see J. Mordaunt Crook, *William Burges and*

the High Victorian Dream, Chicago, 1981, pp. 243–44.

17. Kimball's revised plan was illustrated in the Trinity College catalogue of 1877–78.
18. See the discussion of Stanford in Chapter V. Olmsted surely knew the Trinity design, and it is possible that it contributed to the Stanford plan's provision for growth by the addition of aligned quadrangles—although this concept was not actually followed at Stanford.
19. Letter from T. W. Goodspeed to William R. Harper, September 7, 1890. J. D. Rockefeller Papers, University of Chicago Archives. Information from William T. Georgis.
20. Schuyler, "Architecture of American Colleges. VII," February 1911, p. 159.
21. Ashton R. Willard, "The Development of College Architecture in America," *New England Magazine*, n.s., vol. 16, 1897, pp. 513–34 (quotation, p. 525).
22. Werner Hegemann and Elbert Peets, *The American Vitruvius: An Architects' Handbook of Civic Art*, New York, 1922, p. 115.
23. Information from Professors Dorothy O. Johansen and Charles S. Rhyne, of Reed College. See *Reed College, Its Grounds and Buildings, and Plans for the College for Women: Portland, Oregon*, Portland, 1914.
24. Ralph Adams Cram, "The Work of Messrs. Cope and Stewardson," *Architectural Record*, November 1904, pp. 407–38.
25. M. Carey Thomas, *Closing Address by the President*, Bryn Mawr College, 1910, p. 47; quoted in Buford Pickens and Margaretta J. Darnall, *Washington University in St. Louis: Its Design and Architecture*, St. Louis, 1978, p. 7.
26. Pickens and Darnell, *Washington University*, p. 10.
27. Cram, "Cope and Stewardson," p. 415. Cope & Stewardson's work also was praised by C. Howard Walker, in "The Inspirational Value of Collegiate Architecture," p. 348. Also see Schuyler, "Architecture of American Colleges. V," September 1910, in which the new buildings at Bryn Mawr and the University of Pennsylvania were discussed. Cope & Stewardson's philosophy of planning was similar, in some respects, to the views of the Austrian architect Camillo Sitte, whose *Der Städtebau nach seinen Künstlerischen Grundsätzen* was published in 1889.
28. The Olmsted firm's recommendations are described and illustrated in Pickens and Darnall, *Washington University*, pp. 31–34.
29. *Ibid.*, p. 36.
30. The invited competitors were Carrère & Hastings of New York; Cope & Stewardson of Philadelphia; Eames & Young of St. Louis; Cass Gilbert of St. Paul and New York; McKim, Mead & White of New York; and Shepley, Rutan & Coolidge of Boston.
31. Henry W. Bragdon, *Woodrow Wilson, The Academic Years*, Cambridge, Mass., 1967, p. 272; Dibble, "Architecture, Education, and Atmosphere," pp. 32–38. The Princeton *Trustees' Minutes* reveal that Presbyterian enrollment in the college dropped below 50 percent by 1902, and that Anglican enrollment rose to about 40 percent by 1912 (Dibble, p. 38).
32. Speech by President Patton of 1888. Quotations from the text of the speech were given to me by Professor Robert J. Clark of Princeton, in a letter of September 23, 1982.
33. Bragdon, *Woodrow Wilson*, p. 215.
34. Letter from Wilson to his wife, July 26, 1899, from Cambridge University; quoted in Ray S. Baker, *Woodrow Wilson, Life and Letters*, vol. 2, New York, 1927, p. 92.
35. Schuyler, "Architecture of American Colleges. VII," February 1911, p. 156.
36. *Princeton Alumni Weekly*, December 13, 1902, p. 200; quoted in Dibble, "Architecture, Education, and Atmosphere," p. 45.
37. Cram, "Cope and Stewardson," p. 411.
38. *Princeton Alumni Weekly*, December 13, 1902, pp. 199–200; quoted in Dibble, "Architecture, Education, and Atmosphere," p. 45.
39. Dibble, "Architecture, Education, and Atmosphere," pp. 72ff.
40. See Sarah D. Lanford, "A Gothic Epitome: Ralph Adams Cram as Princeton's Architect," *The Princeton University Library Chronicle*, Spring 1982, pp. 184–220.
41. Five years later, a full issue of the *Architectural Record* was devoted to Cram's firm (Montgomery Schuyler, "The Works of Cram, Goodhue and Ferguson," *Architectural Record*, January 1911, pp. 1–112). Among the illustrated works were buildings by the firm at West Point, Phillips Exeter Academy, the Taft School, and Rice Institute.
42. See: Montgomery Schuyler, "The Architecture of West Point," *Architectural Record*, December 1903, pp. 463–92; "The New West Point," *The American Architect*, November 4, 1908, pp. 145–48; Schuyler, "Cram, Goodhue and Ferguson," pp. 88–109; and Richard Oliver, *Bertram Grosvenor Goodhue*, New York, 1983.
43. See "Recent Collegiate Architecture, as Exemplified in the Work of . . . Cram, Goodhue and Ferguson at Richmond College," *The Brickbuilder*, November 1914, pp. 259–68.
44. Several versions of Cram's master plan are known. One was published in *The American Architect*, July 21, 1909, p. 22. A slightly modified version appeared in Montgomery Schuyler's article on Princeton in *Architectural Record*, February 1910, p. 141. The Princeton University Archives have another, "revised," plan dated December 1911, with several newly proposed buildings added, and omitting the Graduate College from its originally planned location near the center of the campus.
45. Ralph Adams Cram, "Princeton Architecture," *The American Architect*, July 21, 1909, p. 24.
46. *Ibid.*, p. 25.
47. See: Andrew F. West, *The Graduate College of Princeton*, Princeton, 1913; and Willard Thorp, Minor Myers, Jr., and Jeremiah Stanton Fitch, *The Princeton Graduate School: A History*, Princeton, 1978.
48. West, *The Graduate College*, p. 30.
49. See "Charles Z. Klauder, 1872–1938," *Pencil Points*, January 1939, pp. 31–36. Among the schools at which Klauder designed buildings were: Princeton, the University of Pittsburgh, Brown, Cornell, the University of Colorado, Denver University, Pennsylvania State College, Wellesley, Albion, Drew, Concordia Seminary in St. Louis, the University of Chicago, the University of Delaware, Hartford Theological Seminary, Thiel College, Vanderbilt University, Rhode Island School of Design,

and Staunton Military Academy. Klauder used many of his own designs as illustrative material in the book on campus planning he co-authored with Herbert C. Wise—*College Architecture in America*, New York, 1929.

50. Schuyler, "Architecture of American Colleges. III. Princeton," *Architectural Record*, February 1910, pp. 145–46.

51. Constance Greiff et al., *Princeton Architecture*, Princeton, 1967, caption to fig. 181.

52. These included Cuyler Hall (1912), Pyne Hall (1922), The Class of 1901 Hall (1926), and Laughlin Hall (1926). Several of these were illustrated in Robert McLaughlin, "The Planning of Dormitories," *Architectural Forum*, December 1925, pp. 327–32.

53. For the buildings at Wellesley, see *Architectural Forum*, January 1932, pp. 13–20. For Cornell, see *Architectural Forum*, September 1917, plates 49–51.

54. See: Agnes Lynch Starrett, *Through One Hundred and Fifty Years, the University of Pittsburgh*, Pittsburgh, 1937, chapter 15, "John Gabbett Bowman and the Cathedral of Learning"; and Klauder and Wise, *College Architecture*, pp. 292–93.

55. Quoted in Starrett, *University of Pittsburgh*, p. 258.

56. *Ibid.*, pp. 258–59.

57. Information from the University of Delaware, Office of Facilities Planning.

58. See: Aymar Embury II, "The New University of Colorado Buildings," *Architectural Forum*, September 1919, pp. 71–80; and John Morris Dixon, "Colorado University: Respect for a Robust Environment," *Architectural Forum*, October 1966, p. 56.

59. Charles Z. Klauder and Herbert C. Wise, *College Architecture in America, and Its Part in the Development of the Campus*, New York, 1929.

60. *Ibid.*, p. 17.

61. *Ibid.*, p. 33.

62. The Harkness Quadrangle was widely described and illustrated in architectural magazines in the 1920s—for example, in articles in *The American Architect*, October 26, 1921, pp. 299–314, and November 9, 1921, pp. 333–42; *Architecture*, 1921, pp. 287–313; *Architectural Record*, February 1918, pp. 148–59, and September 1921, pp. 163–82; and in an issue of *Architectural Forum* devoted to collegiate buildings, December 1925, p. 324.

63. Among these buildings by Rogers were: Jonathan Edwards College (1925), Sterling Library (1927), Trumbull College (1929), Sterling Law Building (1930), Hall of Graduate Studies (1930), and Pierson and Davenport colleges (1930). See Elizabeth Mills Brown, *New Haven, A Guide to Architecture and Urban Design*, New Haven, 1976, pp. 120–28.

64. Roger Hale Newton, *Town and Davis, Architects*, New York, 1942, p. 242. Newton believed that Davis was the architect of the Yale library (now Dwight Chapel), but it is now generally attributed to Henry Austin.

65. Most of the new colleges were designed by James Gamble Rogers. Calhoun College was designed by John Russell Pope (see *Architectural Forum*, May 1934, pp. 320–29).

66. A couple of the Harvard houses took over groups of buildings that had been constructed in the 1910s as freshman dormitories (designed by Shepley, Rutan & Coolidge), whose quadrangular plans and architectural character anticipated the later houses. They were described and illustrated in an article on "Recent Collegiate Architecture," in *The Brickbuilder*, November 1914.

67. Two of these Harvard houses, Lowell and Dunster, were described in *Architectural Forum*, June 1931. The firm of Coolidge, Shepley, Bulfinch & Abbott (previously Shepley, Rutan & Coolidge; later Shepley, Bulfinch, Richardson & Abbott) produced buildings and designs for many colleges and universities, including Stanford, the University of Chicago, Oklahoma University, Harvard Medical School, Wellesley, Brown, Elmira, Northeastern, and Southern Methodist University. See J. D. Forbes, "Shepley, Bulfinch, Richardson & Abbott, Architects: An Introduction," *J.S.A.H.*, Fall 1958, pp. 19–31.

68. From a letter of 1929; quoted by Douglass Shand Tucci in an article on the Harvard Memorial Church, in *Harvard Magazine*, November–December 1982, p. 45.

69. Widener Library was designed by the Philadelphia architect Horace Trumbauer, whose selection as designer was a condition of the memorial bequest that funded the construction, by the family of Harry Elkins Widener, a Harvard alumnus and bibliophile who perished in the sinking of the Titanic. See Bainbridge Bunting and Robert Nylander, *Survey of Architectural History in Cambridge*, vol. 4, Cambridge, Mass., 1973, p. 177. For Memorial Church, designed by Coolidge, Shepley, Bulfinch & Abbott, see Douglass Shand Tucci, "Does the Tower of Old North Church Belong in Harvard Yard?," *Harvard Magazine*, November–December 1982, pp. 44–54.

70. Bunting and Nylander, *Architectural History in Cambridge*, vol. 4, p. 178.

71. Harriet Hayes, *Planning Residence Halls, For Undergraduate Students in American Colleges and Universities*, New York, 1932. This work deals mainly with the functional aspects of dormitory planning, and reflects few formal preconceptions or biases.

72. *Architectural Forum*, December 1925. The same journal also devoted whole issues to collegiate architecture in June 1926 and June 1931. Klauder and Wise's *College Architecture in America*, of 1929 (as well as Jens F. Larson and Archie M. Palmer, *Architectural Planning of the American College*, New York, 1933) gave more attention to the design of dormitories than to any other single aspect of college planning. For other dormitory designs, see articles in: *The Brickbuilder*, November 1914 (Northwestern University); and *Architectural Forum*, November 1931 (St. Lawrence University).

73. See *Architectural Forum*, June 1931, pp. 671–76.

74. G. H. Edgell, *The American Architecture of Today*, New York, 1928, chapter 2.

75. *Ibid.*, p. 160.

76. William Blackburn, *The Architecture of Duke University*, Durham, N.C., 1937, pp. 7–8.

77. *Ibid.*, p. 6.

Chapter VII

1. "The President's Commission on Higher Education for Democracy," 1947; reprinted in Richard Hofstadter and Wilson Smith, eds., *American Higher Education: A Documentary History*, Chicago, 1961, vol. 2, pp. 970ff.
2. Richard P. Dober, *Campus Planning*, New York, 1963, p. 3.
3. *Ibid.*, p. 3.
4. *Ibid.*, p. 8. "Colleges: The Education Explosion," *Architectural Forum*, February 1962, p. 51. The building programs for the state university systems in New York and California were especially extensive in this period. For that in New York, see *Campus Plans for State University of New York* (n.d., ca. 1965), which describes and illustrates the plans for new or remodeled campuses at twenty-six state schools.
5. "Town and Gown," *Architectural Forum*, March 1963, p. 92.
6. The Society for College and University Planning (S.C.U.P.) was founded in 1966, as a spinoff of the American Institute of Planning. Its journal, *Planning for Higher Education*, began publication in 1972.
7. See Dober, *Campus Planning*, pp. 97ff (section on government-sponsored research at universities).
8. William Harlan Hale, "Old Castles for New Colleges," *Architectural Forum*, June 1931, pp. 729–31. Ironically, the rest of this issue of *Architectural Forum* was devoted to collegiate structures of the sort that Hale was criticizing.
9. The competition was conceived by the head of the Wheaton College Art Department, Esther Seaver, a strong supporter of modern design who had rejected the plans for a Georgian-style arts building presented by the firm of Cram & Ferguson, the college architects. First prize in the composition went to the young architects Richard Bennett and Caleb Hornbostel; second prize went to Walter Gropius and Marcel Breuer, both of whom had recently come to America. (For the design of Gropius and Breuer, see Siegfried Giedion, *Walter Gropius: Work and Teamwork*, New York, 1954, pp. 56–57, 134–35.) Insufficient funds prevented the construction of the building, and Bennett & Hornbostel were given the commission for a smaller project on campus, a student alumnae building, which was erected in 1940. See: *Architectural Forum*, February 1938; August 1938, pp. 143–49; January 1941, pp. 54–55. I am grateful for information from Professor Thomas J. McCormick of Wheaton College, who presented a paper, "The Architecture of Wheaton College: Cram versus the International Style," at the 1982 meeting of the Society of Architectural Historians.
10. *Architectural Forum*, February 1946, pp. 11–12.
11. "Hunter College, New York City," *Architectural Forum*, December 1940, p. 473. The architects of the Hunter College building were Shreve, Lamb & Harmon, in association with Harrison & Fouilhoux.
12. *Architectural Forum*, September 1948, p. 8; September 1945, pp. 105–14.
13. *New York Times Magazine*, October 23, 1949; cited in Albert Bush-Brown, "Cram and Gropius: Traditionalism and Progressivism," *The New England Quarterly*, March 1952, pp. 3–22.
14. Walter L. Creese, "Architecture and Learning: A Collegiate Quandary," *Magazine of Art*, April 1950, pp. 136–41.
15. *Architectural Forum*, for example, called it "the first important group of U.S. educational buildings of modern design" (February 1942, p. 14). Most of Mies van der Rohe's plans for I.I.T. are now at the Museum of Modern Art in New York. Professor Kevin Harrington of I.I.T. is currently conducting research on the evolution of the design of the campus, and is preparing a publication on the subject.
16. See: "Goucher College Campus Competition," *Pencil Points*, December 1938, pp. 735–50; Eleanor P. Spencer, "A College Builds a College: The Goucher Competition," *Magazine of Art*, December 1938, pp. 705–7; and "Mary Fisher Hall, Goucher College," *Pencil Points*, July 1943, pp. 54–67.
17. Program of the Goucher College competition, dated June 1, 1938. I am grateful to Professor Emeritus Clinton I. Winslow of Goucher College for sending me a copy of this document.
18. Two such entries, by the architects Frost & Frost, and Thompson & Holmes, are illustrated in the *Pencil Points* article of December 1938, p. 747. The Saarinens' design also is illustrated.
19. Quoted in the *Pencil Points* article of December 1938, p. 737.
20. See Chapter I.
21. These sketches are illustrated in the *Pencil Points* article of December 1938, pp. 740–42.
22. The literature on Wright's Florida Southern college design, beginning with an article in *Architectural Forum* in 1938, is indexed in Robert L. Sweeney, *Frank Lloyd Wright, An Annotated Bibliography*, Los Angeles, 1978.
23. Conversation reported to me by Professor Emeritus Paul R. Hanna, of Stanford University, for whom Wright was designing a house in 1936.
24. For the chapel, the focal point of the plan (designed by Rudolph in association with the firm of Fry & Welch), see *Architectural Forum*, September 1960, pp. 103ff.
25. See Martin Duberman, *Black Mountain: An Exploration in Community*, New York, 1972. This work was brought to my attention by Neal Benezra.
26. The plan, and a model, of Gropius's design were published in Siegfried Giedion, *Walter Gropius: Work and Teamwork*, New York, 1954, p. 133.
27. For Kocher's plan, see *Architectural Forum*, June 1945, pp. 128–29. Additional information about the designs of Gropius and Kocher is found in Duberman, *Black Mountain*, chapter 6.
28. Response to my survey in 1977, by Dr. Chalmers G. Davidson, Davidson College, North Carolina.
29. Harold Goyette, quoted in an article on new building at Harvard, in *Architectural Forum*, June 1964, p. 116.
30. Joseph Hudnut, "On Form in Universities," *Architectural Forum*, December 1947, pp. 88–93. Hudnut's attitude, and even his language, was echoed in subsequent articles in *Architectural Forum*—for example, in a 1949 article on the new campus of the University of Miami, which was praised for its "informal grouping" of buildings, "uncorseted by yesterday's bi-axial symmetry" (June 1949, p. 71).
31. Hudnut, "On Form in Universities," pp. 90–92.

32. *Ibid.*, p. 92.
33. See: "A Dormitory that Explores New Ideas of Student Life," *Architectural Record*, December 1947, pp. 97–99; "M.I.T. Senior Dormitory," *Architectural Forum*, August 1949, pp. 62–69; and "Saarinen Challenges the Rectangle, Designs a Domed Auditorium and a Cylindrical Chapel for M.I.T.," *Architectural Forum*, January 1953, pp. 126–33.
34. Jonathan Barnett, "The New Collegiate Architecture at Yale," *Architectural Record*, April 1962, p. 125. Griswold was president of Yale from 1950 to 1963.
35. Quoted in Walter McQuade, "The Building Years of a Yale Man," *Architectural Forum*, March 1963, pp. 88, 92.
36. Barnett, "The New Architecture at Yale," p. 126.
37. Mentioned in "Brandeis Under Construction," publication of Rose Art Museum, Brandeis University, 1972. Also see: "Brandeis Builds Three Chapels for Three Faiths," *Architectural Record*, September 1954, pp. 9–11; "Three Religions at One Fount," *Architectural Forum*, September 1954, pp. 134–35; and "An Unusual Design for Collegiate Religion," *Architectural Record*, January 1956, pp. 147–53.
38. See ". . . The United States Air Force Academy," *Architectural Forum*, June 1955, pp. 100–9.
39. Richard P. Dober, *Campus Planning*, New York, 1963.
40. *Ibid.*, p. 61.
41. *Ibid.*, p. 61.
42. See Albert Bush-Brown, "Cram and Gropius: Traditionalism and Progressivism," *The New England Quarterly*, March 1952, pp. 3–22. In this article, Bush-Brown contrasted Gropius's Graduate Center as an expression of the dynamic modern university, with Cram's Graduate College at Princeton as a reflection of that school's conservative educational principles forty years earlier.
43. Walter Gropius, quoted in "Harvard Builds a Graduate Yard," *Architectural Forum*, December 1950, p. 63.
44. *Reader's Digest*, March 1977, p. 192.
45. Plans of these various types are illustrated, for example, in Dober, *Campus Planning*.
46. See "Irvine Campus, University of California," *Architectural Record*, November 1964, pp. 186–88.
47. See Eduard F. Sekler and William Curtis, *Le Corbusier at Work: The Genesis of the Carpenter Center for the Visual Arts*, Cambridge, Mass., 1978, p. 50.
48. See: James Bailey, "Academic Center at Fredonia," *Architectural Forum*, May 1969, pp. 36–47; *Campus Plans for State University of New York*, n.d. (ca. 1965), pp. 38–41; and Daniel D. Reiff, *Architecture in Fredonia, 1811–1972*, Fredonia, 1972, pp. 100–3.
49. "How to Grow a Campus," *Architectural Forum*, April 1966, p. 60. Another article on the Tougaloo plan appeared in *Architectural Record*, November 1973, pp. 110–16.
50. "How to Grow a Campus," p. 57.
51. Josep Lluis Sert, quoted in "Le Corbusier at Harvard . . . ," *Architectural Forum*, October 1963, p. 105.
52. See Knud Bastlund, *José Luis Sert: Architecture, City Planning, Urban Design*, New York, 1967, pp. 202–43.
53. "The Universities: Tall New Symbols of Their Significance," *Architectural Forum*, June 1964, pp. 114–23. The institutions examined included Harvard, M.I.T., and Boston University.
54. See Donlyn Lyndon, "Student Dorms: A University Tries Variety," *Architectural Forum*, March 1966, pp. 62–63.
55. See: Bastlund, *José Luis Sert*, pp. 220–31; *Architectural Forum*, June 1964, pp. 116ff.
56. Oscar Newman, "The New Campus," *Architectural Forum*, May 1966, pp. 44–51.
57. *Ibid.*, p. 45.
58. The history of this process is described and analyzed in detail in George Rosen, *Decision-Making Chicago-Style: The Genesis of a University of Illinois Campus*, Chicago, 1980. See also "Campus City, Chicago," *Architectural Forum*, September 1965, pp. 23–44. I am grateful to Professor Robert Bruegmann, of the University of Illinois at Chicago Circle, for information and observations about the school.
59. Walter Netsch, quoted in "Campus City, Chicago," p. 24.
60. Newman, "The New Campus," p. 50.
61. *Architectural Forum*, September 1965, p. 44.
62. Ian Brown, "Irrelevance of University Architecture," *Architectural Forum*, April 1972, pp. 50–55.
63. *Ibid.*, p. 50.
64. G. M. Kallmann and N. M. McKinnell, "Movement Systems as Generators of Built Form," *Architectural Record*, November 1975, pp. 105–16.
65. "No Other University Has Ever Been Planned in Quite This Way," brochure produced by Caudill Rowlett Scott. I am grateful to Franklin D. Lawyer, of Caudill Rowlett Scott, for information on this and other campus plans by this firm.
66. *Architectural Record*, March 1973, pp. 103ff, and May 1977, pp. 95ff. Also see "Stockton: Campus Planning by Increments," *Planning for Higher Education*, December 1972. "Stockton State College," a description of the design provided to me by the architectural firm of Geddes Brecher Qualls Cunningham, states that the "ancestors" of the design included "London's Burlington Arcade, the Free University of Berlin's walkway-based plan, and the University of East Anglia where the simple linear dimensions are bent to meet the topography."
67. See: "Campus Architecture," *Architectural Record*, January 1975, pp. 123ff; "College Buildings: The Multi-Purpose Building as an Alternative to the Sprawling Campus," *Architectural Record*, November 1977, pp. 109ff; and "Designing the Campus as One Big Building," *Architectural Record*, November 1979, pp. 87ff.
68. Clark Kerr, "California's New Campuses," *Architectural Record*, November 1964, p. 175.
69. *Ibid.*, p. 175.
70. See "Irvine Campus, University of California," *Architectural Record*, November 1964, pp. 186–88.
71. Dean McHenry, "Santa Cruz Campus, University of California," *Architectural Record*, November 1964, pp. 176–78. Also see Gerald Grant and David Riesman, *Perpetual Dream: Reform and Experiment in the American College*, Chicago, 1978, chapter 8, "The Cluster Colleges at Santa Cruz."
72. Grant and Riesman, *Perpetual Dream*, p. 255.

73. *Ibid.*, p. 255.
74. McHenry, "Santa Cruz Campus," p. 178.
75. "A New and Spacious Campus Inspires a Fresh Approach," *Architectural Record*, April 1967, p. 208.
76. Robert Edgar to Dean McHenry, January 1970; quoted in Grant and Riesman, *Perpetual Dream*, p. 80.
77. Sally Woodbridge, "How to Make a Place," *Progressive Architecture*, May 1974, p. 79.
78. Grant and Riesman, *Perpetual Dream*, p. 89.
79. See Chapter II.
80. Christopher Jencks and David Riesman, *The Academic Revolution*, Chicago, 1977, pp. 481ff.
81. "Colleges for the Community," *Architectural Forum*, November 1959, pp. 132–39.
82. *Ibid.*, p. 133. Also see n. 65 above.
83. *Ibid.*, p. 133.
84. Information partly from interviews with the architects, by Stanford student Stephen R. Saul, in 1976.
85. Allan Temko, "Foothill's Campus Is a Community in Itself," *Architectural Forum*, February 1962, pp. 54–57.
86. "Pima County Junior College," brochure produced by Caudill Rowlett Scott. "Pima Community College," *Western Building Design*, July 1976.
87. Elizabeth K. Thompson, "Community Colleges," *Architectural Record*, July 1974, pp. 119–32.
88. "Cypress College: Concept to Reality," brochure produced by the architectural firm.
89. See: *Architectural Record*, November 1979, pp. 87ff, and April 1975, pp. 101ff.
90. "Designing the Campus as One Big Building," *Architectural Record*, November 1979, p. 96.
91. *Architectural Record*, November 1977, pp. 112ff.
92. *Architectural Record*, July 1974, pp. 123ff.
93. "Hunter College Gets a Campus and an Identity on Crowded Streets," *Architectural Record*, September 1975, p. 82.
94. See *Architectural Record*, August 1975, pp. 90–92.
95. "Fitting the Future Into the Past," *Architectural Forum*, December 1956, p. 102. See also "Wellesley's Alternative to 'Collegiate Gothic,'" *Architectural Forum*, July 1959, pp. 88–95.
96. "An Old Village Silhouette for a New College," *Architectural Forum*, December 1954.
97. See: "Modern Medievalism for Yale," *Architectural Forum*, July 1960, p. 100; "Polygonal Architecture," *Architectural Record*, February 1960, pp. 159–64; and "The New Yale Colleges," *Architectural Forum*, December 1962, pp. 105–11.
98. Quoted in Jonathan Barnett, "The New Collegiate Architecture at Yale," *Architectural Record*, April 1962, p. 129.
99. Reyner Banham, in a commentary included in "The New Yale Colleges," *Architectural Forum*, December 1962, p. 110.
100. See *Architectural Forum*, February 1963, pp. 114–15.
101. See "Continuity in New Mexico: University's Varied Plazas," *Architectural Forum*, September 1963, pp. 108–11.
102. This was a competition-winning design for a new law school and a social science building, by Dolf Schnebli, George Anselevicius, and Roger Montgomery. See *Architectural Forum*, April 1966, p. 63.
103. Richard A. Miller, "Harvard's Course in Continuity," *Architectural Forum*, September 1960, pp. 94–101.
104. See *Campus Plans for State University of New York*, n.d. (ca. 1965), pp. 6–9.
105. See "Campus Architecture," *Architectural Record*, January 1975, pp. 123ff.
106. Suzanne Stephens, "Such Good Intentions: Architecture and the Arts at Purchase," *Art Forum*, January 1976, pp. 26–31.
107. Mildred F. Schmertz, "An Art Center by Edward Larrabee Barnes," *Architectural Record*, March 1978, p. 108.
108. James J. Morisseau, "For Planners, That Shrinking Feeling," *Planning for Higher Education*, October 1973. Morisseau was editor of this journal and wrote many of the articles in its first several years.
109. "Build If You Must, But Consider . . . ," series of seven articles, *Planning for Higher Education*, April to August 1974.
110. James J. Morisseau, "Campus Chapels: Case of the Missing Pews," *Planning for Higher Education*, April 1973.
111. "Yale University Is Preserving Its Great Late-19th-Century Architecture By Remodeling the Old Campus," *Architectural Record*, March 1977, pp. 93ff.
112. Mendel, Mesick & Cohen, *The Nott Memorial, A Historic Structure Report*, Schenectady, N.Y., 1973 (historical study and recommendations for preserving the building).
113. *Princeton Alumni Weekly*, November 3, 1980, p. 20.
114. See *Architectural Forum*, September 1957, pp. 138–40.
115. Numerous examples of this could be cited, including Princeton, where the enclosed quadrangles of Cram and Klauder have been followed, on the whole, by much more typically American collegiate buildings and spaces. At Stanford, the original master plan by Olmsted, which called for a succession of enclosed quadrangles, was abandoned immediately after the central group was executed, and construction ever since has consisted of individual structures.

Bibliography

Listed here are writings that deal with American campus planning and architecture in a relatively general way. For works on individual institutions and other specialized topics, see the notes to the discussions of these subjects in the text.

Ackerman, Frederick L., "The Planning of Colleges and Universities," *Architectural Forum*, vol. 54, June 1931, pp. 691–96.

Anonymous, "College Edifices and Their Relations to Education," *American Literary Magazine*, vol. 1, November 1847, pp. 269–74.

Bush-Brown, Albert, "Image of a University: A Study of Architecture as an Expression of Education at Colleges and Universities in the United States between 1800 and 1900," Ph.D. dissertation, Princeton University, 1958.

Cram, Ralph Adams, "Recent University Architecture in the United States," *Journal of the Royal Institute of British Architects*, vol. 19, 25 May 1912, pp. 497–519.

Dean, Eldon L., "Early Colleges and Educational Buildings in New England," *Pencil Points*, vol. 15, December 1934, pp. 597–602.

Dober, Richard P., *Campus Planning*, New York, 1963.

Githens, Alfred M., "The Group Plan" (series of five articles, three dealing with campus planning), *The Brickbuilder*, vols. 15–16, July 1906–December 1907, and "Recent American Group Plans," *The Brickbuilder*, vol. 21, December 1912.

Granger, A. *et al.*, "The Small College" (series of articles), *American Landscape Architect*, vols. 2–4, March 1930–January 1931.

Hamlin, A. D. F., "Recent American College Architecture," *The Outlook*, vol. 74, 1 August 1903, pp. 790–99.

Hegemann, Werner and Elbert Peets, "The Development of the American College Campus," in *The American Vitruvius: An Architect's Handbook of Civic Art*, New York, 1922, pp. 110–26.

Horowitz, Helen L., *Alma Mater: Design and Experience in the Women's Colleges from Their Nineteenth-Century Beginnings to the 1930s*, New York, 1984.

Johannesen, Eric, *Ohio College Architecture Before 1870*, Cleveland, 1969.

Klauder, Charles Z. and Herbert C. Wise, *College Architecture in America and Its Part in the Development of the Campus*, New York, 1929.

Larson, Jens F. and Archie M. Palmer, *Architectural Planning of the American College*, New York, 1933.

Newman, Oscar, "The New Campus," *Architectural Forum*, vol. 124, May 1966, pp. 44–51.

Olmsted, Frederick Law, *A Few Things to Be Thought of Before Proceeding to Plan Buildings for the National Agricultural Colleges*, New York, 1866.

Pine, John B., "Notes on the Building of a University," *The American Architect*, vol. 106, 2 December 1914, pp. 333–40.

Pope, John Russell, *University Architecture*, New York, n.d. [1920s].

Schmertz, Mildred, *Campus Planning*, New York, 1972 (collection of articles previously published in *Architectural Record*).

Schuyler, Montgomery, "Architecture of American Colleges" (series of ten articles), *Architectural Record*, vols. 26–31, October 1909–May 1912.

Society for College and University Planning, *Planning for Higher Education* (journal, published beginning in 1972).

Tolles, Bryant F., "College Architecture in New England Before 1860, in Printed and Sketched Views," *Antiques*, March 1973, pp. 502–9.

Willard, Ashton R., "The Development of College Architecture in America," *The New England Magazine*, vol. 16, July 1897, pp. 513–34.

Index

Numbers in italics indicate illustrations.